SAVAGE LOST

FLORIDA GARAGE BANDS:
THE '60S AND BEYOND

by

JEFFREY M. LEMLICH

dp
DISTINCTIVE PUBLISHING CORPORATION

Savage Lost
by Jeffrey M. Lemlich
© 1992 by Jeffrey M. Lemlich

Published by Distinctive Publishing Corporation
P.O. Box 17868
Plantation, FL 33318-7868
Printed in the United States of America

ISBN: 0-942963-12-1
Library of Congress No.: 91-15241
Price: $19.95

Library of Congress Cataloging-in-Publication Data

Lemlich, Jeffrey M. (Jeffrey Marsh), 1956-
      Savage lost : Florida garage bands—the '60s and beyond/
Jeffrey M. Lemlich
          p.   cm.
      Includes bibliographical references.
      Includes discographies.
      ISBN 0-942963-12-1 (trade soft) : $19.95
      1. Rock music—Florida—History and crticism. 2 Soul music—
Florida—History and criticism. 3. Country music—Florida—
History and criticism.   I. Title.
ML3534.L45   1991
781.66'09729'09046—dc20   91-15241
                                                              CIP

TABLE OF CONTENTS

SECTION IV. NAMES, TAGS, NUMBERS, AND LABELS (For Record Collectors Only)

SECTION V. TRANSISTOR SISTER: OUR BEST FRIEND. OUR RADIO

SECTION VI. GOODBYE HARMONIES . . . HELLO HIPPIES
(South Florida Lets Its Hair Down)

SECTION VII. BEYOND THE '60s:
MAKING IT BACK FROM THE FUTURE

1

GARAGE BANDS... WHY?

Somewhere between the twist and the sit-in was a musical experience unlike any other. Somewhere between the first British invasion and the first rock opera was the most energetic, honest, exciting music ever created.

It didn't come from a producer's console or an overzealous entrepreneur's brain. More accurately, it was an honest outgrowth of street life; of school frustrations and parental regulations; of the greasier, sweatier side of music that no other generation could possibly understand. Yes, somewhere between the Beatles and the Grateful Dead was an often overlooked, and often maligned, yet amazingly powerful force: the American garage band.

As an equalizer it couldn't be beat. Not every kid could make straight A's in school or secure a spot on the varsity baseball team, but nearly any kid was capable of learning three chords on a guitar. For those who could never hit home runs or win spelling bees, it was a way to become more than just a face in the crowd. In this respect, garage bands were bona fide dignity-makers. With even the most average student being able to learn a few simple tunes (just enough to dazzle his peers), this otherwise average student was transformed into something way beyond ordinary — a weekend star, more than just another fish in the difficult sea known as teenage life.

This is the beauty of rock 'n roll and its unique combination of simplicity, emotion, and energy. Despite the endless meanderings of those who strive to demean it, REAL rock 'n roll IS and has ALWAYS BEEN a tremendously positive force and a most creative outlet for one's energies and aggressions.

There is no easy way to describe the music of a mid-'60s garage band; basically, it was third generation rock 'n roll, structurally similar to the sounds of the '50s, but with the added drive of the musical innovations of the decade. The early '60s had seen rock 'n roll lose much of its impact on the music charts; the emphasis shifted toward the safe teenage balladeer and acts that the adult-controlled entertainment world felt were suitable for teenage minds. Very little early '60s music was initiated by teens themselves with the possible exception of the surf-oriented instrumental bands that were especially popular on the west coast.

Prior to 1962, most American teen bands existed merely to create dance music; very little was distinctive or original about the majority of these combos. When surf influences interacted with the rhythm-and-blues base of the dance/twist band, things finally began to escalate. (Keep in mind that surf music, while often maligned by the so-called hip faction, was firmly rooted in rock 'n roll and generally characterized by some of the heaviest tremolo-laden staccato guitar riffs ever played.) The surf/dance band served its purpose, but hindsight shows that this musical genre was rather limited. Clearly, it was the British Merseybeat sound that catalyzed the music scene and made it possible for rock 'n roll to return to the forefront of popular music.

The advent of Beatlemania may have seemed like a radical musical departure; and while in approach it certainly was, the musical base for the early Mersey sound was firmly embedded in American rhythm and blues and rock 'n roll music. It shouldn't be too difficult to understand why the Beatles' arrival in America was such a sociological, as well as musical, phenomenon. The shooting of President John F. Kennedy just eight weeks or so earlier; the subsequent rising to the top of the charts of pap such as "Dominique" by the

Singing Nun, and "There I've Said It Again" by Bobby Vinton; the seeming lack of any kind of genuine teenage culture; above all, the newly emerging generation of teens and preteens who had never before heard a Chuck Berry or Little Richard song. The Beatles not only gave music a well-needed shot in the arm, but also provided a new kind of optimism for young people. The Fab Four's contributions to hair styles, fashion, and music, all spoke to youth, and reached them in a way that no exploitation teen film or innocuous balladeer ever could.

While the music of the Beatles, so obviously influenced by the likes of Berry, Richard, Buddy Holly, and Gene Vincent, was second generation rock 'n roll, there is little doubt that the spark of the originals was far from lost in the translation. The Beatles, as well as their other British and German contemporaries, played American rock 'n roll with an intensity that had been sorely missed on our own shores and provided thousands of American teenagers with the impetus to play rock 'n roll themselves.

It is interesting to note that many of these newly formed American bands didn't even realize that they were playing '50s rock 'n roll songs — to them "Roll Over Beethoven" and "Long Tall Sally" were as British as "Love Me Do" or "Please Please Me." It really didn't matter. What did matter was the spirit and enthusiasm, both of which were alive and contagious to musicians and audiences alike.

Cities throughout the United States were witnessing the rise of bands that were playing an American interpretation of this British interpretation of American rock 'n roll; sure, it was third generation, but that didn't make it any less exciting. In fact, the very innocence that was exuded by these bands made the music all the more appealing, making up in energy and intensity what could never be matched in technical proficiency. The American kids borrowed freely from the British, and with the rise of Motown, Bob Dylan, and folk-rock, the British borrowed freely as well.

All of these diverse approaches to rock 'n roll, coupled with the advent of the British rhythm-and-blues bands, and technical advances such as the fuzztone box, made rock 'n roll more exciting than ever. Add to this the first genuine rock 'n roll television show since the earliest days of *American Bandstand (Shindig)*, its worthy but inferior clone *(Hullabaloo)*, and the rock 'n roll clubs that were opening all over America, and you have the ideal environment for the emergence of the garage band era: a time when nearly every city had dozens... hundreds... maybe even thousands of fledgling rock 'n roll bands, and every block in every town was alive with the sounds of the latest three-chord wonders attempting the latest Rolling Stones or Kinks songs.

The bands that were good enough to learn a dozen or more tunes would play local parties, shopping centers, school dances; whatever modest bookings they could acquire. The better of these bands would headline one of the weekend dances at local clubs or bowling alleys, and maybe even back up one of the major stars that would occasionally come to town. If you were really lucky, you got to cut a record, and maybe, just maybe, this record would get played on a local radio station.

If your record was a local hit, there was always the chance that a national label might decide to pick up the master for national distribution. This was never a guarantee that the record would be an instant million-seller, but one out of every couple of hundred nationally distributed masters did manage to elevate its makers into national stars — at least for a month or two. The Gentrys from Memphis; ? and the Mysterians from Texas (via Michigan); the Gants from Mississippi; the Swingin' Medallions from South Carolina; the Syndicate of Sound and Count Five from San Jose; the Blues Magoos from New York; these were some of the lucky ones. Most local discs were doomed to languish in obscurity along with the musicians that created them.

It is only now that people are beginning to appreciate these discs and to realize the sheer excitement that typified not only these local releases, but each and every performance given by these teenage bands. It may have been hard to see at the time, but it's more apparent than ever today that this so-called "naive period" in American music was one of the most prolific, creative times in the history of the music world.

Some of the more fruitful scenes around the country included Texas, Detroit, Boston, Chicago, Minneapolis/St. Paul, the Pacific Northwest, and even Washington, D.C. Each region had its own slight musical variations, depending on a number of diverse factors, ranging from the make-up of the population to whether or not the city resided on an ocean! The approach may have varied, but in all cases the music was fresh, real, and always rock 'n roll. South Florida was no exception; we had a scene that was comparable to any around the country. Hopefully, through this book, I'll be able to shed some insight into what it was like to live in Florida during this most incredible of eras and bring some long-deserved recognition to those individuals who worked long, hard hours to fill our lives with the sound of music.

It is to the fun-filled garage band era that this book is dedicated: to all the bands, disc jockeys, and energized kids whose legacy of music and memories are a never-ending source of inspiration to those who are fortunate enough to care or remember. To those who truly believe in rock 'n roll as a positive, invigorating force: listen... learn... read on.

2

THE SOUTH FLORIDA BAND SCENE, 1964-1970

RADIO has touched all our lives; it's made us smile, it's made us swing, and lately, it's even made some of us sick. Just like watching a friend in trouble and not being able to help, we've all stood by helplessly while radio changed before our very ears. Remember when originality and personality could be found up and down the dial, day in and day out? Some may blame radio's clone-like atmosphere since then on Bill Drake, whose late-'60s crusade to "clean-up" top-40 radio slowly overtook the nation's leading rock stations. Drake's tightening of music playlists and strict control over his air staffs stifled any kind of creativity; radio became safe and stagnant, and in turn the music we heard grew increasingly bland.

While Drake did not directly program a station in the Miami-Ft. Lauderdale market, his influence was felt nationwide, leaving nary a market unaffected. Today the effects are still felt; the original Drake music machine may be a thing of the past, but the resulting damage proved irreversible as early as two decades ago when personality radio seemed about as rare as a Beach Boys concert at James Watt's house. Although the "morning show" concept has finally returned to major markets, how many radio hosts today are truly doing something different? If you're old enough to remember mid-'60s radio, you remember stations working hard to establish a distinct character and personality. And that made them true entertainers in every sense of the word.

WQAM and WFUN were the perennial powers of the Miami airwaves, thanks to extraordinary air staffs and 24 nonstop hours of great rock 'n roll. WQAM, with a signal that reached into 16 or more counties, usually won the ratings battle, but not without a valiant fight by its more than worthy competitor.

Let's talk briefly about the WQAM and WFUN air staffs since (believe it or not) there actually was a time when disc jockeys would do more than just play records and go home uninvolved. We're talking about an era when each jock knew and respected his music and more times than not became an active part of it.

WQAM's most legendary name is probably Rick Shaw, who boasted the top-rated nighttime show for no less than six years. Shaw shared the Miami Tiger microphone with names (and voices) such as Roby ("The Big Kahuna") Yonge, longtime program director Charlie Murdock, Jim Dunlap (who remained with the station throughout most of the '70s), Lee Sherwood, Dan Chandler, Mac Allen (previously WFUN's all-night man), Stu Bowers, Johnny Knox, John Powers, Clarke Moore, Ron King, Ted Clark, Steve Clark, and Jack Sorbi.

WFUN's lineup was no less impressive. Led by Mike E. Harvey and the late Dick Starr, the Boss Jocks included the now-infamous Morton "Doc" Downey, Jr., Jim Howell, Jerry Smithwick, Bob Gordon, Johnny Summer (nee Knox), Dutch Holland, Greggo Warren, Davey O'Donnell, Stephen W. Morgan, Jack Armstrong, Chris Edwards, Jesse James, Jack Wilder, Al Dunaway, Bill Holley, Dave Archard, and one-time WQAM nighttime man Tom Campbell.

WQAM and WFUN were extremely vital in the development of local bands, through their respective show-dances, the Miami Bandstand and the Florida Bandstand. It was common to see radio personalities working hand-in-hand with musicians and club owners, all of whom pulled together to bring local music to the public. Few club owners worked harder than Steve Palmer, manager of numerous teen hangouts, and supervisor and mentor of dozens of bands. Palmer's involvement with the Florida Bandstand was instrumental in the recording and promotion of many of South Florida's best groups, with his "father figure" guidance (and penchant for laying down the law) helping to turn even the greenest of high school kids into viable, working performers, whether they realized it at the time or not.

Now for the million-dollar question: Just where and when did the Miami scene begin? The logical start would be with Sherlyn Music more than three decades ago. Sherlyn, the main publishing arm of Henry Stone's long list of artists, has been around since the days of the Champions and the Charms, through Tracy Pendarvis, the Birdwatchers, the Last Word, and the Legends, all the way to the more recent sounds of KC & The Sunshine Band and Bobby Caldwell, to name but a few. A handful of '50s hits originated from South Florida, most notably "It's Almost Tomorrow" by the Dream Weavers and "When" by the Kalin Twins (by way of New York City), but very few, if any of these, had any connection with what was to transpire in the mid-to-late '60s. The first local band with any lasting influence was no doubt the Ardells (Bill Ande, lead guitar; Tom Condra, rhythm; Vic Gray/Jim Tolliver, bass; Dave Hieronymus, drums), a veteran West Palm Beach band whose recording history dates back to 1960.

Members of the Ardells first cut their teeth in rockabilly groups such as Wesley Hardin & The Roxters, but once they came together, they crystallized quickly. WFUN's Jim Howell sang his first song in public with the group and fondly recalls that they were one of the town's most exciting bands . . . certainly the one that drew the largest crowds at the Florida Bandstand. It was no surprise when the Ardells were snatched away for an international tour, including a phenomenal stay in South America . . . and we don't use the word phenomenal lightly. Stories abound of mass hysteria among adoring teenage fans who thought the Yankee rockers were the American Beatles . . . a tag the group even adopted as its new name.

But once back on our shores, America made it clear it didn't need another Beatles. Despite a tour with Murray the K, and about half-a-dozen singles (as the American "Beetles"), it was time to change to a name that wouldn't be such a hindrance. So when someone suggested the "Razor's Edge," the rest became history for the band about to enter its sixth year of existence.

1966 saw the release of "Let's Call It A Day Girl" (later covered by Bobby Vee), which made it onto *Billboard's* "Hot 100," thanks to monster airplay in New York and Florida. But three other singles on the Buffalo-based Pow label failed to keep the momentum going, and by 1967, the Razor's Edge planned their move back to Florida . . . where they came up with a song that traded their Four Seasons-style harmonies for psychedelic punk, without any compromises whatsoever!

"Get Yourself Together" would have been great, even if it didn't have the most obscure lyrics this side of the Suwanee River. "If you go on feeling disturbed, I'm gonna set you free just like the Byrds," was an obvious jab at the Byrds' folk-rock classic "Set You Free This Time," and might have been a bit too esoteric, even during the Summer Of Love. The record succeeded everywhere but on the charts; its commercial crash seemed to foreshadow the end for the Razor's Edge, who not long after "called it a day." Jim Tolliver would later be found in the early '70s band Peace & Quiet, while drummer Hieronymus went on to engineer recordings for numerous bands, including the Heroes of Cranberry Farm, Maxima, and the Tasmanians. (Hieronymus now runs his own studio in Nashville.)

As a general rule, South Florida bands of the early '60s were heavily influenced by the Everly Brothers, Buddy Holly, and the top instrumental bands of the day. When the British explosion took hold, Beatlemania ran rampant in South Florida, with many bands making the smooth, necessary transition to the Mersey approach to music. No band made the move more successfully than the Legends (Sam McCue, vocals and lead guitar; Larry Foster, rhythm guitar; Jerry Schils, bass; Jim Sessody, drums), or, as manager Steve Palmer decided to call them, the Canadian Legends (even though none of the members came from Canada!)

In their earliest days, the Legends played mainly rockabilly and instrumentals in their hometown of Milwaukee. It's no understatement to call the Legends the teenagers' choice. If *Happy Days* had shown the real Milwaukee, instead of some crude fictionalized burlesque of the '50s and '60s, it would have been the Legends blasting the breweries and burger joints instead of the neo-'70s warblings of Anson Williams and Suzi Quatro. But that was fiction; in real life, the Legends outscored most national bands on the charts, with a cover of the Mel Tillis/Ronnie Self classic "Bop-A-Lena" turning up the heat on many a cold Milwaukee night, and their cool cover of "Say Mama" going all the way to number one on a tri-state survey.

Somewhere behind those wild Go-Go girls were the **Canadian Legends**, fighting the Summertime Blues from the stage of the Tiger-A-Go-Go. *Photo courtesy Jim Sessody*

But like most regional bands, the Legends were virtually unknown outside of their little corner of the world. That was about to change, with a move to South Florida, that not-so-coincidentally coincided with the coming of Beatlemania. Don't think for one minute the newly dubbed Canadian Legends couldn't bring their sound up-to-date; their packed shows at the Balmoral and Diplomat Hotels not only attracted young people by the score, but the best-looking go-go girls in town. The Legends even managed a mention (and photograph) in a *New York Times* article about the Miami Beach teen scene . . . and when their sizzling version of "Alright" (allegedly covered from a Philippines import single by the Searchers!) stormed its way onto the local charts, the song was well on its way to becoming a Miami garage band staple.

It's said that all good things come to an end, and for the Canadian Legends, a pair of draft notices brought down the curtain. Sam McCue returned to the Everly Brothers' band, where his guitar was heard from coast to coast, while Jerry Schils joined forces with the Birdwatchers, playing on most of their best singles. Drummer Jim Sessody turned to management and production, unleashing nearly a dozen Miami punk classics in conjunction with the Florida Bandstand. The Legends re-formed for a reunion concert in November, 1979, and recorded an album at Criteria Studios that showed they never lost a step. More on this unfortunately unreleased album in a later chapter.

Another band to successfully mix the traditional Everly's influence with the nascent British sounds was the Birdwatchers, formed in 1964 by former members of the West Palm Beach-based Apollos. The early incarnations of the group (Bobby Puccetti, keyboards; Jim Tolliver, bass; Eddie Martinez, drums; Dave Chiodo, guitar) played primarily at a Broward County (Ft. Lauderdale area) club called Porky's (no relation to the fictitious South Florida club in the movie of the same name), with Trader John's in North Miami later becoming the group's home base. The Birdwatchers' first two releases, "Love, Emotion, Desire" and "Blue Suede

Shoes," both managed to get some local airplay as did "Real
Appeal," which featured producer Gary Stites on lead vocals.
Yet it wasn't until a major personnel switch early in 1966
that the Birdwatchers began to gain its reputation as
Miami's state-of-the-art local band.

Puccetti and Martinez remained with the group while
three important additions were made: Joey Murcia, a versatile guitarist-songwriter who had previously played with
the Kingsmen and the Busy Signals; Sammy Hall, former
lead vocalist of the Mor-Loks and the Trolls; and Jerry Schils,
bass player with the aforementioned Canadian Legends.
This was the lineup that produced "Girl I Got News For You,"
a haunting, mid-tempo ballad that shot up the charts in
April, 1966, reaching number one on WFUN and number
four on WQAM.

Also receiving immediate attention was the follow-up, "I'm
Gonna Love You Anyway," which although inspired by the
McCoys' "Hang On Sloopy," still managed to maintain its
own character. "I'm Gonna Love You Anyway" peaked locally
at number two, behind the Supremes' national smash "You
Can't Hurry Love." (With the coming of major hits like
"Cherish" by the Association and "Yellow Submarine" by the
Beatles, the record seemed unavoidably doomed to remain
in the runner-up spot.)

The Birdwatchers' next three releases, "I'm Gonna Do It
To You," "Mary Mary (It's To You That I Belong)," and "Turn
Around Girl," all received local airplay, but were unable to
match the success of their predecessors. Still, "Mary Mary"
was without question their finest record, with an opening riff
resembling the Monkees' then current "I'm Not Your Step-
ping Stone," and lyrics bearing hints that maybe the Mary
in question was none other than the evil weed! All this, plus
a savage beat and just enough echoey effects . . . it was sure
top ten material, and probably would have been, had the title
and overall sound not been so similar to the Monkees.

It might be said that what the New Colony Six was to
Chicago and what the Choir was to Cleveland, the
Birdwatchers were to Miami. They were a solid, often com-

mercial band and always one step away from that elusive "big break." The group's ambition, as stated in the March 10, 1967, issue of *GO Magazine*, was "to become one of the top groups in the nation and to have a million-seller." It never quite happened.

Puccetti, Schils, and Martinez kept the Birdwatchers going throughout the early '70s while Joey Murcia joined a group called Magic early in 1969 and resurfaced years later as an integral part of Andy Gibb's backup band. Sammy Hall left the group in February, 1968, and later took to the Christian folk route, releasing several successful inspirational albums and a truly amazing single, "Drug Talk," which not only recalls his early days with the band, but also mentions their famed appearances on ABC-TV's *Where The Action Is*. Hall also authored a revealing book called *Hooked On A Good Thing*, which is well worth seeking out. The Birdwatchers may not have reached their magic goals, but certainly produced a wealth of great music in their pursuit.

Like the Birdwatchers, Ft. Lauderdale's Mor-Loks also stood on the brink of stardom, a goal that may have been obtainable had the draft not stood in the way. The first group of Mor-Loks (Sammy Hall, lead vocals; Johnny Hartigan, lead guitar; Mike Wall, drums; Don Henry, rhythm guitar; Ron Armstrong, bass) was formerly known as the Impressions V and had a local chart hit with "There Goes Life," a strong folk-rock ballad.

The Mor-Loks even had their own fan club. They were wild!

The second group of Mor-Loks (Craig Held, lead guitar;
Ron Armstrong, bass; Mike Wall, drums; Bill "Nappy" Lynn,
lead vocals; Billy Burke, keyboards) signed a two-year
recording contract with Decca Records in February, 1966,
and appeared to be on the verge of success when Uncle Sam
intervened in September, stealing away some key members.
Still, they managed to stick around just long enough to
record "What My Baby Wants," an excellent Legends rip-off
that remains their finest moment.

No discussion of Mersey-oriented bands would be complete without the Clefs of Lavender Hill, a short-lived but
nonetheless well-remembered quartet. "Stop! Get A Ticket,"
the band's debut single, was so popular locally that even
WQAM was forced to play it despite the fact that the Clefs
had always been a Florida Bandstand group. Leader Travis
Fairchild, who claimed to be John Lennon's cousin, drew
heavily upon his contemporaries across the sea as evidenced
on "So I'll Try," and the Clefs' excellent version of the Beatles'
"It Won't Be Long." The Clefs evolved from the Twilites, whose
upbeat, Legends-influenced version of Joe Tex's "Take What
I Got" was a local hit in the summer of 1965.

Other groups, such as the London Chymes, the Blue
Beatles, the Limeys, and the Echoes Of Carnaby Street,
expressed an admiration of English ways in their names as
well as in their music. Groups dressed British; sounded
British; acted British. The high school kids who were "with
it" did the same. While "The Ballad Of The Green Berets" and
"Strangers In The Night" were topping the charts, the hip
kids were listening to the Pretty Things, the Who, and Small
Faces. It was only natural that a scene that was once
comprised of Beatle imitators and misplaced folkies would
soon turn into a full-fledged punk scene!

The hub of much of this emerging action was Southwest
Senior High School, which has also given the world such
luminaries as musician Charlie McCoy and power-hitting
outfielder Andre Dawson. Three extremely influential bands
to come from Southwest High were the Shaggs, the Montells,

and Evil, all of whom were vital in shaping the local scene. The Shaggs were born when members of the Voyagers and the Deltonas merged, creating one six-piece group (Richie Chimelis, vocals; Mike Latona, bass; Cleve Johns, rhythm guitar and vocals; Gregg Shaw, drums; Craig Caraglior, guitar and vocals; Dennis O'Barry, lead guitar).

The early Shaggs mixed harmony and beat with incredible ease, modeling their sound after their idols, the Beatles. The Shaggs recorded "Ring Around The Rosie" during an extended stay in Detroit, but a philosophical disagreement literally split the group in half with Latona, Chimelis, and Shaw leaving to form the Kollektion with three other musicians. The remaining Shaggs also added three members and switched to a blue-eyed soul sound, complete with Young Rascals-style organ. The Shaggs kept it going until late 1968, but by then no original members remained, and the interest had all but died. If the later Shaggs never reached their full potential, the same can't be said about the band formed by its defectors. And what a band it was!

With the release of "Savage Lost," a group original and local smash, the Kollektion secured its rightful place as a group to be reckoned with. The Kollektion was one of 1967's most progressive bands with a style similar to the Pigeons, a local favorite at South Dade's Par-Tee Lounge. The Pigeons, of course, were to go on to fame and fortune as Vanilla Fudge while the Kollektion would stay on top but a year, later struggling to stay alive in the wake of numerous defections (including vocalist Angel Rissoff to the fledgling Blues Image) and a growing reputation by "adults" as a band promoting drugs. If Miami teens accepted, and appreciated, the Kollektion's hard rock and light show, it's due in no small part to a pair of bands that paved the way, proving anything can happen in rock 'n roll.

The Montells and Evil both built solid reputations as punks, labels that certainly were well deserved. The Montells could only be described in terms of extremes. From a standpoint of awareness and progression, they were undoubtedly Miami's most advanced band of 1965, as well as the wildest, and in many ways one of the strangest. To say that the Montells were unpredictable would be the grossest of understatements. Consider that the band's first single, a cover of the Pretty Things' "Don't Bring Me Down," was forced to carry both a censored and an uncensored side due to self-proclaimed "critics" objecting to the band's repeated use of the word "lay" in the lyrics.

Consider also that drummer Jeffrey Allen, a confirmed Pretty Things fanatic, made a number of trips to England to visit his idols and pick up the latest British R & B records months before the discs were released on our shores (if at all). This enabled the Montells to feature such underrated classics as "Get Yourself Home" by the Fairies and "I Am So Blue" by the Poets in live performance as well as nearly every Pretty Things song ever recorded. The Montells also did a remarkable live version of "Gloria" that was so immensely popular that local stations flatly refused to play the Shadows Of Knight's inferior cover. This was the main reason that Them's original version became a number one hit in April, 1966; if local fans couldn't have the Montells' version, only the original British disc would do!

One of the Montells' most popular live numbers, a cover of the Who's "Daddy Rolling Stone" (originally recorded by Otis Blackwell), became the group's second release. "Daddy Rolling Stone" was an instant classic with Carter Ragsdale's aggressively snotty vocals, Danny Murphy's throbbing bass, and George Walden and John Weatherford's ringing guitars mixing with Allen's drums to form an amalgamation of glorious, controlled noise. The flip side, "You Can't Make Me," was co-written by bass player Murphy and Hustlers' guitarist Bob Leavitt and was another exercise in frantic musical distortion.

As far as wild, energetic, anything-goes rock 'n roll bands are concerned, only one band was even remotely close to being in the Montells' class: A band that shook Miami's musical foundation to its very core through wild antics on and off the stage; a group whose rockin' reputation was amply captured, even in its name. Imagine a band destroying the stage at the 1966 Youth Fair Battle Of The Bands after a super-charged version of "My Generation" and still managing to win first prize! Or a band that dared to wear dresses on stage (in 1967, no less) at their reunion concert before proceeding to destroy nearly everything around them!

Evil may not have been your typical clean-cut American kids, but they **WERE** everything that made '60s rock 'n roll so spontaneous and exciting. One listen to their classic cover of the Small Faces' "Whatcha Gonna Do About It" will confirm this. Producer Jim Sessody took special care in capturing the group's sound, using 16-track overdubs on the middle section, which not only featured lots of feedback, but also a guitar and a kazoo played at the same time! Capitol Records picked up the master for national distribution, but unfortunately, edited out most of the middle, a move that made about as much sense as their decision not to promote a record with that much potential.

Lots of bands have called themselves "punk" in the last few years, but none have matched the vitality or pure energy of Evil or the Montells. Try as they may, it's quite unlikely any ever will.

In contrast to the mid-'60s punks were the surfers: the clean-cut kids who frequented Roby Yonge's surf meets and helped push "Surfer Joe" by the Surfaris back to the number one position on WQAM midway through 1965. Two popular surf bands were the Gents Five, who specialized in Four Freshmen-like harmonies, and the Aerovons (Chuck Kirkpatrick, lead guitar; Dick Cook, rhythm guitar; Dennis Williams, bass; Vince Corrao, drums), whose home base was the Pompano Teen Center. The Aerovons gained much notoriety throughout their two-year existence for their clean-cut appearance and smooth, Beach Boys-style vocals and recorded a fine, British-influenced single at Storz Studios in 1965.

Upon the Aerovons' demise in September, 1966, Chuck Kirkpatrick joined the Gas Company (Sandy Meyer, drums; Ken Byers, Jr., organ; Gary Carter, lead guitar; George Terry, bass; Kirkpatrick, guitar), a popular Ft. Lauderdale band.

The Gas Company easily won a local Battle Of The Bands, winning the right to compete in the National Tea Council finals in Lambertville, New Jersey.

The Gas Company later become known as the Proctor Amusement Company and scored a local top-ten smash with "Heard You Went Away," composed by the Birdwatchers' Bobby Puccetti. (The B-side, "Call Out My Name," was written by Chuck Conlon of the Nightcrawlers.) The Proctors were best known for their vocal abilities, often astounding audiences with four-part harmonies and offbeat material such as the Association's "Requiem For The Masses." With the acquisition of Eddie Keating, Scott Kirkpatrick, and Les Luhring (all formerly of the Ambassadors and the very progressive Bridge), the Proctor Amusement Company eventually became known as Game, releasing two relatively successful albums in 1970-71.

Chuck Kirkpatrick went on to work for a number of years at Criteria Studios, ending up on tour with brother Scott as a member of Firefall. George Terry is a respected session musician, best known perhaps for his work with Eric Clapton, for whom he co-wrote the national top-three hit "Lay Down Sally." (Game was introduced to Clapton by Floridian Duane Allman during the Derek & The Dominoes sessions.) Terry also played at one time with the Vandals, a Hollywood-based band whose organ-dominated sound won much fan support at the Miami Bandstand. (Coincidentally, Vandals guitarist John Sambataro would go on to join Kirkpatrick as a member of Firefall, which in its own strange way brings the story full circle.)

Another local band worth mentioning is the Squiremen IV (Jim Oliver, organ; Jerry Molina, rhythm guitar; Don O'-Connell, bass; Sandy Torano, lead; Bennie Buchacher, drums), which by the late '60s evolved into the Heroes Of Cranberry Farm and, more recently, the Heroes. The Squiremen IV are not to be confused with the Squires V, whose late 1965 version of Travis Fairchild's "Bucket Of Tears" is another example of the Mersey influence so prevalent in Miami bands of the era.

Like most major scenes, Miami had its share of perennials; those individuals whose careers spanned many years and whose appeal defied any age barriers. One such man was Wayne Cochran, a Georgia-born singer who spent many years playing at a club called The Barn. Cochran became a longtime favorite with his unique brand of blue-eyed soul. Besides writing J. Frank Wilson's 1964 smash "Last Kiss," Cochran had a number of regional hits, including "Get Down With It," "Get Ready," and the auspicious "Goin' Back To Miami," covered in 1981 by the Blues Brothers (who openly referred to Cochran as their main influence). Cochran continued to play real, pure soul music for a number of years in South Miami clubs and now heads a successful ministry.

Other perennials, such as Gary Stites and Steve Alaimo, also made major contributions to the local scene. Stites, a pop singer of the late '50s and early '60s, worked with a number of artists and continued to dent the local charts with pop ballads such as "Hurting," reportedly written for the Mor-Loks.

But when South Florida perennials are mentioned, without a doubt Steve Alaimo stands out as the most important and influential figure of all. Alaimo began his musical career in the late '50s while attending medical school at the University of Miami. Along with the Redcoats (his backup group), Alaimo had a small degree of local success on numerous labels, eventually leading to a contract with Checker Records and his first nationally charted tune, "Mashed Potatoes."

Alaimo continued to be a local chart-topper throughout the '60s and early '70s with "I Don't Know," "Happy" (a two-time smash), "Cast Your Fate To The Wind," and "You Don't Know Like I Know," all reaching the top ten despite the fact that he never again hit the national top fifty after "Everyday I Have To Cry" in 1963. Fortunately, Alaimo started dabbling in production around this time and along with partner Bradley Shapiro produced an impressive string of hit singles which were both commercially and aesthetically successful. Locally, he contributed to the success of acts such as the Birdwatchers, the Nightcrawlers (actually from Daytona Beach but still part of the local scene), the Last Word, Kanes Cousins, Mercy, the 31st of February, and many, many more (including early sessions by Duane and Gregg Allman, who at one time were in the house band at Hialeah's Tone Studios). Alaimo continued to remain active in Florida music, serving many years as a writer/producer and eventually securing the job of vice president of TK Productions. It should be noted that Alaimo managed to record over 50 singles during his prolific singing career, a truly staggering amount by anyone's standards.

Obviously, any history of a local scene is bound to contain certain loose ends which may never be resolved. South Florida had its share of "common name" bands as did most other cities. What scene didn't have a group named the Road Runners, the Sting Rays, or the New Breed? How about the Bossmen, Apaches, Mystics, Noblemen, Nomads, Showmen, Drones, Bonnevilles, Aztecs, Coachmen, Misfits, Avengers, Kids, Cobras, Impacts, Strangers, or Trolls? South Florida had them all. Countless records were released by groups bearing these names, and whether any belong to South Florida bands remains to be seen.

Most groups were so shortlived that even band members tend to forget the names of the people they played with. A few shortlived bands (Shades Inc., Lansirs 5) did, in fact, release singles, which leads one to believe that perhaps a few of the records floating around by groups with names previously mentioned may be by the same bands that once graced the stages of the Place, the World, the Hollywood Armory, or the Par-Tee Lounge.

By 1968, the local scene was noticeably succumbing to the pressures of the hippie world. December saw the first (and only) Miami Pop Festival, which exposed South Florida to then little-known acts such as Three Dog Night and Fleetwood Mac. In a few months, these bands were to catapult to stardom along with Blood, Sweat & Tears, Crosby, Stills & Nash, and countless others. It was no longer important (or, for that matter, not necessarily complimentary) to be hyped as the next Beatles — instead, musicians liked being compared to Jimi Hendrix or Ginger Baker. The Who, a perennial inspiration of newly formed bands, traded in their pictures of Lily for a deaf, dumb, and blind kid. Anybody who was anybody wanted to witness the "happening" at Woodstock. A rock musical had danced its way to the slick stages of Broadway... even Bar-Mitzvah bands were adding "Aquarius" and "Spinning Wheel" to their repertoires. And still, through all this dilution of essence, people persisted in calling it "rock 'n roll."

The whole complexion of the local scene had changed as well with the few quality bands which remained now feeling the effects of the "peace/love/jam session" syndrome. The unity of the scene was being defeated by all kinds of polarization (Latins vs. non-Latins; hippies vs. straights; druggies vs. non-users) and a number of factors that slowly gnawed away at its very foundation (see the "Life In The Bloodstream" chapter for more on this). While very few local bands really seemed to matter anymore, two are worth noting, if for no other reason than the national attention they received.

Fantasy worked its way up from its members' garages to the better local clubs, thanks in no small part to the powerful voice of young Jamene Miller. The group scored a local number one smash with the instrumental "Stoned Cowboy" in 1970 and issued a futuristic two-album set under the name of Year One in 1974. Fantasy is still around and occasionally performs in area clubs, despite a profusion of personnel changes.

Blues Image emigrated from Tampa in 1968 and rapidly established itself as the hottest new band in town. While playing at Thee Image (Miami's top club of the late '60s), Blues Image caught the attention of Jimmy Page, who at the time was looking for a vocalist for his "New Yardbirds" band. Page publicly referred to Blues Image as "the most dynamic sound in the country." While this statement can certainly be debated, there's little doubt that it didn't hurt Atco Records' decision to make the band a top priority.

Blues Image struck gold early in 1970 with the national top-five hit "Ride Captain Ride," but despite a strong follow-up in "Gas Lamps And Clay," another hit record was nowhere to be found. Lead guitarist Mike Pinera left the band in 1970 and went on to enjoy varying degrees of success in bands such as Iron Butterfly, Ramatam, Cactus, Alice Cooper, and, appropriately enough, Thee Image, while drummer Joe Lala became a member of Stephen Stills' Manassas and is now a respected session musician.

By the late '60s, Criteria was establishing itself as one of the nation's top recording studios with Aretha Franklin and Wilson Pickett leading the way for an awesome group of artists which would someday include the Bee Gees, the Rolling Stones, the Eagles, Eddie Money, and even the Dead Boys. Miami had firmly established itself as a viable recording center, attracting successful artists from all over. Yet local music was on its way toward what would soon become an all-time low, with only the slimmest reminders of the once-lucrative scene remaining.

Bands in Miami seemed prone to take one of two very different, yet equally cliched routes as the '70s wore on. There were the thunderously loud, hopelessly boring bands that unrelentingly played every Grand Funk Railroad tune they could get their hands on. Even worse than these "heavy metal doldrums" were the countless bands that were seemingly stuck in a dismal "singer-songwriter" time warp, churning out mundane versions of "Take Me Home Country Roads" and "You've Got A Friend" with a little "We've Only Just Begun" thrown in for good measure. In their original forms these songs may have had meaning, but when performed by the umpteenth cover band, the meaning bordered more on insincerity than anything else, and let's face it . . . if the singer sounds bored, the audience is bound to **BE** bored . . . and the down tempo of the music sure didn't do anything to change that.

It may have seemed that things couldn't possibly get worse, but by 1974 the dreaded "D" had firmly enveloped local clubs. When "Kung Fu Fighting" and "Doctor's Orders" became the new "Little Black Egg," it was clear that disco-mania had hit Dolphin City. KC & The Sunshine Band, George & Gwen McCrae, and a host of others would go on to create music that would be known the world over as "The Miami Sound." While this may have been an accurate tag at the time, it certainly serves no justice to the non-disco talent that it seems this city (and the rest of the world) has chosen to ignore. South Florida demanded the survival of disco and certainly got its way. Even as disco started waning in other locales, Boogie Fever ran rampant in Florida with the Latin musical influence proving way too strong to overcome.

It's ironic that the great bands of the past were not able to make a national breakthrough while today's mellow and dance bands have. Could you imagine Evil or the Montells playing "Shake Your Booty?" The mid-to-late '70s saw many talented artists selling out to disco drivel or heavy metal excesses, if for no other reason than having to make a living or needing to find a place to play. Many acts found themselves having to compromise quality in order to draw the discotheque crowd — and the ones that refused found that they just couldn't make it.

It took a number of years for things to pick up steam, but by the late '70s (and the "bounce back" year, 1980), young bands such as the Reactions, Z-Cars, Critical Mass, Charlie Pickett & The Eggs, the Cichlids, and the Eat started to attract strong followings in local nightspots. Later into the '80s it was Pickett, the Chant, and dozens of others trying to keep the spirit alive. (See "THE '80s: A RETURN TO CLUBLAND?" for more.)

But it would be "track music" making tracks on the FM blasterjams (you know — faceless groups with trendy names, singing generically over preproduced tracks. Drum machines, synthesizers . . . about as close to pure rock 'n roll as *The Love Boat* is to Shakespeare.) So Exposé, Company B, and Treniere became known as "The New Miami Sound." Any musical success is good for the city, but the powers that be only fooled themselves into thinking "track groups" could bring even a fraction of the excitement of teen bands entering uncharted territory. Producers found themselves going to the bank, but rarely going to the edge. The age of innocence didn't just end . . . it echoplexed!

Yet, I find great optimism in the young bands of the early 1990s with their do-it-yourself cassettes, hand-printed concert flyers, colorful names, and insistence on playing originals. It's very exciting to see the bands support each other, but I still don't see the masses rallying behind them. Hopefully, the pages of this book will help prevent the errors that ended the first golden era; a time a lot less complicated and a lot less calculated . . . and darn if we didn't have a scene. Boy, did we **EVER** have a scene.

3

THE SOUTH FLORIDA BAND SCENE, 1964-1970

SINGLES DISCOGRAPHY

Aerovons
  Was It Meant To Be/Be Bop A-Lula
  (Winterhurst, No #)   (8-65)

American Beetles
  Don't Be Unkind/You Did It To Me
  (Roulette 4550)   (3-64)
  School Days/Hey Hey Girl (Roulette 4559)   (5-64)
  She's Mine/Theme Of A.B.'s (BYP 1001)   (64)
  It's My Last Night In Town/You're Getting To Me
  (BYP 101/102)
  It's My Last Night In Town/You're Getting To Me
  (Mammoth 102)
  I Wish You Everything/Say You Do (Yorey 1001)
  (Barry 3307- Canada)   (1-65)
  [For later releases, see Razor's Edge.]

Ardells - See Related South Florida Releases section.

Beaver Patrol
  ESP/Just Like A Lady (Columbia 44139)   (5-67)

Belles
  La Bamba/Sleep Walk (Tiara 703)   (65)
  Melvin/Come Back (Tiara 100)   (66)

Birdwatchers
    I Don't Care/Love Emotion Desire (Tara 100)   (8-64)
    Blue Suede Shoes/She Tears Me Up
    (Tara 1001)   (10-64)
    Wake Up Little Susie/She Tears Me Up
    (Tara 1002)   (65)
    It's A Long Way Home/It Doesn't Matter
    (Marlin 1902)   (65)
    Girl I Got News For You/Eddie's Tune
    (Scott 27)   (2-66)
    Girl I Got News For You/Eddie's Tune
    (Mala 527)   (3-66)
    I'm Gonna Love You Anyway/A Little Bit Of Lovin'
    (Mala 536)   (7-66)
    I'm Gonna Do It To You/I Have No Worried Mind
    (Mala 548)   (11-66)
    Mary Mary (It's To You That I Belong)/Cry A Little
    Bit (Mala 555)   (2-67)
    Turn Around Girl/You Got It (Scott 29)   (7-67)
    Turn Around Girl/You Got It (Laurie 3399)   (8-67)
    Put A Little Sunshine In My Day/Then You Say
    Boh Bah (Scott 30)   (11-67)
    Mr. Skin/Come Home Baby (Geminix 5501)   (72)
    [Also see Glass Bubble, Sammy Hall, Legendary
    Street Singers, Mousetrap, New Rock Band,
    Security Blankets, Gary Stites and Birdwatchers.]
Blues Image
    Can't You Believe In Forever/Parchman Farm
    (Image 5833)   (9-68)
    Lay Your Sweet Love On Me/Outside Was Night
    (Atco 6718)   (10-69)
    Ride Captain Ride/Pay My Dues (Atco 6746)   (4-70)
    Clean Love/Pay My Dues/Parchman Farm
    (EP) (Atco 33317)   (70)
    Gas Lamps and Clay/Running The Water
    (Atco 6777)   (9-70)
    Rise Up/Take Me Back (Atco 6798)   (12-70)
    Behind Every Man/It's The Truth (Atco 6814)   (4-71)

Ride Captain Ride/Van Morrison-Into The Mystic
(WB PRO 499) (DJ only)   (71)
Ride Captain Ride/Robert John-The Lion Sleeps
Tonight (Atlantic 13119 - reissue)

Blues Messengers
   Yesterday Girl/I Won't Ask For More (Adonis 0702)
   High Wednesday (I'll Stay With You)/Whad'ja
   Come Back For? (Adonis 05/06)

Briarwoods
   Woman, Play Your Music/What A Fool I've Been
   (Rising Sons 718)   (69)
   [For earlier releases as the Briarwood Singers, see
   Related South Florida Releases section.]

Brim
   There Must Be/She's No Good For You
   (Atlantic 2597)   (1-69)

Brimstone
   Blowin' In The Wind/Trinket (Firebird 1800)   (69)

Burgundy Blues
   Nothing Without You/I'll Get You Back Again
   (Argee 100)   (66)

Busy Signals
   Wild Hooten/This Is Something New
   (Freshman 301)   (1-64)
   I Don't Know/The Losers (Marina 1001)   (65)

Bernadette Castro
   Tell Him For Me/They Don't Understand
   (P.P.X. 719)
   His Lips Get In The Way/Sports Car Sally
   (Colpix 747)   (8-64)
   A Girl In Love Forgives/Get Rid Of Him
   (Colpix 759)   (11-64)
   [For earlier releases as Bernadette, see Related
   South Florida Releases section.]

Cavemen
   The Pillow Bit/It's Trash (Chelle 148)   (66)

Chessmen
  The Lycra Stretch/One And Only (Suncrest 2454)   (64)
  [This group appears to have a connection to the
  Canadian Legends on White Cliffs and Polar —
  which is definitely not connected to the better-
  known Canadian Legends.]

Clefs of Lavender Hill
  Stop—Get A Ticket/First Tell Me Why
  (Thames 100/101)   (4-66)
  Stop—Get A Ticket/First Tell Me Why
  (Date 1510)   (5-66)
  One More Time/So I'll Try (Date 1530)   (8-66)
  It Won't Be Long/Play With Fire (Date 1533)   (11-66)
  Oh Say My Love/Gimme One Good Reason
  (Date 1567)   (6-67)
  [Above release shown as Travis & Coventry/The
  Clefs of Lavender Hill.]

Wayne Cochran - See separate discography.

College
  Travlin' The Road/O My Love (Sherlyn 002)   (70)

Cousins
  Take Your Love And Shove It!/National Anthem
  (Shove Love 0069)   (69)
  Take Your Love And Shove It!(Shove Love
  069)/National Anthem (USA 069)   (69)
  [See Kane's Cousins for all subsequent releases.]

Crystalline Silence
  Space Kid's Science Fair Project/Papa's Hung Up
  On The T.V. Newsman (Twin Oaks 6274/6275)   (69)
  [Closely related to bands such as Fantasy and the
  Force.]

Art Dallaire and The Watchmen
  A Cryin' Shame/Insignificant Me (Flip 201/202)   (64)

Dee & Tee
  Something's Comin/When The Cold Winds Blow
  (Coral 62507)   (12-66)

Andy Dio
    Sass-Afras/Shout (Musicor 1118)   (9-65)
    Sorrento/Dancing Bull (Musicor 1162)   (3-66)
    [Trumpetmaster Dio attended the University of
    Miami and blew up a storm from the stages of the
    Florida Bandstand. It's not clear if this is the same
    Andy Dio who recorded for labels such as
    Johnson, Thor, Crusade, Joy, and Gone.]

Dr. T. & The Undertakers
    Times Have Changed/Deceased
    (Undertakers Theme) (Epitaph 0001)   (1-66)
    Blue Blue Feeling/Undertakers Theme
    (Target 101)   (8-66)
    It's Easy Child/Times Have Changed
    (Target 4610)   (4-67)

Mort (Doc) Downey, Jr.
    The Ballad Of Billy Brown/Flattery
    (Magic Lamp 517)   (61)
    The Ballad Of Billy Brown/Flattery
    (Cadence 1407)   (11-61)
    [Many other nonlocal releases throughout the '60s
    and '70s. This 1961 track was resurrected in 1965
    while Downey was a popular WFUN disc jockey.]

Echoes
    Wild Mother/Every Second Of The Day (Art 198)   (66)
    Don't Know Why/Young People (Rebound 001)
    (as the Echo)   (67)
    Shadows/Cheatin' Girl (Argee)   (7-68)

Echoes of Carnaby Street
    No Place Or Time/Baby Doesn't Know
    (Thames 105)   (8-66)

Evil
    Whatcha Gonna Do About It/Always Runnin'
    Around (Living Legend 108)   (4-67)
    Whatcha Gonna Do About It/Always Runnin'
    Around (Capitol 2038)   (10-67)
    [The Capitol issue is an edited version of Living
    Legend 108. Evil also had three limited-pressing

demo 45s issued following the band's victory in
the 1966 Youth Fair Battle of the Bands. "Always
Runnin' Around" came from these sessions.]

Fantasy
I Got The Fever/Painted Horse
(Imperial 66394)   (7-69)
Stoned Cowboy/Understand (Liberty 56190)   (7-70)
Rock 'N Roll Nights/Morning Lights
(Above + Beyond 311)   (74)
Now You're In The Puzzle/We Look Out At You
(Year One 52347/52377)   (6-76)
[Above 45 recorded by Fantasy under the name
Year One.]

Harrison Freese, Jr. - See Related South Florida
Releases section.

Funky Five
The White Baron/Turn Me Loose (Dazey 1001)   (67)
[Actually Wayne Cochran's C.C. Riders.]

Game
My Kind Of Morning/Things For Me
(Scarlet 7001)   (11-69)
When Love Begins To Look Like You/Julie (The
Song I Sing Is You) (Commonwealth United 3009) (2-70)
Stop Look And Listen/Fat Mama
(Faithful Virtue 7005)   (70)
Fat Mama/Girl Next Door (Evolution 1042)   (4-71)
Two Songs For The Señorita/
(Evolution 1053)   (12-71)
["Sunshine 79" is also rumored to exist on a
single.]

Generation Gap
Small Things/Plastic Faces/Losing Every Trace
(EP) (Century 34184)   (69)
Trumpets/Movin' On Strong (Trip Universal 12)   (69)
Letter From Seattle/Ball (Trip Universal 19)   (11-69)

Gents Five
A Wave Awaits/Straight Shooter (March 7734)   (4-67)

I'll Remember You/Legendary Street Singers -
While I'm Gone (Legend 110)   (67)
[The Legendary Street Singers were actually Gary
Stites with the Birdwatchers.]

Gladstone Bag
Baby You Sure Know How To Do It/Emily
(Kangi 075)   (70)

Glass Bubble
Dreamin' In The Rain/You Don't Need A Reason
(Victory 2000)   (6-68)
[Also the Birdwatchers under one of their many
aliases.]

Graduates
Right Or Wrong/Theme For A Little Girl
(Penni 5391)   (68)

Grand-Prees
Heartbreak Hotel/Four Strong Winds
(Go-Go 101-45)   (64)

H. M. Subjects - See the Montells.

Sammy Hall
Weeping Analeah/Just Be Yourself (Parrot 332)   (67)
[Future releases in the Christian folk vein listed in
the Related South Florida Releases section.]

Harry
Emily, My Darlin'/If You're Ever in Miami
(Case 001)   (69)
[Many releases in the '70s and '80s as KC, of KC
and the Sunshine Band.]

Heroes of Cranberry Farm
Fellow John/Who In The World (Trip Universal 16)   (69)
Man/Secrets (Trip Universal 18)   (69)
Will You Love Me Tomorrow/Fellow John
(Trip Universal 22)   (12-69)
Will You Love Me Tomorrow/Fellow John
(Lancelot 201)   (70)
Big City Miss Ruth Ann/Fellow John (Jamie 1386)   (70)

Love Me While You Can/Christians (Back In The
Arena) (GWS 19)   (70)
Christians (Back In The Arena)/Children (Save
The World) (Trip Universal 61)   (71)
Children Save The World/Back Home
(Lionel 3209)   (71)

Hustlers
If You Try/My Mind's Made Up (Chelle 145)   (66)

Illusions - See Jacksonville discography.

Invaders
She's A Tiger/"Honda" Come Back
(Suncrest 3344)   (9-65)

Kane's Cousins
Take Your Love And Shove It!/Good Loven Women
of Bismark, North Dakota
(Shove Love 0069/0073)   (5-69)
Take Your Love (And Shove It!)/Support Your
Local Bands (Shove Love 500)   (5-69)
Alice's Restaurant/Drive In Window Tap Tapper
(Shove Love 0070/0071)   (69)
Alice's Restaurant/Drive In Window Tap Tapper
(Shove Love 501)   (9-69)

Kollektion
Savage Lost/My World Is Empty Without You
(Heads Up 101)   (8-67)

Lansirs 5
Little Girl/Listen To Your Man (Chief, No #)   (67)

Last Word
Can't Stop Loving You/Don't Fight It
(Atco 6498)   (7-67)
I Wish I Had Time/One More Time (Atco 6542)
(As the Last Words)   (12-67)
Mor'een/Runnin' And Hidin' (Atco 6579)   (5-68)

Leaves of Grass
All This Is Right/City In The Rain
(Platinum 2001)   (68)

Legendary Street Singers - See Gents Five.

Legends
  Lariat/Gail (Key 1002) (PS)   (61)
  Say Mama/My Love For You (Ermine 39)   (62)
  Lariat/Late Train (Ermine 41)   (62)
  Bop-A-Lena/I Wish I Knew (Ermine 43) (PS)   (62)
  Temptation/Marionette (Ermine 45) (PS)   (62)
  Run To The Movies/Summertime Blues
  (Capitol 5014)   (7-63)
  Here Comes The Pain/Don't Be Ashamed
  (Warner Bros. 5457)   (7-64)
  Just In Case/If I Only Had Her Back
  (Parrot 45010)   (3-65)
  Alright/How Can I Find Her (Parrot 45011)   (6-65)
  Raining In My Heart/How Can I Find Her
  (Thames 104)   (5-66)
  Raining In My Heart/How Can I Find Her
  (Date 1521) (as the Legend)   (6-66)
  [All releases through "Run To The Movies" were
  recorded while the group was based in Milwaukee.
  "Here Comes The Pain" was the beginning of a new
  South Florida home and sound for the group.]

Jon Jon Lewis
  I'm A Nut/World Full Of Sadness
  (World Pacific 77810)   (12-65)
  Sure Lookin' Good/Shame On You
  (World Pacific 77836)   (66)
  [Not credited on the above is Jon Jon's backup
  group, the Rave Ons, which helped him share the
  bill at a December, 1965, concert by the Dave
  Clark Five.]

Lid
  Girl, I Love You/My Place (Judd 9E01)

Limeys With London Sounds
  Come Back/Green And Blue
  (Sherwood 1715) (PS)   (5-66)
  Come Back/Green And Blue (Scepter 12156)   (7-66)
  [Although the above is listed in Scepter's company

files, it's doubtful the national release ever saw the
light of day.]

Magic
Keep On Movin' On/One Minus Two
(Armadillo 0022)   (10-69)
Sound Of Tears Is Silent/California
(Armadillo 0023)   (70)
I Think I Love You/That's How Strong My Love Is
(Monster 0001)
[The above was issued on a Detroit-based label
just prior to the band's 1971 album for Rare Earth
Records.]

Mark Markham and the Jesters
Goin' Back To Marlboro Country/I Don't Need You
(Power 4225)   (9-66)

Mark Markham and His Jesters
Marlboro Country/I Don't Need You
(RCA Victor 8992)   (10-66)
[Promotional copies on RCA Victor erroneously
show "I Don't Need You" as the plug side. Note the
slight differences in band name and song titles.]

Milktruck - See Sweet Basil.

Minority
Where Was My Mind/High Flyer (Hyperbolic 105)   (69)

Minute Men
I Won't Lead You On/Mr. Mistake (Parrot 318)   (2-67)

Monopoly
There's Gotta Be Some Goodtimes/Shame
(Power, No #)   (7-68)

Montells
Don't Put Me Down (Censored)/Don't Put Me
Down (Uncensored) (Blue Saint 1001)   (6-65)
Don't Bring Me Down Part 1/Part 2 (Saint 1001)   (6-65)
[Both issued under the pseudonym H.M. Subjects.
Despite the differences in label markings, the
above two singles are identical.]

Daddy Rolling Stone/You Can't Make Me
(Thames 102)   (5-66)

Mor-Loks
There Goes Life/Elaine (Loks 1/2)   (8-65)
There Goes Life/Elaine (Living Legend 100)   (9-65)
What My Baby Wants/Looking For A New Day
(Decca 31950)   (4-66)

Mousetrap
Spinning Wheel/Rhymetyme (Scott 402)   (5-69)
[The Birdwatchers' attempt at soul. It didn't work!]

(Nation Rocking) Shadows - See Orlando
discography.

Neighborhood of Love
Count Yourself Out Of Bounds/Miss Blue Three
Quarter (Twin 102)   (69)
Count Yourself Out Of Bounds/Miss Blue Three
Quarter (Trip 102)   (69)
[B-side of the above is an edited version of Twin
102.]

New Chains III
The End/Like A Friend (Enterprise 5242/5243)   (9-67)

New Rock Band
Rock Steady/Little David (Scott 401)   (10-68)
Rock Steady/Little David (Laurie 3480)   (1-69)
[Actually members of the Birdwatchers, joined on
bass by Duane Allman.)

New Society Band
Margie May/Minek A Szoke Ennekem
(Trip Universal 28)   (3-70)

Nightcrawlers - See Daytona Beach discography.

Novas
Whenever You're Ready/Please Ask Her
(Chelle 162)   (1-67)

NRBQ - See Related South Florida Releases section.

On The Other Hand
I'll Get You Back Again/It's Too Late (Argee 101)

Orange Pineapple Tree
  Baby You Sure Know How To Do It/She Smiled At
  Me (Kangi 101)   (6-69)

Peach - See Related South Florida Releases section.

Proctor Amusement Company
  Heard You Went Away/Call Out My Name
  (Scott 168)   (6-67)
  Heard You Went Away/Call Out My Name
  (Laurie 3396)   (8-67)
  You Don't Need A Reason/Two Wonderful Girls
  (Scott 31)   (11-67)
  [See Game for future releases.]

Prowlers
  Summertime/Bongo Rock (The Prowlers, No #)   (65)

Razor's Edge
  Let's Call It A Day Girl/April (Avril) (Pow 101)   (7-66)
  Let's Call It A Day Girl/April (Avril) (Arc 1141 -
  Canada)   (7-66)
  Don't Let Me Catch You In His Arms/Night And
  Day (Pow 103)   (11-66)
  Night And Day/True Patron Of The Arts (Pow 103)   (67)
  Baby's On His Way/True Patron Of The Arts
  (Pow 105)   (67)
  Get Yourself Together/Cloudy Day (Power 4932)   (8-67)

Rhodes Brothers
  Wings Like A Dove/Don't Close The Door On Love
  (United Artists 50060)   (8-66)
  [Many other less interesting releases through the
  '70s.]

Roustabouts
  Doin' The Dock/Don't Turn Away (Paradise 67-1)   (67)

Security Blankets
  Schroeder/(Marlin)   (1-67)
  [The Birdwatchers answered the Snoopy craze
  with this Peanuts novelty.]

Seven of Us
  How Could You/The Way To Your Heart
  (Red Bird 10-069)   (6-66)
  Jamboree/It's Not Easy To Forget
  (Red Bird 10-080)   (66)
  [For future releases as NRBQ, see Related South
  Florida Releases section.]

Shades, Inc.
  Who Loved Her/Sights (Abstract 4604)   (3-67)

Shaggs
  Ring Around The Rosie/The Way I Care
  (Palmer 5010)   (9-66)
  Hummin/I Who Have Nothing (Power 103)   (9-67)

Cynthia Williams & Shaggs - It's Too Late/Perry
  Gordon & Shaggs - Anytime (Abco 1002)   (65)

Six Pak
  There Was A Time/Midnight Brew
  (Trip Universal 15)   (69)

Sounds Unlimited
  Nobody But You/Why Doesn't She Believe Me
  (ABC 10803)   (4-66)

Speed Limit
  You're Too Young To Know/Speed
  (Hyperbolic 108)   (69)

Spellbinders
  Poor Little Girl/Spellbound (Sound 401)   (6-67)

Squiremen Four
  What's On Your Mind/Bitter End (Squire 14-15)   (6/67)
  Who In The World/Secrets (Trip 110) (as the
  Squiremen)   (69)
  [For future releases, see Heroes of Cranberry
  Farm.]

Squires V
  Bucket Of Tears/I'm Thru (Blue Saint 1002)   (12-65)

Still Life
  Dear Robert/Midnight Brew (Trip Universal 21)   (11-69)

Gary Stites
  You've Known So Many (I've Known So Few)/Find
  Yourself Another Fool (Mala 474)   (2-64)
  Hurting/Thinking Of You (Epic 10064)   (8-66)
  [Many other non-local releases in the '50s and
  '60s.]

Gary Stites and the Birdwatchers
  Real Appeal/While I'm Gone (Living Legend 101)   (7-65)
  [B-side reissued 2 years later as by the Legendary
  Street Singers.]

Stix & Stonz
  Bad News/Gator Tails And Monkey Ribs
  (Pat 100/101)

Stix & Stonz
  A Love That's Real/Take A Bus
  (Columbia 45029)   (11-69)
  [The above are two entirely different groups.]

Strat-O-Tones
  Jenny Jenny/Never On Sunday/A Taste Of
  Honey/Do You Want To Dance (EP)
  (SSI 0013) (PS)   (66)

Sweet Basil
  The Shield/Milktruck - Girl I Love You
  (Junior Achievement 500) (PS)   (70)
  [Forget the Sweet Basil single on A&M, which is
  not related to Miami's top local band of the early
  '70s.]

Tasmanians
  Love, Love, Love/Baby (Conda 101)   (67)
  I Can't Explain This Feeling/If I Don't
  (Power 4933)   (8-67)

31st of February - See Jacksonville discography.

Sandy Torano & Nimo Spliff
  A Year Ago Today/I Wanna Know
  (Platinum 101/102)

Travis & Coventry - See Clefs of Lavender Hill.

Tropicals
  Say Goodbye/Pat Phillips - You Tell Me Your Love
  Is True (AIR 1593)

Twilights
  Take What I Got/She's There (Parrot 45013)   (6-65)

Upper Hand - See South Florida Soul discography.

Vandals
  Mystery/We're The Vandals (Parole, No #)   (65)
  I Saw Her In A Mustang/The Joker (Tiara 200)   (65)
  I Saw Her In A Mustang/The Joker (Tiara 200-2)   (65)
  [The Montells weren't the only band being
  censored in 1965. The Vandals had to redub the
  original version of "Mustang" due to references to
  "poontang" and "going to bed." The "clean" version
  is easy to spot with the "2" tacked onto the record
  number.]

Jimmy Velvet - See Related South Florida Releases
  section.

Mike Vetro & Cellar Dwellers
  That's Not True/You Got Me Running/Mustang/I
  Want To Go Home/Summertime/Slow Motion (EP)
  (Art 2006) (PS)   (65)
  [The above EP includes an uncensored cover of the
  Vandals' "Mustang!"]

Edie Walker
  Don't Cry Soldier/I Don't Need You Anymore
  (Mew 102)   (10-66)
  Baby Angel/Your Unusual Love (Mew 103)   (68)
  Young Tears Don't Fall Forever/Good Guys
  (Rising Sons 713)   (68)
  Living On A Prayer, A Hope And A
  Hand-Me-Down/A Stop Along The Way
  (Rising Sons 719)   (11-69)

Young Strangers
  She's Gone/You Are (TYS 1)   (6-67)

STEVE ALAIMO SINGLES DISCOGRAPHY

Kite 2003 — Perkin (also shown as PERKINS)/Hi Ho
(as the Redcoats)

Lifetime 6112/6113 — Jelly/The Girl Can't Help It
(with the Redcoats)   (57)

Marlin 6064 — I Want You to Love Me/Blue Skies
(with the Redcoats)

Marlin 6065 — The Weekend's Over/Girls! Girls!
Girls! (with the Redcoats)   (59)

Marlin 6067 — She's My Baby/Should I Care (with
the Redcoats)   (7-59)

Dade 1800 — Home By Eleven/ (with the Redcoats)   (59)

Dade 1805 — Love Letters/You Can Fall In Love
(with the Redcoats)   (60)

Dickson 6444/6445 — Blue Fire/My Heart Never
Said Goodbye (with the Redcoats)   (7-60)

Imperial 5699 — Blue Fire/My Heart Never Said
Goodbye   (7-60)

Imperial 5717 — Unchained Melody/It Happens
Ev'ry Time   (2-61)

Marlin 6103 — Spooky/The Redcoats Are Coming (as
Count Stephen)   (61)

Checker 981 — Big Bad Beulah/I Cried All The Way
Home   (61)

Checker 989 — All Night Long/I'm Thankful   (61)

Checker 998 — The Waiting's So Hard/You Got Me
Whistling   (61)

Checker 1006 — Mashed Potatoes/Mashed Potatoes
Part 2   (2-62)

Checker 1018 — My Friends/Going Back To Mary   (7-62)

Checker 1024 — One Good Reason/
Cry Myself To Sleep   (9-62)

Checker 1032 — Everyday I Have To Cry/Little Girl
(Please Take A Chance With Me)   (12-62)

Checker 1042 — A Lifetime Of Loneliness/It's A Long
    Long Way To Happiness   (3-63)
Checker 1047 — Don't Let The Sun Catch You
    Crying/I Told You So   (6-63)
Checker 1054 — Michael/Michael Part 2   (8-63)
Imperial 66003 — Gotta Lotta Love/Happy Pappy   (10-63)
ABC-Par. 10540 — Love's Gonna Live Here
    /Let Her Go   (3-64)
ABC-Par. 10553 — Love Is A Many Splendored
    Thing/Fade Out Fade In   (4-64)
ABC-Par. 10580 — I Don't Know/That's What Love
    Will Do   (7-64)
ABC-Par. 10605 — Happy/Everybody Knows
    But Her   (10-64)
ABC-Par. 10620 — Real Live Girl/Need You   (1-65)
ABC-Par. 10643 — Tomorrow Is Another
    Day/Laughing On The Outside   (3-65)
ABC-Par. 10680 — Cast Your Fate To The
    Wind/Mais Oui   (5-65)
ABC-Par. 10712 — Blowin' In The Wind/Lady Of The
    House   (7-65)
ABC-Par. 10764 — Once A Day/Bright Lights Big City (1-66)
ABC-Par. 10805 — So Much Love/Truer Than True   (4-66)
ABC-Par. 10833 — Happy/On The Beach   (6-66)
ABC 10873 — Pardon Me (It's My First Day
    Alone)/Savin' All My Love   (10-66)
ABC 10917 — You Don't Know Like I Know/You
    Don't Love Me   (3-67)
Atco 6512 — New Orleans/Ooh Poo Pah Doo   (8-67)
Atco 6560 — Cuando Yo Vuelva A Mi Tierra/Todavia (2-68)
Atco 6561 — Denver/I Do   (2-68)
Atco 6589 — My Friend/1 X's 1 Ain't 2   (6-68)
Atco 6620 — Watching The Trains Go By/Thank You
    For The Sunshine Days   (11-68)

Atco 6659 — After The Smoke Is Gone/I'm Thankful
   (with Betty Wright)   (3-69)
Atco 6710 — One Woman/And Then I Tripped Over
   Your Goodbye   (8-69)
Atco 6732 — Smilin' In My Sleep/Melissa   (2-70)
Atco 6797 — Wild Side Of Life/Can't You See   (12-70)
Tone Latino 5051 — Yo No Se Que Voy A Hacer Sin
   Ti/No Quiero Dejarla Ya   (70)
GWS 58 — Sleeping Giant/Going Thru The Motions   (71)
Entrance 7501 — When My Little Girl Is
   Smiling/Gemini   (5-71)
Entrance 7503 — Nobody's Fool/Thorn In Our Roses   (71)
Entrance 7507 — Amerikan Music/Nobody's Fool   (4-72)
Entrance 7513 — Sand In My Pocket/Gemini   (72)
Marlin 3301 — Tip Toe/Truckload (as ALLEY)   (75)

EPs

Checker EP-5135 — Don't Cry/I Wake Up
   Crying/Cry/Don't Let The Sun Catch You Crying   (63)
ABC-Par. 531 — Where The Action Is/Sweet Little
   16/500 Miles/Papa's Got A Brand New
   Bag/Personality/Blowing' In The Wind   (65)
Sylvania, No # — Papa's Got A Brand New Bag (on 7"
   EP *Sylvania Blue Dot Flash A Go Go*) (PS)   (65)
[There is also a reissue of "Everyday I Have To Cry"
   in existence on Eric 234.]

WAYNE COCHRAN
SINGLES DISCOGRAPHY

The Naughty Coo/The Naughty Coo (Rebel 1333 1/2)
  (as THE GREAT SEBASTIAN)   (59)

The Coo/My Little Girl (Scottie 1303)

The Last Kiss/Funny Feeling (Galico 105)

The Last Kiss/Funny Feeling (Gala 117)

Liza Jane/No Return (Gala 120)

Dreams/Linda Lu (Confederate 155) (with THE
  ROCKIN' CAPRIS)

Monkey Monkey (You Do It Like This)/Little Orphan
  Annie (Deck 151)   (63)

Monkey Monkey (You Do It Like This)/Little Orphan
  Annie (King 5832)   (11-63)

Last Kiss/I Dreamed, I Gambled, I Lost (King 5856)   (2-64)
  ["Last Kiss" was redone, inserting a chorus.]

The Coo/Cindy Marie (King 5874)   (6-64)

Mr. Lonely/Wrong Number-Wrong Gal (King 5950)   (11-64)

Think/You Left The Water Running (King 5994)   (6-65)
  ["Think" is considered to be Wayne's transitional
  record from country-influenced rock 'n roll to a
  new, James Brown-type soul sound.]

Harlem Shuffle/Somebody Please (Soft 779)   (65)

Harlem Shuffle/Somebody Please (Mercury 72507)
  (with picture sleeve)   (11-65)
  [Above record credited on some pressings as by
  WAYNE COCHRAN & THE FABULOUS C.C.
  RIDERS.]

Get Down With It (2:27 version)/Get Down With It
  (2:15 version) (Mercury DJ-78)   (3-66)

Get Down With It (2:27 version)/No Rest For The
  Wicked (Mercury 72552)   (3-66)

Goin' Back To Miami/I'm In Trouble
  (Mercury 72623)   (10-66)

Shout VOCAL/INSTRUMENTAL (Sound City Studios
    Demo, Ft. Worth)   (66)

Some-A' Your Sweet Love/When My Baby Cries
    (Chess 2020) (with picture sleeve)   (8-67)

Get Ready/Hootchie Cootchie Man (Chess 2029)   (10-67)

You Can't Judge A Book By The Cover/Up In My
    Mind (Chess 2054)   (7-68)

Hang On Sloopy (Live At The Barn)/
    Hey! Baby (Soft 1009)

Last Kiss II/Hey! Baby (Boblo 101)   (68)
    ["Last Kiss II" has different lyrics than the better-
    known version. Probably a studio out-take.]

Please, Please, Please/Hey! Baby (Soft 1009)   (68)
    [The above three releases were probably issued by
    Texas entrepreneur Major Bill Smith in an effort to
    try to cash in on Wayne's success on Chess.]

Hey Jude-Eleanor Rigby Medley Part 1/Part 2
    (Bethlehem 3097)   (69)

Life's Little Ups And Downs Part 1/Part 2
    (King 6253)   (9-69)
    [The above two releases credit THE C.C. RIDERS
    as backing band.]

If I Were A Carpenter/I Can't Turn You Loose
    (King 6288)   (1-70)

Harlem Shuffle/Chopper 70 (King 6326)   (9-70)

Let Me Come Home With You Part 1/
    Part 2 (King 6358)   (2-71)

Last Kiss/C.C. Rider (King 517)
    [Part of King's reissue series. This is the 1964
    version of "Last Kiss" while this is the only 45
    appearance of "C.C. Rider.")

Do You Like The Sound Of The Music/Somebody's
    Been Cuttin' In On My Groove (Epic 10859)
    (with THE C.C. RIDERS)   (5-72)

Long Long Day/Sleepless Nights (Epic 10893)
    (with THE C.C. RIDERS)   (10-72)

Long Long Day +3 tracks by other artists
   (Playback EP 32)   (72)
Shoot The Model/Sea Cruise (Drive 6249) (Shown as
   by WAYNE COCHRAN & HIS C.C. RIDERS)

Wayne Cochran's albums could never match his electrifying live performances. What could? Oh, that hair! *Photo courtesy Wayne Cochran*

WAYNE COCHRAN INVOLVEMENT

Bobby Cash
  I Don't Need Your Love & Kisses/Answer To My
  Dreams (King 5894)   (64)
  [A side written by Cochran and Cash. Also
  reissued in the early '80s as part of King EP
  25327.]

Alane Cochran & The Nomads
  Gone Twisting/How To Love (Conco 149)

Funky Five
  The White Baron/Turn Me Loose (Dazey 1001)   (67)
  [Actually the C.C. Riders. Cochran co-produced
  both sides. This was the theme song to a locally
  produced children's show called *The White Baron.*]

Ritchie Kall
  King Lover/Come On Let's Sing (King 5888)   (64)
  [B-side written by Wayne Cochran.]

Buddy Leach (& The Playboys)
  In The Blue/These Arms Of Mine (Confederate 150)
  [Circa 1961. Rumored to be the earliest version or
  at least the earliest cover of the famous Otis
  Redding tune. Cochran co-owned the Confederate
  label and owned both tunes at this time.]

Otis Redding & The Pinetoppers
  Shout Bamalama/Fat Gal (Confederate 135, Orbit
  135, Bethlehem 3083, King 6149)
  [Cochran plays bass on "Fat Gal."]

Rocking Capris
  Money/Lights Out (Confederate 145
  and Conco 145)
  Lights Out/A-OK (Bethlehem 3084)
  ["Lights Out" was published by Cochran Music.]

Alice Rozier
  My Candy Man/George, BB & Roy (King 5896)   (64)
  [A-side written by Cochran.]

Bobby Lee Smith
    I'm Gonna Put You Down/Have You Any Love
    (King 5843)   (64)
    [A-side written by Cochran.]
Three Jays
    Pool Party/Little Orphan Annie (Nova 120)   (66)
    [Both sides produced by Cochran.]
Dennis Wheeler
    Down In Daytona/Rock Bottom (King 5898)   (64)
    [A-side written by Cochran.]

UNISSUED
SOUTH FLORIDA DEMOS

All of the following exist in demo or acetate form but were never released to the public. It's a shame that some of the great music contained on these is doomed to remain so obscure.

Atoms
   Wolf of Manhattan/Come On Up
   (Master Studios, Hialeah)
   [This early version of the Union South Band chose covers of the Kingsmen and the Young Rascals for their first and only demo.]

Bartocks Mts.
   Midnight Hour and 2 originals (Dukoff Studios)
   [Including Tom Staley, later of NRBQ.]

Cliques
   Summertime
   [Early track by the band that included Evil bass player Mike Hughes.]

Dave & The Wanderers
   What's Wrong With You? (one-sided)

Deltonas
   Lisa/The Unlucky Man (Criteria Studios, October, 1964)

[Featuring Craig Caraglior on lead vocals. This
band later evolved into the Shaggs.]

Evil

Always Running Around/From A Curbstone
I'm Movin' On/I Know I'll Die
[Superlatives do these demos no justice. Whole
nations have toppled for much less than Evil's
resplendent mixture of the Yardbirds, Pretty
Things, and Zombies.]

Exit

Hold Onto Me/Hey Little People
[1969 recordings by the Birdwatchers under one of
their many aliases. Craig Caraglior also sings lead
here.]

Friends & Lovers

Very Last Day (one-sided) (Dukoff Studios, 1966)

The Fugue

So Lonely/Love (Criteria Studios)

Heat Machine

Oedipus Rex/I Know You (Criteria Studios, 1969)
["Oedipus Rex" sounds like a cross between Procol
Harum and the early Bee Gees.]

Hustlers

I Don't Know/Try To Forget Her/We Were In
Love/Vivid In My Mind (Voice Inc. 8965)

Impressions

Nothin' But Lies/Elaine (Stevens Sound Studios,
1964)
[First recordings by the band that became the
Mor-Loks.]

Intruders

Turn Down The Lights/He's No Good For You
(1965)

Invaders

Keep-a Knockin'/Little Things You Do (1965)
[Excellent tracks! These should have been number
one hits!]

Legends
    Make Believe
    [Recorded during the brief period when Sam
    McCue was not in the group. The Legends also
    recorded a demo in Milwaukee with Roland Stone
    called "Shotgun Haircut."]
Modds
    Don't Be Late/So In Love (Dukoff Studios,
    April, 1965)

The **Modds** made the scene in September 1965. Their demo,"Don't Be Late,"
is garage band music at its best. L-R: Don Ricketts, bass; Dean Liapis (seated),
lead vocals; Dewey Bond, drums; John Mascaro, rhythm guitar and vocals;
Dennis O'Barry, lead guitar. *Photo courtesy John Mascaro*

Montells

  Can't Explain/For Your Love (Dukoff Studios,
  May, 1965)
  Watch Out For That Guy/Don't Bring Me Down
  (Dukoff Studios, May, 1965)
  [It should be pointed out that at the time these
  demos were recorded, "For Your Love" had not yet
  hit the American charts for the Yardbirds; and the
  Who was going nowhere fast with "Can't Explain."
  But the real prize is the alternate take of "Don't
  Bring Me Down." You might say the Montells really
  "lay" into the lyrics, which are definitely
  uncensored here.]

Joey Murcia & Kingsmen

  You Can't Sit Down/Since You're Gone
  (Gulfstream Studios)
  [First recordings of future Busy
  Signals/Birdwatchers/Magic/Andy Gibb,
  guitarist.]

New Society Band

  Up In The Air (1970)

Novas

  Frog Eyeballs/Whenever You're Ready
  (alternate take) (Late 1966)

Perfections

  Bony Moronie/Mother-In-Law (Dukoff Studios,
  February, 1965)

Proctor Amusement Company

  Night And Day (Criteria Studios, 1968)
  [There are also 13 other unissued Proctor
  Amusement Company tracks on tape as well as
  literally hours of live recordings.]

Renegades

  It's Easy Child (1965)

Sabres

  Caravan/Mildew/You Lie

Shades Inc.
Don't Run My Life/There Goes My Life (Criteria
Studios)
Just Walk Away (one-sided) (Criteria Studios)
Shaggs
The Very Last Day/The Way I Care/Ring Around
The Rosie/A Lot More Where It Came From
(Criteria Studios, 1966)
[The above versions of "Ring Around The Rosie"
and "The Way I Care" are different from those
released on Palmer 5010.]
Stix & Stonz
The World/I Can't Quit (Pat/Criteria 101/102)
[Two tracks by the "original" group, apparently
unrelated to the Columbia group.]
Charles Sylvestry with the Echoes
Dusty Said Goodbye/Everything But Time
Joel Tessler/Jack Blanchard
Why?
[Excellent Bob Dylan-inspired track.]
Travis & Coventry
You
[British invasion-influenced track recorded just
prior to the formation of the Clefs of Lavender Hill.]

SOUTH FLORIDA ALBUM DISCOGRAPHY

Steve Alaimo -*Twist With* (Checker 2981)   (12-61)
The Twist/Let's Go! Let's Go! Let's Go!/Good Good
Lovin'/I've Got it!/Do The Mashed
Potatoes/Lucille/Boppin' The Blues/Hoochie
Coochie Coo/Let's Twist Again/Do The Hully
Gully/This Little Girl's Gone Rockin'/Twist All
Night
Mashed Potatoes (Checker 2983)   (62)
Mashed Potatoes, Part 1/Ooh Poo Pah Doo/She's
My Baby/I Like It Like That/Peanut Butter/You're
SO Fine/Mashed Potatoes, Part 2/Ya-Ya/Hully
Gully With Me/Heart Break/Baby What You Want
Me To Do/I Got A Woman
Everyday I Have To Cry (Checker 2986)   (63)
Everyday I Have To Cry/I Don't Want To Cry/My
Heart Cries For You/I Cried All The Way
Home/Cry Me A River/I Wake Up Crying/Cry/She
Cried/Don't Cry/Cry Of The Wild Goose/Cry
Myself To Sleep/Don't Let The Sun Catch You
Crying
Sensational (Crown 382)   (2-63)
I Want You To Love Me/You Can Fall In Love/Blue
Skies/I Wanna Kiss You/Home By Eleven/She's

My Baby/The Weekend's Over/Girls! Girls!
Girls!/Should I Care/Love Letters
[The above is a reissue of early Dade and Marlin
tracks.]
Starring (ABC-Paramount 501)   (64)
I Don't Know/Ya-Ya/Nobody Loves Me Like You/I
Don't Wanna Cry/Sammy Dead/People Act
Funny/Everybody Likes To Do The Ska/Stand By
Me/Behold/Soon You'll Be Gone/You're Driving
Me Crazy/I Won't Let You Go
From The ABC TV Show Where The Action Is
(ABC-Paramount 531)   (65)
Where The Action Is/Hitch Hike/Don't Let
Go/Long Tall Sally/Sweet Little Sixteen/500
Miles/Papa's Got A Brand New
Bag/Personality/Blowin' In The Wind/
All Around The World/Mr. Pitiful/Talkin' 'Bout You
Sings & Swings (ABC-Paramount 551)   (66)
Cast Your Fate To The Wind/Lady Of The
House/Love Is A Many Splendored Thing/Let Her
Go/Need You/Real Live Girl/Mais Oui/Fade
Out-Fade In/Truer Than True/Bright Lights, Big
City/Once A Day/Love's Gonna Live Here
En Español Con Los Violines De Pego
(Tone Latino 1455)   (70)
Yo No Se Que Voy A Hacer/Maria Isabel/Niña/Ya
No Me Vuelvo A Enamorar/Son Esas Cosas/No
Quiero Dejarla Ya/Cuando Yo Vuelva A Mi Tierra/
Todavia/Se Acabo/Alguien Canto
[Steve Alaimo also contributed six previously
unissued tracks to the album *Something From The
Air Force Academy*, USAFA 70.]
Bethlehem Asylum - See Related South Florida
Releases section.
Birdwatchers -*South Florida's 60s Sounds*
(Florida-Rock 4001)   (12-80)
I'm Gonna Do It To You/A Little Bit Of Lovin'/Just
Be Yourself/Then You Say Boh Bah/Can I Do

It/You Got It/I'm Gonna Love You Anyway/Mary
Mary (It's To You That I Belong)/Girl I Got News
For You/It's A Long Way Home/It Doesn't Matter/I
Have No Worried Mind/Cry A Little Bit/Eddie's
Tune/Hey Schroeder
[The above is a legal reissue of classic and
unreleased tracks.]

Blue Beatles - No information available, but it
definitely exists!

Blues Image -*Blues Image* (Atco 33-300)   (7-69)
Take Me to The Sunrise/Leaving My Troubles
Behind/Outside Was Night/In Front Behind
You/Lay Your Sweet Love On Me/(Do You Have)
Something To Say/Lazy Day Blues/Yesterday
Could Be Today/Reality Does Not Inspire
Open (Atco 33-317)   (4-70)
Love Is The Answer/Running The Water/Clean
Love/La Bamba/Consuelate/Ride Captain
Ride/Pay My Dues/Fugue U/Parchman
Farm/Wrath Of Daisey/Take Me
Red White & Blues Image (Atco 33-348)   (9-70)
Rise Up/Behind Every Man/Gas Lamps And
Clay/Take Me Back/It Happens All The
Time/Good Life/It's The Truth/Let's Take A
Ride/Ain't No Rules In California
Something To Say (Illusion 2006)   (77)
In Front Behind You/Something To Say/Take Me
To The Sunrise/Outside Was Night/Prelude Full
Moon Blues/Yesterday Could Be Today/Lazy Day
Blues/New York City Blackout
Leavin' My Troubles Behind (Illusion 2007)   (77)
Leavin' My Troubles Behind/Pay My
Dues/Parchman Farm/Reality Does Not
Inspire/Drums Of Reason/Full Moon Blues
Ride Captain Ride (Illusion 2008)   (77)
Ride Captain Ride/Take Me, Make Me/People Get
Ready/Running The Water/Gimme Some
Lovin'/Anchors/Imagination

Can't You Believe In Forever (Illusion 2009)
Rapture Of The Deep/Good To You/Alone With
You/Fly Away/For Another Day/So Hard To
Say/Can't You Believe In Forever
Clean Love (Illusion 2010)
Show Your Love/Blues Star/Daddy's Not
Gone/Clean Love/Madre Mia/Milk Man
[The above Illusion albums were recorded in the
mid-to- late 70s by Mike Pinera and other
musicians, including drummer Donny Vosburgh.]
Briarwood Singers - See Related South Florida
    Releases section.

Wayne Cochran -*Wayne Cochran* (Chess 1519)   (67)
Get Ready/Boom Boom/The Peak Of Love/You
Don't Know Like I Know/Some-A Your Sweet
Love/I'm Leaving It Up To You/You Can't Judge A
Book By Its Cover/Big City Woman/Little Bitty
Pretty One/I'm Your Hoochie Coochie Man/Get
Down With It/When My Baby Cries
High & Ridin (also known as *Rappin'*)
(Bethlehem 10002)   (68)
Sister Sadie/Ode To Billie Joe/Critic's Choice/Hey
Jude- Eleanor Rigby Medley/Satisfaction/Better
Get It In Your Soul/I Was Made To Love
Her/Mo-Lasses
[Basically an instrumental album.]
Alive & Well & Living (King 1116)   (70)
Overture/My Machine/Riders Blues/If I Were A
Carpenter/Sunday Driver/Let Me Come With
You/C.C. Rider/Chopper 70
Cochran (Epic 30989)   (72)
Do You Like The Sound Of The Music/Long Long
Day/Somebody's Been Cutting In On My
Groove/Sleepless Nights/Boogie/Circles/Sittin' In
A World Of Snow/I Will/We're Gonna Make It
Love Love Love (WMC 245)   (82)
Hosanna/Love Love Love/Jump No Pews/Like He
Said He Would/Trumpet Of Jesus/Power In The

Blood/Amazing Grace
[Gospel album distributed by Wayne Cochran
himself.]

Fantasy -*Fantasy* (Liberty LST-7643)   (70)
   Happy/Come/Wages Of Sin/Circus Of Invisible
   Men/Stoned Cowboy/Understand/What's Next
   Year One (Year One, No #)   (74)
   A Legend An Anthem And A Cause/E Equals
   M-C-Squared/Planet, Where Are You/Come Along
   To The Stairway/Now You're In The
   Puzzle/Morning Lights/Jubilation/Tales (Your
   Love Shines)/ The Juggler/Transitory
   River/Universal Love Song/Year One/ Kings And
   Queens In Exile/We Look Out At You/As Much As
   I Know You/Rock 'N Roll Nites/Boxcar
   Lillee/Above You (Traveled Many Miles)/True My
   Lord/Champion
   [The above was a futuristic 2-LP set issued by
   members of FANTASY under the name YEAR ONE.]
   Fantasy/Year One (Above + Beyond, No #)   (76)
   Morning Lights/E = MC2 [superscript 2]/Rock 'N
   Roll Nights/Jubilation/Year One/We Look Out At
   You/Come Along To The Stairway/Now You're In
   The Puzzle/Transitory River/Juggler/ Champion
   [A condensed, single-album version of the*Year One*
   concept album.]

Game -*Game* (Faithful Virtue 2003)   (70)
   Game (Evolution 2021)   (71)
   Entrance/What's Goin' Through My
   Head/Discovering You/Fat Mama/Make Some
   Music/Stop Look & Listen/Disturbance/We Turn
   To You/Sermon/Girl Next Door/Exit
   [The above two albums share the same tracks and
   cover design.]
   Long Hot Summer (Evolution 3008)   (71)
   The Rock & Roll Medley/Man In Black/Sunshine
   79/Two Songs For The Señorita/I'll Be Back

Someday/Laying Back/Animal Friends/Feeling
Good/Changes/The Same Mountain

Kane's Cousins -*Undergum Bubbleground*
(Shove Love ST-9827)   (69)
Take Your Love & Shove It/Drive In Window Tap
Tapper/Plastic, Plastic, Plastic/Alice's
Restaurant/Taster/Don't Touch My Body/Why
Don't You Go Love Yourself/Man Eating Vine/Ace
In The Hole/Morrison (Jim)/ Rushes

Last Words -*Last Words* (Atco 235)   (1-68)
One More Time/Be My Baby/Mor'een/No Reply/A
Basket Of Flowers/The Kids Are Alright/Can't
Stop Lovin' You/You've Lost That Lovin'
Feelin'/It's Not Over/I Wish I Had Time

Legends -*Let Loose* (Ermine 101)   (62)
Let Loose (Capitol 1925)   (62)
Say Mama/Lariat/I Wish I
Knew/Bop-A-Lena/Late
Train/Legendermaine/How The Time
Flies/Fever/Shout Part 1/Shout Part 2/It's So
Easy/Summertime
[Although the selections on the above two albums
are identical, the cover artwork and order of tracks
are different.]
Run To The Movies (Capitol Custom, No #)   (6-63)
Run To The Movies/Hey Little One/Peggy
Sue/Memphis/Fancy Nancy/Da Doo Ron
Ron/Summertime Blues/Killer
Joe/Pipeline/Lucille/Things/I'll Be Forever Loving
You

Magic -*Enclosed* (Armadillo 8031)   (69)
Keep On Movin'/Indian Sadie/You Must Believe
She's Gone/ETS- Zero/Wake Up Girl/One Minus
Two/Who Am I To Say?/I'll Just Play
Magic (Rare Earth 527)   (8-71)
Keep On Movin' On/No, Know/Alexis/Velvet
Underwear/Don't Use Your Love To Blind
Me/Pacifying Burn/Absolutely

Free/Duckbutter/I'm Your Landlord/Our Hearts
Are In Our Heads (We Can't Be Wrong)

Nightcrawlers - See Florida Album Discography later
in this book.

NRBQ - See Related South Florida Releases section.

Rhodes Brothers -*The Rhodes Brothers* (United
Artists 6531 - stereo)   (66)
The Rhodes Brothers (United Artists 3531 - mono)
Fine Again, Mine Again/Wings Like A Dove/Do
Lord/Try To Remember/I Ain't Got Nothin' (Except
That Little Girl You Want)/Soft Lights And Sweet
Music/Black Cloud/Don't Close The Door On
Love/Be Cool Slick/What Now My Love/You Were
On My Mind
[The Rhodes Brothers had many other less
interesting releases throughout the 70s.]

Jimmy Velvet - See Related South Florida Releases
section.

RELATED SOUTH FLORIDA RELEASES

Duane & Gregg Allman
Morning Dew/I'll Change For You (Bold 200)   (72)
[Promotional copies feature "Morning Dew" on
both sides and were pressed on red wax.]
(LP) *Duane & Gregg Allman* (Bold 301)   (72)
(LP) *Duane & Gregg Allman* (Bold 302)   (73)
[The above two albums are packaged very
differently, yet include exactly the same tracks.]
[Reissue of tracks recorded in Hialeah in the
summer and fall of 1968, with the 31st of
February. These same tracks were later reissued
in 1974 on K-Tel 471.]

Apollos
Rockin' Horses/Just Dreaming (Mercury 71614)   (4-60)
Walk By Myself/I Found A New Girl (GLO 5218)
[This early West Palm Beach band included Keith
MacKendrick, formerly of the Roxters and later of
the Champs, as well as a handful of members who
would later form the Birdwatchers.]

Ardells
You Say/You Know Baby (Dade 1806)
(as the R-Dells)   (60)

Roll On/Every Little Day Of The Week
(Marco 102)   (61)
Candy Stick Twist/That's What I Want
(Gone 5128) (as the R-Dells)   (5-62)
You Can Fall In Love/Seven Lonely Nights
(Selma 4001)   (3-63)
Eefananny/Lonely Valley (Epic 9621) (PS)   (8-63)
[Longtime South Florida band which later became
known as the American Beetles and the Razor's
Edge. The Ardells also provide vocal backup on the
Twist With Steve Alaimo album. Also see the
Tones.]

Bernadette
I Knew You When/It's Almost Tomorrow
(Gold Coast 61-22)   (61)
When You're Dancin With Me/Crazy Yogi
(Gold Coast 6134)   (61)
When You're Dancin With Me/Crazy Yogi
(Beach 1001)   (61)
Class Ring/Gimme Gimme (Beach 1002)
Set Me Free/Don't Count Your Dreams
(Beach 1003)
My Babe/Small Talk (Beach 1004)
The Slosh/Silver Platter (Beach 5) (PS)
[Early singles by Bernadette Castro, whose father
owns Castro Convertibles, a large Miami company
and a major sponsor of '60s radio programs.
Bernadette also had an early '60s LP on Gold
Coast 61-8.]

Bethlehem Asylum
Talkin' 'Bout Love/Child Of The Mountain
(Ampex 11009)   (10-70)
Ring My Bell/ (Ampex 11041)   (10-71)
(LP) *Commit Yourself* (Ampex 10106)   (10-70)
(LP) *Bethlehem Asylum* (Ampex 10124)   (71)
(LP) *Paragon Agency Presents* (Paragon PR-162)
(includes "Child Of The Mountain" by Bethlehem
Asylum)   (71)

[Not one of Miami's more exciting bands!
Saxophone player Charlie DeChant is now with
Daryl Hall & John Oates while drummer Buddy
Helm once played in the Tampa band Those Five.]

Jack Blanchard Group
    Gemini/New World (Zodiac 3341)   (9-65)
    [While Blanchard was one of the most important
    names in the local country music scene, these
    "spacy" instrumentals were more in the vein of the
    Tornadoes' 1962 smash "Telstar." Both sides were
    later overdubbed with vocals and reissued as
    "Strange New World/Runaway" by Jacqueline
    Hyde and the Moonfolk (Zodiac 1040/41).]

John Braden
    Hand Me Down Man/What A Friend We Have In
    Jesus (A & M 1066)   (6-69)
    (LP) *John Braden* (A & M 4172)   (69)
    [Folk-influenced artist who was a 1960's graduate
    of Southwest High School. John went on to record
    "cartoon albums" for a Hollywood firm, including a
    recent "Nancy & Sluggo" release.]

Briarwood Singers
    Hush Little Baby/Walk Me Out In The Morning
    Dew (United Artists 661)   (10-63)
    He Was A Friend Of Mine/Bound For The Freedom
    Land (United Artists 686)   (12-63)
    Love Tastes Like Strawberries/Two Brothers
    (United Artists 709)   (4-64)
    (LP) *Well, Well, Well!* (United Artists 3318)   (63)
    [One of Miami's all-time greatest folk groups whose
    "He Was A Friend Of Mine" has become a classic
    within the genre. Also see Dorinda Duncan.]

Tom Carlile & Craftsmen
    Roses Are Red/The Work Song
    (Gulfstream 1058) (PS)
    Can't Win For Losin'/Run Man Run
    (Criteria Rec. Demo 1/2)

[Both of the above are shown as Tom & The
Craftsmen.]
I Saw The Light/Nightingale (Columbia 44372)   (12-67)
I Believe In Miracles/Born Free (MARC 1001)
(LP) *The Original Sounds Of Tom Carlile*
(Cherry 101)   (69)
[Tom's later country recordings for labels such as
Door Knob and Aragon brought him national
attention in the early '80s.]

Crane
  Oh Dancer/Everyday (Capitol 4471)
  (Capitol CL 15941 - demo pressing)   (8-77)
  (LP) *Crane* (Capitol 11742)   (1-78)
  (LP) *What's In-Store For You #4 CAP-FM*
  (Capitol 8802/8803)   (78)
  [Includes "Why Does Love Got To Be So Sad" by
  Crane.]
  [Post-Game endeavor by local veteran Chuck
  Kirkpatrick. Many former Proctor Amusement
  Company and Game members are involved.]

Ginny Dale
  Wishful Thinking/Just Thinking Of You
  (Alston 235)   (12-63)
  Wishful Thinking/Just Thinking Of You
  (Lawn 242)   (64)
  [Ginny, whose real name was Virginia Ragsdale,
  came from Broward County and was a one-time
  classmate to Chuck Kirkpatrick.]

Dream Weavers
  It's Almost Tomorrow/You've Got Me Wondering
  (Decca 29683)   (9-55)
  Into The Night/You're Mine (Decca 29818)   (1-56)
  A Little Love Can Go A Long, Long Way/Is There
  Somebody Else (Decca 29905)   (4-56)
  Give Us This Day/Why I Chose You (Decca 29990) (6-56)
  All This Is Home/Till We Meet Again
  (Decca 30156)   (12-56)
  Fool's Gold/I'll Try, I'll Try (Decca 30276)   (4-57)

(EP) *Dream Weavers* (Decca ED 2376) (PS)   (56)
[Two guys and one girl from Coral Gables. Their
version of "It's Almost Tomorrow," recorded in the
studios of Art Records, was not only a national top
ten hit in 1955, but also topped the British charts
in March, 1956.]

Dorinda Duncan
  It's Christmas Time/Happy Little Star
  (Glendale 1004)
  You're Something Special/Caddy Daddy
  (Glendale 1011) (with the Capris)
  Little People/They'll Love You (Ascot 2174)   (3-65)
  (LP) *The Songs Of Bob Dylan Through The Heart Of
  A Girl* (United Artists 6436)   (65)
  [Solo releases by the distaff member of the
  Briarwood Singers.]

Sam Early
  You Are The Greatest Of Them All/Do You Love Me
  (APT 25041)   (60)
  Question Mark/Trust Me Baby (Dade 1822)
  Never Love A Woman Like You Part 1/Part 2
  (Cat 1975)   (70)
  [Sam & The Sweet Daddys were mainstays of the
  local rock & soul scenes.]

Sammy Early
  If You Really Love Me/I'm Gonna Find Me A Girl
  (Marlin 6066)   (59)

Fans
  Middle Class Blues/Day In Day Out
  (Fave, No #) (PS)   (80)
  [Included two members of the New Society Band.]

Faustus
  We've Got It All/Deal For Yourself (Faustus 001)   (75)
  [Country-rock sides by band which included
  ex-Pods/Leaves of Grass guitarist Alberto DeAlmar
  and former Nimo Spliff members Mark Skola and
  Jimmy Rivas.]

Foxy -Local disco band that had a huge national hit
    with "Get Off" (Dash 5046) late in 1978. Included
    former members of the Birdwatchers, Brimstone,
    Kracker, Dave & The Wanderers, and numerous
    bands. Otherwise, nothing much to boast about.
    Also see OXO.

Harrison Freese
    Earth Angel/Mary Lou (Freshman 302)   (1-64)
    He Cares/Would You Still Bother (Eagle 101) (PS)
    [Above is a '70s issue — ol' Harrison had become a
    Ft. Lauderdale police detective by this time.]

Harrison Freese, Jr.
    You Better Let Him Go/I Am (Roulette 4496)   (6-63)

Harrison J. Freese, Jr.
    I Hope It's Soon/Just Say No (Roulette 4429)   (6-62)

Freestone
    Bummer Bitch/Church (Akhashic 2001) (PS)   (78)
    [Included three members of the New Society Band.
    Freestone was part of the late '70s New York
    CBGB punk scene.]

Ernie Coyote Garza
    Nights Are Cold/Life Ain't Easy (PJP 070)   (81)
    Sure Like To Get To Know You/I The Sun
    (Coyote, No #)   (81)
    (LP) Don't Touch My Guitar! (Coyote 685)   (1-82)
    [Formerly of the Renegades, Peach, Maxima, and
    the later Birdwatchers.]

Sammy Hall
    Walk A Mile In My Shoes/Drug Talk
    (Woodstock 1703)
    Let's Make Tomorrow Together/Love
    (Woodstock 1077)   (71)
    Put Your Hand In The Hand/Bridge Over Troubled
    Water (Woodstock 1078)   (71)
    I Lost It All To Find Everything/ (Newpax 45018) (76)
    Guess Who Moved/We're Not Getting Older
    (Impact 5180)

I've Got A Piece Of The Rock/ (HRT 5199)
Hey, The Moon Is Falling/Keep On Keepin' On
(Neoteric 2713) (PS)   (78)
(LP) *What's It All about* (Christian Folk 1972)
(LP) *All Things Are New* (Christian Folk 1973)   (11-70)
(LP) *Get Together* (Christian Folk 1975)
(LP) *Let's Make Tomorrow Together*
(Christian Folk 1977)   (8-71)
(LP) *Plenty* (Christian Folk 1979)
(LP) *Hooked On A Good Thing*
(Christian Folk 1980)   (72)
(LP) *King Jesus* (Skylite 1981)   (73)
(LP) *Power* (Christian Folk 1982)   (73)
(LP) *The Sammy Hall Trio* (Praise 127)
(LP) *If Nobody Loves You... Create The Demand*
(Impact 3313)   (74)
(LP) *Live* (Impact 3399)
(LP) *Christian Grit* (Newpax 33015)   (76)
(LP) *A Funny Thing Happened On The Way To Hell*
(Newpax 33018)   (76)
(LP) *Don't Let Anyone Steal Your Dream*
(Newpax 33038)   (77)
(LP) *If You Can't Believe In Love* (HRT 3376)
(LP) *Love Is A Puzzle* (Tudor 114604)
(LP) *Reminisce* (Tudor 112202)
[Christian-oriented releases by the former
Mor-Loks/Birdwatcher vocalist.]

Joel Hamilton
    Pretty Girls Everywhere/Starlight (Roulette 4462)(12-62)
    Can't Wait/Vicki Is Her Name (Roulette 4484)   (3-63)
    [Hamilton is best known today to local television
    viewers for his automobile advertisements.]

Kris Jensen
    Bonnie Baby/Staying Up Late (Colpix 118)   (7-59)
    School Bus/Perfect Lover (Leader 808)   (8-60)
    Please Let Me Love You Tonight/Your Daddy Don't
    Like Me (Leader 813)

Tender Hearted Baby/The Jackie Look
(Kapp 393)   (4-61)
3 Vanilla, 2 Chocolate, 1 Pistachio Ice Cream
Cone/Danny's Dreams (Kapp 410)   (7-61)
Busy Signal/Mary Mary (Kapp 493)   (62)
[Above releases were recorded while Jensen was a
resident of Ft. Lauderdale. Jensen had 11 later
singles on three different labels, including the
national hit "Torture" in 1962.]

Kalin Twins
Jumpin' Jack/Walkin' To School (Decca 30552)   (58)
When/Three O'Clock Thrill (Decca 30642)   (5-58)
Forget Me Not/Dream Of Me (Decca 30745)   (9-58)
It's Only The Beginning/Oh! My Goodness
(Decca 30807)   (12-58)
Cool/When I Look In The Mirror (Decca 30868)   (3-59)
Sweet Sugar Lips/Moody (Decca 30911)   (6-59)
Why Don't You Believe Me/Meaning Of The Blues
(Decca 30977) (PS)   (9-59)
Chicken Thief/Loneliness (Decca 31064)   (2-60)
True To You/Blue, Blue Town (Decca 31111)   (60)
Zing! Went The Strings Of My Heart/No Money
Can Buy (Decca 31169)   (10-60)
You Mean The World To Me/Momma-Poppa
(Decca 31220)   (9-61)
One More Time/Bubbles (Decca 31286)   (61)
Trouble/Picture Of You (Decca 31410)   (6-62)
Sometimes It Comes, Sometimes It Goes/Thinkin'
About You Baby (Amy 969)   (10-66)
(LP) Kalin Twins (Decca DL 8812/78812)   (58)
(LP) When (Vocalion VL 3771/73371)
(EP) When (Decca EP 2623)   (58)
Jumpin' Jack/Walkin' To School/When/Three
O'Clock Thrill
(EP) Forget Me Not (Decca EP 2641)   (58)
[Miami answered the Everly Brothers craze with
this pair of former New Yorkers.]

Katmandu
    (LP) *Katmandu* (Mainstream 6131)   (11-70)
    [Included Bobby Jabo, formerly of Dr. T & The
    Undertakers, and Bobby Caldwell, who eight years
    later surprised everyone with a national top ten
    hit.]

Chuck Kirkpatrick
    Surf's Up (4:37)/I'm That One (Good Sounds 713) (8-81)
    (12") Surf's Up (8:43)/I'm That One
    (Good Sounds 112)   (8-81)

Kracker
    Because Of You (The Sun Don't Set)/City Blues
    (Dunhill 4329)   (11-72)
    Song For Polly/Medicated Goo (Dunhill 4368)   (9-73)
    Song For Polly/Medicated Goo
    (Rolling Stones 19 106) (Germany) (PS)   (9-73)
    (LP) *La Familia* (Dunhill 50134)   (72)
    (LP) *Kracker Brand* (Dunhill 50154)   (73)
    (LP) *Hot* (Dash 30003)   (76)
    [Top Miami Latin-oriented band with roots
    including the Queen's Kids, Chango, Nimo Spliff,
    and Dave & The Wanderers.]

Laddins
    [(Sonny Johnson, lead; Ernest "Mickey" Goody,
    first tenor; Earl Marcus, second tenor; John
    Marcus, baritone; Robert Jeffers, bass.) An
    outstanding vocal group from New York that
    produced eight excellent singles from 1957
    through 1963. In the mid-'60s, the group played
    South Florida as part of the Miami Bandstand and
    recorded its final singles at North Miami's Criteria
    Studios. The Laddins have the distinction of
    having been at Criteria recording "Dream Baby"
    and party-like "Dizzy Jones Birdland" (also issued
    by the Marvells) when news arrived of President
    John Kennedy's assassination. In 1966, the
    Laddins became known as the Steinways and
    recorded some excellent tracks for the

ABC-distributed Oliver label. Longtime members
David Coleman (who replaced Sonny Johnson in
1960) and Earl Marcus died in the early '70s,
while bass singer Jeffers made a name for himself
in New York radio as Bobby Jay.]
Now You're Gone/Did It (Central 2601)   (57)
Yes, Oh Baby Yes/Light A Candle (Grey Cliff 721) (7-59)
She's The One/Come On (Isle 801)   (2-60)
Did It/Now You're Gone (Times Square #3)
(reissue)   (61)
There Once Was A Time/Oh How I Hate To Go
Home (Theatre 111)   (6-61)
That's What You Do To Me/Try, Try Again
(Groove 4-5)   (1-62)
I'll Kiss Your Teardrops Away/I'll Be There
(Angie 1790)   (11-62)
Push Shake Kick & Shout (Vocal)/(Instrumental)
(Angie 1003)   (63)
Push Shake Kick & Shout (Vocal)/(Instrumental)
(Bardell 776)   (63)
Dream Baby/Dizzy Jones Birdland (Butane 779) (1-64)
(LP) *Bobby Jay Presents The Laddins*
(Central 5018)   (74)
[The above is a compilation of the Laddins' best
tracks.]

Laddins (as the Steinways)
  My Heart's Not In It Anymore (Babe, Babe,
  Babe)/You've Been Leadin' Me On (Oliver 2002)   (3-66)
  One Angel Less/ (Oliver)   (66)
  Don't Wonder Why/Call Me (Oliver 2007)   (10-66)

David Coleman (solo)
  My Foolish Heart/Drown My Heart (Barry 1013)   (67)
  [David "Pinky" Coleman left the Laddins in 1965
  and was replaced by Frankie Gearing, formerly of
  the Miami vocal group the Co-Eds. When the
  Steinways broke up in 1967, Frankie teamed up
  with two other women to form the Glories, whose
  first single, "I Stand Accused" (Date 1553), was

originally intended to be the next Steinways'
single. The Glories recorded eight singles for Date
(including a cover of Della Humphrey's "Don't
Make The Good Girls Go Bad") before changing
their name to Quiet Elegance. Quiet Elegance later
recorded for Hi Records and went on to sing
backup vocals for a number of well-known acts.]

Bonnie Lane
Long Lonely Night/The Dance Is Over (Gone 5124) (1-62)
[Ft. Lauderdale girl Linda Kane changed her name
for a shot at the big time.]

Life
Cool Down/Whatever It Takes (Elektra 47128)   (3-81)
Let Me Down Easy/ (Elektra 47158)   (5-81)
Don't Go Wanderin'/When You Gonna Feel Right
(Elektra 47207)   (9-81)
(LP) *Life* (Elektra 6E-339)   (3-81)
[Led by vocalist Kitty Woodson and guitarist
George Terry, formerly of the Vandals, Proctor
Amusement Company, Game, and the Eric
Clapton Band.]

John Lombardo
Sing Sing Sing/Lady Jane (Paramount 0105)   (6-71)
I Apologize/Love Song (Paramount 0150)   (72)
[Early '70s releases by former lead vocalist of the
Last Word. Tommy James produced both of the
above.]

Mandarin Gate
It's A Revolution Mother/Mount Reality (It's A
Revolution Mother 001)   (70)
[A side was actually the group Skin under an alias.
Bobby Caldwell, Bill DeMoya, Chris Martell, and
former Shagg Mark Watson are among the players
here. From the early '70s soundtrack to the film
It's A Revolution Mother (It's A Revolution Mother
EW-01.)]

Mark & Clark

One Past Summer Afternoon/Please Do Yourself A
Favor (MTA 179)   (70)
Jigsaw Woman/Sidestreets (Columbia 10500)   (2-77)
When It Comes To Love/Drinking Man's Concerto
(Columbia 10594)   (7-77)
[The above Columbia singles shown as the Mark &
Clark Band.]
(LP) *From The Inside Out* (Twin Co. 521/2)   (69)
(LP) *The Best Of* (Phase II 3301)
[Both of the above LPs credit Mark & Clark
Seymour.]
(LP) *Double Take* (Columbia 34498) (as the Mark
& Clark Band)   (77)
[Twin piano players/singers who can best be
described as a mix between Peter & Gordon and
Ferrante & Teicher!]

Mark Markham

(LP) *If This Is Love Then I Want My Money Back*
(Athens Free Enterprise, No #)   (80)
[Recorded at Criteria Studios around Christmas,
1978, by Markham and members of the local band
Tight Squeeze, whose lead guitarist Coz Canler is
now with the Romantics. Markham, who scored a
local hit in 1966 with "Goin' Back To Marlboro
Country," is the cousin of Florida rock 'n roller
Charlie Pickett.]

Eddie Martinez

Oh Dad/Harmonizing Love (Magic Minstrel 3003)
[Mid-'70s solo single by longtime Birdwatchers
drummer.]

Max Demian Band

Paradise/Still Hosed (RCA 11525) (PS)   (2-79)
Havin' Such A Good Day/The Lizard Song
(RCA 11644)   (79)
(LP) *Takin It To The Max* (RCA AFLI-3273)   (1-79)
(LP) *The Call Of The Wild* (RCA AFLI-3525)   (2-80)

(12") Havin' Such A Good Day/See Me Comin'
Down (RCA 11467)   (1-79)
(12") Paradise (one-sided, DJ-only release) (RCA) (2-79)
[Late '70s band which included former members of
the Novas, Drones, Sounds Unlimited, and Stix &
Stonz.]

Maxima
Together Again/Four Dead In Ohio (GWS 42)   (70)
[Included local veteran Ernie Garza.]

Charlie McCoy

Charlie was born in Oak Hill, West Virginia, but
an inadequate hometown school system, coupled
with an anemic condition, prompted a move to
Miami at the age of nine. McCoy didn't give much
thought to a career in music until his junior year
at Southwest High School, where he started
paying his dues as a singer and guitarist in local
rock 'n roll bands.

McCoy's first break came through a meeting with
Happy Harold, Miami's most influential country
disc jockey. Harold hosted a live radio show called
The Old South Jamboree that emanated from the
porch of a Miami used car lot. He was impressed
enough with the young rock musician to feature
him on the Saturday night radio show. McCoy's
job was to play rock 'n roll for the predominantly
country-western audience, and somehow the
combination worked. (Incidentally, McCoy's bass
player at the time was Donny Young, who years
later would find fame and fortune in Nashville as
Johnny Paycheck.)

While attending the University of Miami, McCoy
decided to heed the advice of both Harold and
fellow Floridian Mel Tillis and head out to
Nashville. After spending most of the summer of
1960 playing drums for Stonewall Jackson, McCoy
heard from Jim Denney of Cedarwood Music, who
had gotten word of the fledgling musician through

friend Tillis. Denney referred McCoy to Archie Bleyer of Cadence Records, for whom he recorded "Cherry Berry Wine," a minor hit that peaked in the '90s on *Billboard Magazine's* Hot 100. From there it was session work under the guidance of Chet Atkins ("I Just Don't Understand," a top 20 hit for Ann-Margaret) and Fred Foster (Roy Orbison's classic, "Candy Man"). McCoy's stellar harmonica work on the latter contributed in no small way to its success and helped lead not only to a plethora of session work, but also a solo shot on Foster's Monument label, for whom he has now recorded for over two decades.

While McCoy's career as a session player has spanned a staggering four thousand sessions through the years (including many of Bob Dylan's classic works), his solo releases of the 1960s were generally based in rock 'n roll and rhythm and blues and are well worth checking out. "Harper Valley PTA" in 1968 was the start of a new sound for McCoy; a new, countryfied image that was to prove very successful throughout the 1970s. Still, the early Cadence and Monument releases show McCoy's rock roots and overall versatility and just what made him the number one session man in Nashville.

Charlie McCoy - releases through 1968
Cherry Berry Wine/My Little Woman
(Cadence 1390) (1-61)
I Just Want To Make Love To You/Rooster Blues
(Cadence 1415) (4-62)
Will You Love Me Tomorrow/My Babe
(Monument 842) (5-64)
Harpoon Man/I'm Ready (Monument 870) (2-65)
It's A Man Down There/Girl (Those Were The Good Old Days) (Monument 893) (7-65)
Let Him Go/Screamin Shoutin Beggin Pleadin
(Monument 926) (66)

Stubborn Kind Of Fellow/My Baby's Back Again
(Monument 975)   (66)
Cold Cold World/You've Got To Face Life
(Monument 998)   (67)
Gimme Some Lovin'/The Boy From England
(Monument 1076)   (7-68)
Harper Valley PTA/Juke (Monument 1093)   (9-68)
(LP) *The World Of Charlie McCoy*
(Monument 18097)   (68)
[Monument releases prior to #1076 were with the
Escorts.]

Sam McCue
What To Do (To Forget You)/Valley Of Tears
(Flight 616)   (4-64)
[Solo single by Legends lead guitarist and vocalist.
McCue also sings background vocals and plays
rhythm guitar on "You" by the Apollos & Paul
Steffan (Cite 5008) and resurfaced in the San
Francisco '70s band Crowfoot.]

Metaphysical Animation
(LP) *Metaphysical Animation*
(no label name 151/152)   (7-73)
[Includes former members of the Burgundy Blues,
Pods, and Leaves Of Grass.]

Fred Neil
Love's Funny/Secret, Secret (Epic 9334)   (10-59)
Slippin' Around/You Don't Have To Be A Baby To
Cry (Epic 9403)   (60)
Four Chaplains/A Rainbow & A Rose (Epic 9435)   (12-60)
Tear Down The Walls/I Know You Rider
(Elektra 45009)   (65)
The Dolphins/Badi-Da (Capitol 5786)   (2-67)
The Dolphins/I've Got A Secret (Capitol 2047)   (10-67)
Felicity/Please Send Me Someone To Love
(Capitol 2091)   (1-68)
Everybody's Talkin'/That's The Bag I'm In
(Capitol 2256)   (7-68)
Everybody's Talkin'/Badi-Da (Capitol 2604)   (8-69)

(LP) *Tear Down The Walls* (with Vince Martin)
(Elektra 248/7248)   (65)
(LP) *Bleecker & Mac Dougal* (Elektra 293/7293)   (5-65)
(LP) *Fred Neil* (Capitol 2665)   (2-67)
(LP) *Sessions* (Capitol 2862)   (12-67)
(LP) *Everybody's Talkin'* (Capitol 294)   (10-69)
(LP) *The Other Side Of This Life* (Capitol 657)   (71)
(LP) *Little Bit Of Rain* (Elektra 74073)
[Above is a '70s reissue of the *Bleecker & Mac
Dougal* album.]

Freddie Neil
Heartbreak Bound/Trav'lin' Man
(ABC-Paramount 9935)   (6-58)
Listen Kitten/Take Me Back Again
(Brunswick 55117)   (2-59)
You Ain't Treatin' Me Right/Don't Put The Blame
On Me (Look 1002)
[Keep reading these pages for much more on this
multitalented folk legend, whose writing credits
include Nilsson's "Everybody's Talkin'" and Roy
Orbison's "Candy Man." Let's also not forget the
influence of Neil's mid-'60s singing partner, Vince
Martin, who once fronted the famous folk group
The Tarriers and left behind at least six 45s on
Glory Records. You won't find a better folk album
than the duo's *Tear Down The Walls*, which
practically puts you smack dab in the middle of a
smoky coffeehouse every time it hits the turntable!]

NRBQ
Stomp/I Don't Know Myself (Columbia 44865)   (5-69)
C'mon Everybody/Rocket Number 9
(Columbia 44937)   (7-69)
Down In My Heart/Sure To Fall (In Love With You)
(Columbia 45019)   (10-69)
All Mama's Children/Step Aside
(Columbia 45107) (as Carl Perkins & NRBQ)   (3-70)
Howard Johnston's Got His Hojo Working/Do You
Feel It (Kama Sutra 544)   (7-72)

Magnet/Only You (Kama Sutra 549)   (8-72)
C'mon If You're Comin'/RC Cola And A Moon Pie
(Kama Sutra 575)   (6-73)
Get That Gasoline Blues/Mona
(Kama Sutra 586)   (11-73)
Rumors/Sourpuss (S.O.H. 022)
Froggy Went A Courtin'/Bless Your Beautiful Hide
(Button 037)
Ridin' In My Car/Do The Bump
(Red Rooster 1001)   (77)
I Got A Rocket In My Pocket/Tapdancin' Bats
(Red Rooster 1002)   (77)
I Love Her, She Loves Me/Green Lights
(Mercury 73991)   (3-78)
Get That Gasoline Blues/Wacky Tobacky
(Red Rooster 1003)   (7-79)
Hot Biscuits And Sweet Marie/Don't She Look
Good (Red Rooster 1004)
Me And The Boys/People (Red Rooster 1005)   (80)
Christmas Wish/Jolly Old St. Nicholas
(Red Rooster 1006)   (80)
Never Take The Place Of You/Captain Lou Albano
For "Tiddlywinks" (Radio Spot/TV Spot)
(Red Rooster 1007)
Captain Lou/Boardin' House Pie
(Red Rooster 1010) (with Lou Albano)   (82)
Rain At The Drive In/Smackaroo
(Bearsville 29588)   (4-83)
(EP) Merry Christmas From NRBQ
Christmas Wish/Here Comes Santa Claus/God
Rest Ye Merry Gentlemen/Message From The
North Pole
(Red Rooster EP-1)   (12-78)
(EP) NRBQ In Person
Do You Feel It/Alone Again Naturally/Please Don't
Talk About Me When I'm Gone/Time And Place)
(Red Rooster Ep-2)   (82)
(LP) NRBQ (Columbia 9858)   (69)

(LP) *Boppin' The Blues* (Columbia 9981)
(as Carl Perkins & NRBQ)   (70)
(LP) *Scraps* (Kama Sutra 2045)   (72)
(LP) *Workshop* (Kama Sutra 2065)   (73)
(LP) *Scraps/Workshop* (Annuit Coeptis 1001 2)   (74)
(LP) *All Hopped Up* (Red Rooster LP 101)   (77)
(LP) *At Yankee Stadium* (Mercury SRM 1 3712)   (78)
(LP) *All Hopped Up* (Red Rooster 101)
(second pressing)   (79)
(LP) *Kick Me Hard* (Red Rooster 102)   (79)
(LP) *Tiddlywinks* (Red Rooster 1004)   (80)
(LP) *Grooves In Orbit* (Bearsville 23817)   (4-83)
(LP) *Tapdancin' Bats* (Red Rooster)   (84)
(EP) *Dig This* (Columbia AS 3) (includes "Boppin'
The Blues" by Carl Perkins & NRBQ)   (70)
(LP) *Somethin' Else Again* (CSP 5386) (includes
"Stomp" by NRBQ plus 25 other bands)   (69)
(LP) *Top Of The Rock* (CSP 5428) (includes "C'mon
Everybody" by NRBQ plus 29 other bands)   (69)
(LP) *More Heavy Sounds* (Columbia CS 1016)
(includes NRBQ)   (70)
(LP) *Heavy Hands* (Columbia 1048)
(NRBQ and lots more)   (70)
[Evolved from the 7 of Us, a New York rock/soul
band that came down to Miami in the mid-'60s.
After changing its name to NRBQ, the group
headed back to New York once more.]

Hoppy Ferguson & Wild Dogs
I Need Good Lovin'/You Snooze, You Lose
(Renegade 5603)   (71)
[Solo release by former NRBQ guitarist.]

OXO
Whirly Girl/In The Stars (Geffen 29765)   (83)
(LP) *OXO* (Geffen 4001)   (83)
[This '80s-style version of the disco group Foxy
continued to record throughout the early '80s.
OXO was led by Ish Angel (nee Ledesma), lead

singer of the final incarnation of the Birdwatchers
and later Miami's top "track" producer.]

Peace & Quiet
(LP) *Peace & Quiet* (Kinetic 30315)   (71)
[Included former members of the Birdwatchers,
Razor's Edge, Villagers, and Convairs.]

Peach
Hide/Public Servant (Platinum 108)   (70)
Love's The Thing/Lady (Geminix 5502)   (72)
[Long-lasting band that included at various times
local musicians Russ Smith, Chris Dieguez, Kooky
Berrios, Ernie Garza, and Omar Martinez.]

Pigeons
(In The) Midnight Hour/Stick In My Corner Baby
(Musicor 1199)   (66)
(LP) *While The World Was Eating Vanilla Fudge*
(Wand 687)
[The pride of the Par-Tee Lounge later struck it
rich as Vanilla Fudge.]

Mike Pinera
Alone With You/Lady Divine (Capricorn 0288)   (77)
Can't You Believe/I Am The Bubble (SRI 00002)   (79)
Goodnight My Love/Looking For The Light
(SRI 00003)   (12-79)
(LP) *Come And Get It* (SRI 3216)   (77)
(LP) *Isla* (Capricorn 0202)   (78)
(LP) *Forever* (SRI 00001)   (12-79)
(12") Can't You Believe/Can't You Believe
(SRI 2104)   (79)

Professor Bug
Beatlemania Part 1/ Part 2 (Beetle 1600)   (64)
[Break-in novelty produced by WFUN Radio,
featuring disc jockeys Dick Starr and Bill Holley.]

Ramatam
Changing Days/Wild Like Wine (Atlantic 2916)   (9-72)
(LP) *Ramatam* (Atlantic 7236)   (72)

RELATED SOUTH FLORIDA RELEASES

(LP) *In April Came The Dawning Of The Red Suns*
(Atlantic 7261)   (6-73)
(LP) *Heavies For June* (Atlantic PR-187) (includes
"The Land/Rainy Sunday Evening" by Ramatam) (6-73)
[Formed by local veterans Mike Pinera and Russ
Smith along with April Lawton and former Jimi
Hendrix Experience member Mitch Mitchell.]

Roxters
So Long/Goodbye Baby (Art 175)

Wesley Hardin & Roxters
Anyway/A Thing Called Love (AFS 302)
['50s rockabilly band featuring Butch Watts, lead;
Don Ward, rhythm; Keith MacKendrick, sax (later
to the Apollos and Champs); and Dave
Hieronymus, drums (pre-Ardells/American
Beetles/Razor's Edge). Roxters tracks have been
reissued on the albums *Miami Rockabilly,
Volumes 1 & 3*.]

Salvation
Tomorrow Is The First Day Of The Rest Of My
Life/Someday The Gray Will Come (United Artists
50695)   (8-70)
[Included former members of the Kidds.]

Seven Blends
(LP) *Twistin' At The Miami Beach Peppermint
Lounge* (Roulette 25172)
[Excellent show band that specialized in original
R&B music. Well remembered by patrons of the
Peppermint Lounge.]

Shandi
Nobody Loves You Better/ (Dreamland 101)   (80)
(LP) *Shandi* (Dreamland 5001)   (80)
(LP) *Flashdance* (Casablanca 0501) (includes
"He's A Dream" by Shandi)   (83)
(LP) *The Karate Kid* (Casablanca 822 213)
(includes "Tough Love" by Shandi)   (6-84)
(12" EP) *Shandi AOR Special* (Dreamland 1201)
Walk The Streets/Heart Beat/Bottom Line   (80)

(10" EP) *Music From Dreamland Records*
(Dreamland DO-2000) (includes "Nobody Loves
You Better")   (80)

Shandi Sinnamon
Rainbow In My Heart/Be Easy (Asylum 45303)   (1-76)
Will You Still Love Me Tomorrow/I Never Knew
How Much I Loved You (Asylum 45321)   (5-76)
(LP) *Shandi Sinnamon* (Asylum 1054)   (76)
[Shandi sang with Friends & Lovers for a very
short time in the late '60s. She may still make it
some day.]

Southern Steel
San Francisco Man/24 Hours A Day (Earth 4444)
(LP) *Get On Through* (Earth 00003)
[Included former members of Shades, Inc., Heat
Machine, Willy Bogg, and The Force.]

Jimmy Summers & Slicks
I Love You, You Love Me/Long Lost Love
(Space 001)
[A good, early Steve Alaimo production.
Jimmy is Steve's cousin.]

Teen Tones
The Rockin' Rumble/Latino Part 2 (Gone 5061)   (59)

Jimmie Tennant -See Jimmy Velvet.

Thee Image
It Happens All The Time/Come To Me
(Manticore 7001)   (75)
Good Thing/So Hard To Say (Manticore 7005)   (75)
Alone With You/Far Away Places
(Manticore 7006)   (75)
(LP) *Thee Image* (Manticore 50451)   (75)
(LP) *Inside The Triangle* (Manticore 50651)   (75)
[Blues Image-related band led by Mike Pinera.]

Theze Vizitors
Happy Man/For Mary's Sake (Capitol 2163)   (4-68)
[Palm Beach's Curtis Brothers were involved with
the above. The Curtis Brothers later joined bands

such as Red Dog Kin and Crazy Horse. They
recorded on their own for Polydor Records in 1976.
Richard and Michael also wrote songs for
Fleetwood Mac ("Blue Letter") and Crosby Stills &
Nash ("Southern Cross.")]

Thingies
It's A Long Way Down/Merry-Go-Round Of Life
(Casino 2305/06)   (66)
English Eyes/
Mass Confusion/Rainy Sunday Morning
(Sonobeat 104)   (68)
[A Topeka-based band that spent the summer of
1967 playing at the Miami teen club The World.
Included Larry Joe Miller, now a local rockabilly
star, with two singles on By My Records to his
credit. The Thingies evolved from the TR-4, which
recorded "Surfin' TR/Peter Rabbit" in 1964.]

Timmy Thomas
Have Some Boogaloo/Liquid Mood (Goldwax 320) (3-67)
It's My Life/Whole Lotta Shaking Going On
(Goldwax 327)   (7-67)
[The above singles were recorded in Memphis prior
to Thomas' relocation to Florida.]

Tiger-Tiger
Hi-Ya-No-Mie'/My Heart Is With Nature
(Miccosukee Hopanke 1001)   (75)
Thank You Ancestors/Your Best Is Good Enough
(Miccosukee Hopanke 1002)   (75)
Dog Legs/Red Man (Miccosukee Hopanke 1003)   (75)
Brown Girl (Tiger-Tiger, No #)   (80)
Taste My Love/Your Best
(Miccosukee Hopanke 1001)   (81)
(LP) Eye Of The Tiger (Clouds 8806)   (80)
[Lee and Stephen Tiger, the pride of Florida's
Miccosukee Indian Village, were formerly with the
Renegades, Bangles, Sun Country, 7 of Us, and
very early NRBQ. "Dog Legs" is one of the best
unknown gems of the '70s.]

Tones
  Paula Is Mine/Love Such As You (Elmor 6001)   (3-63)
  [Actually the Ardells. "Paula Is Mine" is an answer
  to Paul & Paula's popular "Hey Paula."]
Truth
  Wade In The Water/Love Locked (Mega 0023)   (3-71)
  [Included Johnny Hartigan of the Mor-Loks.]
Union South
  Act Naturally/Come Home To Me (Atoms 001)   (71)
  [Formerly the Atoms.]
Unknowns
  Melody For An Unknown Girl/Peith's Song
  (Parrot 307)   (9-66)
  Tighter/Young Enough To Cry (Marlin 16008)   (9-67)
  [Studio group reportedly led by Steve Alaimo,
  Keith Allison, and Mark Lindsay. A direct
  by-product of ABC-TV's *Where The Action Is*.]
David Vance
  Be Mine Again/How Can I Know (Torch 101)   (66)
  [Vance, A North Miami photographer, recorded
  this in Detroit around the same time the Shaggs
  invaded the Motor City.]
Jimmy Velvet
  The Witness/Giggle Wiggle (Thunder 1000) (as
  Jimmie Tennant with Buddy Lucas & His
  Dynatones)   (59)
  You're The Beat Within My Heart/Heartbreak
  Avenue (Amp 790) (as Jimmie Tennant)   (59)
  First Star/Across The Moon (Warwick 523)
  (as Kitt & Kory)   (3-60)
  Salute/The Big Retreat (Warwick 533)
  (as Jimmie Tennant)   (60)
  You're Mine & We Belong Together/I'm Gonna Try
  (To Forget The One I Love) (Velvet 201)
  (Witch 115)   (62)
  We Belong Together/I'm Gonna Try (Cub 9105)   (62)
  We Belong Together/The History Of Love
  (ABC-Paramount 10488)   (9-63)

To The Aisle/Lonely Lonely Night
(ABC-Paramount 10528)   (2-64)
Teen Angel/ (Velvet Tone 101)   (10-64)
Teen Angel/Mission Bell (Tollie 9037)   (11-64)
It's Almost Tomorrow/Young Hearts
(Velvet Tone 102)
It's Almost Tomorrow/Blue Eyes (Don't Run Away)
(Philips 40285)   (4-65)
I Won't Be Back This Year/Young Hearts
(Philips 40314)   (7-65)
Take Me Tonight/Young Hearts (Velvet Tone 106)
Take Me Tonight/Young Hearts (Cameo 464)   (2-67)
Roses Are Blue/A Touch Of Velvet (Cameo 488) (7-67)
Candy Heart/Sigma Alpha Lonely
(Velvet Tone 112)   (68)
Candy Heart/Sigma Alpha Lonely
(United Artists 50279)   (2-68)
Good Good Lovin'/Heart Breakin' Misery
(Velvet Tone 114)   (1-68)
Good Good Lovin'/Heart Breakin' Misery (United
Artists 50272)   (2-68)
[While both of the above were issued under the
name The Jimmy Velvet Five, they were actually
recorded in 1965 and first released on Velvet Tone
104, as Gene and Gare with The Velvet Tones. The
rare original release features a much longer
version of "Good Lovin'" — with a guitar break!]
(EP) *Golden Hits* (Velvet Tone 201)
We Belong Together/Teen Angel/It's Almost
Tomorrow/Mission Bell
You're Mine & We Belong Together/The History Of
Love (Velvet Tone 444) (issued as The Velvet View)
It's You/A Woman (Royal American 286)   (12-68)
Missing You/Blue Velvet (Royal American 291) (69)
It's You/Wasted Years (Music City 888)   (70)
(Things That Make A Woman) A Woman/Wasted
Years (Sundi 7101)   (2-71)
(LP) *Sings A Touch Of Velvet* (Velvet Tone VTR 501) (68)

(LP) *Sings A Touch Of Velvet* (United Artists 6653)   (68)
(LP) *Jimmy Velvet* (Music City 502)

[Now here's a guy who's really hard to figure out.
Velvet (real name James Tennant) was basically an
innocuous balladeer; sort of a cross between
Bobby Vinton and Johnny Tillotson, with lots of
sappy, obnoxious ballads to his credit. But
occasionally Velvet would really let loose and
record an excellent track or two — the rockabilly
styling of Thunder 1000; the horn band R&B
influence of The Jimmy Velvet Five tracks; the
great folk-rock rendition of "Run Run Mister Sun"
on his otherwise awful *A Touch Of Velvet* album...
all are superlative recordings. So Velvet certainly
was not incapable, nor without merit — just
inconsistent. When he was good, he was very, very
good, but when he was bad, forget it.

There was a second, unrelated singer who also
went by the name of Jimmy Velvet; a cat from
Dallas named Jimmy Mullins. This second Jimmy
Velvet recorded for labels such as Alta, Division,
Startime, Teardrop, Abnak, BI, and Bell, and even
signed with ABC-Paramount at the same time as
our Velvet. ABC had to think fast, making the
Dallas-based singer change his name — at least
temporarily — to Jimmy Satin! The "Mullins"
Velvet also recorded for Cub, which of course
released a version of "We Belong Together," further
complicating matters.

Velvet also claims to have recorded "Go Little Go
Cart/Spark Plug" with the Champs. Go pay him a
visit the next time he brings his traveling Elvis
museum to your town.]

Mike Vetro

(LP) *Live 'N Kickin' At The Losers* (Vetrix 8070)   (70)
[Very forgettable Las Vegas-style album by the
former Continentals/Cellar Dwellers leader.]

Wild Oats
   (LP) *Wild Oats* (Clouds 8803)   (12-76)
   [Included two former members of the local '60s
   band The Pyramids.]
World of Matter
   No Such Thing/What's Your Name
   (Trip Universal 41)   (70)
   [Early '70s club band.]
Wowii
   Rock 'N Roll Singer/I'm So Bad (Cartoon 1)   (77)
   [With members whose backgrounds reportedly
   include the Echoes of Carnaby Street and the
   pre-"Stoned Cowboy"-Fantasy. Wowii came real
   close to the big time, signing a lucrative deal with
   Elektra that fell apart when the corporate tie-guys
   heard how "uncommercial" their unreleased album
   was. Strange, considering one of those tracks,
   "Shake It Up," sounded suspiciously like a top ten
   smash many years later for another Elektra band,
   the Cars!]

7

SOUTH FLORIDA '60s ARTISTS ON COMPILATION ALBUMS

Steve Alaimo

    Best Is Yet To Come (*Trade Secrets Vol. 1*, Smash 422 830 408-1)

    Cold Sweat (*Something From The Air Force Academy*, USAFA 70)

    Girls! Girls! Girls! (*Steve Alaimo & Johnny Rivers*, Custom 1100)

    Hey Jude (*Something From The Air Force Academy*, USAFA 70)

    Home By Eleven (*Come To A Shindig Dance Party*, Custom 1038; *Steve Alaimo & Johnny Rivers*, Custom 1100)

    I Don't Know (*Smart*, Kent 052)

    I Wanna Kiss You (*Steve Alaimo & Johnny Rivers*, Custom 1100)

    I Want You To Love Me (*Steve Alaimo & Johnny Rivers*, Custom 1100)

    Knock On Wood (*Something From The Air Force Academy*, USAFA 70)

    Let It Be (*Something From The Air Force Academy*, USAFA 70)

    Let's Twist Again (*Dance Tunes From The Vault*, Chess 1476)

Love Letters (*Steve Alaimo & Johnny Rivers*, Custom 1100)

Nobody Cries For Me (*Based On The ABC-TV Shindig!*, ABC- Paramount 504)

Raindrops Keep Falling On My Head (*Something From The Air Force Academy*, USAFA 70)

She's My Baby (*Steve Alaimo & Johnny Rivers*, Custom 1100)

Should I Care (*Desperate Rock 'N Roll Vol. 9*)

Ticket to Ride (*Something From The Air Force Academy*, USAFA 70)

The Twist (*Dance Tunes From The Vault*, Chess 1476)

The Weekend's Over (*Steve Alaimo & Johnny Rivers*, Custom 1100)

You Can Fall In Love (*Steve Alaimo & Johnny Rivers*, Custom 1100)

Beaver Patrol

ESP (*Boulders Vol. 4*, 61 MLP 07; *Pebbles Vol. 11*, BFD)

Belles

Come Back (*Girls In The Garage Vol. 1*, Romulan UFO X02)

Melvin (*Garage Punk Unknowns, Vol. 4*, Stone Age 664; *Riot City!*, Satan 1003)

Birdwatchers

Girl I Got News For You (*Nuggets Vol. 5*, Rhino 029; *WFUN Son Of 21 Golden Rocks*, Take 6 2013; *WQAM Roaring 30*, Post 560)

Blues Image

Ride Captain Ride (*Atco Sales Meeting, Winter 1970*, Atco SD CSM 2; *Dusty And Sweets McGee Original Soundtrack*, Warner Bros. 1936; *Heavy Metal*, Warner Special Prod. 2001; *96X Home Grown*, Phoenix 76; *Super Hits Vol. 5*, Atlantic 8274)

Cavemen
> It's Trash (*Off The Wall Vol. 2*, Wreckord Wrack 1301)

Clefs Of Lavender Hill
> Stop! Get A Ticket (*Open Up Yer Door*, Frog Death Inc. 101; *WFUN Son Of 21 Golden Rocks*, Take 6 2013)
> [An '80s bootleg from France known as *Everywhere Chainsaw Sound (Interferences)* includes 8 Clefs tracks: First Tell Me Why, Gimme One Good Reason, It Won't Be Long, Oh Say My Love, One More Time, Play With Fire, So I'll Try, and Stop! Get A Ticket.]

Wayne Cochran
> Get Down With It (*WQAM's Roaring 30*, Post 560)
> Long Long Day (*The Music People*, Columbia C3X 31280)

Dee & Tee
> Something's Comin' (*Pebbles Vol. 14*, AIP 10014)

Echoes
> Every Second Of The Day (*Garage Punk Unknowns Vol. 7*, SA 667)

Echoes Of Carnaby Street
> Baby Doesn't Know (*Louisiana Punk*, Eva 12051)
> No Place Or Time (*Louisiana Punk*, Eva 12051)
> [Somehow the makers of this French compilation must have figured Florida was part of the Louisiana bayou!]

Evil
> Always Runnin' Around (*Boulders Vol. 3*, MAX MLP 04)
> Whatcha Gonna Do About It (*Boulders Vol. 3*, MAX MLP 04; *Scum Of The Earth Vol. 2*, Killdozer)
> [*Boulders* features a poor-quality reproduction of the edited Capitol version while *Scum Of The Earth* uses the full Living Legend track.]

H.M. Subjects - See The Montells.

Hip City Five
  Hound Dog
  Jamaica Ska
  Mashed Potatoes
  The Twist
  Twist And Shout
  [All five of the above appear on the 1964 album
  Arthur Murray Presents Discotheque Dance Party,
  RCA Victor 2998. Mickey Carroll, later a solo
  singer in the '70s and '80s, is the lead singer for
  this band, which used to be known as The
  Checkmates. Coincidentally, Carroll's first solo
  album, some twelve years later, was also on RCA.]

Immortals
  Laugh Laugh/Just A Little (*Braintree Battle Of The
  Bands*, Normandy)
  [This national Battle Of The Bands compilation
  featured acts from all over the country. The
  Immortals won the right to compete by winning
  the state Battle Of The Bands in St. Petersburg on
  May 20, 1967.]

Legends
  Alright (*Off The Wall*, Wreckord Wrack 1025)
  Say Mama (*Exciting New Releases From Sound
  Capitol Of The World*, Capitol 2376/77)
  [The Capitol LP was issued to disc jockeys in June,
  1963, while *Off The Wall* appeared as a bootleg in
  February, 1981.]

Mark Markham & The Jesters
  Goin' Back To Marlboro Country (*Florida Punk
  Groups From The Sixties*, Eva 12026)
  I Don't Need You (*Florida Punk Groups From The
  Sixties*, Eva 12026)
  [From a poorly put-together 1983 French bootleg.]

Minority
  Where Was My Mind (*Psychedelic Unknowns Vol.
  5*, Starglow- Neon 00001)
  [August, 1983, bootleg.]

Montells

>Don't Bring Me Down (*Good Roots; Psychotic Moose
>And The Soul Searchers*, Psychotic Moose 101)
>You Can't Make Me (*Back From The Grave Vol. 3*,
>Crypt 003)
>[The makers of the Autumn, 1982, *Psychotic
>Moose* bootleg neither realized that this was the
>Montells nor that it was even from Florida!]

The **Montells** tear up The Place in the summer of '66, twenty years before
appearing on several compilation albums. That's rhythm player John Weatherford on the left, and bassist extra-ordinaire Danny Murphy on the right. *Photo
courtesy Jeffrey Allen/The Montells*

Razor's Edge

>Get Yourself Together (*Garage Zone Vol. 2*,
>Moxie 17)

Tasmanians

>Baby (*Florida Punk Groups From The Sixties*,
>Eva 12026)

>Love Love Love (*Florida Punk Groups From The
>Sixties*, Eva 12026)

Vandals

>I Saw Her In A Mustang (*Garage Punk Unknowns
>Vol. 3*, Stone Age 663; *Riot City*, Satan 1003)

>[Artists from other sections of Florida are covered later in
>this book.]

8

PHASES AND STAGES

You'll always remember the first time you saw them. Maybe it was the Beatles. Maybe Jimi Hendrix, U2, or whomever. Something inside made it clear your life would never be the same. You were touched and somewhat transposed. A fool would call it infatuation. The poet knows it as inspiration.

It's the natural order of the music world: *Revolver* inspires *Pet Sounds*, which inspires *Sgt. Pepper*, which inspires *Their Satanic Majesties Request*. Inspiration breeds inspiration; no, INSPIRES inspiration. Musicians can't help but grow in a competitive, creative atmosphere, whether a national megagroup recording for one of the Big Six or a weekend musician recording for the first time.

In the first golden era of the weekend musician — the mid-'60s — there were countless ways to conjure up inspiration (starting with cool TV shows such as *Shindig* and *Hullabaloo*). As our local scene grew, bands sought inspiration not only from their English heroes, but from each other — musicians turning to other musicians for tips and tunes and serving as role models to help mold musical careers.

Especially artists who were a little older or more experienced. The impact a seasoned performer such as Fred Neil, who'd lived every lyric and done it all, could have on a young Travis Fairchild before he'd stopped and gotten his ticket... or what seeing the Legends meant to the guys who'd later bear names such as the Invaders or Shaggs. Below, you'll find a short list of local musicians from the South Florida '60s scene who share the names of their fellow scenesetters they considered the best or most influential to their careers:

The **Catalinas**, particularly rhythm player Ronnie Luke (second from left), were a huge influence on the Montells' Jeffrey Allen. Luke, a paratrooper in Viet Nam, died just six months after this picture was taken. *Photo courtesy John Mascaro*

Jeffrey Allen (Montells, Evil): "The Catalinas... especially their leader, Ronnie Luke. He's the guy who showed me that not just sissies play music."

Ronnie Armstrong (The Mor-Loks): The Ardells, The Twilites

Craig Ball (The New Society Band): The Shaggs and The Legends

Burt Compton (Oxfords, Heroes Of Cranberry Farm): The Shaggs

Bill DeMoya (Heirs Of Lorelei, Carter's Pills): The Montells, Squires V, and The Renegades

Donnie Goodson (The Invaders, The Echoes): The Canadian Legends

Mike Hughes (Evil): The Backbeats

Cleve Johns (The Shaggs): "The Legends... especially lead guitarist/singer Sam McCue."

Chuck Kirkpatrick (The Aerovons, Proctor Amusement Co.): "The Ardells were really hot!"

Dick Miller (Friends & Lovers, The Collegians): The Shaggs

Steve Palmer (Manager of dozens of bands): "The Canadian Legends were by far the best of all my bands."

John Sirocco (The Checkmates): "The Seven Blends at the Peppermint Lounge. I thought they were better than the Beatles."

Travis (Fairchild) Ximenes (Clefs Of Lavender Hill): "Fred Neil with Vince Martin."

[Fred Neil, the writer of "Everybody's Talkin'," "The Dolphins," "The Other Side Of This Life," and Roy Orbison's "Candy Man," influenced a wide range of artists, including Dion, John Sebastian, Dino Valenti, and the Jefferson Airplane. Speaking of inspiration, the late Jaco Pastorius once said the local band he dug the most while growing up was none other than the Shaggs!]

BANDS IN SOUTH FLORIDA

Here's where the mind really boggles. In the transient '60s, when change and expansion in music were commonplace, bands were prone to come and go at the drop of an amp. This makes it very difficult to chronicle just who was playing with whom at any given time. Still, I have attempted to list, to the best of my knowledge, a chronological installment of bands in South Florida. My apologies to anyone who may have been inadvertently omitted, and any additions or corrections, as always, are greatly appreciated!

1962 - Early 1965

Abstracts (Broward) (Gary Carter, guitar; Brad Roydhouse, drums . . .)

Agendas (Miami) (Ron Davis, vocals; Bert DeBois, guitar; Shelley Resnick, bass; Joe Garcia, drums)

American Beetles (West Palm Beach) (formerly The Ardells)

Apollos (West Palm Beach) (Dave Chiodo, guitar; Frank Nagy, sax; Bobby Puccetti, piano; Eddie Martinez, drums; Jim Tolliver/Vic Gray, bass. Keith McKendrick also played sax through 1961.)

Ardells (West Palm Beach) (Bill Ande, lead guitar; Tom Condra, rhythm guitar; Dave Hieronymus,

drums; Vic Gray/Jim Tolliver, bass, replacing
original bass player Johnny Burgess. It should be
noted that Tolliver and Gray played concurrently
in the Apollos and Ardells.)

Aztecs (Larry, Barry...)

Backbeats (I) (Lee Norman, lead guitar; Paul St.
Pierre, bass; Allan Mason, drums; Tommy
Strickland, guitar. Dennis Regan also filled in on
bass from time to time.)

Bailiffs

Birdwatchers (I) (originally West Palm Beach) (Bobby
Puccetti, keyboards; Eddie Martinez, drums; Jim
Tolliver, bass; Dave Chiodo, guitar.)

Blue Notes (Miami)

Bonnevilles (Broward) (John Marino, guitar...)

Briarwood Singers (Miami) (Stan Beach, Bob
Hoffman, Harry Scholes, Barry Bobst, Dorinda
Duncan)

Busy Signals (I) (Ft. Lauderdale) (John Archer,
guitar; Larry, guitar...)

Busy Signals (II) (Ft. Lauderdale) Joey Murcia, guitar;
Mike Dukes...)

Bystanders (Broward)

Canadian Legends (II) (Miami, via Milwaukee) (Jim
Sessody, drums; Jerry Schils, bass; Larry Foster,
rhythm guitar; Johnny Rondel, lead guitar; Billy
Joe Barnett, vocals, replaced by Ron Davis. Rondel
and Barnett replaced original lead guitarist and
vocalist Sam McCue, who rejoined the group early
in 1965.)

Candymen (Ft. Lauderdale) (Bob Ungerer, guitar...)

Caravelles (Broward) (Bruce Chandler, guitar...)

Catalinas (Miami) (Ronnie Luke, rhythm guitar;
Ronnie Sexton, lead guitar; Al Lavoie, drums;
Jimmy Cortez, bass)

Changing Tides (North Miami) (Bill Pelham, bass;
Ricky LaBresi, rhythm; Jeff Bolan, lead guitar;
Billy DeMoya, drums and vocals)

Chantels (Miami) (Mike Hughes, bass; Doug
Romanella, drums; Brian Grossman, guitar...)

Checkmates (Miami) (John Siracco, keyboards; Bert
DeBois, guitar, replaced by Ron Hutchinson;
Walter Williams, horn; Ronnie Pall, bass; George
Mora, drums. Also see HIP CITY 5).

Classics (Jack, Kurt, Bill...)

Cliques (Miami) (Mike Hughes, bass and guitar; Paul
Sosa, lead vocals; Dave Buser, guitar; David
Lerner, keyboards and sax; Rick Taylor, drums;
Mike Joseph)

Coachmen (Russ, Steve, Chuck, Bruce)

Coachmen (Broward) (Rick Tarquin, bass; Gary
Carter, guitar; Brad Roydhouse, drums; Danny
Skidmore, vocals)

Cobras (Broward) (Jimmy Smith, guitar; Tim
Yaquinto, guitar...)

Cobras (Hialeah) (Tom Bova, accordion; Charlie
Molter, guitar; Alan Alverson/Tom Vroga, drums...)

Continentals (Ft. Lauderdale) (Mike Vetro, vocals;
Mike Day, bass; Tony Sarandes, drums, replaced
by Brent Leckie)

Corvettes (John Seaton, Jim Crooke, Henry Senerth)

Crossfires

Deltonas (I) (Miami) (Craig Caraglior, vocals and
guitar; Don Ricketts, bass; Austin Huhn, rhythm;
Bob Kellett, drums)

Deltonas (II) (Craig Caraglior, vocals and guitar; Don
Ricketts, bass; John Mascaro, rhythm; Dewey
Bond, drums, replaced by Gregg Shaw)

The **Deltonas**, December 1964, at the P.A.L. Dance Hall (AKA Palmetto Bandstand). Three of the four members would soon join the Shaggs. Back row: Don Ricketts, bass; Gregg Shaw, drums. Front row: Craig Caraglior, lead guitar and vocals; John Mascaro, rhythm guitar and vocals. *Photo courtesy John Mascaro*

Dixons (Miami) (Stuart Colby, lead guitar; Bob Margolin, rhythm; Don Gillett, lead vocals; Mike Johannsen, drums; Jim Rush, piano)

Don & The Juniors (Miami) (Craig Caraglior, guitar; Dewey Bond, drums; Don Yocum, rhythm. The earliest pre-Shaggs band.)

Dukes (Miami) (Billy Vasquez, rhythm; Gene Salom, lead; Mario, drums; Louis, bass)

Dynamics (Miami) (Ron Hutchinson, guitar; George Mora, drums; Ron Pall, bass; Clair, sax)

Dynamics (Ft. Lauderdale) (Mike Chumley, guitar;
   Ron Pelleteri, lead and rhythm...)

Eldorados (Ft. Lauderdale) (Chuck Kirkpatrick,
   guitar; Allan Mason, drums; Rick Tarquin; Paul St.
   Pierre)

Elgins (Carol City)

Elites (Broward) (George Terry, guitar...)

Emanons (Miami) (Josh Marks, guitar; Eddie Harris,
   organ; Gary Waldman, drums...)

Explosions Plus Five (Miami)

Four Dimensions (Bob Wolfkill, rhythm; Frank
   Malone, lead; Jim O'Connell, bass; Tony Capallino,
   drums)

Four Speeds

Fugitives (Miami)

Golden Nuggets (Miami) (Bob White, sax; Carl Wells,
   guitar; Billy Meyer, guitar; John Bartee, drums)

Granadas (Miami)

Green Onions (Broward) (Randall Peters...)

Hip City 5 (Miami) (John Siracco, keyboards; Mickey
   Carroll, guitar; Walter Williams, horn; Ronnie Pail,
   bass, replaced by Nick Antonetti; George Mora,
   drums)

Impalas (Miami) (George Walden, lead guitar; John
   Weatherford, rhythm; George Hall, bass; Jeffrey
   Allen, drums; Gene Murray, part-time vocals,
   replaced by Carter Ragsdale. Originally known as
   The Emanons (No Names backwards), this was the
   lineup that became The Montells in 1964.)

Impalas (Ft. Lauderdale) (Chuck Kirkpatrick, guitar;
   Tommy Strickland, guitar; Paul St. Pierre, bass;
   Jim McCutcheon, drums, replaced by Dennis
   Potakar)

Impressions (also known as The Impressions V) (Ft.
   Lauderdale) (Sammy Hall, vocals; Johnny
   Hartigan, lead guitar; Mike Wall, drums; Don

Henry, rhythm; Ron Armstrong, bass. This lineup
changed its name to The Mor-Loks in 1965.)

Intruders (I) (Miami) (Chuck Guy, lead vocals; Kenny
Simons, lead guitar and bass; Phil Griffin, bass;
John Mascaro, rhythm guitar and vocals; Gene
Geiger and Bob Kellett, drums. Wes Brasse also
played guitar for a while.)

Intruders (II) (Chuck Guy, lead vocals; Phil Griffin,
bass; Austin Huhn, rhythm guitar and harmonica;
Kenny Simons, lead guitar and vocals; Bob Kellett,
drums and vocals.)

Jerry & Jesters (Jerry Phillips, guitar; Bill Kerti,
bass...)

Keynotes (Miami) (George Walden, guitar; John
Weatherford, rhythm... The earliest of the
pre-Montells bands.)

King Bees (Ft. Lauderdale) (Joe Moriello, guitar; John
Archer, guitar... Closely related to The Shadows.)

Kingsmen (Ft. Lauderdale) (Joey Murcia, guitar...)

Midnighters

Mistics (Miami)

Monarchs (Hialeah) (Charlie Molter, lead guitar;
Jimmy Cardinelli, drums; Chick Frissora,
accordion and sax; Wayne Wetley, rhythm; Jim
Ryan, rhythm)

Montells (I) (Miami) (George Walden, lead guitar;
John Weatherford, rhythm; George Hall, bass;
Jeffrey Allen, drums; Carter Ragsdale, lead vocals)

Mystics (Miami Beach) (Stan, Joey...)

Bobby Naylor & Saints (Ft. Lauderdale) (Bobby
Naylor, guitar and vocals; Chuck Kirkpatrick,
guitar; Fred Reed, drums)

Nomads (Miami) (Tom Bassing, drums; Kenny
Simons, guitar; Tim Metters, guitar...)

Novas (I) (Miami) (Jim LeFevre, bass; John Bernard, drums; Kenny Wynn, guitar; Bill Campbell, vocals; Rick Calaboro, guitar)

Nutones (Norland) (Roger Shane, guitar...)

Paragons (Miami) (Bill Kerti, bass; Jim Smith, lead guitar; Carl Keese, drums; Gary Ballman, rhythm)

Penetrations (Bob, lead guitar; Steve, drums; Pat, rhythm...)

Peridots (Miami) (Greg Monaco, bass; Bob Monaco, guitar; Pat Appochelli, guitar and vocals...)

Playboys (I) (Frank, Terry, Bill, Randy)

Playboys (II) (Frank, Terry, Bryan, Jimmy)

Proteges (Pompano) (Craig Chanson, Rick, Mike, Bob, Steve)

Quart Jesters (North Miami) (Billy DeMoya, vocals and drums; Bill Pelham, drums; Norman Shank, vocals; Jeff Nichols, lead guitar; Mark Watson, organ)

Rebels (Miami) (John Hurtak, bass; Chuck Cruz, guitar; Paul, drums...)

Regents (Broward)

Rock 'N Ramrods (Miami) (Dave McCafferty, Richard Groom, Carlos Linares...)

Sensations (North Miami) (Albert Costello, lead vocals and guitar; Don Norris, bass; Bill Cherry, rhythm...)

Shadows (Ft. Lauderdale) (John Archer, guitar; Joe Moriello, guitar; Dennis Regan, occasionally on bass . . .)

Shadows (also known as the Nation Rocking Shadows. Actually from Leesburg, but still a part of the Ft. Lauderdale Armory scene: Ronnie Skinner, lead guitar; David Friedman, drums; Bill Thacker, bass and vocals; Sherman McGreggor, rhythm guitar and vocals; Randy Boyte, organ)

Silent Knights (Miami) (Ernie Garza, vocals...)

Squires (Miami) (Austin Huhn, guitar; Roy Engleking, guitar; Dewey Bond, drums)

Stardusters (Hollywood) (Danny Lavrich, guitar; Mike Wilder, rhythm; Tim Mitchell, bass; Ted Burke, drums)

Stingrays (Broward) (Ron Armstrong, lead guitar; Ron Pelleteri, rhythm; Jim McCoy, sax; Mike Manion, keyboards and later bass; Joe Barnett/Brad Roydhouse, drums)

Surfin' Vibrations (Miami) (Ray Finn, lead guitar; John Mascaro, guitar; Kenny Christian, guitar; Gene Geiger, drums; Chuck Guy, vocals)

Swinging Rocks (Miami) (included a female vocalist)

Temptations

Tides (Broward)

Times Of Greenwich (Gary Vandy, rhythm...)

Torquays

Tradewinds (Miami) (Kenny Ahern, guitar; Jack Kinsell, rhythm; Jay Kolinski, saxophone; Bill Angus, drums)

Travelin' Wanderers (Chris Dieguez, guitar; Alberto DeAlmar, guitar; Mario, drums...)

Travellers (Coral Gables) (Kirby Howell, bass; Dan Brock, lead guitar; Bob Garvin, guitar; Bill Campbell, vocals; Randy Johnson, drums, replaced by Henry Matta. Later known as The Collegians.)

Tresspassers (Roy Sluzis...)

Twilites (North Miami) (Bill Moss, guitar; Fred Moss, drums; Gordon, bass)

Valiants

Velairs (Broward) (Joe Costa...)

Velvetones (Broward) (Bill Kluenie, guitar; Ted Burke, drums)

Villagers (Miami) (Peggi Greene, Scotty Greene)

Voyagers (Miami) (Richie Chimelis, vocals; Mike
  Latona, bass; Dewey Bond; drums; Dennis
  O'Barry, lead guitar; Cleve Johns, rhythm guitar)

Weeds (Boca Raton, via Lakeland) (Skip Sheffield,
  bass and vocals; Bobby Johns, lead guitar; John
  Baldwin, drums)

Yellow Jackets (Miami) (Gregg Shaw, drums; Tim
  Yero, guitar...)

1965-1966

A-Men (Miami) (Bill Sabella, keyboards and vocals;
  Bob Lewis, bass; Tim Yero, guitar and vocals;
  Keith Van Shoik, drums)

Aerovons (Ft. Lauderdale) (Chuck Kirkpatrick, lead
  guitar; Dennis Williams, bass; Vince Corrao,
  drums; Dick Cook, rhythm guitar)

Aesop and The Fables

Alley Kats (Miami) (Frank, Danny...)

Amazing Aztecs

Avengers (Dade) (Chuck Stewart, drums; Ronny
  Maurno, guitar; John, bass; Carlos, vocals; Randy,
  rhythm)

Avengers (Dade) (Nick, Steve, Tom, Nick)

Avengers (Broward) (Bill, organ; Glenn, lead; Tom,
  vocals; Dick, rhythm; Keith, bass; Dick, drums)

Back Beats (II) (Lee Norman, rhythm; Paul St. Pierre,
  bass; Allan Mason, drums; Larry, guitar) (House
  band at the Palmetto Bandstand)

Barons (Miami) (Rocky Mountain, guitar; Jerry Avick,
  drums; Bill Marks, bass; Rich, guitar)

Bartocks' Mts. (Ft. Lauderdale) (Bob Hertzog, vocals;
  Bill Burke, organ; Tom Staley, drums; Ken
  Gemmer, guitar)

Beethoven's Fifth (Hollywood) (Girls!)

Belles (North Miami Beach) (Debbie Teaver, rhythm guitar and vocals; Pam Kent, drums; Marina Perez, bass and vocals; May Perez, lead guitar)

Birdwatchers (II) (now Miami-based) (Bobby Puccetti, organ; Sammy Hall, vocals; Eddie Martinez, drums; Joey Murcia, lead guitar; Jerry Schils, bass)

Blazing Daddy-O's (Miami) (John Siracco, keyboards; Ron Davis, vocals and guitar; Joe Hevia, drums)

Blokes (Miami) (Gary Salem, vocals; Frank Rebello, keyboards; Harold, Roger, Norman)

Blue Beatles (Miami) (Bob Breen, guitar; Bob Bach, drum; Ken Medder, bass)

Blue Notes (I) (Miami) (Doug Carter, sax; Jeff Masari, organ; Tim Boynton, bass; John Bartee, drums)

Bluetones (Hialeah) (Noel Perez, bass; Joe Pla, lead guitar; Joe Livermore, rhythm; Joe Gonzalez, drums)

Bods + 1 (Miami)

Body Shoppe (Hollywood) (Jimmy Bowers, Ricky Bowers... Also known as The Calientes.)

Bossmen

Boston Tea Party (Miami) (Bob Halley, bass; Chris Dieguez, guitar; Steve Chase, guitar...)

Brewins (Miami) (John Moore, Greg Fuote, Joe Mancuso...)

Bushmen

Caesar's Four (Miami) (Ronnie Pall, bass; George Mora, drums; Pete Gill, lead guitar; Gene, vocals...)

Calliatis

Calientes (Hollywood) (see Body Shoppe)

Canadian Legends (III) (Miami) (Sam McCue, lead guitar and vocals; Jim Sessody, drums; Larry Foster, rhythm guitar; Jerry Schils, bass. The Legends broke up on January 1, 1966.)

Carry-Ons

Castaways (North Miami) (Ricky LeBresi, rhythm;
    Jeff Bolan, lead guitar; Don Granda, vocals;
    Danny Alexander, bass)

Cavemen (John Brouillard, guitar; Jeff Delgarn,
    drums; Tony Avella; Bill Condrone; Matt Prespy)

Cellar Dwellers (Broward) (Mike Vetro, vocals; Dave
    Bonovitch and Brent Leckie, drums; Jim
    McClung...)

Centaurs (Miami) (Bob, drums...)

Chayns (Miami) (Dave Stevens, drums; Chuck
    Blazek...)
    [There seems to have been at least four different
    groups in South Florida using this name.]

Checkmates (Miami) (Ron Blecha, bass; Steve Hood,
    rhythm; Allen Haller, lead; Pete Nantovech, drums;
    John Cheek)

Chevels (Coral Gables) (Bob Alley, guitar; David
    Chiles, guitar; Jack Liberman, vocals; Steve
    Metzger, bass; Randy Johnson, drums)

Chordells (Miami)

Chosen Few (Broward) (Mike Caplan, guitar and
    trumpet; Tony Sarandes, drums; Scott Faunce,
    bass; John Sly, organ; Tom Dismuke, guitar)

Clefs Of Lavender Hill (I) (North Miami) (Travis
    Fairchild, guitar and vocals; Coventry, guitar and
    vocals; Bill Moss, bass; Fred Moss, drums)

Coastwatchers (Vic, John, Al, Mike)

Collegians (I) (Coral Gables/Miami) (Dick Miller,
    guitar; Kirby Howell, bass; Dan Brock, guitar; Bill
    Campbell, vocals; Bob Garvin, rhythm; Henry
    Matta, drums)

Collegians (II) (Dick Miller, guitar; Dan Brock, guitar;
    Henry Matta, drums; Dick Lee, bass and electric
    piano)
    [It should be noted that around this time The

Collegians and The Novas became virtually interchangeable, and any of the preceding musicians could have been a Nova at any time.]

Convairs (I) (Miami) (Bob Del Poso, Wayne Powell, Fred, John, Pete)

Convairs (II) (included Greg Williams, drums, and Chuck Witherow, keyboards)

Cro-Magnons (Carol City/Opa-Locka) (Gary Gott, vocals; Arthur Payne, drums; Dave Simmons, guitar; Bill Kerti, bass; Jim Smith, lead guitar)

Crumbums (Miami) (Randee Lemlich, vocals and drums; Debbie Friedman, vocals; Jeff Lemlich, vocals)

John Dante and English Americans (Jimmy Redding, drums...)

Dave & The Wanderers (Miami) (Gene Salom, lead guitar; Billy Vasquez, rhythm; Carlos Driggs, drums; Paul Gonzalez, bass; Dave and Norman, vocals)

December's Children (Miami) (Al Costello, vocals...)

Dedd (Miami)

Dr. T. & The Undertakers (I) (Miami) (Tony Asci, organ and vocals; Jerry Johnson, drums and vocals; Sal Gonzalez, guitar; Bob Barbara, rhythm; Louie, bass)

Down Beats (Miami) (Gary Selken, Craig Nash, Jeff Myers, Ronnie Perkins)

Drones (Hialeah) (Paul Rose, lead guitar and vocals; Brim Leal, rhythm guitar and vocals...)

Duke & Counts (Miami)

Early Times (Miami) (Al Yanes, guitar; Jimmy Goodman, rhythm; Greg Orsini, drums...)

Echoes (I) (Miami) (Jim Crosbie, drums; Kenny Ahern, guitar and vocals; Scott Lamb, bass; Wayne Magley, rhythm)

Echoes of Carnaby Street

Esquires

Essex of Sound (Miami) (Jim, lead vocals; Phil, bass; Jerry, rhythm; Tom, drums; Steve, lead guitar)

Evil (I) (Miami) (John Doyle, lead vocals; Stan Kinchen, lead guitar; Al Banyai, rhythm; Doug Romanella, drums; Larry O'Connell, bass)

Evil (II) - same as above, with George Hall, followed by Mike Hughes, replacing O'Connell on bass.

Existers (John, Butch, Blair, Chris)

Falcons (Miami) (Steve Griffin, John Molin, Jeff Lovell, Jim Haizlip, Dan Haizlip)

Finders Keepers (Miami)

Fugitives (Miami)

Gents Five (Northwest Dade) (Chris; Steve; Dave; Jerry Cohn, guitar; Ronnie Chassner, vocals)

Good Reasons (Ft. Lauderdale) (Dean Goodwin, bass; Tom Strickland, lead guitar; Bob Fausett, rhythm; Jim Sindelar, drums; Aaron Dagovitz, piano)

Grim Reapers (Miami)

Grotesque

Hares (I) (Miami) (Chuck Guy, vocals; Phil Griffin, bass; Austin Huhn, rhythm; Kenny Simons, lead guitar; Bob Kellett, drums. Formerly The Intruders.)

Hares (II) (Pete Gill, lead guitar; Phil Griffin, bass; Bob Kellett, drums; Austin Huhn, rhythm; Chuck Guy, vocals)

Harlequins

Heirs of Lorilei (North Miami) (Billy DeMoya, drums & vocals; Mark Watson, organ; Bill Cherry, rhythm and lead guitars; Craig Cherry, bass; Jim Kabori, rhythm)

Henchmen (Miami) (Brian King, guitar; Burt Compton, drums; Clint Collins, guitar; Rocky Mountain, guitar)

Hide Aways (Miami)

High Society (Broward)

Hustlers (Miami) (Johnny McNicol, guitar; Bob
Leavitt, rhythm...)

Ideals (Miami) (Alberto Guerra, lead guitar and
vocals; Tony, keyboards; Renee, drums; Gustavo...)

Impacts (Miami) (Terry McGarey, guitar; Ron Blades;
Ken Summers, replaced by Rene; Rocky Gimenez,
replaced by Mike)

Innkeepers (Miami)

Invaders (Miami) (Bob Haas, keyboards; Steve Seitz,
bass; Jeff Glass, saxophone and horn; Donnie
Goodson, drums; Dave Davis, lead guitar and
vocals, replacing Kenny Ahern)

Jades (Miami) (Mike, lead; George, rhythm, Kelly,
bass; Steve, organ; Tom, drums)

Jagged Edge (Miami)

Jesters (Miami) (Richard White, Bob Ammarell, Mike
Linet, Pete Mooy)

Jokers Wild (Miami)

Kegs (Miami) (Steve Sexton; Bob Berke, drums;
Richard Peacock, guitar)

Knowmads (Miami Beach)

Legends (unrelated to Canadian Legends) (Bob,
Steve, Greg, Bud)

Limeys (Miami) (Andrea Gennard, Stephen Gennard)

London Chymes (North Miami) (Steve Bates, lead
guitar; Tom Murasso, lead vocals; John Hair,
drums; Vince Deegan, bass; Bill Cherry, rhythm
guitar)

Lovin' Kind (Bill, George...)

Madmen (Miami) (Frank Trabonello, guitar; Tony
Trabonello, saxophone...)

Mark V (Jerry, Butch, Jim, Rick, Wayne)

Mark Markham & Jesters (Ft. Lauderdale) (Mark Markham, vocals and guitar; Scott Austin, drums...)

Me And The Others (Miami) (Alan, George, Dave, Pat)

Michael & The Strangers (Mike, Leroy, Ron, Ken)

Minute Men (Hialeah) (Don Wetzel, Terry Wetzel...)

Mis Fits (Bob Howard, Joe Andrules...)

Missing Links (Miami) (Sandy, organ; Scott, lead; Mac, drums; Ronny, Rhythm)

Modds (Miami) (Bob Nimmer, lead guitar; Dean Liapis, vocals; Dennis O'Barry, 2nd lead guitar; Dewey Bond, drums; John Mascaro, rhythm and vocals; Don Ricketts, bass)

Montells (II) (Miami) (George Walden, lead guitar; John Weatherford, rhythm; Carter Ragsdale, lead vocals; Danny Murphy, bass and vocals; Jeffrey Allen, drums. Also Don Ricketts on bass for a time.)

Mor-Loks (I) (Ft. Lauderdale) (Sammy Hall, lead vocals; Johnny Hartigan, lead guitar; Don Henry, rhythm; Ron Armstrong, bass; Mike Wall, drums)

Mor-Loks (II) (Bill "Nappy" Lynn, lead vocals; Craig Held, lead guitar; Ron Armstrong, bass; Billy Burke, keyboards; Mike Wall, drums, replaced by Jim Leach)

Morticians

Mustangs (Miami) (John Smith, Gary Sorensen, Steve Felts, George Goodridge, Rob Goodridge)

Mystics (Miami Beach) (Joey Posnick, keyboards; Stanley Soloman, drums...)

New Society Band (I) (Miami) (Craig Ball, lead guitar; Andy Berlin, rhythm; Jimmy Muller, bass; Alan Wall, drums. This lineup remained intact through 1970.)

Nightriders (Jan, Steve...)

Nightwalkers (I) (Miami) (Chris Horn, guitar; Bob Caldwell; Mike Fogarty; Chip Kinsey)

No Names

Noblemen (Miami)

Nobles (Miami) (Joe Smith, Eddie Smith, Jack Jones, Ray Harris)

Nomads (Andy Berlin, rhythm; Craig Ball, lead guitar; Robert Vigman, keyboards; Malcolm Teitzer, bass)

Our Generation (Broward)

Oxfords (Miami) (Pat McMakin, rhythm; Jim Kemp, vocals; Brian King, lead guitar; Burt Compton, drums)

Outcasts (Miami) (Jeff Levine, vocals; Irv, bass; Walt, rhythm; Mike, drums; Mike, lead guitar)

Paxtons

Plunket's Canoe (Broward)

Pods (Miami) (Alberto DeAlmar, guitar; Chris Dieguez, guitar; Gene Salom, part-time guitar; Mario, drums)

Poets (Miami) (Bob Goodridge, sax; George Goodridge...)

Prowlers

Pyramids (Marc Levy, guitar; Kippy Paulin, bass; Benjie Lieberman, drums; Lenny, lead; Stew, rhythm)

Remnants (Miami) (Chuck, Jeff...)

Renegades (Miami) (Lee Tiger, lead guitar; Steve Tiger, rhythm; Ernie Garza, guitar; Tommy Higgs, drums)

Roadrunners (Homestead) (Jim, John, Butch, Buddy)

Roadrunners (Hollywood)

Robin And The Sherwoods

Rogues (Miami) (Vince Deegan, bass; Jack Horner, keyboards; John Bartee, drums; John Toto, guitar)

Roustabouts (I) (Miami) (Ivan Bailey, bass and lead vocals; Chalice Bailey, drums; John McLaughlin, lead guitar and vocals; Jim Taylor, guitar)

Royal Headhunters

Sabres (Miami) (Frank Beckett, lead guitar; Connally Addington, bass; Jack Horner, keyboards; John Bernard, drums)

Saints Of Labour (Miami) (Ernie, Bill, George, Fritos, Freddy)

Senecas (Broward)

Serfs (Miami)

7 Of Us (I) (Miami, formerly of New York) (Frankie Gadler, vocals; Terry Adams, keyboards; Jody Spampanato, bass; Johnny, vocals...)

Shadells (Eddie Baquero...)

Shaggs (I) (Miami) (Richie Chimelis, vocals; Craig Caraglior, vocals and guitar; Mike Latona, bass; Cleve Johns, rhythm guitar and vocals; Dennis O'Barry, lead guitar; Gregg Shaw, drums)

Shaggs (II) (Craig Caraglior, lead guitar and vocals; Cleve Johns, rhythm guitar and vocals; Richie Chimelis, vocals; Don Ricketts, bass; Gregg Shaw, drums)

Shandels (Miami) (Terry Mongole, Bob Jennings...)

Sherlock And The Spies

Shires (Miami) (Joe, Al, Mike, Mickey)

Showmen (Miami) (Robbie, lead; Randy, bass; Ramon, drums; George, rhythm)

Something Good (North Miami) (George Bennett, bass; Carl Wells, lead guitar; Bob White, rhythm guitar; Tom Kounelis, drums, Jack Horner, keyboards)

Soul Riders (North Miami) (Bill Lachmiller, guitar; Ike Borac, keyboards; Cliff LaRue, trumpet; Dale Mathews; Steve, Paul, Ronnie)

Sound Merchants (Miami) (Tony Metka, rhythm; Jim Metka, bass; Don Neuman; Don Snyder; Jim McLaughlin; (later) Joe Parent)

Sounds Of Silent

Sounds V (Miami) (Frank Trabonello, guitar; Tony Trabonello, sax; Frank Milone, bass; Sal De La Rosa, drums)

Sovereigns

Squires V (North Miami) (Steve Bates, lead guitar; Al Costello, vocals; Vince Deegan, bass; Bill Cherry, rhythm; Fred Samms, drums)

Stingrays (Miami) (Howie Albert, keyboards...)

Stones (Mike, Ted, Steve, Mike)

Stops (Hialeah) (Wayne Wetley, rhythm...)

Strat-O-Tones (Miami Beach) (Bill, drums; Carl, rhythm; Martin, rhythm and bass; Barry, organ; Irene, guitar; Andrea, guitar)

Streetmen

Summits (Miami) (Rick Calaboro, guitar; George Taylor, drums; Mel Phillips; Mark Carlson)

Tensions (Key Biscayne) (later known as The Wild Ones)

Trods (Miami) (Denis, Alfred, Tom, Mike)

Trolls (Ft. Lauderdale) (Sammy Hall, lead vocals; Johnny Hartigan, lead guitar; Brad Roydhouse, drums; Rick Tarquin, bass)

Tyrants (Miami) (Ronnie B., lead; David M., drums; Robert G., bass; Howard S., vocals; Jerry L., rhythm)

Upper Hand (Broward) (Tommy Strand, lead vocals...)

Vampyres (Miami) (Hector, organ; Mandy, bass; Al, guitar; Raul, drums)

Vandals (Hollywood) (George Terry, lead guitar; Johnny Sambataro, rhythm guitar and bass; Augie Bucci, keyboards; Richie Kutcher, drums; Bill

Cosford, guitar and tambourine (part-time member); Russ Sepielli, vocals (part-time member)

Vigils (Miami) (Butch, John, Steve, Mark, Joe)

Villagers (I) (West Palm Beach) (Jeff Teague, drums; Brian Rich, guitar; Bill Donahue, keyboards; Roger Berger, bass; Rick Steele, lead vocals)

Wet Paint (Miami)

What's Left? (Ft. Lauderdale) (Brent Leckie, drums; Danny Skidmore, vocals...)

Wild Ones (Key Biscayne) (Mark Fielden...)

Wyrd (Miami/Hialeah) (Frank Trabonello, lead guitar; Frank Milone, rhythm; Tom Cooper, bass; Sal De La Rosa, drums; Tony Trabonello, sax)

LATE 1966 - 1967

Agents (Miami) (Bud Bradbury, keyboards and sax; Andy Charlton, guitar; Dick Whiting, guitar; Gary Walker, drums)

Ambassadors (I) (Ft. Lauderdale) (Joe Mayer, lead guitar; Dick Newbauer, rhythm; Galen Barker, bass; Les Luhring, keyboards; Scott Kirkpatrick, drums)

Apaches

Apple (Miami) (Bill Cherry, guitar; Craig Cherry, bass; Tom Murasso, vocals; Billy DeMoya, vocals; Stan Crawl, organ; Tom Cherney, drums)

Atoms (Miami) Gidge Miller, lead guitar; Gabriel Sanchez, drums; Jorge Sanchez, bass)

Bangles (also known as Bangs) (I) (Miami) Lee Tiger, lead guitar; Stephen Tiger, rhythm; Mike Latona, bass; Tommy Higgs, drums)

Beaver Patrol (Hollywood) (Jim Bledsoe, bass; Floyd Humphrys, guitar; Jimmy Becker, drums; Gary Vandy, rhythm. Vandy does not appear on the group's Columbia 45.)

Birds & The Bees (North Miami) (Mike White, vocals and organ; Bill Moss, bass; Fred Moss; drums)

Bitter Ind (Ft. Lauderdale, via Jacksonville) (David Brown, bass; Scott Boyer, guitar; Butch Trucks, drums. This group later became The 31st Of February.)

Blue Notes (II) (Miami) (John Bartee, drums; Jack Horner, keyboards; Tim Boynton, bass)

Bo Pete & His Playboys (North Miami)

Buddha & The Idols (Miami) (Bill Marks, bass; Terry Kaiser, drums; Rocky Mountain, guitar; Glenn, keyboards)

Burgundy Blues (Miami) (Tim Yero, guitar and vocals; Bill Sabella, organ; Bob Lewis, bass; Burt Compton, drums. Compton does not appear on the group's Argee 45.)

Carter's Pills (Miami) (Carter Ragsdale, lead vocals; Steve Chase, guitar; Bob Halley, bass; Billy DeMoya, drums; Mark Watson, organ)

Chelsea's Children

Chessmen (Miami) (Craig Houghton, drums; Mike, Ray, John)

Clefs Of Lavender Hill (II) (North Miami) (Travis Fairchild, guitar and vocals; Coventry, guitar and vocals; John Hair, drums...)

Countdowns (Miami) (Scott Lamb, bass; Roger Pavlica, guitar...)

Cowboys & Indians (Miami) (Travis Fairchild, guitar and vocals; Coventry, guitar and vocals...)

December's Children (Hollywood)

Dead End Kids (Miami) (Tim Metters, guitar; Bob Bach, drums...)

Dedd Set (Miami) (John Elroy, Ray Harris, Bill Wrightson, Tom Grantz, Butch Walders)

Dirt Merchants (Miami)

Dr. T. & The Undertakers (II) (Miami) (Tony Asci,
    organ and vocals; Jerry Johnson, drums and
    vocals; Bob Barbara, rhythm; Bobby Jabo, lead
    guitar; Bob Usherson, bass)

Druids (Miami) (Bruce Balint, guitar; Bruce
    Starbuck, drums; Mike Goad; Craig Throssell)

Echoes (II) (Miami) (Kenny Ahern, lead guitar; Bill
    Kerti, bass; Wayne Magley, rhythm; Donnie
    Goodson, drums; Don Fedele, keyboards)

Eighth Day (West Palm Beach)

End (South Dade) (Bill Layton...)

Evil (III) (Miami) (John Doyle, lead vocals; Mike
    Hughes, bass; Stan Kinchen, lead guitar; John
    Dalton, rhythm; Jeffrey Allen, drums)

Evil (IV) (John Doyle, lead vocals; Stan Kinchen, lead
    guitar; Frank Milone, bass...)

Faces (Miami) (Danny Murphy, bass and vocals;
    George Walden, lead guitar; Jeffrey Allen, drums.
    This trio of ex-Montells was also known as The
    Flowers for a short time.)

Five Too Many (Miami) (Jon...)

Fortune Tellers (Hialeah) (Dan, organ; Fred, drums;
    Glen, rhythm; Richard, lead; Mike, vocals)

Friends & Lovers (I) (Coral Gables/Miami) (Dick
    Miller, guitar; Dan Brock, Jr., rhythm; Randy
    Johnson, drums; David Chiles, bass; Jack
    Liberman, vocals; Marjorie and Nancy Leonard,
    vocals, replaced by Jane Margulis)

Fugue (North Miami) (Bill Cherry, guitar; Craig
    Cherry, bass; Pete Bartell, rhythm; Bob Rose,
    organ; Lou Kramer, drums; Vince Deegan, vocals,
    replaced by Alpart Zugar)

Gas Company (Ft. Lauderdale) (Ken Byers, Jr.,
    organ; Gary Carter, guitar; George Terry, bass and
    guitar; Sandy Meyer, drums; Chuck Kirkpatrick,

rhythm and lead. This lineup became The Proctor
Amusement Company.)

Gemini & The Planets

Grapes Of Wrath (Miami) (Bobby Brooks...)

Grievance Committee (Miami) (Bill Sabella,
keyboards and vocals; Burt Compton, drums; Tim
Yero, guitar and vocals; Bob Lewis, bass)

Hares (III) (Miami) (Pete Gill, lead guitar and vocals;
Austin Huhn, rhythm and bass; Allan Mason,
drums, replaced by Bennie Becker, Sam Harris,
Tony Novello, and Leo)

Immortals (Hollywood) (Denis Barberio, Steve
Barberio, Dan Hess, Louis Mowad, John Battaglia)

Intrigues (Broward) (Gino Moretta...)

Intruders (Miami) (George Budachis, vocals; Bill
DeMoya, vocals; Tom Tyree, rhythm; John
O'Donnell, lead guitar; Bob Mercagliano, drums;
Don Borgese, bass)

Kidds (Miami) (Chuck Guy, vocals; Slaton Shaw,
organ; Ronnie Sexton, lead guitar; Bob Bach,
drums; Jimmie, bass. Formerly the Tradgidies)

Knight Riders (Miami) (Jim, Mike T., Mike M., Ken)

Kollektion (I) (Miami) (Richie Chimelis, vocals; Angel
Rissoff, vocals; Mike Latona, bass; Bobby Jabo,
lead guitar; Richie Borkin, keyboards; Gregg
Shaw, drums, replacing Doug Romanella)

Krypt Kickers (Ft. Lauderdale) (Jim Smith...)

Lansirs V (Roy Spaulding, lead vocals...)

Las Olas Brass (Broward) (Danny Skidmore, vocals...)

Last Word (Miami, via New York) (John Lombardo,
lead vocals and tambourine; Mike Byrnes, guitar;
Rick Cook, drums; Steve Sechak, organ)

Marat Sade (Miami) (Jim Hilley, guitar and vocals;
Bob Wessells, lead vocals; Andy Charlton, guitar
and vocals; Dan Oelker, bass; Buddy Palmer,
keyboards; Bob Quirk, drums)

Mass Confusion (I) (Miami) (Mark Elfenbein, lead; Steve Griffin, bass; Chuck Gomez, rhythm; Chuck Spivak, drums)

Montells (III) (Miami) George Walden, lead guitar; Danny Murphy, bass and vocals; Carter Ragsdale, lead vocals; John Weatherford, rhythm; Ted Napoleon, drums)

Mystics (Miami) (Lee, Peter...)

Myth (Miami Beach)

Myths (Miami) (Joe, Alan, Bill, Harry, Frankie)

New Breed (Miami) (Mark Fielden, guitar; Bill Sabella, keyboards; Drew Donnelly, guitar; Al Albert, bass; Rusty, drums)

New Chains III (Hollywood) (Rob Campbell, bass; Ron Fontes, organ; Steve Sallaz, rhythm; Steve Bacall, lead singer-guitarist; Ed Doros, drums)

New York Square Library (I) (Miami) (Brooks Reid, guitar; John Monroe, drums; Kjeld Kristensen; Chris Martin)

Nightwalkers (II) (Miami) (Bob Goodridge, sax; Bob Caldwell, guitar; George Goodridge; Chip Kinsey; Dave Brooks)

Nomads (I) (Miami) (Shannon Thomas, bass; Dan Halyburton, lead vocal and guitar; Bruce King, lead guitar; Maury Sheets, drums)

Norwegians (Miami) (Jeff Bodry, vocals; Frank Milone, bass; Gary Santarcangelo, rhythm; Ken, lead guitar)

Novas (II) (Miami) (Kenny Wynn, lead guitar; Jim LeFevre, bass; Rick Calaboro, guitar; John Bernard, drums)

Odds And Ends (Miami) (Richard Ashley, Rik Rasmussen, Mike Murphy, Lance Shotwell, Steve Fletcher)

Outcasts (Miami) (Duke, Phil, Chuck, Don, Dave)

Pawns (Miami)

Pigeons (South Dade, via New York) (Mark Stein, organ and vocals; Vinnie Martell, lead guitar; Tim Bogert, bass; Joe Brenan/Carmine Appice, drums)

Plagues (Miami)

Potions

Proctor Amusement Company (I) (Ft. Lauderdale) (Ken Byers, Jr., organ; Gary Carter, guitar; Chuck Kirkpatrick, rhythm and lead; George Terry, bass and guitar; Sandy Meyer, drums)

Quantrels (Miami) (George Brown, Bob Rush, Ken Price, Bob Tanner)

Razor's Edge (West Palm Beach) (Bill Ande, lead guitar; Tom Condra, rhythm; Jim Tolliver, bass; Dave Hieronymus, drums)

Roustabouts (II) (Miami) (Ivan Bailey, bass and lead vocals; Chalice Bailey, drums; John McLaughlin, lead guitar and vocals; John Hulzing, sax and flute; Manny Lopez)

Royal Ascots (Hollywood)

Sceptors (Miami) (Eric, Terry...)

Sensations (Miami)

Sentrys (South Miami) (Bobby Roberts, guitar; Chuck Spivak, drums and vocals; Steve Griffin, bass; Mark Elfenbein, guitar)

Shades Inc. (I) (Miami) (Pat Smith, bass; Spike Warner, lead guitar; Randy Wooley, vocals; Jim States, guitar; Mario Combo, drums)

Shades Of Jade

Shaggs (III) (Miami) (Craig Caraglior, lead guitar and vocals; Cleve Johns, rhythm guitar and vocals; Jacques Heideier, vocals and some percussion; Mark Watson, organ; Doug Romanella, drums; Don Ricketts, bass; replaced by Chris Dieguez)

Short Sircuits (Miami) (Clint Border, bass; Dave Darlington, guitar; Jim Hilley, lead guitar and

vocals; John Hilley, drums, Scott Truax,
keyboards)

Slaves Of Sound (Miami) (Burt Compton, drums;
Brian King, lead guitar; John Austin, rhythm;
Barry Barnard, bass; Marc Steinhauer, keyboards;
Bruce Merwin, lead vocals)

Sounds Of Soul (John Gallagher, drums; Bill, Ward)

Sound Waves (Miami) (How, Ches, Lou, Dan)

Sounds Unlimited (Hialeah/Miami) (Paul Rose, lead
guitar; George Bennett/Larry Hines, bass; Randy
Rhodes, drums; Richard Dow, rhythm; Richie
Borkin, organ)

Spellbinders (Hialeah) (Charlie Molter, lead guitar;
Harry Jones, keyboards; Russ McKinley/Greg
Carpenter, lead vocals; Mel Weinberg, drums;
Dennis Beres, bass)

Squiremen IV (I) (Miami) (Jim Oliver, organ; Jerry
Molina, rhythm guitar; Don O'Connell, bass;
Sandy Torano, lead guitar; Bennie Buchacher,
drums)

Squires (Miami)

Squires III (Miami)

St. John's Wood (Miami) (Rick, Davy, John, Mark)

Stoned (Miami) (Doug Burke, bass; Bruce Starbuck,
drums; Bruce Balint, guitar; Craig Trossel)

Strangers (Miami)

Stix & Stonz (I) (Miami) (Larry Sharp...)

Take Five (West Palm Beach) (Lee Davis, Don
Zaniewski, Jim Wilson, Bob Brown, Jim Bielick)

Thingies (Miami, via Topeka, Kansas) (Larry Joe
Miller, bass and vocals; Gordon Marcellus, drums;
John Dalton, guitar; Bob Cole, organ; Phil Weaver,
vocals. The Thingies arrived from Topeka in July,
1967, and left for Austin, Texas, in September.)

Trashmen (Miami)

Victims (Miami)

Villagers (II) (West Palm Beach) (Jeff Teague, drums; Brian Rich, guitar; Bill Donahue, keyboards; Joe Dunlop, bass; Rick Steele, lead vocals)

Warlocks (Hialeah) (Kooky Berrios, keyboards; Bob Gonzalez, bass; Ricky Murciano, lead guitar; Donnie Jarrells)

The What (Miami) (George Parrott, lead guitar; Jamene Miller, vocals; Rick S.; John C.; Chris L.)

Wretched Souls

Yeknom (Miami) (Randee Lemlich, drums; George Tershakovec, organ; Andrew Tershakovec, guitar) [Later called the Purple Flurp.]

Young Strangers (Miami) (Greg Risca, Jim Culliton, Bob Weaver, Alan Papas, Russ Killinger)

Zodiacs

1968 - 1969

Aboriginal Missionary (Miami) (Chris Horn, first guitar; Bob Lamoreaux, second guitar; Al Banyai, vocals; Bill Banyai, bass; Tom Lamons, drums)

Ambassadors (II) (Broward) (Les Luhring, keyboards; Eddie Keating, vocals and guitar; Jim Godwin, lead guitar; Dick Newbauer, rhythm guitar; Scott Kirkpatrick/Rich Franks, drums. Evolved into Bridge.)

Bangs (II) (Miami) (Mike Hughes, bass; Steve Chase, guitar; Steve Tiger, rhythm; Terry McGarey, guitar; Tom Cherney, drums)

Bangs/Bangles (III) (Steve Tiger, rhythm; Lee Tiger, bass; Frank Trabonello, lead guitar; Tommy Higgs, drums)

Birdwatchers (III) (Miami) (Bobby Puccetti, organ; Eddie Martinez, drums and vocals; Jerry Schils, bass; Craig Caraglior, guitar and vocals; Joey Murcia, lead guitar until January, 1969)

Blues Image (I) (North Miami, via Tampa) (Mike
    Pinera, lead guitar and vocals; Angel Rissoff,
    vocals; Frank Skip Konte, organ; Joe Lala (also
    known as Sabu Schwartz), drums; Manuel
    Bertematti, drums; Malcolm Jones, bass; Bob
    Hoffman, lead and rhythm guitar)

Blue Jam (Miami) (Billy DeMoya, vocals and drums;
    Tom Tyree, rhythm guitar; John O'Donnell, lead
    guitar; Bob Mercagliano, drums; Don Borgese,
    bass; Mark Watson, organ)

Blues Messengers (Hollywood)

Briarwoods (Miami) (Dorinda Duncan, vocals; Barry
    Monroe, 12-string guitar and vocals; Charles Fye,
    bass; Russell Howard, lead guitar; Bob Smith,
    keyboards; Paul Joseph (Zlotucha), drums and
    vocals)

Bridge (Ft. Lauderdale) (see The Ambassadors)

Chaps (Miami) (Joe Livermore, rhythm; Bobby
    Isidrin, vocals; Louie Martinez, drums; Joe Pla,
    lead guitar...)

Clefs Of Lavender Hill (III) (Miami) (Coventry, lead
    vocals; Travis Fairchild, lead guitar and vocals;
    Frank Milone, bass; Steve Zaricki, drums,
    replacing Ted Napoleon)

Crystalline Silence (Miami) (Harold Pettit, guitar;
    Billy Robbins, guitar; Bobby Robbins, bass; Greg
    Kimple, drums. Future lineups with Vince DeMeo
    on guitar and Mario Russo on keyboards went by
    the name of Heat before evolving into Fantasy.)

Echo (III) (Miami) (Kenny Ahern, lead guitar; Bill
    Kerti, bass; Don Fedele, keyboards; Donnie
    Goodson, drums)

Electric Earth

F.E.C. (Fruit Eating Chicken) (Miami) (Danny
    Murphy, bass and vocals; Pedro Riera, lead guitar;
    Greg Osborne, drums)

Fire (Miami) (Sandy Torano, guitar; Dick Miller, guitar; Russ Smith, bass; Burt Compton, drums; John Harper, keyboards)

Force (Miami) (Dave Brophy, vocals; Ed Olszewski, guitar; Greg Minek, guitar; Al Greenberg, bass; Bobby Ronco, drums)

Generation Gap (West Palm Beach) (Craig Hawkings, vocal; Jim Seagraves, lead guitar; Dana Brindle, drums; Pat Seminara, bass; Richard Held, keyboards; Rick Hawkings, second guitar)

George (Miami) (Dick Miller, guitar; Bill Sabella, keyboards; Gary Salem, lead vocals; Burt Compton, drums)

George Washington Helicoptre (Miami) (Jeff Pomeranz...)

Glass Menagerie (Miami) (Chris Martell, vocals; Howie Albert, keyboards; Frank Trabonello, lead guitar; Bob Miller, bass)

Heat Machine (North Miami) (Tom Murasso, vocals; Greg Orsini, drums; Pat Smith, bass; Jimmy Goodman, guitar; Al Yanes, guitar)

Jayne & Electric Jive Wire

Joined Venture (Homestead) (Will Hyde, vocals; Ron Hoben, guitar; Larry Hoben, bass; Joe Mansir, drums; Santi Lomillo, piano)

Kanes Cousins (Ft. Lauderdale) (Galen Barker, bass; Dick, Jim, Sue, Nancy)

Leaves Of Grass (Miami) (Alberto DeAlmar, lead guitar; Bill Sabella, keyboards; Doug Damico, lead vocals; Kenny Thomas, bass; Rick Thomas, drums)

Mass Confuzion (II) (Miami) (Mark Elfenbein, rhythm; Steve Griffin, bass; Gary Salem, vocals; Chuck Spivak, drums and vocals; Dick Miller, lead guitar; Carrie Williams, keyboards)

NRBQ (North Miami) (Steve Ferguson, guitar and vocals; Frankie Gadler, vocals; Jody St. Nicholas, bass and vocals; Terry Adams, keyboards and harmonica; Tom Staley, drums. Lee Tiger also played guitar in the early days, and Joe Lala also filled in on drums. This lineup, which evolved from the 7 Of Us, moved to Passaic, New Jersey, and then to New York City, where, as they say, the rest is history.)

New York Square Library (II) (Miami) (Gary Walker, drums; Kenny Wynn, guitar; Andy Charlton, guitar; Brooks Reid, bass and vocals. This group also worked as a trio without Charlton.)

Nimo Spliff (Mark Skola, guitar; Carlos Garcia, bass; Jimmy Rivas, drums)

No Plans (Miami) (Jack Horner, organ; Chuck Polk, bass; Alan Yott, guitar; Jimmy, drums)

Nomads (II) (Miami) (Shannon Thomas, bass; Dan Halyburton, vocals and guitar; Maury Sheets, drums; Bruce King, lead guitar; Mike Dirse, keyboards and vocals)

Package

Peach (I) (Miami) (Chris Dieguez, guitar; Ernie Garza, bass; Omar Martinez, drums...)

Pooh Groupe (Miami) (Bud Bradbury, lead vocals and organ; Bob Quirk, drums; Andy Charlton, lead guitar; Dan Oelker, bass; Ed Black, light man)

Proctor Amusement Company (II) (Ft. Lauderdale) (Ken Byers, Jr., organ; Gary Carter, guitar; Chuck Kirkpatrick, bass and guitar; George Terry, bass and guitar; Sandy Meyer, drums; Cleve Johns, vocals)

Queen's Kids (Miami) (Carlos Driggs, drums; Dave, vocals; Norman, vocals...)

The Rush (Miami) (Paul Chevalier, guitar; Dave Robinson, drums; Heppy Pettit, guitar...)

Sands Of Time (Miami)

Sault Shaquer (North Miami) (Pat Smith, bass; Tom Murasso, lead vocals; Al Yanes, guitar; Jim Goodman, rhythm...)

Self (Miami) (George Parrott, lead guitar; Edwin Ward, rhythm; Sandy Rubin, drums; Joe Riccobene, percussion and harmonica; George Bennett, bass)

7 Of Us (III) (Miami) (Lee Tiger, guitar; Frankie Gadler, vocals; Terry Adams, keyboards; G. T. Staley, drums; Jody Spampanato, bass. Evolved into NRBQ.)

Shades Inc. (II) (North Miami) (Pat Smith, bass; Spike Warner, lead guitar; Randy Wooley, vocals; Jim States, guitar; Tom Murasso, vocals)

Shaggs (IV) (Miami) (Terry McGarey, lead guitar; Larry O'Connell, bass; Jacques Heideier, lead vocals; Doug Romanella, drums; Mark Watson, keyboards. It's interesting to note that at this point no original Shaggs were left in the group!)

Showmen (Miami)

Six Pak (Miami)

Skin (I) (Miami) (Mark Watson, organ; Randy Wooley, harmonica and lead vocals; Tom Cherney, drums; Terry McGarey, guitar)

Smack (Miami) (George Walden, lead guitar; Ted Napoleon, drums; Danny Murphy, bass, replaced by Frank Milone)

Squiremen IV (II) (Miami) (Jim Oliver, organ; Jerry Molina, guitar; Don O'Connell, bass; Bennie Buchacher, drums)

Still Life (North Miami) (Bill Cherry, guitar; Craig Cherry, bass; Larry Hirt, drums; Eleanor Hill, vocals; Bob Rose, organ, replaced by Tim Murphy)

Stix & Stonz (II) (Miami) (Paul Rose, guitar; Randy Rhodes, drums...)

Tasmanians (West Palm Beach) (Robin Thompson, Mike Carnes...)

Tropical Trip Company (Miami) (Al Costello, vocals...)

Universal Joynt (Miami) (Dave Stevens, guitar; Rick Murciano, guitar; Kooky Berrios, organ; Ray Tirador, lead vocals; Tony Robledo, drums; Bob Gonzalez, bass)

Zookeepers (Miami) (Jim Hayek, bass and vocals; Alan Cease, keyboards; Moe Cease, drums; John Crimi, guitar)

LATE 1969 - INTO THE 1970s

America's Five (Miami)

Angels of Heaven (Brian Voight, lead vocals . . .)

Bangles (IV)/Sun Country (I) (Miami) (Lee Tiger, bass; Steve Tiger, lead vocals; Frank Trabonello, lead guitar; Norman Harris, keyboards; Tommy Higgs, drums)

Bethlehem Asylum (originally from Clearwater/Tampa) (Danny Finley, guitar and vocals; Charlie DeChant, acoustic piano, sax, flute, moog and vocals; Christian Gandhi, piano, trombone, alto flute; Jim Neiman, bass and vocals; Buddy Helm, percussion. Helm played in the mid-'60s Tampa group Those Five.)

Blues Image (II) (North Miami) (Mike Pinera, lead vocals and guitar; Skip Konte, piano and organ; Joe Lala, drums and congas; Manuel Bertematti, percussion; Malcolm Jones, bass)

Brimstone (Miami) (Brim Leal, lead guitar and vocals; Joe Livermore, bass; Terry Weiss, keyboards; Joe Galdo, drums)

Buttermilk Shoehorn

Mickey Carroll Four (Miami) (Mickey Carroll, vocals...)

Celebration (Gainesville, via Miami) (Bill Sabella, keyboards and vocals; Alberto DeAlmar, guitar;

Debbie Shane, lead vocals; Jerry Greenhouse, drums; Steve Margolis, bass; Oden Powell, flute and saxophone)

Collage (Miami) (Paul Solo, vocals; Dick Miller, guitar; Connally Addington, bass; Randy Johnson, drums)

Cottonwood (South Miami) (Brooks Reid, bass and vocals; Jim Hilley, guitar and vocals; Frank Quinn, keyboards and vocals; Denny Alonzo, percussion; Bob Quirk, drums and marimba)

Coventry Carol (Bob McNeely, vocals; John, guitar...)

Dakota (North Miami) (Pat Smith, bass; Jimmy Goodman, rhythm; Tom Murasso, vocals... Short-lived band that served as a bridge between The Heat Machine and Willy Bogg.)

Echo (IV) (Miami) (Bill Kerti, bass; Don Fedele, keyboards; Donnie Goodson, drums; Dave Stevens, guitar)

Ewing St. Times

Fantasy (II) (Miami) (Bobby Robbins, bass; Mario Russo, keyboards; Jamene Miller, lead vocals; Gregory Kimple, drums; Vincent DeMeo, Jr., lead guitar and vocals)

Game (I) (Ft. Lauderdale) (George Terry, bass and guitar; Eddie Keating, guitar and bass; Chuck Kirkpatrick, guitar; Les Luhring, keyboards; Scott Kirkpatrick, drums)

Heroes Of Cranberry Farm (I) (Miami) (Jim Oliver, organ; Jerry Molina, guitar; Don O'Connell, bass; Bennie Buchacher, drums, Jack Vino, guitar)

Willie Hop & Soul Setters (Miami)

Institutional Conspiracy (Miami) (Steve, Jon, Bob, Jay)

Katmandu (Miami) (Bobby Jabo, lead guitar and vocals; Norman Harris, keyboards and lead vocals; Bobby Caldwell, bass; Kenny Zale, drums)

The Lid (Broward)

John Mace Group (Miami) (John Mascaro, lead guitar
and vocals; Nick Mascaro, rhythm and vocals;
Frank Whitney, bass; Al Lavoie and Art Gnaegy,
drums)

Magic (Miami) (Joey Murcia, guitar; Duane King,
guitar and vocals; Nick King, bass; Gary Harger,
drums)

Maxima (Miami) (Ernie Garza, bass; Clay Cropper,
guitar; Kevin McManus, drums...)

Milktruck (Miami) (Noel Cleland, keyboards; Bob
Morris, lead vocals; Bob Marcus, bass; Terry
Jones, guitar; Terry Nicholson, drums)

Monopoly (West Palm Beach) (Art Groom...)

Moon (Miami)

9th Floor Simfony (North Miami)

Only Exit (Miami)

Peach (II) (Miami) (Chris Dieguez, guitar; Russ Smith,
bass; Omar Martinez, drums; Kooky Berrios,
keyboards, replaced by Bob Wooley)

Rose Creek (North Miami) (Mike Smith, drums; Alvin
Crawford, bass; John Clemmons, guitar and
vocals; Ron Schwartz, organ)

Rubber Soul (Miami) (Dino, vocals; John G., bass;
John L., lead; Jeff, drums; Jack, rhythm)

Rubberband (Miami) (Ray Harris, bass...)

Sheffield Brothers Band (Boca Raton) (Skip Sheffield,
bass and vocals; Richard Sheffield, guitar and
vocals; John Sheffield, drums; Dave Hebert,
keyboards; Warren Guess, lead guitar)

Speed Limit (Broward)

Stone Fence (Miami)

Stuck Zipper (Miami)

Sun Country (II) (Lee Tiger, rhythm guitar; Steve
Tiger, lead vocals; Frank Milone, bass; Frank
Trabonello, lead guitar; Tommy Higgs, drums)

Sweet Basil (Miami) (Moss Jacobs, drums; Rick
Rolfes, bass and lead vocals; Don Blanchone, lead
guitar and vocals...)

Truth (Broward) (Johnny Hartigan, lead guitar...)

Union South (Miami) (Gidge Miller, lead guitar;
Gabriel Sanchez, drums; Jorge Sanchez, bass)

Mike Vetro's Soul Brothers (Miami Beach) (Mike
Vetro, John Bineiro, Bill Burke, Richie Corso,
Bobby Curbello, Clint Oakley. Teddy Washington)

Willy Bogg (I) (North Miami) (Jim Goodman, rhythm;
Pat Smith, bass; Tom Murasso, vocals; Mike
Mastaler, organ; Al Yanes, guitar; Greg Orsini,
drums)

Willy Bogg (II) (Pat Smith, bass; Spike Warner, lead
guitar; Tom Murasso, lead vocals and guitar;
Jimmy, drums)

World Of Matter

10

CAN'T YOU
BELIEVE IN FOREVER?

Band Reunions Beyond The 1980's

Thanksgiving Night, 1979, while millions of Americans are gorging themselves on the limbs and vital organs of a deceased, much-maligned bird, an unusually large, enthusiastic crowd makes its way through the entrance of Milwaukee's legendary Eagles Club, the very same club which once hosted such luminaries as Bill Haley & The Comets and Buddy Holly (in one of his last appearances). On this night, an air of thankfulness is prevalent as Milwaukee's rock 'n roll heroes have returned. After a nearly fourteen-year hiatus, the Legends (Sam McCue, lead guitar and vocals; Larry Foster, rhythm guitar; Jerry Schils, bass; Jim Sessody, drums) have re-formed for one final concert, nearly twenty years to the day they first took to a stage.

It was on New Year's Day, 1966, at a club called Beneath The Street that the Legends played their final show as a band. In the fourteen years that passed, only Foster and McCue remained active as performers. Schils played with Miami's Birdwatchers through much of the early '70s, but had not played his bass in years. Outside of a few practice sessions with former Echoes Bill Kerti and Kenny Ahern, Jim Sessody had not touched his drum set since the 1960s.

Clearly, this reunion was to mean much more than just a show at a nightclub; this reunion would represent the culmination of many years of rock 'n roll repression just waiting to explode in its practitioners.

Schils, Sessody, and Foster arrived at McCue's Milwaukee home three days before the show; it was the first time that all four had been in the same place since the break-up of the group. The results of the first few practice sessions were nothing short of astounding. "It was as though nothing had ever happened," said Sessody. "We all picked up exactly where we left off."

As showtime grew nearer, the media attention grew more intense. Photographers followed their every move; local television and radio stations (particularly WOKY) treated them as if they were the Beatles; and, as Sessody notes, the comparison is not a farfetched one. "We were Milwaukee's own rock 'n roll band in the early '60s, and our following has always been loyal. We always figured they'd like to see us give it another try."

Milwaukee's love affair with the Legends was dealt a severe blow in 1964 when the group moved its home base to South Florida. (For further details, see BLITZ #36.) As one of Miami's top bands, the Legends constantly reached the upper portions of the local charts and always attracted a large group of fans to their shows at the Balmoral and Diplomat Hotels. Sessody, Schils, and Foster all decided to live in Florida with only McCue opting to stay in Wisconsin. Yet, Milwaukee was always home, and on this night of November 22, one would have thought that the Legends had never left.

The crowd that night could best be described as rabid. Among those in attendance were Roland Stone, himself a rockabilly legend and former bandmate of Sessody's, as well as Bill Taylor, a former Milwaukee disc jockey and long-time Legends' supporter. As showtime approached, an air of apprehension overtook the band. All those years of inactivity were taking their mental toll, making each second seem like a minute, and each minute seem like an hour. Yet it was an anxiety that the Legends would not have traded for all the serenity of the world; the indescribable agony of anticipation could not have been any sweeter. When Sessody walked up to his long-ignored set of drums and pounded out the opening beats of "Lariat," the rock 'n roll-starved crowd clapped its hands, moved in unison, and roared with un-bridled approval.

"Lariat" was a little rough as the sound mix wasn't quite right — yet it's unlikely that anyone in attendance really noticed. By the time the second song (Little Richard's "Lucille") began, it was clear that the Legends had put everything together. Foster and McCue shared lead guitar duties on this selection (something they had rarely done), and the sublime merging of their guitars seemed to energize the crowd. Although Larry Williams' "Slow Down" was next, there certainly was no slowing down during the Legends' two-and-a-quarter-hour set. By the time the night was over, the group had not only played most of their old hits, but also dozens of rock 'n roll classics, ranging from Larry Williams' "Bony Moronie" to the Beatles' "Get Back," with a few special requests thrown in (including Buddy Holly's "That'll Be The Day," a song the Legends hadn't attempted in over fifteen years and never even planned on playing). Everyone in the house was totally satisfied, particularly the band members themselves, who admittedly could have played all night. "It was the most fun I've had in thirteen years," exclaimed Sessody. "It made me wonder why we had waited so long."

The tremendous success of the show led the group to give two more performances at Sam McCue's own nightclub, McCue's Last Legends Saloon. Both times a crowd of people were turned away at the door, but those who were fortunate enough to be in attendance were treated to another excep-tional blend of pure, simple, uncluttered rock 'n roll. It was clear that the Legends story could not end on this November night.

And, so it began once again, when all four original Legends gathered together in May, 1980, to record a comeback album at Criteria Studios. The twelve new tracks included updated versions of three Legends' chestnuts ("Say Mama," "Bop-A-Lena," and "Lariat") as well as rock 'n roll classics by Eddie Cochran ("C'mon Everybody"), Chuck Berry ("Brown Eyed Handsome Man"), and Fats Domino ("Blue Monday"). The album would have surely pleased both longtime Legends' fans and those who had never before heard the group, but all the encouragement never materialized in a recording contract. Over a decade later, the twelve tracks have yet to see the light of day, and at this point it's not likely they ever will.

McCue and Foster returned to Milwaukee, where they teamed up with McCue's young son, Sean, in a country band called Wanted Dead Or Alive. Sessody hung in there as a recording engineer at Criteria Studios while Schils, for the most part, has left his playing days behind. A third reunion is not out of the question, but for now, you can only imagine the power of "Blue Monday," played as only the Legends can!

MORE REUNIONS

Both the Backbeats and the Spellbinders held private reunions in the early '80s; the Backbeats got together around Christmas, 1980, and the Spellbinders gathered at Palm Springs Methodist Church on August 7, 1981. The Spellbinders reunion attracted some attention in the local press, and lead guitarist Charlie Molter reported that the experiment was a "great success."

The Montells reunion now appears more unlikely than ever. A practice session was held at guitarist John Weatherford's house on May 1, 1982; everyone involved had lots of fun, but it was apparent that major work needed to be done on the musical front. The Shaggs also discussed getting together for a series of concerts, but as so often happens, the commitment to the idea just didn't seem to be there.

As for future band reunions, only the sky (and the ravaging years) is the limit. I held a general reunion party at my house in October, 1981, that attracted former members of the Birdwatchers, Montells, Shaggs, Proctor Amusement Company, Legends, Evil, Dr. T. & The Undertakers, Kollektion, and numerous others. If nothing else, it proved these musicians are not only alive and well, but still have a great deal of musical talent to contribute. The saga of the South Florida '60s music scene COULD conceivably grow throughout this century, but only if those who made it happen stay determined... and keep a-knockin'!

'60s band members gather for a reunion party at the author's home, October 1981: L-R Gregg Shaw (Shaggs/Kollektion); Craig and Bernadette Caraglior (Shaggs/Birdwatchers); Billy DeMoya (Carter's Pills/Heirs of Lorelei); Pam Sessody (covered) and Jim Sessody (Canadian Legends); Craig Cherry (The Apple/London Chymes); Jeffrey Allen (Montells/Evil); Jeff Lemlich (the author); Kurt Curtis ('60s historian); Paula Curtis, John Weatherford (Montells). *Photo by Wendy Gilson*

11

NO PLACE OR TIME

Bits And Pieces Of
The South Florida Scene

Remember the Alamo! Travis Fairchild certainly did. The
Clefs of Lavender Hill's leader (born Joseph Ximenes) legally
changed his first name to that of his Alamo hero, Lt. Col.
William B. Travis. His sister Coventry (born Lorraine
Ximenes) took HER name, in Travis' words, "from a bombed
out city in England."... Both Travis and Coventry claimed to
be British, but were actually born in Brooklyn, where they
began their careers as vaudeville performers... Former Clefs
Bill and Fred Moss occasionally shared the stage with
recording star Andy Dio, while leading a trio known as The
Twilites... Among the later Clefs were Montells' replacement
drummer Ted Napoleon, and Frank Milone, who later joined
Napoleon in the power trio Smack...

The Canadian Legends had a tremendous influence on
innumerable mid-'60s bands. Three records with an unmistakable Legends' sound are "Take What I Got" by the Twilites,
"What My Baby Wants" by the Mor-Loks, and "That's Not
True" by Mike Vetro & The Cellar Dwellers...

A slowed-down version of Chuck Conlon's "A Basket Of
Flowers" appears on the Last Words' LP...

The Echoes (or as they were later known, The Echo) lasted well into the '70s and had the dubious distinction of opening for Jim Morrison and the Doors at the March, 1969, "indecent exposure" concert. Dinner Key Auditorium never shook so hard... Echoes' guitarist Kenny Ahern played for a short time in the Invaders but didn't appear on their 1965 single "She's A Tiger" — at one time WQAM's second most requested song...'

The **Clefs Of Lavender Hill**, around the time they recorded their ill-fated LP for CBS' Date subsidiary. That album was reportedly shelved when it was decided the Cyrkle ("Red Rubber Ball") deserved a break instead. That's Travis and his sister Coventry on the left, and the Moss Brothers on the right. *Photo courtesy Travis Ximenes*

You can thank the pen of local songwriter Rick Tyson for "Ring Around The Rosie" by the Shaggs and both "Man" and "Fellow John" by the Heroes of Cranberry Farm. Tyson once tried unsuccessfully to interest Capitol Records in the Montells...

The man responsible for the Shaggs' 1966 stay in Detroit was Ray Skop, a Southwest High teacher, who briefly managed the group. The Shaggs played at a Detroit club

called "The Rooster's Tail" alongside the Lourds, an early
incarnation of Ted Nugent's Amboy Dukes. Skop worked
closely with Punch Andrews, manager of Detroit's legendary
Hideout Records...

The Shaggs' single on Capitol Records, "Mean Woman
Blues"/ "She Makes Me Happy," was not by the Miami group,
but rather by a Detroit band assembled by Skop after the
Miami Shaggs returned to South Florida... Skop also
managed the Intruders, the Miami band that later took off
for Wisconsin as the Hares... Craig Caraglior of the Shaggs
went on to replace Sammy Hall in the Birdwatchers, before
a brief association with Peace And Quiet... Fellow Shagg
Cleve Johns left the band for a short stint with Proctor
Amusement Company. Cleve can still knock 'em out with his
killer Beatle harmonies!...

Original Montells' drummer Jeffrey Allen replaced Doug
Romanella in Evil while Romanella was migrating to the
Shaggs (via the Kollektion). Evil almost didn't record
"Whatcha Gonna Do About It" as its single — band members
seriously considered a slowed-down, R&B version of Lulu's
"I'll Come Running"... Original Evil rhythm player Al Banyai
later joined a five-piece band called Aboriginal Missionary,
best known for its live recreation of the Beatles' "A Day In
The Life"...

The first band in town to learn and perform the Beatles'
"Paperback Writer" and "Rain" was Hialeah's Spellbinders,
which used the tunes to help them win second prize in a
Variety Children's Hospital Battle Of The Bands...

Brim, whose late-'60s single for Atlantic was produced by
Chicago's renowned Dunwich Company, was formerly a
member of the Hialeah-based Drones. Former Drones'
guitarist Paul Rose (who also played in Sounds Unlimited
and Stix & Stonz) joined ex- Novas' bass player Jim LeFevre
in the late-'70s band Max Demian, whose two RCA albums
received some national attention...

The longest-enduring mid-'60s band has to be The New
Society Band (later known as the Rockerfellas), whose members are strongly influenced by '60s bands such as the

Montells and Legends, and keep that raw, rock 'n roll spirit alive today... The New Society Band once took its show on the road to Vegas — but they weren't the only ones. Bobby Caldwell's early-'70s band Katmandu was "discovered" by Little Richard and hired to share the bill with him on a tour of Las Vegas, Lake Tahoe, and California...

One-time Caldwell sideman Omar Martinez beat the skins with the popular late-'60s/early-'70s band Peach. Omar went on to become a member of Paul Revere & The Raiders, only to be joined years later by fellow Miamian Carl Driggs (ex-Queen's Kids/Dave & The Wanderers/Kracker). Jimmy Miller, best known as former producer of the Rolling Stones and Traffic, also worked the controls for Kracker's two Dunhill albums...

If you were in New York City in 1964, attending WMCA Radio's Easter Parade Of Stars, you may have seen the American Beetles sharing the stage with dozens of nationally known acts...

You would have had to have been at the Par-Tee Lounge to catch The Blue Beatles and The Minutemen appearing together throughout 1965...

But to catch the Limeys, a brother and sister act, you only had to watch the "Skipper Chuck" TV program. Their backup band, shown on disc as "The London Sounds," was actually The Outcasts...

Former WFUN Program Director Jack Merker won $100,000 on TV's "Name That Tune" in the late '70s...

Due to the unwritten rule that WFUN and WQAM's bands could only play their respective gigs, WQAM's Mor-Loks secretly became the Buckingham Palace Guards for about a month in order to play the lucrative WFUN dances — and nearly got away with it! The Mor-Loks were also known as the Bald Eagles for one night, appearing as skinheads while opening for a local Beach Boys concert...

Other bands appearing at that April 9, 1966, Beach Boys extravaganza were the Lovin' Spoonful, the Birdwatchers, and the Dedd...

The Birdwatchers used many aliases through the years, including the Security Blankets, Glass Bubble, New Rock Band, Mousetrap, the Marlins, and Exit... Joey Murcia of the Birdwatchers was once in a group called the Kingsmen. When "Louie Louie" broke nationally, many locals believed it was Joey's group that was enjoying such great success... The place to catch Murcia's early licks was Ft. Lauderdale's War Memorial Auditorium, site of some of South Florida's best dances. In addition to local bands, dance directors Sally Duke and June Krczwicki also booked a number of national acts, including the Knickerbockers, Music Machine, and Grass Roots...

The nationally-known disco/jazz group Nite Flyte (of "If You Want It" fame) boasts former Squiremen IV guitarist Sandy Torano, playing alongside Miami soul star Howard Johnson...

Talk about persistence, Mike Pinera continues to keep his old Blues Image material alive and even had a local hit with a remake of "Can't You Believe In Forever." Pinera shared lead vocal duties in the early Blues Image days with Angel Rissoff, who also sang with the Kollektion...

Another popular Miami band worth mentioning is the Bangles (also known as the Bangs), which originally included Lee and Stephen Tiger from the Renegades and former Shaggs bass player Mike Latona, who later helped form the Kollektion. The second incarnation of the Bangs featured Steve Tiger, Mike Hughes of Evil, and longtime musicians Steve Chase, Terry McGarey, and Tom Cherney. The final version of the Bangs changed its name to Sun Country and stayed together until 1975, despite numerous personnel changes. Sun Country guitarist Frank Trabonello is still remembered as the featured model on the infamous "Beautify America — Get A Haircut" billboards...

Billboard Magazine recognizes Steve Alaimo as holding a dubious distinction: No artist has ever had as many singles hit the national Hot 100 (nine) without once cracking the Top 40...

Former Eric Clapton sideman George Terry shouldn't have been surprised when some radio stations found his composition "Lay Down Sally" offensive. Terry encountered the same problem way back in 1965, when his band, the Vandals, had to re-cut their song "I Saw Her In A Mustang." That's not too surprising, when you consider the original lyrics referred to "poontang" and "going to bed"...

Clapton's Derek & The Dominoes might have helped Criteria Studios establish its reputation, but it was Atlantic Records producer Tom Dowd who really put it on the map. The veteran music man's work at Criteria with Aretha Franklin, Wilson Pickett, the Rascals, and many others, helped bring long-deserved recognition to the studio and its owner, Mack Emmerman...

Mention should also be made of producer Bob Yorey, whose credits include the American Beetles, the Razor's Edge, the Marvells, Bill Robinson & The Quails, the Laddins, and the Glories...

Old folkies still sing the glories of Coconut Grove, a small village just south of downtown Miami and the center of a very lucrative folk scene throughout the '60s. Luis Bravo, the Southwinds, and the Briarwood Singers could be seen nightly as could Spanky & Our Gang (who immortalized the local folk scene in "It Ain't Necessarily Bird Avenue"), Fred Neil, and countless others. Another hotbed of folk activity was a Coral Gables coffee house called "The Flick," which in addition to featuring local talent, was very instrumental in relaunching the career of Dion DiMucci, now a South Florida resident...

Folk enthusiasts should be on the lookout for the superb compilation album "Night At The Hootenanny Coffee House" (Yale 1001), which features Mike Piel, Luis Bravo, Helene Slack, Phil Koss, the Southwinds, Carrol Morris, Oz Bach (later of Spanky & Our Gang), Dave Robinson, the New Coachmen, and Barry Simms. Also suggested is "Well Well Well" by Miami's Briarwood Singers (United Artists 3318)... Briarwood Singers' member Stan Beach is the former husband of newscaster Jill Beach...

Another artist with roots in folk music is John Braden, a Southwest High graduate who recorded an album for A&M Records in 1969... Southwest students were shocked to learn of Ronnie Luke's death in Viet Nam in November, 1965. The Catalinas' guitarist was killed in combat just one year after graduation...

12

GARAGE BANDS
AROUND FLORIDA

Geographically speaking, few states are as unusual as Florida. A low-lying peninsula with a coastline second in length only to Alaska, Florida is basically a north-south state, with only the panhandle boasting much in the way of east-west mass. These geographic features were instrumental in separating all of Florida's local scenes, with South Florida, for example, being totally independent of what was happening in, say, Jacksonville.

There is no clearcut definition of what constitutes South Florida. For simplicity's sake, I have defined the scene as anything south of West Palm Beach (inclusive) or the basic coverage area of WFUN radio. While WQAM was undoubtedly South Florida's number one station, its exceptional signal reached into 16 or more counties, way too broad an area for our purposes here. WQAM was great for spreading local music to other parts of the state while WFUN covered just the limited area, which in essence defined the perimeters of the scene.

Tampa was probably the most prolific of all of Florida's remaining scenes with Charles Fuller (Boss, CFP/Fuller), Gil Cabot (Paris Tower), and H & H (Hit Cat, Knight) recording the bulk of the area's bands. When those groups weren't recording, they were probably playing at one of Big Moose

Vosburgh's many teen clubs. Big Moose booked just about every name that passed through the South, from the Byrds to Bobby Fuller to the Shangri-Las, and gave so many bands their start that it's almost beyond belief. Being a Tampa rocker just wouldn't have been the same without the Eldorado Showcase, White Rabbit, or the many other Vosburgh venues.

THE **SWINGINGEST** *PLACE*

SATURDAY OCTOBER 17th

IS

ELDORADO

SHOW CASE

37 Street & 38 Avenue South

National Recording Artist

Italian American Club Across From the Armory

✱✱✱ *JOE HINTON* IN PERSON

"Funny"

✱✱ *LITTLE JUNIOR PARKER* IN PERSON

"Annie Get Your Yo-Yo"

✱ *TWO TOP BANDS*

Admission $1.00

DANCING 8:00 till 12:00

Big Moose Vosburgh's Eldorado Showcase brought in all the top rock and soul acts — including, of course, the **Eldorados** (which featured Moose's son, Donny, and his pal, Mike Pinera!)

Yet Big Moose wasn't alone in the "man behind the scene" department. You kind of get the feeling Daytona Beach would have been just sand and stockcars without the hand of Robert Quimby. The man behind Tropical Records and Alison Music recorded literally thousands of hours of tapes by everyone from the Nightcrawlers and Hank Ballard, to *"those Allman Boys"* (as he calls them) and... oh yes... hundreds of teenage garage bands, many of whom never got any further than the magnetic tape stage. Quimby, like Steve Palmer in Miami and Bee Jay Studios in Orlando, gave '60s collectors a gift which we can never repay. Thankfully, we'll never know how many more unrecorded bands there would have been if these pioneering few had not devoted their free time, and finances, to giving teenage tunesmiths a chance to record.

As for Florida's other scenes, there's more than enough to choose from. From Ft. Myers to the west, to Jacksonville to the north, there was no shortage of groups or guitars. Florida's panhandle, too, gave us both garage rock and the Carolina beach sound, although it's admittedly very tough to tell how many bands that appear to be from Northern Florida were actually nomadic neighbors from the north. I've tried to list only groups that called Florida their home, although a lot of Alabama/Georgia bands, particularly the Candymen, Rubber Band, James Gang, and K- Otics, had enough of an impact here to almost justify their inclusion. But that's another story.

So on the next few pages, we'll take you from the college campus at Gainesville to the fertile farmlands of Ocala, to the launch pads of Cape Canaveral, and anywhere the silence of suburbia was shattered by a beat. Here's to a time when the guardsmen were royal, the rogues were Canadian, the shadows rocked the nation, and every day was the 31st of February!

13

FLORIDA GARAGE BAND
DISCOGRAPHIES

DAYTONA BEACH/DeLAND

Allman Joys
    Spoonful/You Deserve Each Other (Dial 4046)   (9-66)

Brewed
    Lifeless Love/State Of Mind (Tropical 126)   (68)
    Love In Them There Hills/I Can't Take No More
    (Atlantic 2716)   (2-70)

Chosen Lot
    Time Was/If You Want To (Sidra 9004)   (11-66)
    [Although Sidra is a Michigan label, I have a tape
    box that shows this track was recorded in DeLand.]

Chuck Conlon
    Won't You Say Yes To Me, Girl/Midnight Reader
    (Marlin 16007)   (8-67)
    Mighty Lighty Moon/I Wish I Could Have Told You
    (Warner- Curb 8136)   (9-75)
    You Are A Woman/ (Wheel 001)   (10-84)
    [Chuck, of course, was the leader of The
    Nightcrawlers and Conlon & The Crawlers. See the
    Tropical Records discography for his early demos
    for the National Songwriter's Guild.]

Conlon & The Crawlers
  I Won't Tell/You're Comin' On (Marlin 16006)   (3-67)

Dead Beats
  Can't Go On This Way/Trust Me (Coe West 002)   (9-67)

Ron Fraiser & Consolidations
  Summer With You/Another Girl (Catalina 335)   (3-67)
  [Disc jockey Fraiser had other releases before
  teaming with the Daytona-based Consolidations.]

Roger Hamilton & Odds & Ends
  I'm A Mojo Man/Something's Wrong (Tropical 147)

Hungry I's
  Half Your Life/Comin' Round (Paris Tower 127)   (11-67)

Rayna Leggett
  Let The Little Girl Love/Now The Shoe Is On The
  Other Foot (King 6026)   (2-66)
  [As featured in the low-budget epic *Teenage Beach
  Blast*. Rayna cut countless demos for the National
  Songwriter's Guild, some of which can be found in
  the Tropical Records discography. Rayna's demo of
  "L.O.D." was somehow heard in Sweden where it
  was covered by the '60s beat group The Lee Kings!]

Mixed Emotions
  I Lied/Marie (Tropical 18591/92)   (2-67)

Newports
  Life Must Go On/Feelin' Low (Zebb 155)   (5/67)

Nightcrawlers
  Cry/Marie (Lee 101)
  The Little Black Egg/If I Were You (Lee 1012)   (8-65)
  The Little Black Egg/You're Running Wild
  (Kapp 709)   (11-65)
  A Basket Of Flowers/Washboard (Marlin 1904)   (1-66)
  A Basket Of Flowers/Washboard (Kapp 746)   (3-66)
  I Don't Remember/What Time Is It (Scott 28)   (6-66)
  The Little Black Egg/You're Running Wild
  (Kapp KE-110)   (67)
  The Little Black Egg/You're Running Wild

(London 10109—UK issue)   (67)
My Butterfly/Today I'm Happy (Kapp 826)   (4-67)
Third Condition
Charisma/ (Sundi 6814)   (70)
Monday In May (The Kent State Tragedy)/Nickel
(Sundi 6815)   (5-70)

2-3rds
All Cried Out/2-3 Baby (April 101)   (4-67)
[The 2-3rds were an early version of The Third
Condition. This band, also known as The Rock
Garden and Duck, included Pete Carr, later part of
the successful duo Le Blanc & Carr. Another
member, Gene McCormick, went on to record for
Epic Records with the Syracuse, New York, band
Jam Factory.]

TROPICAL RECORDS
(Based In DeLand, Florida)

17419/20 Laney Jones & Chordvettes -
          Almost Persuaded Him/Little Heartthrob

18591/92 Mixed Emotions - I Lied/Marie

100

101

102

103

104

105

106 Bar Room Boys - Border Queen/Bad Gin
     Charles Vickers - Come On, Baby/Betty Jayne
     - In The Darkness

107

108 Lee Hazen - Don't Know A Thing About
     Money/Rayna Leggett - One More Lesson

109 OffBeets - Double Trouble/She Lied

110 Craftsmen - Diddy Wah Doo/Today In Omaha

111   Craftsmen - My Honey/Big Foot Wallace
112   Charles Conlon - When God Comes To
         Call/Charles Vickers - He'll Understand
113
114
115
116   Rayna - The Bank Of Love/Lee Hazen - My Love
         For You Has Come Back Again
117
118   Charles Vickers - Did You Have A Good
         Time/Every Day's Blue Monday
119   William Austin - Somewhere Along The Way/I'll
         Never Forget Her
120   William Austin - Feudin' & Shootin'/F-86
121
122   Arnold Fowler & Golden Valley Boys - Dim Lights
         & Thick Smoke/Soldier's Last Letter
123   Earthmen - Hey, Hands Off She's Mine/
124   Charles Vickers - Mammy Lou/Surftones - Secret
         Admirer
125   Charles Vickers - Where Do The Teardrops
         Go/I'm Trying To Believe I'm Through
126   The Brewed - State Of Mind/Lifeless Love
127
128   Country Church Singers - (EP) Jesus Was A
         Helpful Man/And He Heard Me/Who Else Is
         Listening/Divine Guidance & Revelation
129   Ronnie Knull & The Sand - Crawfish/Leah
130   Bobby Williams & His Mar Kings - Darling, Here
         Is My Heart/All The Time
131
132
133
134

135   Betty Bond - I Couldn't Leave You
      Lonely/Country Church Singers - A Perfect
      Way

136   True Heavenly Gospel Singers - Nobody But You,
      Lord/Ain't It Sweet To Know

137   Earthmen - She's My Girl/Save Your Love For Me

138   Jim Lea - World Without Love/I Better Go

139   Charles Vickers - (EP) No, No More Tears/Can't
      Get Anywhere With You/If I/Wondering,
      Wondering

140

141   Mighty Willing Gospel Singers - All The Way With
      Jesus/Have You Got Your Ticket

142

143

144

145

146   Pancho And Cherie - Danny Boy/El Rancho
      Grande

147   Roger Hamilton & Odds & Ends - I'm A Mojo
      Man/Something's Wrong

148   Blue Brass - Every Day The Sun Will Rise/One
      Night Stand

149

150

151

152

153   Gospel Keys - I've Tried Jesus/Holdin' On By
      Faith

154   Whipperdoos - Playback/Daytona Beach

155   Lance Hall - I'll Light Another Candle/Betty Bond
      - A Bit Of The Sunshine

156   Jim Lea - Just Pass Me By/Country Church
      Singers - Let's Pray Every Day

157   Rubber Band - Oh, What It Is/Flashback

158

159   Surftones - Be My Girl/I'm One Of The Bad Guys
      Earthmen - Happiness/You've Got To Be
      Kidding

160   Earthmen - I'm Living It Up/Holy Cow, Great
      Balls Of Fire!

161

162   Jim Lea - Flower Child/Leftover Love

163

164   Charles Vickers - That Little Honey Bee/You Can
      Light Another Candle (By Jim Lea)

165   (LP) Charles Vickers - *The Charles Vickers Album*

166

167   Heavenly Trumpets - I Want To Rest/Not Enough
      Love

168   Bruce Eller - The Little Sports Car/The Florida
      Waltz

169   Betty Bond - I Remember/Night

170   Sensational Spiritualaires - Give Up The
      World/Son Of God
      Jim Lea - The Doing Of Our Thing/5 O'Clock
      Friday

171   Charles Vickers - Thunder Bay/Yes-es Of
      Yesterday

172   Charles Vickers - Let There Be Another
      Tomorrow/Let's Go Back
      Betty Bond - Where In The World/Sentimental
      Tears

173

174

175   John E. Dallas & Heavenly Trumpets - He Woke
      Me Up This Morning/Lord, You Know My Heart

176   Steve Sams - Down The Trail/Whipperdoos -
      Thank You For Thinking Of Me

177   Dan Feather - Touch And Go/Memories

178

179

180 Northerners - Sweetie Pie/Be A Packer Backer

181

182

183

184 Whipperdoos - Happy Day/Betty Jayne &
Whipperdoos - Don't Cling To Me

185

186 Frederica LaFleur & Greater Faith Cathedral
Choir - Rock My Soul/Nobody Knows The
Trouble I've Seen

187

188

189

190

191 Steve Summers - I Could Love You So Easy/It's
Easier To Say Than To Do

192

193

194

195

196

197

198

199

200

201 Ronnie Layne - The Four
Commandments/Broken Promise

202

203 Betty Jayne - Witch Doctor Say/Black Candle &
The Ghost
Diana Lee - Allison's Candle/The Black Candle

204

205   Jerry & Johnny And The Buttermilk Biscuits -
       Country Rock and Roll/Baby, Baby, Where
       You Been?

206   William Austin - Wanting To Feel You Close To
       Me/Sweet Love

207

208   Whipperdoos - Let Freedom Ring/Charles Vickers
       - How Many Times

209   Lonnie Dahl & Joanne Westmoreland -
       Abraham/Let Them Live

210

211   Bobby Franklin - Dangerous/Baby Sittin' Baby

212   Whipperdoos - Loving America/

213

214

215

216

217   Ronnie-D - Office Lounge/Hey Lawdy Mama

No #   Dixie Ramblers - Riding That Midnight
       Train/Pathway Of Teardrops

No #   (EP) David West/Earthmen - Bar On Heartache
       Row/Turn The Light Off/City Of Stone/He's
       Way On Top, Baby

402   (LP) Charles Vickers - *Does Disco*

403   (LP) Charles Vickers - *Disco Pop For The '80s*

CARELLEN RECORDS

101   Betty Jayne & Teenettes - The Sun Will
       Rise/Show Your Love (PS)   (12-60)

102   Billy Jones & Teenettes - Johnny Preacher/Night
       Angel (PS)

103

104

105

106   Johnny Redd - Fixed For Life/Rockin' Peg   (2-61)
107   Betty Jayne & Teenettes - I'm No Longer Jimmy's
        Girl/Tag Along
108
109
110
111   Charles Vickers - Little Sally Walker/Friendly
        Advice
112   Betty Jayne - Dreamy/Betty Jayne & Dudley -
        Dudley
113   Betty Jayne - Loneliness In My Heart/Now
        There's You
   1   Billy Jones & Teenettes - Dixie Belle/I'm Sorry
        You're Sorry
   2   Betty Jayne & Teenettes - The Man I'm Going to
        Marry/June Bug
   3
   4   Betty Jayne - My Billy Boy/I'm Rehearsing
   5   Betty Jayne - Softly And Tenderly/Maybe Sooner
        Than We Know
   6   Charles Vickers - Are Ya For Me Or Agin' Me/He's
        My Everything
   7   Billy Jones - The More I See You/Teenager's
        Dream
   8   Betty Jayne - What's She Got (That I Ain't
        Got?)/Cry Baby Heart
   9
  10   Charles Vickers - Double Knott/Who's Putting
        Stardust In Your Eyes
  11   Johnny Redd - I Flipped My Top/
 125   Houston & Dorsey - The Wreck Of The John
        B/Hootenanny Annie   (64)

[Early label operated by Bob Quimby as an outlet for
compositions by the National Songwriters Guild. Carellen
was virtually replaced by the Tropical label in 1964.]

FLORIDA PANHANDLE

Bangs
  Then I'll Cry/Tab Top (Orchid 503)   (5-65)
  [Folk rock from tiny Marianna, Florida.]

Bob Carnes & Chaotics
  Come Back Lauree/So Tough (Phi Delts 101)
  [Plus a 1965 recording, titles unknown, on
  Carnival Records out of Tallahassee.]

Kleen-Kuts
  (You're My) Summer Love/I've Found A New Love
  (Vitality 701)   (66)

Larry & Loafers
  Let's Go To The Beach/Who (Shurfine 017)   (66)
  [This Pensacola band also recorded "Panama City
  Blues" way back in the early '60s for both the Reed
  and Heart labels. Group leader Larry Parker
  reissued "Panama City Blues" in the early '80s on
  Rock & Roll Reunion 31041.]

Many Others
  (Tell Me Why) I'm Alone/Can I Get A Witness
  (Orchid 504)   (12-65)

Missing Links
  Run And Hide/I Really Ought To Go
  (Bamboo 111380/81)   (66)
  ["Run And Hide" was obviously influenced by the
  Beatles' "Run For Your Life." From the town of
  Quincy.]

Mystics
  Oo-Poo-Pah-Doo/Snoopy (Black Cat 501)   (8-64)
  [An early version of Many Others. From
  Tallahassee.]

Pagans
  Strawman/You're Gonna Lose That Girl
  (Orchid 9693)   (65)
  [Recorded in Panama City.]

Don Schroeder
  Sweet Violets/I'm Hurtin' (R And H)   (5-65)

[The man behind Papa Don Studios was a disc jockey on WNVY Radio in Pensacola at the time of this recording. Schroeder's first waxings appeared in 1959 on Vee Jay Records, followed by releases on Philips and Sound Stage 7 and a mysterious recording on Ace 606 as Little Jerry & The Chants.]

Truths
Pending/Why (Circle 953)   (8-65)

Zig Zag Paper Co.
I Feel Free/The Greatest Show On Earth (Bell 741)(8-68)
Just As Long As You Hold Out/Cast Out Your
Worries (Bell 752)   (11-68)
[Papa Don Schroeder remembers this group as James & Bobby Purify's backing band.]

APACHE RECORDS
(Blues label based in Crestview, Florida)

1786 Crook, Jr. - Wiggle It Baby/Please Believe Me
      Darling
1788 Clifford King - Chicken Shack Boogie/Want To
      Jump With You Baby
1830 Big Jesse & Blue Aces - Come On Baby/Blue
      Aces - Rugged
      [All the above are RCA pressings and were
      released in 1960.]

FT. MYERS

Bees
Shy Boy/Jadoo (Bees 3622)   (1-66)
[Also see Wally Naylor & Bees.]

Jesters
I'll Laugh At You/You Can Have Her
(no label or number)
Just Let Me Love You/I'll Laugh At You
(The Jesters no #)

Don't Try To Crawl Back/Leave Me Alone
(Sidewalk 910)   (12- 66)
Unchain My Heart/Blue Feeling (Qualicon 5003)   (67)
Hands Of Time/If You Love Her, Tell Her So
(Sidewalk 916)   (67)
(LP) *Freakout U.S.A.* (Sidewalk 5901)   (67)
[Includes "Don't Try To Crawl Back" by the Jesters
plus seven more groups.]

Painted Faces
Things We See/I Need You (Qualicon 5002)   (4-67)
Anxious Color/Things We See (Manhattan 808)   (6-67)
I Lost You In My Mind/I Think I'm Going Mad
(Manhattan 811)   (9-67)
In The Heat Of The Night/Don't Say She's Gone
(Manhattan 814)   (12-67)
[Who says high school students don't read? The
Painted Faces took their unusual name from
Tolkien's *The Lord Of The Rings* in much the same
way Ft. Lauderdale's Mor-Loks took theirs from H.
G. Wells' *The Time Machine*. The Painted Faces
rose out of the remnants of two Ft. Myers bands,
The Hightones and The Fifth Dimension, and
recorded a demo album that has never been
released. Maybe one day we'll be lucky enough to
hear the Faces blare out "Incense and
Peppermints," but that day will probably never
come.]

Wally Naylor & Bees
Shy Boy/Where Is My Baby (Sunville 495)   (5-66)

Spades
I'm Alright/I Won't Want You Anymore (Ace no #)

Spyders
New Boy Came To Our School/Just For You
(Spyder 3220)   (7- 65)

GAINESVILLE

Flow
  Mr. Invisible/Daddy (CTI 503)   (70)

...Incidentals
  It's In Your Mind/Baby, I Want You Back Again
  (Paris Tower 126)   (11-67)

Maundy Quintet
  2's Better Than 3/I'm Not Alone (Paris Tower 103) (3-67)
  [Both the Maundy Quintet and Flow featured
  members that would later go on to play with the
  Eagles.]

Tom Petty
  No recordings in the 1960s, but plenty of local
  appearances with his bands, the Sundowners and
  Epics. The latter band became Mudcrutch in the
  early '70s, releasing two singles: "Up The
  Mississippi"/"Cause is Understood" on Pepper
  9449 in 1971 and "Depot Street"/"Wild Eyes" on
  Shelter 40357 in 1975. Among Mudcrutch's early
  members was Tommy Leadon, whose brother
  Bernie (one of the future Eagles alluded to above)
  had played in the Maundy Quintet. In 1976, Petty
  joined with former Mudcrutch members Benmont
  Tench and Mike Campbell, former Road Turkey
  drummer Stan Lynch, and bassist Ron Blair, from
  the Gainesville band RGF. Together they became
  the highly successful Tom Petty & The
  Heartbreakers. Another short-time member (and
  fellow Gainesville boy) Jeff Jourard later helped
  form the L.A. band, the Motels.]

Rare Breed
  In The Night/I Need You (Cool As A Moose 012)
  Don't Blow Your Cool/I Talk To The Sun (Cool As
  A Moose 3250)
  [The Rare Breed reportedly signed with
  Mainstream Records, but it's not clear if anything
  ever came of it.]

Rhodes Scholars
   You're Gonna Love Your Daughter/Baby Let Me
   Try (Buddah 13)   (9-67)
   [Seven-piece band which called both Atlanta and
   Gainesville home.]

Sole Survivors
   Good Times-Bad Times/David's Mood
   (D And B 101)   (66)

JACKSONVILLE

Bitter Ind
   Hands Are Only To See/Baby Blue (ACP 380)
   [Also see The 31st Of February and Tiffany
   System.]

Boys
   Sticks And Stones/Rocks In My Head (Lowery
   Music NRC 511)
   [Also see Mouse & The Boys.]

Chosen Few
   Little Darlin'/Love Is A Hurtin' Thing (Viking 377)
   [Related to The Morrison on the same label.]

Classics IV
   It's Too Late/Don't Make Me Wait (Arlen 746)
   Pollyanna/Cry Baby (Capitol 5710) (as The
   Classics)   (7-66)
   Little Darlin'/Nothing To Lose (Capitol 5816)   (2-67)
   Spooky/Poor People (Imperial 66259)   (9-67)
   Soul Train/Strange Changes (Imperial 66293)   (4-68)
   Mamas & Papas/Waves (Imperial 66304)   (5-68)
   Stormy/Ladies Man
   (Imperial 66328-DJ issue only)   (10-68)
   Stormy/24 Hours Of Loneliness (Imperial 66328) (10-68)
   Traces/Mary Mary Row Your Boat
   (Imperial 66352)   (1-69)
   Everyday With You Girl/Sentimental Lady
   (Imperial 66378)   (4-69)
   Change Of Heart/Rainy Day (Imperial 66393)   (7-69)

Midnight/The Comic (Imperial 66424)   (10-69)
[Above two shown as Dennis Yost & The Classics
IV. Early releases include two singles as The
Crescents: "When You Wish Upon A Star"/"Hey
There (I Want To Walk You Home)", issued on both
Hamilton 50033 and Dot 16447, and "Smoke Gets
In Your Eyes"/"Johnny Won't Run Around" on
Arlen 743. Leader Dennis Yost was also a member
of The Echoes, who recorded "House
Warming"/"Restless" on Ace 657 in 1962. The
Classics IV continued to record throughout the
1970s, but most of these releases were rather
bland and not worthy of mention here.]

Rita Coolidge
Rainbow Child/Secret Places, Hiding Faces
(Pepper 442)
Turn Around And Love You/Walking In The
Morning (Pepper 443)   (2-69)
[Rita attended Andrew Jackson High in
Jacksonville and was an unknown when she
recorded the above two singles.]

Coronados
Angel/Florida Sun (Arlingwood 6467)   (6-67)
["Angel" — a cover of Dave Meadows & The
Neanderthals' 1960 recording (Magnum 41160) —
might have been the A-side, but it was "Florida
Sun" that rode high on the WAPE Tuff Thirty in
July, 1967.]

The Crypt
You Keep Me Hanging On/Love, I'll Never Know
(The Crypt 68- 940)   (68)

Dalton Gang
Our Love/Stubborn Kind Of Fellow
(Kimberly-Ann 127)   (4-67)
["Our Love" was originally recorded on Arlingwood
8601 by Ernie & Petie — way back in 1962. The
Dalton Gang played a key role in Channel 12's TV
program *Shakin' Up Summer* in 1967. In fact, a

demo of the title song soared up the WPDQ charts,
as did another apparently unreleased tune called
"Jody" (which even predates the Kimberly-Ann
single!).]

Deep Six
   One And One/Last Time Around (Soft 960)   (66)

Florida Deep Six
   I Don't Wanna Cry/Start From Here (Charay 16)   (66)
   [Both Deep Six recordings feature former members
   of The Vikings and future members of Mouse &
   The Boys.]

Illusions
   I Know/Take My Heart (ACP 375)   (66)
   I Know/Take My Heart (Columbia 43700)   (6-66)
   [This Palatka group also had a TV program on
   Channel 12!]

Lynyrd Skynyrd
   Need All My Friends/Michelle (Atina 129)   (78)
   [Reissue of tracks allegedly recorded in 1968.]

Male Bachs
   Tears As My Consolation/Sugar Dee (Truce 3351)(11-67)

Mind's Eye
   Mind's Eye Theme/Donna, Where Can You Be
   (Arlingwood 9567)   (9-67)

Monarchs
   Girl, You Know/Do You Love Me (Bruno 539)   (66)

The Morrison
   Every Part Of You/Gonna Have That Girl (Viking
   376)

Mouse & The Boys
   Love Is Free/Xcedrin Headache #69
   (Rubiat 68-1043)   (9-68)
   [The number one record in Jacksonville on
   October 21, 1968!]

Mouse & The Boys With Brass
   Dancing To The Beat/Tears In My Eyes (SSS 716) (9-67)
   [According to an old WAPE survey, this apparently

first came out in June on the Wild Moose label —
perhaps simply as The Boys.]

M.O.U.S.E.
Knock On My Door/Where's The Little Girl (Bell
870)   (3-70)
Woman Or A Girl/I Can Only Touch You With My
Eyes (Bell 918)   (9-70)
Different Drummer (one-sided) (Bell Sound
Studios demo — unissued)
[Yes, this is Maurice "Mouse" Samples of Mouse &
The Boys!]

Dennis Ott
Quick Draw McGraw/I Need You (Continental Ltd.
692C-0895)   (9-65)
[Featuring backing by The Vikings.]

Second Coming
I Feel Free/She Has Funny Cars (Steady 001)   (69)
[Included, at various stages, Dickey Betts, Berry
Oakley, Larry Reinhardt, Reese Wynans, and
Bruce Morford. Betts got his start in 1960 with a
group called The Swingin' Saints and then went on
to The Fabulous Flambeaus. Oakley played
rhythm guitar for The Roemans, whose drummer,
Bertie Higgins, had a top ten hit in 1982 with "Key
Largo." Morford played bass in the legendary
garage band, The Painted Faces, while Reinhardt
paid his dues in The Thunderbeats, which also
included Bobby Shea of The Tropics. Reinhardt
later went on to Iron Butterfly and Captain
Beyond, joining piano player Wynans in the latter
group . . . and, of course, Betts and Oakley stuck
together, hitting it big in the Allman Brothers
Band.]

31st Of February
Sandcastles/Pick A Gripe (Vanguard 35066)   (4-68)
In The Morning When I'm Real/Porcelain Mirrors
(Vanguard 35087)   (12-68)
[Formerly The Bitter Ind. Lead guitarist Scott

Boyer joined Tommy Talton and Tom Wynn of We
The People and George Clarke and Pete Kowalke of
The Go Mads/Plant Life, becoming the
country-rock band Cowboy. Drummer Butch
Trucks became a mainstay in the Allman Brothers,
joining Betts and Oakley from Second Coming.]

Tiffany System
Let's Get Together/Wayward One (Minaret 128)   (9-67)
[Also The Bitter Ind in disguise, before being forced
to take the name 31st Of February.]

Vikings
Rosemary/You're The One (The Vikings 2101) (PS)   (64)
[With two future members of Deep Six/Mouse &
The Boys — plus Butch Trucks on drums!]

Yo Yos
Leaning On You/I Can't Forget You (Goldwax 303)   (66)
Gotta Find A New Love/I've Got Something In My
Eye (Goldwax 310)   (8-66)

RELATED JACKSONVILLE RELEASES

Phil Cay
Key To My Heart/Blue Eyes (Ron 338)

Phil Cay & Bluenotes
Meet Me In The Barnyard/If They Ask Me (Hart
1001)   (57)
Take My Everything/Tell Me (Hart 1003)

Phil Cay & Chantells - Mid-'60s LP on Climax Records

Cowboy
It's Time/Pretty Friend (Capricorn 8015)   (71)
A Patch & A Pain Killer/Coming Back To You
(Capricorn 0078)   (74)
Takin' It All The Way/River To The Sea (Capricorn
0283)   (12-77)
I Will Be There (Pat's Song)/What Can I Call It
(Capricorn 0289)   (78)
(LP) *Reach For The Sky* (Atco/Capricorn 351)   (70)
(LP) *5'll Getcha 10* (Capricorn 864)   (10-71)

(LP) *Why Quit When You're Losing* (Capricorn 0121) (73)
(LP) *Cowboy/Boyer & Talton* (Capricorn 0127)   (3-74)
(LP) *Cowboy* (Capricorn 0194)   (11-77)
(LP) *Paragon Agency Presents* (Paragon PR-162)   (71)
(includes "It's Time" and "Everything's Here" by
Cowboy)
(Related LP: Talton, Stewart & Sandlin - *Happy To
Be Alive* (Capricorn 0167)   (76))
[Country-rock band that included former members
of We The People, Plant Life, and Bitter Ind/31st
Of February.]

Bob Currie
Where Does The Time Go/Cheers To You
(Arlingwood 8614)   (11-65)

Ernie & Petie
Cold Fire/One Day (Ace 659)   (62)
You Don't Even Care/Our Love (Arlingwood 8601)   (62)
Nosey Neighbors/I'll Have A Broken Heart
(Arlingwood 8602)   (63)
[Ernie & Petie would be remembered mainly as a
Kalin Twins/Arena Twins clone had The Dalton
Gang not turned their composition "Our Love" into
a garage classic.]

Fabulous Fabuliers
I Found My Baby/She Is The Girl For Me
(Angletone 539)
[An answer to the Drifters' hit "There Goes My
Baby".]

Fabulous Imperials
My Little Nita/Moonbeat (Impra 1269/70)
[Also see Four Jays & Fabulous Imperials.]

Fidelitys
The Things I Love/Hold On To Whatcha Got
(Baton 252)
Memories Of You/Can't You Come Out (Baton 256)
Captain Of My Ship/My Greatest Thrill (Baton 261)
Walk With The Wind/Only To You (Sir 274)
This Girl Of Mine/Brand New House (Sir 276)

Wishing Star/Broken Love (Sir 277)
[Long-enduring R&B group.]

Five Fleets
I Been Cryin'/Oh What A Feeling (Felsted 8513)
Slight Case Of Love/You Good Lovin (Felsted 8522)

Five Knights with The Dukes
She's All Right/Take Me In Your Arms (Tau 104)   (63)
[Actually The Five Knights Of Brooklyn, featuring
John Standberry, Jr., of The Fabulous Imperials.
Brooklyn was a black suburb of Jacksonville.]

Five Men-Its
I Don't Love You No More/The Old Man (R And H
1006)   (64)
[Included future Almanac/Hour Glass members
Johnny Sandlin and Paul Hornsby.]

Four Jays & Fabulous Imperials
Weird/Class Ring (Impra 1267/68)   (58)
Class Ring/Weird (MGM 12687)   (7-58)

Hour Glass
Heartbeat/Nothing But Tears (Liberty 56002)   (10-67)
Power Of Love/I Still Want Your Love (Liberty
56029)   (3- 68)
D-I-V-O-R-C-E/Changing Of The Guard (Liberty
56053)   (8-68)
She Is My Woman/Going Nowhere (Liberty 56065)   (68)
Now Is The Time/She Is My Woman (Liberty 56072) (10-68)
I've Been Trying/Silently (Liberty 56091)   (3-69)
(LP) *Hour Glass* (Liberty 3536/7536)   (10-67)
(LP) *Power Of Love* (Liberty 3555/7555)   (68)
(LP) *The Hour Glass 1967-1969*
(United Artists 13-G2)
(LP) *Gregg & Duane Allman* (Springboard 4046)
(The above is a '70s reissue of Hour Glass tracks.)
[Formerly The Almanac. While this band was
based in Los Angeles, it featured former members
of the Allman Joys and musicians who would later
merge with members of the Second Coming to
form The Allman Brothers Band. Some of the

Liberty singles were billed as Gregg Allman & The Hour Glass.]

King Crooners
Lonely Nights/ (Hart 1002)   (57)
Now That She's Gone/Won't You Let Me Know (Excello 2168)

King Crooners/Little Rico
Memoirs/School Daze (Excello 2187)
[Some pressings show the group's name as King Krooners.]

Mike Reineri
No Money Down/Michael Row The Boat Ashore (Wholewheat 21067)
[Recorded before Reineri settled in South Florida where he spent decades anchoring WIOD's morning drive show. He also recorded "Crazy Ellen's Blueberry Jam" with Reineri's Raiders on Buddah 280.]

Jan Rivers
My Last Love/Nice (Impra 7493/1271)
[Related to the Fabulous Imperials.]

Spindles
To Make You Mine/And The Band Played On (ABC-Par. 10802)   (4-66)
No One Loves You (The Way I Do)/Ten Shades Of Blue (ABC- Par. 10850)   (8-66)

DAVCO RECORDS

[Tiny label based in the tiny community of Hilliard, just northwest of Jacksonville. Most Davco releases mixed country sounds with the typical teen idol sounds of the early '60s.]

101   Johnny Folkston - The Twistin' Freeze/April Fool

102   Merlene Garner - You're It/My Search Has Ended

103   Jimmy Strickland - A Little Too Late/Living Alone

104   Jimmy Strickland - Touch Of Heaven/Just As
      Plain As Day
105   Merlene Garner - (It's Over) Casanova/Will You
      Remember Mine
106
107   Jimmy Strickland - (I Have A) Ring In My
      Pocket/My Dream Of A Lifetime
7479 Johnny Folkston - Dance Little Leaves/You Said
      I'd Never Love Again

OCALA

Reason Why
    Sweetest One Around/One More Time (Strike 001) (6-67)
Royal Guardsmen
    Baby Let's Wait/Leaving Me (Laurie 3359)   (9-66)
    Snoopy Vs. The Red Baron/I Needed You (Laurie
    3366)   (11-66)
    Squeaky Vs. The Black Knight/I Needed You
    (Laurie 3366-X) (Canada)   (12-66)
    The Return Of The Red Baron/Sweetmeats Slide
    (Laurie 3379)   (2-67)
    Airplane Song (My Airplane)/OM (Laurie 3391)   (5-67)
    Wednesday/So Right (To Be In Love) (Laurie 3397)
    (also shown on some pressings as Any Wednesday)(8-67)
    Snoopy's Christmas/It Kinda Looks Like
    Christmas (Laurie 3416) (PS)   (11-67)
    I Say Love/I'm Not Gonna Stay (Laurie 3428)   (1-68)
    Snoopy For President/Down Behind The Lines
    (Laurie 3451)   (6-68)
    Biplane "Evermore"/Baby Let's Wait (Laurie 3461) (9-68)
    Baby Let's Wait/So Right (To Be In Love) (Laurie
    3461A)   (10-68)
    Mother Where's Your Daughter/Magic Window
    (Laurie 3494)   (3-69)
    Snoopy For President/Down Behind The Lines
    (Laurie 3590)   (6-72)

Snoopy For President/Sweetmeats Slide
(Laurie 3646)   (76)
[#3590 was reissued for the 1972 election with NO
INTRO and the date "68" in the opening line
dubbed out. #3646 features an entirely new
beginning and end and substitutes "76" for "68" in
the first line of the song.]

Billy Sandlin & Embers
I Kept On Walking/You'll Always Have Someone
(Viking 1001/02)   (66)

Billy Sandlin & Interns
Poor Rich Girl/Here Comes That Feeling (Royale
326)   (4-66)
[Billy started his career in the early '60s on labels
such as Gala and Vim and was recording for Mega
in the early '70s at the time of his death.]

Barry Winslow
The Smallest Astronaut (A Race To The Moon With
The Red Baron)/Quality Woman (Laurie 3509)   (7-69)
Get To Know Me/Where There's Love There's Fire
(Big Tree 16000)   (73)
[Barry Winslow and Billy Sandlin recorded one
single together, "Have You Seen A Rainbow
Lately"/"Peace Time," on Mega 0044, released in
September, 1971.]

ORLANDO

Big Don Adams
Grasshopper Pizza/It Won't Be Long (Kam 111)
[Also see Don & The Holidays.]

Barons
Drawbridge/Lovin' Man (Tener 1011)   (66)
Reach For The Sky/Colors Of Love (Tener 1021)   (67)

Blues People
(EP) *Blame It On Florida* (Introduction/Psychedelic
Bubblegum/Wade In The Water/Goin' Up To ABC
News/Can't Be As Bad As It Seems
INST./C.B.E.S./Can't Be As Bad As It Seems

VOCAL) (GP 6346/6347) (PS)   (69)
[This 33 1/3 Cocoa recording comes from the
motion picture *Blame It On Florida*.]

Bobby Cash
Mona Lisa/Teen Love (King 5844)   (1-64)
Only Make Believe/Run Fool Run (King 5864)   (3-64)
I Don't Need Your Love And Kisses/Answer to My
Dreams (King 5894)   (64)
Do Wah Diddy Diddy (Hit 43)   (65)

Bobby Cash & Niteflyers
Nobody Knows/Only With You (Kap-Tal
1001/1002)   (12-66)
[Four of the King recordings by Cocoa's Bobby
Cash were reissued in the early '80s on King EP
25327.]

Custer's Last Band
Another Year/Mind Rhymes (Legend 111)   (68)
[It's not clear if this is the same band that released
"I Couldn't Last A Day Without Your Love" on
Golden Chariot 70001.]

December's Children
A Girl Like Me (A Boy Like You)/Makin' Music
(Capitol 5883)   (4-67)
Backwards And Forwards/Kissin' Time
(World Pacific 77887)   (4-68)
The Lovin' Things/Extraordinary Man
(World Pacific 77895)   (68)
I've Been Hurt/Good Time Boy
(World Pacific 77910)   (3-69)
You're My Girl (I Don't Want To Discuss It)/Dirty
City (Liberty 56195)   (7-70)

Don & The Holidays
Grasshopper Pizza/It Won't Be Long (Kam 104)   (66)

Edgin-Inds
Don't Try To Hide It/U.F.O. (Tener 1012)
Whatever's Right/Grandma (Tener 1029)   (68)

Enalpria
You Keep Me Hanging On/Purple Haze
(Moonport 100)   (68)
Rose Water/Shredded Heat (Enko 6200/6201)   (69)
Speed Limit/Sliding (Ron Sound Productions 128)   (70)
[From Cocoa Beach. "Enalpria" is "airplane"
spelled backwards.]

Fabulous Thunder
So Hold Me Tight/Jealous of You (Tight 3606)   (1-66)

Mark Ferrell
Go Go Girl/I'll Never Forget You (Kam 103)   (66)

Mark Ferrell & New Blue Angels
Sweet Donna Lee/I'll Never Forget You (Bion 1)

J. Walker & Pedestrians
Thinking Of You/Life's Too Short (PH 112)

Kolor Korporation
Love That Drives Me Crazy/Sunshine On Our Love
(Hype 1015)
[From Leesburg. Included Barry Ferguson, the
brother of We The People's Lee Ferguson.]

Little Willie & The Adolescents
Get Out Of My Life/Stop It (Tener 1009)   (11-66)
Looking For Love/The Push Song (Tener 1013)   (67)
[Formerly known as The Starfires. Group member
Eric Schabacker later operated Bee Jay Studios in
Orlando.]

Magic Circle
I Put A Spell On You/She Means All The World To
Me (Paris Tower 119)   (67)
[From Leesburg.]

Malemen
My Little Girl/She Means The World To Me (PH
2455)   (66)
[The Malemen also back Sue Pennie on Dunmar
103 — "Ghost Town"/"He's Everything I Need."]

Mysteries
My True Love/Pink Panther (JDL 3554)   (11-65)

Please Agree/I Find It's True Love
(Manhattan 815)   (12-67)
I Can't Wait For Love/Satisfaction Guaranteed
(Manhattan 817)   (68)

Nation Rocking Shadows
Anesthesia/Going Down (F-S no #) (PS)   (64)
[The organ player for this group, Randy Boyte,
later went on to We The People. "Anesthesia" is
one of the greatest instrumentals ever recorded.]

Leesburg's **"Nation Rocking" Shadows,** wishing you a Merry Christmas in
1964. Note guitarist Ron Skinner's signature on the card; Skinner is presently
serving a life sentence for a grenade attack on two Orange County deputies.

Nonchalants
Double Trouble/I Wanna Do It (unissued demo)   (4-64)
[Also see The Offbeets.]

Offbeets
Double Trouble/She Lied (Tropical 109)   (64)
[Formerly The Nonchalants. This band and the
Trademarks Unlimited evolved into the nucleus of
We The People.]

Oxford Blue
Will You Still Love Me Tomorrow/Alice in
Wonderland (Hype 1043)

Plant Life
   Flower Girl/Say It Over Again (Date 1572)   (8-67)
   [Known as The Go-mads prior to this recording.]

Rockin' Roadrunners
   Go Away/My Window (Lee C. 696)   (5-66)
   King Of The Jungle/You Ain't Gonna Cry
   (Lee C. 970)   (9-66)
   Down/Urban Meadows (Tener 1015)   (67)
   [Rockin' all the way from Sanford, Florida.
   Also see The Yak.]

Shy Guys
   Goodbye To You/Black Lightening Light
   (M-U 5941/5942)   (68)
   [Sanford's Shy Guys later evolved into King
   recording artists Miami.]

Soul Tenders
   Somebody Help Me/Glitter And Gold (JD 4663)   (4-67)
   Heard It Through The Grapevine/The Dock Of The
   Bay (Tener 1028)   (68)

Trademarks
   Don't Say You Love Me Too/Here Come Elmer's
   Boys (Arlingwood 8610)   (64)
   Everything Will Be Alright/Crying Gun (Criteria
   Studios Acetate)   (64)
   Crying Gun/Everything Will Be Alright/Don't Say
   You Love Me Too (upbeat version)/Hallelujah I
   Love Her So (Criteria Acetate)   (64)
   [Yet another pre-We The People band.]

Twelfth Night
   I Don't Believe You/Grim Reaper
   (Whiteholme 1984)
   [The name Twelfth Night was used only for this
   recording. The band was really called The
   Emotions and later evolved into Birnam Wood —
   the early '70s band that released "If It's
   Alright"/"Country Living" on Souncot 1123.]

Undertakers
  Searching/The Reason Why (PH 110)   (3-67)
  Love So Dear/Loneliness To Happiness (PH 115)
  [The Undertakers also back H. F. Gore on "No One
  Will Ever Know"/"Washington Report," PH 117, a
  very mediocre country recording.]

We The People
  My Brother, The Man/Proceed With Caution
  (Hotline 3680)   (1-66)
  Mirror Of Your Mind/The Color Of Love (Challenge
  59333)   (6-66)
  He Doesn't Go About It Right/You Burn Me Up
  And Down (Challenge 59340) (Apex 77011 -
  Canada)   (9-66)
  (EP) *We The People* - You Burn Me Up And
  Down/He Doesn't Go About It Right/Mirror Of
  Your Mind/The Color of Love (London 10.181 -
  France)   (66)
  St. John's Shop/In The Past (Challenge 59351)   (11-66)
  Follow Me Back To Louisville/Fluorescent Hearts
  (RCA 9292)   (8-67)
  The Day She Dies/Love Is A Beautiful Thing
  (RCA 9393)   (12- 67)
  Ain't Gonna Find Nobody (Better Than You)/When
  I Arrive (RCA 9498)   (3-68)
  [We The People also recorded an unissued acetate
  under the name of Fresh Air. "Love Wears Black
  (Nun)" was recorded at Bradley's Barn in Nashville
  circa 1967.]

Wrong Numbers
  The Way I Feel/I Wonder Why (Hit Cat 201)   (12-65)
  I'm Gonna Go Now/I'm Your Puppet (Paris Tower
  111)   (67)
  [From the small community of Mt. Dora.]

Yak
  Every Little Thing/Eric Cleveland (Tooth 533)   (69)
  Every Little Thing/Eric Cleveland
  (Avco Embassy 4514)   (69)

[With two former members of the Rockin'
Roadrunners, which explains why Nightcrawlers'
leader Chuck Conlon contributed the B-side.]

For more Orlando-based releases, see Tener Records discography.

TENER RECORDS - Singles Discography

1001-02 Suzanne Goddard - Anything Can
        Happen/It's Too Bad

1003-04 Paul Sindab - I'm Up Tight/Since I Met
        You (Hype Records)

1005-06 The Band - Mr. Guitar Man/Lovin' Zone

1007-08 Paul Sindab - Do Whatcha Wanna Do/
        Give Me Your Heart (Hype Records)

1009 Little Willie & Adolescents - Get Out Of My
      Life/Stop It

1010 Flower Power - I Can Feel It/Stop

1011 Barons - Drawbridge/Lovin' Man

1012 Edgin-Inds - Don't Try To Hide It/U.F.O.

1013 Little Willie & Adolescents - Lookin' For
      Love/The Push Song

1014 (LP) *Bee Jay Demo Vol. II* - Various Artists
      (LP) *Bee Jay Video Soundtrack* - Various Artists

1015 Rockin' Roadrunners - Down/Urban Meadows
      Kolor Korporation - Love That Drives Me
      Crazy/Sunshine On Our Love (Hype Records)

1016 Burlington Squires - World/Back Up

1017 State Of Mind - Time Will Tell/City Life

1018 First National Band - Flying Away/My
      Generation

1019 Bob Johnson - For God, Our Country, And
      You/Fleet Reserve Association

1020 Mind Ration - Always And A Day/It's Your
      Mother

1021 Barons - Reach For The Sky/Colors Of Love

1022

1023

1024 Ron & The Starfires - Be Sincere/The Grass Is
Greener

1025

1026

1027 Clarence McGill & Blue Devils - Pauline/Forever
My Darling

1028 Soul Tenders - Heard It Through The
Grapevine/The Dock Of The Bay

1029 Edgin-Inds - Whatever's Right/Grandma

1030 Cosmic Camel - The Suzanne Love Mirage/The
King's Winetaster

1031

1032

1033 Ecumenical Drugstore - I'd Really Like To
Watch You Fly/I'm Tired

1034 Fabulous Soul Masters - Funky Thing/Can't
See Nobody

1035

1036

1037

1038 (EP) *Bee Jay Sampler* (Oxford Blue, Barons,
Cinnamon, Soul Tenders, Brewed)

1039 (EP) *Bee Jay Sampler* (The Riff, The Rab, The
Image, People's Choice, One Is-We The People)

1040

1041

1042

1043 Oxford Blue - Will You Still Love Me
Tomorrow/Alice In Wonderland (Hype Records)

1044

1045

1046

1047

1048

1049

150/151   Denny Noie & The In-Crowd -
Dee-Dee/Don't Follow Me
[Also issued as Denny Noie & The 4th Of
Never.]

1052

1053   Universouls - New Generation/The Way A Girl
Should Be

154   Wave-Riders - Ain't It A Shame/

1055   (LP) *Bee Jay Sampler* - Various Artists

[Tener had at least 45 other releases throughout the early
'70s . . . very few are of interest to '60s collectors.]

RELATED ORLANDO RELEASES

Boot

Hey Little Girl/Liza Brown (Agape 9008)	(72)
(LP) *Boot* (Agape 2601)	(72)
(LP) *Turn The Other Cheek* (Guinness 36002)	(77)

[Originally known as The Allusions, and later The
Split Ends, whose "Rich With Nothin'" is a '60s
killer! I'm told Boot stood for "Blues Of Our Time."]

Ral Donner

Good Golly Miss Molly (demo only — as Ral Donner & Gents)	(58)
Tell Me Why/That's All Right With Me (Scottie 1310)	(59)
Girl Of My Best Friend/It's Been A Long Time (Gone 5102)	(4-61)
To Love/And Then (Gone 5108)	(6-61)
You Don't Know What You've Got (Until You Lose It)/So Close To Heaven (Gone 5108)	(7-61)

[Both of the above were issued with the same
number.]

[Ral was born in Chicago but moved to Orlando in
the late '50s. At a studio in the Orlando suburb of
Winter Park, Ral cut five tracks with a band called
The Starfires, most of which resulted in the Gone
releases shown above. Other tracks from those
sessions turned up on the local Tau label, but not
until 1963 ("Loneliness Of A Star"/"And Then," on
Tau 105). Ral moved away from Florida but
continued to record for no less than a dozen
additional record labels. Ral died of lung cancer in
April, 1984, at the age of 41.]

International Submarine Band
   The Russians Are Coming The Russians Are
   Coming/Truck Driving Man (Ascot 2218) (PS)   (6-66)
   Sum Up Broke/One Day Week (Columbia 43935) (1-67)
   Luxury Liner/Blue Eyes (LHI 1205)   (2-68)
   Miller's Cave/I Must Be Somebody Else You've
   Known (LHI 1217)   (68)
   (LP) *Safe At Home* (LHI 12001)   (2-68)
   [Legendary band led by Winter Haven's Gram
   Parsons. *Safe At Home* has been reissued in
   various forms through the years.]

Miami
   Just Can't Wait/She Don't Need No Other (King
   6331)   (10-70)
   [Included former members of The Shy Guys.]

Tin House
   Be Good And Be Kind/I Want Your Body (Epic
   10739)   (71)
   (LP) *Tin House* (Epic 30511)   (71)
   [Produced by Rick Derringer.]

TAMPA/ST. PETERSBURG

Agency
   Sunset Strip/Love So Fine (Sundi 6805)   (68)

Blues Image - See South Florida discography.

Boozers
    The Crow/Bon Soir Baby (Columbia 2269-Belgium)   (66)
    No No No/Cry Cry Cry (Columbia 2420-Belgium)   (66)
    (EP) The Crow/Bon Soir Baby/No No No/Cry Cry
    Cry (Columbia- Belgium, also Disc AZ EP
    1075-France)   (66)
    [Actually Travis Rogers & The Continentals. The
    above releases, recorded while the group was on a
    four-month tour of Belgium, included two future
    members of Blues Image. A later version of The
    Continentals included the nucleus of Mighty
    Manfred & The Wonder Dogs.]

Canadian Rogues
    Have You Found Somebody New/You Better Stop
    (Fuller 2597)   (7-65)
    Ooh Poo Pah Doo/Keep In Touch (Charay 19)   (66)
    Ooh Poo Pah Doo/Keep In Touch (Palmer 5017)   (67)
    Run And Hide/Love And Dreams (Paris Tower 112)   (67)
    Do You Love Me/Mickey's Monkey (Rogue 1967)   (12-67)
    [From Lakeland, Florida.]

Chipper - See The Tropics.

Elderados
    Mojo/My Soul (Soft 103)   (64)
    [This late 1964 release included drummer Donny
    Vosburgh and guitarist Mike Pinera, both later of
    Blues Image, The New Cactus Band, Iron
    Butterfly, and many more. The Elderados are said
    to have had a pair of later recordings.]

Emotions
    Sometimes/Why Must It Be (Century 24742)   (66)

Forvus With Brooke Chamberlain & Rovin' Flames
    Now That Summer Is Here/It's Nothing New
    (Tampa Bay 1110)   (9-66)
    [Also see The Rovin' Flames.]

Four Letter Words
    Quadruple Feature/Goodbye (Paris Tower 107)   (67)

[An early version of the country-rock band The
Outlaws.]

Alan Franklin Explosion/Blues Climax
Bye Bye Baby/Piece Of Your Love (Horne 888-4)   (70)

Gap
Sheriff/Theme From The Sheriff (Laurie 3491)   (3-69)

Pam Hall
Run From Her/Let Them Whisper
(ABC-Paramount 10597)   (11-64)
[Pam was from Clearwater and sang with a group
called The Catalinas.]

Hoppi & Beau Heems
I Missed My Cloud/So Hard (Laurie 3411)   (9-67)
When I Get Home/So Hard (Laurie 3439)   (3-68)

Hyperions
Theme/The Truth Always Hurts (Paris Tower 102)   (67)
[Just in case you were curious, mythology tells us
that Hyperion was a Titan; more precisely, the
father of Helios, the sun god. There was another
Hyperions single on Chattahoochie #669: "Why Do
You Wanna Treat Me Like You Do"/"Believe In
Me," but it's unlikely that this was the same
group. It is, however, just as unlikely that two
different mid-'60s groups would select the name
Hyperions.]

Impacs
Lost Love/Great Falls, Montana (Impac 61-59)
(as Pat Scot with the Impacs.)   (7-61)
Tru-Fine Twister/Forever And A Day (Impac 6160)   (61)
I'm Gonna Make You Cry/Tears In My Heart
(Parkway 865)   (2-63)
Hold-Out/Forever And A Day (Arlen 741)   (63)
Jo Ann/Two Strangers (King 5851)   (1-64)
Shimmy Shimmy/Zot (King 5863)   (3-64)
She Didn't Even Say Hello/Kool It (King 5891)   (64)
Ain't That The Way Life Is/Don't Cry Baby
(Things Couldn't Be That Bad) (King 5910)   (64)

Your Mama Put The Hurt On Me/Cape Kennedy,
Fla. (King 5965)   (11-64)
Soul And Inspiration/In The Midnight Hour
(Sundi 6807/6808)   (68)
[Also see Vic Waters & The Entertainers.]

Kent Lavoie
Happy Days In New York City/My Friend Is Here
(Laurie 3526)   (10-69)
[Dedicated to the 1969 New York Mets. Kent had
many others throughout the '70s and '80s as
Lobo. Also see Me & The Other Guys, the Sugar
Beats, and the U.S. Male.]

Lonely Souls
I Can't Stop Now/Paths Of My Mind
(Paris Tower 137) (PS)   (68)
[This five-man Clearwater band placed third in the
state Battle Of The Bands championship on May
20, 1967.]

Mama's Boys
Please Don't Let Me/Leading Me On (Shadow 113)

Me And The Other Guys
Skinny Minnie/Crazy (Hit Cat 102)   (66)
Runaround Girl/Everybody Knew But Me
(Boss 009)
[From Madeira Beach. A much later version of this
group recorded an album in 1974 called "Be
Young Be Foolish Be Happy"
(Copahog 0069/0070)

Members
Wish I'd Never Met You/Jenny Jenny (Label 101) (12-65)
Come On Everybody/I'll Get By Without You
(Label 102)   (4-66)
[Included Jay Lee Angelo, co-founder of the
Impacs.]

Mercy
Love (Can Make You Happy)/Fireball
(Sundi 6811)   (10-68)

[The above exists in three different forms — local
and national issue as well as flexi-disc — all with
the same number.

Love (Can Make You Happy)/Fire Ball
(Vogue 14882-Germany)   (69)
Love Can Make You Happy/Never My Love
(Warner Bros. 7291- Canada)   (69)
Forever/The Morning's Come
(Warner Bros.-7 Arts 7297)   (6- 69)
Hello Baby/Heard You Went Away
(Warner Bros.-7 Arts 7331)   (9-69)
Feelin' Easy/To Whom It May Involve (Marlin 2301) (70)
["Love Can Make You Happy" has been reissued on
Goldisc 3096 and Jamie 917.]

Mighty Manfred & The Wonder Dogs
Bo Diddley/By The Time I Get To Phoenix
(Paris Tower 140)
You Can I Can (Join Hands)/She (Atco 6823)   (5-71)
[Mighty Manfred also backed Mercy on their Sundi
LP.]

Mods
Sweets For My Sweet/Empty Heart (Knight 105)   (66)

Movers
Birmingham/Leave Me Loose (123 1700)   (7-68)
Hello L.A. (Bye Bye Birmingham)/Hey You, Hey Me
(123 1705)
[Formerly known as The Intruders.]

Noah's Ark
I Get All The Luck/Love In (Decca 32153)   (6-67)
Paper Man/Please Don't Talk About Yesterday
(Decca 32217)   (10-67)
Purple Heart/Stormy (Liberty 56157)   (1-70)
[Included members of The Outsiders,
Go-mads/Plant Life, and The Candymen.]

Noblemen
Two Faced Woman/You Didn't Have To Be So Nice
(Paris Tower 110)   (67)
[From Clearwater.]

Non-Pariels
  Willow Tree/Painter Man (5 Star Productions 101) (1-67)
Other Side
  Wild Rebels/Come See About Me (Sundi 103/104)
  (PS)   (11-67)
Outsiders
  Just Let Me Be/She's Comin' On Stronger (Knight
  103)   (1-66)
  Summertime Blues/Set You Free This Time
  (Knight 104)   (4-66)
  [Also see The Soul Trippers.]
Paradox
  There's A Flower Shop/With Someone To Love
  (Fuljac 6803)   (68)
Promise
  Sundown Sky/Love Is (Scepter 12220)   (6-68)
  That's A No No/What Have You Got Left To Give
  (Scepter 12243)   (2-69)
  [Actually The Paragons, featuring
  singer/songwriter Steve Bogard.]
Purple Underground
  Count Back/Soon (Boss 010)
  On Broadway/Rain Come Down (Boss 0095)   (68)
Ravens
  Reaching For The Sun/Things We Said Today
  (Boss 003)   (66)
  Calamity Jane/Now She's Gone (Rust 5123)   (2-68)
  [Artist on the above shown as The Raven.]
Tommy Roe & Roemans
  I Think I Love You/Oh So Right
  (ABC-Paramount 10579)   (7-64)
  Diane From Manchester Square/Love Me, Love Me
  (ABC- Paramount 10623 & Sparton 1333-Canada) (1-65)
  [Above release was also issued erroneously as
  Tommy Roe & Oremans.]
Roemans
  Give Me A Chance/Your Friend

(ABC-Paramount 10583)   (7-64)
Misirlou/Don't (ABC-Paramount 10671)   (5-65)
Universal Soldier/Lost Little Girl
(ABC-Paramount 10723)   (9-65)
Listen To Me/You Make Me Feel Good
(ABC-Paramount 10757)   (12-65)
When The Sun Shines In The Mornin'/Love (That's
All I Want) (ABC 10814)   (6-66)
All The Good Things/Pleasing You Pleases Me
(ABC 10871)   (10-66)
Smokey Rose/On The Road Again (SSS Intl. 842)
(as The Romans)   (71)
[Clearwater's top mid-'60s group originally spelled
its name "Romans" until Tommy Roe's producer,
Felton Jarvis, took them under his wing.]

Travis Rogers & Continentals
  Only Friends/Hey Baby (Nugget 1014)
  Why/Rheumatiz (T 'N T 2001)   (65)
  [Also see The Boozers.]

Ron & The Starfires
  Why Did You Cry/The Grass Is Greener
  (Lee-C 1014)   (65)
  Midnight Reader/   (8-66)
  Be Sincere/The Grass Is Greener (Tener 1024)
  [From Auburndale. Ron & The Starfires later
  became known as Cinnamon. Also see Ron Starr.]

Rovin' Flames
  Gloria/J.J.J.P. (Fuller 2627)   (65)
  I'm Afraid To Go Home/I Can't (Boss 002)   (66)
  Seven Million People/Bo Diddley (Tampa Bay 1111)   (66)
  How Many Times/Love Song #6 (Decca 32191)   (9-67)

St. Petersburg Paradox
  Where's She Gone/Won't You Take Me
  (TS 9755/56)

Savages
  Everynight/So Much In Love (National 2001)   (65)

Little Miss Sad/If You Left Me (National 2002)   (12-65)
Little Miss Sad/If You Left Me (Laurie 3328)   (2-66)

Senders
Party Line/Love Me Too (Leopard 201)   (1-66)
Chintz And Rubies/What's Your Sister's Name
(Marlin 1910)

Sir Michael & The Sounds
Can You/Love Your Fellow Man (Dig 333)   (5-67)
[From Clearwater. Dig Records was run by
manager Allen Diggs.]

Soul Trippers
King Bee/Girl Of Mine (Providence 415)   (7-66)
[Formerly The Outsiders.]

Split Ends
Rich With Nothin'/Endless Sea (CFP 4)   (66)
[Formerly known as The Allusions.]

Sugar Beats
Have You Ever Had The Blues/What Am I Doing
Here (Knight 101)   (65)

Ron Starr
Crawl Into My Shoulder/Lyla (Kim 7546)   (6-67)

Surprize
Too Bad/I Will Make History (Cent no #)

Those Five
Love/Because You Love Me
Sidewalks/Challenge Of A Fantasy Man
(Paris Tower 117)   (9-67)
[Included John DeLise, one-time vocalist for the
Soul Trippers and the Rovin' Flames, along with
Buddy Helm, later of Bethlehem Asylum, and
future H.Y. Sledge bass player Jan Pulver.]

Trojans
The Kids Are Allright/Leave Me Be (Boss 006)   (66)
[Included Tommy Saussy, the brother of Neon
Philharmonic writer/founder Tupper Saussy.]

Tropics
I Want More/Goodbye My Love (Knight 102)   (65)

I Want More/Goodbye My Love (Freeport 1006)   (1-66)
It's You I Miss/You Better Move (Laurie 3330)   (2-66)
For A Long Time/Black Jacket Woman
(Thames 103)   (5-66)
Time/As Time's Gone (Columbia 43976)   (1-67)
Summertime Blues-Land Of A Thousand
Dances/This Must Be The Place
(Columbia 44248)   (8-67)
Sunshine Man (Allegro Sound Studios acetate —
unissued)   (67)
Groovy Christmas/Toy Soldier (Malaco 2002)   (11-68)
[Above shown as by Chipper.]
Tired Of Waitin'/Talkin 'Bout Love (Malaco 2003) (1-69)
[Rumored Tropics demos include "Stupidity,"
"Alright," and "Hitch Hike." Half the group left in
1969 to form Bacchus while other members
persisted into the '70s under the name White
Witch, meant to designate "good over evil." The
Tropics' Columbia recordings followed their victory
in a 1966 national Battle Of The Bands in
Chicago, where they claimed top prize with their
versions of "Misirlou," "I'm A Man," and "Black
Jacket Woman." Tropic Dave Burke, who co-wrote
the group's wildest rocker, "You Better Move," later
moved to greater success with the Standells.]

U.S. Male (Uglies)
It's Gonna Be So Hard/Is This Guy (United
American Productions 1002)   (2-67)

Vic Waters & The Entertainers
Taking Inventory/The Greatest Love (Capitol 2406)(1-69)
I'm White-I'm Alright/Dreamer (Crazy Horse 1309)   (69)
I'm White-I'm Alright (2:32 vers./3:46 vers.) (Crazy
Horse SPRO-4750) (A promotional-only version of
Crazy Horse 1309.)   (69)
The Greatest Love/Dreamer (Crazy Horse 1316)
[Vic released numerous country records in the '70s
and '80s, including three solo albums.]

BOSS RECORDS

001

002 Rovin' Flames - I'm Afraid To Go Home/I Can't

003 Ravens - Reaching For The Sun/Things We Said Today

004 Berkley Five - You're Gonna Cry/In The Midnight Hour

005

006 Trojans - The Kids Are Allright/Leave Me Be

007 Souldiers - Would You Kiss Me/Lemon Sun

008 Journey Men - She's Sorry/Short And Sweet

009 Me And The Other Guys - Runaround Girl/Everybody Knew But Me

010 Purple Underground - Count Back/Soon

0095 Purple Underground - On Broadway/Rain Come Down

CFP/FULLER RECORDS

2   Esquires - Heat/Heartaches Stay The Night

3   Jr. And The Dimensions - Keep On Trying/I Heard You Love Me Again

4   Split Ends - Rich With Nothin'/Endless Sea

1925 Tommy Williams - Rockin' Drums/

6438 Little Junior & Butler-Aires - Jackie, Don't You Weep/That's What's The Matter With Church Today

2522 Harold White - God Sent An Angel/

2533 Little Junior - The Last Mile Of The Way/

2597 Canadian Rogues - Have You Found Somebody New/You Better Stop

2627 Rovin' Flames - Gloria/J.J.J.P.

2646 Intrigues - Sunset/Why?

2679 Mighty Kings - Swing Low/Fly Away

2680 Epics - Cruel World/I'll Be Glad

2681 Mk. III - Thunderbolt/The Wild Boar

2682 Florida Spiritualaires - The Bible Tells Me/Good
      News

2683 Don Scott And His Orchestra - Pretty Girls
      Everywhere/Baby It's Allright

2684 Jesters IV - (Bye Bye Bye Bye) So Long/She Lied
      (I Know Why)

2685 Hank Williamson - You Talk About
      Troubles/Hand In Heaven

2686

2687 Sandy Phelps - Free Movin' Spirit/Here Was
      Love

3180 David Carlton - Do You Even Care/Fuller
      Chorale - One Gun-Two Gun (Do You Even
      Care)

0031 Lewis Clark - Green Power/Here's My Heart

TIGERTOWN RECORDS

001

002   Lewis Clark & Explorers - Let's Do It Now/I Need
      Your Lovin' So Bad

003   Mk. III - Blues For George C./Mocha Nova

004   Lewis Clark - Here's My Heart/If You Ever, Ever
      Leave Me

PARIS TOWER

101   Joshua Dyke - Cheating/Confessing The Blues

102   Hyperions - Theme/The Truth Always Hurts

103   Maundy Quintet - 2's Better Than 3/I'm Not
      Alone

104   Richard Lee and the Country Four - Trouble
      Makin' Woman/Cloudy and Cool

105   Inner Thoughts - Smokestack Lightning/1,000
      Miles (Cheating On Me)

106   Early Americans - It's So Cool Outside/Night After Night

107   Four Letter Words - Quadruple Feature/Goodbye

108   Swaydes - Anymore/Why

109   Lost Generation - I'd Gladly Pay/Milk Cow Blues

110   Noblemen - Two Faced Woman/You Didn't Have To Be So Nice

111   Wrong Numbers - I'm Gonna Go Now/I'm Your Puppet

112   Canadian Rogues - Run And Hide/Love And Dreams

113   Wisdoms - Outer Limits '67/I'm All Right

114   John Bolan Quintet - There Is A Limit/The Shadow Of Your Smile

115   Missing Links - Get Out Of My Life/Where Were You Last Night

116   Last Knights - The Way You Do The Things You Do/Twenty Four Hours A Day

117   Those Five - Sidewalks/Challenge Of A Fantasy Man

118

119   Magic Circle - I Put A Spell On You/She Means All The World To Me

120   Ernie Benet - Sandy/Cheerful Tearful

121   Justis Brothers - Count On Me/I'D Do It For You

122

123   Steve Gibbs - Beautiful Thoughts/Steve & Karen Gibbs - Meditation

124   Star Dolls & Astros - Nothing Can Change/Baby I Need (Your Love So Bad)

125   Jackson Investment Co. - What Can I Do/Not This Time

126   The . . . incidentals - It's In Your Mind/Baby, I Want You Back Again

127   Hungry I's - Half Your Life/Comin' Round

128   Sand Trippers - Say You Love Me/Give A Little
129
130   Guild - I Believe Her/In My Mind
131   Last Knights - Twenty Four Hours A Day/The
      Way You Do The Things You Do
132   Enticers - Turn On Your Lovelight/What's Easy
      For Two Is Hard For One
133
134   Sweet Soul Generation - Knock On Wood/In My
      Tree
135   James Brown - If Somebody Breaks Your
      Heart/Open Your Heart
136
137   Lonely Souls - I Can't Stop Now/Paths Of My
      Mind
138   Absolutes - Yesterday I/Nobody But Me
139   Del Rays - Love Came/The Day
140   Mighty Manfred and the Wonder Dogs - Bo
      Diddley/By The Time I Get To Phoenix

KNIGHT

101   Sugar Beats - What Am I Doing Here/Have You
      Ever Had The Blues
102   Tropics - I Want More/Goodbye My Love
103   Outsiders - Just Let Me Be/She's Comin' On
      Stronger
104   Outsiders - Summertime Blues/Set You Free
      This Time
105   Mods - Sweets For My Sweet/Empty Heart

SUNDI

103/104 Other Side - Wild Rebels/Come See About Me (PS)
6801 Pat Henry - (LP) *Lookin' For A Free-Way!*

6803 Paradox - There's A Flower Shop/With Someone
To Love (Fuljac Records)

6804

6805 Agency - Sunset Strip/Love So Fine

6806

6807/6808 Impacs - (You're My) Soul And
Inspiration/In The Midnight Hour

6809 Jim Downing & Renegade Brass - Good Bye
Judy/It May All Be Over Now (PS)

6810

6811 Mercy - Love (Can Make You Happy)/Fire Ball

6812 Joey Ray & Shays - For A Little Of Her
Sunshine/Would I Still Be Loving You
Panacea - Witch Hunt/Little Bird

6813

6814 Third Condition - Charisma/

6815 Third Condition - Monday In May (The Kent
State Tragedy)/Nickel

6901 The Class - Windy/Girl From Ipanema/I Know
A Place (Fuljac Records)

[Sundi moved its base to Hollywood, California, in
1971, and issued a handful of uninteresting
releases, including sides by George Wallace,
Jr., Jimmy Velvet, Alex Brown, and Benny
Strong & His Orchestra.]

NUGGET

1000 Dreamers - Don't Cry/It's Gonna Be Alright

1001 Frank Evans - Gotta Get Some Money/

1002 Starlighters - A Fool's Understanding/

1003 Bobby Sands & Royal Teentones - Teenage
Joy/Secret Lover

1004 Mack King - You Look Better Going/No Special
Reason

1005 Jimmy Padgett - Some Glad Tomorrow/

1006 Eden Rocs - Walkin' With Satan/Eden Rock

1007 Ernie Lee - In The Hobo Heaven Train/Round Round The Universe

1008 Clyde Guthrie - My World Keeps Rollin' On And On/I Forgot

1009 Satellites - Moody/Needless To Say

1010 Dusty & Laura Anne - Halfway Down The Stairs/I'm Loving You

1011 Bee Clark - Sleepless Nights/Two Wrongs Don't Make One Right

1012 Dusty & Laura Anne - Passing Fancy/It's A Fine Time To Tell Me

1013 Dave Lee - Step It Up And Go/They'll Understand

1014 Travis & Continentals - Only Friends/Hey Baby

1015 Mack King - Go Ahead/Second Choice

1016 Bee Clark - Old Memories/Why Do I Want The Wrong One

1017 Lonzo & Oscar - Waltz Me Around Again Willie/Peelin' Taters In The Army

1018 Don Holly - Back Again/Nothing To Remind Me Of You

1019 Pine Mt. Boys - Has Anybody Seen My Baby/Pine Mt. Stomp

1020 Papa Joe - Closing Time/Speakeasy, 1929

[Tampa-based label run by country satirists Lonzo & Oscar until its late-60's purchase by guitarist Fred Carter, Jr. Nugget later moved to Goodlettsville, Tennessee, but by then the label was turning out strictly country releases. Only Nugget's earliest releases are listed here.]

RELATED TAMPA RELEASES

Arena Twins
Mama Cara Mama/Little Pig (Kapp 252)   (12-58)
In My Wallet/No One Else (Kapp 288)   (7-59)

This Could Be The Night/Jambalaya (Kapp 315) (11-59)
Notify The F.B.I./Oh! What A Show
(Columbia 41081)   (10-60)
Judy Says/I'D Just As Soon Forget
(Columbia 42026)   (61)
Love Is A Many Splendored Thing/Heartaches Are
Bad (Nob 104)
Master Of My Fate/You Think She's Yours
(Nob 105)   (63)
[Back in the late '50s, nearly every major label was
looking for a duo to cash in on the success of the
Everly Brothers. Sammy and Andrew Arena were
Tampa's contribution to the Everly's sweepstakes.]

Bacchus
Celebration/Carry My Load (Johnson 745)   (6-71)
We Like To Boogie/Ya Ya Ya (Boblo 500)   (75)
(LP) *Live At The Zodiac* (no label 29981/82)   (8-72)
(includes "Where Are You Going" by Bacchus)
[Boring '70s band which included former members
of The Tropics.]

Dennis Ballew & Plain Truth
You Don't Need My Love/You Could Be Falling In
Love (Marlin 3303)   (75)
[Former guitarist for Vic Waters & The
Entertainers.]

Chuck Boris
Talking Back To Echoes/You'll Wake Up Wiser
(Enterprise 9007)   (12-69)
Maryanna/Why Did It Take You So Long
(Enterprise 9023)   (70)
My Baby's Comin' Back/I Don't Know Any Better
(Scepter 12357)   (6-72)
Smokey Mountain Lullabye/Love Words
(Springfield 1002)   (77)
[Longtime member of The Rockers, Tampa's top
early '60s group. Boris also wrote tunes recorded
by B. J. Thomas, Marvin Gaye, Barbara Lewis,

Ronnie Dove, Merrilee Rush, and Tommy
Overstreet.]

Jim Downing & Renegade Brass
Good Bye Judy/It May All Be Over Now
(Sundi 6809) (PS)   (68)
[Included former members of The Rockers.]

Dreamers
Only Time/Dear I (Tri-Dec 8757)
Don't Cry/It's Gonna Be Alright (Nugget 1000)
[Someone once told me this early white Tampa
group is the same Dreamers on ABC-Paramount
from September, 1956. Personally, I don't buy it.]

Duckbutter
Gospel Trip (Medley)/Mountain Dream Song
(Paramount 0099)   (5-71)
[1970s band featuring former members of The
Outsiders, Soul Trippers, Emotions, Noah's Ark,
and more. Pete Yorkunas of The Swimming Pool
Q's was also a member. Anyone who saw
Duckbutter's crazy act at the "Young Summer' 70"
concert on Miami Beach knows how disappointing
this record is.]

Steve Gibbs
[Florida singer/songwriter who had a late '60s
release on Paris Tower. Gibbs hit it big in 1979
with his composition, "She Believes In Me," a top
five hit for Kenny Rogers.]

Bertie Higgins
Key Largo/White Line Fever (Kat Family 02524)   (81)
[The ex-Roemans drummer had many more
releases throughout the '80s, but few of these have
any interest to '60s collectors. "Key Largo" turned
out to be a surprise national top ten hit in 1982.]

Mark Holly
Dues/Cross Country Driver (Grit 107)   (73)
(LP) *Mark Holly* (Grit 2002)   (73)

[Actually Chuck Kaniss, The Impacs' second lead
singer.]

Rodney Justo
  Miss Brown/Tell Her That You Care
  (Sound Stage 7 2531)   (64)
  [Roy Orbison discovered the former leader of
  Clearwater's Rodney & The Mystics and brought
  him together with The Webs, the Alabama group
  that was to become The Candymen. Rodney later
  sang with Noah's Ark, Beaverteeth, and The
  Atlanta Rhythm Section.]

Manitoba/Joe Dowen
  Something In You/You'll Never Get Back
  (RCA 9908)   (10-70)
  Dead End Street/Come On Down To My Boat
  (RCA 0417)   (1-71)
  [Although based out of Saratoga Springs, New
  York, most band members grew up in St.
  Petersburg and paid their dues in Florida bands
  such as The Ravens, Rolling V, and The Tempests.]

Chalker McKay & Backroom Boys
  Lost Stop Sign/T. Zero (Amphion 101)   (64)
  [Chalker was the first Impacs vocalist.]

Opposite Sexes
  We Can Work It Out/Dark Days   (70)
  Hosanna-Simon Medley/No More Love
  (Opposite 1261/2) (PS)   (3-71)
  [Late releases by long-enduring Tampa band
  formerly known as The Mist.]

Raindrops
  Rock-A-Baby Rock/Rain (Capitol 4136)   (2-59)
  [Actually Tampa's Skyliners in need of a name
  change when the Pittsburgh Skyliners made a
  national breakthrough.]

Satellites
  Moody/Needless To Say (Nugget 1009) (PS)   (60)

Skyliners
I Can't Sleep/Why Should You Taunt Me
(DOC 496/7)
Rock-A-Baby Rock/Rain (Suncoast 1002)
[Featuring vocalist Tini Williams. Also see The
Raindrops above.]

Spinners
Happy Hootenanny/Nothin' (Smash 1845)   (9-63)
[This is the group that merged with The Impacs to
form Vic Waters & The Entertainers. Originally
from Roanoke, Virginia.]

Starliters
Whomp! Whomp!/Until You Return
(Suncoast 1001)

Big John Taylor
Stompin'/So Lonely (Tri-Dec 8457)
[See the Florida Rockabilly section for John's
recordings with the late Benny Joy. John also had
an early '60s recording called "The Raid" as part of
Big John & The Untouchables (which also
included country songwriter Bobby Braddock.)

Tides
Would I Still Be Loving You/Stranger
(Warwick 653)   (6-61)

Onelio Ochoa With Mafala Kootchie Whistlers
Listen To My Heart-Beat/Donna Lynn with Mafala
Kootchie Whistlers - Here Comes That Feeling
(Hurricane 106)
[Both The Tides and Mafala Kootchie Whistlers
were actually The Rockers, a very popular and
influential early '60s Tampa band. The group's
manager, Robert Bernstein, was reportedly
responsible for all the unusual pseudonyms.
Bernstein, incidentally, was known to thousands
of radio listeners as Rock Robbins, a one-time
popular disc jockey both in Tampa and Miami.]

White Witch
  And I'm Leaving/Parabrahm Greeting-
  Dwellers Of The Threshold (Capricorn 0012)   (72)
  Don't Close Your Mind/You're The One
  (Capricorn 0016)   (73)
  Home Grown Girl/It's So Nice To Be Stoned
  (Capricorn 0023)   (7-73)
  Home Grown Girl/Help Me Lord (Capricorn 0025) (7-73)
  Walk On/Showdown (Capricorn 0080)   (74)
  (LP) *White Witch* (Capricorn 0107)   (72)
  (LP) *A Spiritual Greeting* (Capricorn 0129)   (5-74)
  (LP) *Peaches Pick Of The Crop* (Capricorn PRO-588) (74)
  [Includes "Black Widow Lover" by White Witch,
  plus 23 cuts by other artists.]
  [White Witch was actually an early '70s version of
  The Tropics minus the members who left to form
  Bacchus. The name change was gradual with band
  members at first using White Witch while on the
  road and The Tropics while playing at home. White
  Witch caused a bit of a stir while recording its
  second album in Miami when word leaked out
  "The Tropics are recording again!" The band also
  featured former Noah's Ark guitarist Buddy
  Richardson and finally called it quits in the
  mid-'70s when the "spiritual greetings" became
  dust in the wind.]

MORE FLORIDA RELEASES
City Of Origin Unknown

Dark Horsemen
  You Lied/Girl, Stand By Me (The Dark Horsemen
  3720)   (3-66)
Eye Zooms
  She's Gone/On The Line (Atila 213)   (10-65)
Gang Of Saints
  Yes, It's Too Bad/This Feeling (PKB's 000)   (4-66)
Satans
  Gone From Me/Big Boss Man (Seller 007)   (2-66)

[All of the above records were mastered in Miami by
engineer Jack Davis — but no one I know remembers these
bands.]

14

FLORIDA ALBUM
DISCOGRAPHY

Duane & Gregg Allman
Duane & Gregg Allman (Bold 301)
Duane & Gregg Allman (Bold 302)
Morning Dew/God Rest His Soul/Nobody Knows
You When You're Down And Out/Come Down And
Get Me/Melissa/I'll Change For You/Back Down
Home With You/Well I Know Too Well/In The
Morning When I'm Real
[Reissue of 1968 tracks recorded in Hialeah; the
31st Of February is featured on every track. #301
and #302 were issued with different covers and
liner notes but contain the same tracks.]

Allman Joys - *Early Allman* (Dial 6005)   (73)
Gotta Get Away/Oh John/Street Singer/You'll
Learn Someday/Old Man River/Bell Bottom
Britches/Spoonful/Stalling For Time/Doctor Fone
Bone/Changing Of The Guard/The Forest For The
Trees/Northern Boundary
[Reissue of early Allman Joys' tracks. The Allmans
never sounded this good again!]

Blues Climax/The Alan Franklin Explosion -
First album (Horne 333-7)
[No information available.]

GIGANTIC
SHOW and DANCE
The Allman Joys

Playing their smash hit "SPOONFUL"

on Dial Records

Fort Brandon Armory
TUSCALOOSA
Friday, November 25

Admission $1.50   8:00 — 12:00 —

Don't Miss the NEW Psychedelic Sound

The **Allman Joys** were popular ALL throughout the south, but it was Daytona Beach's Martinique Club they called home. Most of their early tracks weren't released to the public until the early '70s.

The Blues Climax (Horne 888)   (70)
    Bye Bye Baby/Say You Love Me At Last/Got To
    Make You Mine/Piece Of Your Love/Love In My
    Heart/Down Hearted/Climax
    [Other Franklin releases include the ultra-rare,
    psychedelic *Alan Roy Franklin* (Underground
    OVL-86-2) and the so-so '80s comeback album,
    Come Home Baby.

Flow - *Flow* (CTI 1003)   (70)
    Daddy/Here We Are Again/Line 'Em/Gotta Get
    Behind Your Trip/Chicken Farm/No Lack Of
    Room/Summer's Gone/Mr. Invisible/Arlene
    [This relatively unexciting album featured Don
    Felder, later of the Eagles. This group was related
    to the Incidentals, who recorded for Paris Tower in
    the late '60s.]

Impacs - *Impact!* (King 886)   (64)
    She Didn't Even Say Hello/Kool It/Shimmy
    Shimmy/Big Boy/Jo- Ann/Black Lace/Voo Doo
    U.S.A./Two Strangers/Midnight Mist/Don't Cry
    Baby/Hide Away/Good, Good, Lovin'
    A Weekend With (King 916)   (64)
    Your Mama Put The Hurt On Me/Zot/Let's Go,
    Let's Go/I Love You More Today/Cape Kennedy,
    Fla./These Young Girls/Ain't That The Way Life
    Is/Music For A Space Station/Finger Poppin'
    Time/A Million Light Years Away/Walking Down
    That Lonely Street/You're Gonna Need My Love
    Again

Mercy - & *Love (Can Make You Happy)*
    (Sundi LP 803)   (5-69)
    Love (Can Make You Happy)/Hey Jude/I've Been
    Lonely Too Long/The Tracks Of My Tears/Hooked
    On A Feeling/Back In My Arms
    Again/Daydream/My Girl/Worst That Can
    Happen/Our Winter Love
    Love Can Make You Happy
    (Warner Bros.-7 Arts 1799)   (69)

Love Can Make You Happy/Heard You Went
Away/Never My Love/Forever/Sounds Of
Silence/The Morning's Come/Aquarius/Walking
By/Come Softly To Me/Love Is Blue/Do I Wanna
Live My Life With You/Ob-La-Di, Ob-La-Da
   [Mighty Manfred & The Wonder Dogs provide
instrumental backing on the Sundi album. The
track "Love Can Make You Happy" also appears on
the compilation album "Rock Classics" (Warner
Bros. 2590).]

Nightcrawlers - *The Little Black Egg*
   (Kapp KL-1520 - mono)   (6-67)
   The Little Black Egg (Kapp KL-3520 -
   rechanneled stereo) (6-67)
   The Little Black Egg/You're Running Wild/Me For
   Me/If You Want My Love/I Don't Remember/A
   Basket Of Flowers/Show Me The Way/What Time
   Is It/Who Knows/Washboard
   The Little Black Egg (Eva 12042)   (84)
   The Little Black Egg/You're Running Wild/Me For
   Me/If You Want My Love/I Don't
   Remember/Today I'm Happy/You're Comin'
   On/Midnight Reader/A Basket Of Flowers/Show
   Me The Way/What Time Is It/Who
   Knows/Washboard/My Butterfly/I Won't
   Tell/Won't You Say Yes To Me, Girl
   [Poorly programmed French bootleg.]

Royal Guardsmen - *Snoopy Vs. The Red Baron*
   (Laurie 2038)   (12-66)
   Snoopy Vs. The Red Baron/Liberty
   Valance/Bears/Peanut Butter/Battle Of New
   Orleans/Baby Let's Wait/Bo Diddley/Road
   Runner/Sweetmeats Slide/Alley Oop/Li'l Red
   Riding Hood/Jolly Green Giant
   The Return Of The Red Baron (Laurie 2039)   (3-67)
   Airplane Song (My Airplane)/I'm A Man/Any
   Wednesday/Shot Down/I'm Not Gonna Stay/So
   You Want To Be A Rock 'N Roll Star/The Return

Of The Red Baron/Gimme Some
Lovin'/OM/Searchin' For The Good Times/I Need
You Girl/Leaving Me

Snoopy And His Friends (Laurie 2042)   (12-67)
The Story Of & Snoopy Vs. The Red Baron/The
Story Of & The Return Of The Red Baron/The
Story Of & Snoopy's Christmas/I Say Love/Down
Behind The Lines/It's Sopwith Camel Time/So
Right (To Be In Love)/Airplane Song (My
Airplane)/It Kinda Looks Like Christmas

Snoopy For President (Laurie 2046)   (68)
Snoopy For President/Cry Like A Baby-The
Letter/Bonnie & Clyde/By The Time I Get To
Phoenix/Bottle Of Wine/Biplane
"Evermore"/Come On Down To My Boat/Simon
Says/Honey/Yummy Yummy Yummy

Merry Snoopy's Christmas (Mistletoe 1238)   (11-78)
  [Same tracks as *Snoopy And His Friends*.]
[The tracks "Snoopy Vs. The Red Baron" and "The
Return Of The Red Baron" also appear on the
album *Laurie Golden Goodies* (Laurie 2041), later
reissued under the title *Nostalgia* (Big Tree 2011).
The Guardsmen also recorded a public service
jingle for the U.S. Army which can be found on
many *The Hit Heard Round The World* albums from
the late '60s.]

Starfires - *The Starfires Play* (ORS 34/35)   (64)
Do It/Well, You're Wrong/Misty/Nobody But
You/Stranger From Durango/Broken
Glass/Country Girl/If You Should Lose Me/I Want
To Hold Your Hand/I Cover The
Waterfront/Grandma/New York
  [Extremely rare album by central Florida band
which later evolved into Little Willie & The
Adolescents.]

31st Of February - *The 31st Of February*
(Vanguard 6503)   (68)
Sandcastles/Porcelain Mirrors/Broken

Day/Wrong/The Greener Isle/Cod'ine/A Different
Kind Of Head/Pedestals/Free/A Nickel's Worth Of
Benny's Help/Pick A Gripe/Cries Of Treason

Tropics - (no label or track information available.)
[This early '60s private pressing signaled the
beginning of the Tropics' recording career and is
undoubtedly a far cry from the White Witch
albums which followed a decade later!]

We The People - *Declaration Of Independence*
(Eva 12009 - France   (1-83)
Mirror Of Your Mind/The Color Of Love/You Burn
Me Up And Down/He Doesn't Go About It Right/In
The Past/Lovin' Son Of A Gun/St. John's Shop
(1st version)/Declaration Of Independence/Follow
Me Back To Louisville/Love Is A Beautiful
Thing/The Day She Dies/When I Arrive/Ain't
Gonna Find Nobody (Better Than You)/St. John's
Shop (2nd version)
[French reissue of classic tracks by this legendary
Leesburg/Orlando band.]

BEE JAY SAMPLER ALBUMS

Bee-Jay Booking Agency of Winter Park, Florida, issued
sampler albums of local talent throughout the late '60s and
early '70s. Only those of interest to '60s fanatics are listed
here.

12 Groovy Hits, 12 Florida Bands (Tener 154)   (1966)
(Starfires, Swinging Temptations, Mysteries,
Moonrakers, Soul Tenders, Malemen, New
Englanders, Nooney Rickett IV, Fabulous Thunder,
Wrong Numbers, Pratts Bottom "5", Nation
Rocking Shadows)

Bee Jay Demo Vol. II (Tener 1014)   (Spring, 1967)
(Little Willie & Adolescents, New Dimensions In
Sound, New Generations, Him And The Others,
Chapter 5, Traditions, Barons, Minutemen, Back
Pages, Mourning After, Consolidation, Hungri I's,

Undertakers, New Englanders, Rhythm's Children,
State Of Mind, Midnight Suns, Kolors, Beau Jests,
Warlocs, Orlando Rogues, Flower Power, Mustard
Jar, Bomarcs)

Bee Jay Video Soundtrack (Tener 1014)   (Winter, 1968)
[For some reason, this had the same release
number as the above album.]
(Ron & The Starfires, The Beloved, Rovin' Flames,
Wrong Numbers, Barons, Tom Tom & Pipers,
Enticers, Plant Life, Custers Last Band, Story
Tellers, Soultenders, Shadows, Warlocs, Sweet
Soul Generation)

Bee Jay Sampler (Tener 1055)   (1970)
(We The People, Soultenders, Brewed, Barons,
Missin Links, 8 lesser bands)

Do It Up Right! (Tener 1067)   (1971)
(The Brewed, East Coast Supply, Oxford Blue, +12)

Bee Jay Does It Again! (Tener 1070)   (1971)
(The Brewed, In The Beginning, East Coast
Supply, 15 more turkeys)

15

FLORIDA '60s ARTISTS ON COMPILATION ALBUMS

Canadian Rogues
    Keep In Touch (*Back From The Grave Vol. 2*)

Esquires
    Heartaches Stay The Night (*Florida Punk Groups From The '60s*)
    Heat (*Florida Punk Groups From The '60s*)

Hoppi & Beau Heems
    When I Get Home (*Psychedelic Unknowns Vol. 8*)
    I Missed My Cloud (*Glimpses 2*)

Illusions
    I Know (*Midwest Vs. The Rest Vol. 1*)

Larry & Loafers
    Let's Go To The Beach (*What A Way To Die*)

Little Willie & Adolescents
    Get Out Of My Life (*Back From The Grave 3*)

Lost Generation
    I'd Gladly Pay (*Garage Punk Unknowns Vol. 1*)

Magi
    You Don't Know Me (*Pebbles Vol. 5*)
    [Why this early '70s hippie record was ever booted is beyond me!]

Missing Links
  Where Were You Last Night (*Garage Punk Unknowns Vol. 5*)

Mods
  Empty Heart (*Florida Punk Groups From The '60s*)
  Sweets For My Sweet (*Florida Punk Groups From The '60s*)

Mystics
  Snoopy (*Back From The Grave Vol. 2*)

Outsiders
  She's Coming On Stronger (*Back From The Grave Vol. 2*)
  Summertime Blues (*Back From The Grave Vol. 2*)

Fort Myers' **Painted Faces** are well-known to '60s collectors through their appearances on several '80s compilation albums — most of which listed them as an L.A. band! *Photo courtesy Jerry Turano.*

Painted Faces
    Anxious Color (*The Cicadelic Sixties, Acid Dream,
    Journey to Tyme*)
    I Lost You In My Mind (*Magic Cube*)
    I Think I'm Going Mad (*Highs In The Mid '60s Vol. 3*)
    Things We See (*Journey To Tyme*)
Purple Underground
    Count Back (*Off The Wall Vol. 1, Mayhem &
    Psychosis Vol. 2*)
Rovin' Flames
    How Many Times (*Pebbles Vol. 8*)
Royal Guardsmen
    Leaving Me (*Mindrocker 10*)
    So Right (*Collector's Records Of The '50s & '60s
    Vol. 19*)
Shy Guys
    Black Lightening Light (*Florida Punk Groups From
    The '60s*)
    Goodbye To You (*Florida Punk Groups
    From The '60s*)
    [In addition to the Florida bands listed here, this
    French compilation also includes bands from as
    far away as Ohio!! Come on, guys, what's going on
    here?]
Sir Michael & Sounds
    Can You (*The Chosen Few Vol. 2*)
Soul Trippers
    King Bee (*Mindrocker Vol. 5*)
Split Ends
    Rich With Nothin' (*I Was A Teenage Caveman,
    Pebbles Vol. 1, Psychedelic Unknowns Vol. 1,
    Psychedelic Unknowns Vol. 2 EP*)
Tropics
    As Time's Gone (*Mindblowers Vol. 1*)
    You Better Move (*I Was A Teenage Caveman,
    Riot City!*)

Twelfth Night
  Grim Reaper (*The Chosen Few Vol. 2*)

Undertakers
  Love So Dear (*Pebbles 17*)

We The People
  By The Rule (*Psychedelic Microdots Vol. 1*)
  Free Information (*Psychedelic Microdots Vol. 1*)
  Half Of Wednesday (*Psychedelic Microdots Vol. 1*)
  He Doesn't Go About It Right (*Mindrocker Vol. 6*)
  In The Past (*Mindrocker Vol. 5, Psychedelic
  Microdots Vol. 1, Psychedelic Unknowns Vol. 1,
  Psychedelic Unknowns Vol. 2 EP*)
  Mirror Of Your Mind (*Mayhem & Psychosis Vol. 2,
  More Nuggets Vol. 3, Psychedelic Microdots Vol. 1*)
  My Brother, The Man (*Garage Punk Unknowns Vol.
  4, Psychedelic Microdots Vol. 1*)
  Too Much Noise (*Psychedelic Microdots Vol. 1*)
  When I Arrive (*Pebbles Vol. 7*)
  You Burn Me Up And Down (*Mindrocker 6,
  Psychedelic Unknowns Vol. 4, Sounds Of The
  Sixties*)
  ["By The Rule," "Free Information," "Half Of
  Wednesday," and "Too Much Noise" made their
  first appearance EVER on the 1989 compact disk
  Psychedelic Microdots Vol. 1.]

Wrong Numbers
  I'm Gonna Go Now (*Off The Wall Vol. 2*)

  (For South Florida compilation appearances, see
  Chapter 7.)

16

POSSIBLE FLORIDA RELEASES

OBSCURE: Webster's defines it as vague. Enigmatic. Cryptic.

Sort of like the records on the next few pages. Yeah, you music moguls of the '50s and '60s: You did a wonderful thing by allowing regional talent to leave behind vinyl souvenirs of their brief moment in the sun. Yeah, you delivered the wax, but most of you fell short on the facts: Where and when the record was released; who you were, where you were, and wherefore art thou rocking 'n rolling! (Not Shakespeare, but shake 'n shimmy, with answers about as scarce as a Montague at a Capulet rock 'n roll party!)

In a moment, we'll discuss DEAD WAX MARKINGS and how they made up for the short-sightedness of many a label owner. But for now, some orphic obscurities: some with label graphics that resemble local releases (Donna And The Dees, Chain Reaction, Mumy, Castaways Five); some by artists that share the same name as Florida acts (Sounds Of Tyme, Shades Of Jade, Eighth Day, Bushmen, Smack, etc.). A few were regional hits (Chosen Few, Teddy Bears, Finders Keepers, Roosters), but all have one thing in common: unknown origin. Needless to say, if anyone has any information on the following releases, please let me know. Let's get to the bottom of these musical mysteries!

Archers
   Hey Rube/Unwind It (Laurie 3207)
   [1963 Phil Gernhard production. Phil went on to
   great succcess with Florida acts ranging from the
   Tropics and Royal Guardsmen in the '60s to Jim
   Stafford, Lobo, and the Bellamy Bros. in the '70s.]

Band
   Mr. Guitar Man/The Lovin' Zone (Pride 3007)
   Mr. Guitar Man/The Lovin' Zone (Tener 1005/6)
   [Pride is an Oklahoma label. Tener is a Florida
   label. YOU figure it out!]

Barking Spyders
   Hard World/I Want Your Love
   (Audio Precision 4201)

Bushmen
   Friends And Lovers Forever/You've Been With Him
   (Smash 2054)
   St. James Infirmary/You're The Girl
   (SSS Intl. 705)
   [Probably from Atlanta. The Bushmen had a studio
   there where they recorded and produced a single
   for the Celtics: "Looking For You"/"For Your Love,"
   on Dante 2295.]

Cash
   I'm In Love/How Much More Must They Cry
   (Corlyn 67-101)

Cash Holiday
   Long Tall Sally/I'm In Love (Corlyn 67-102)
   I'm In Love With You (Ip Bip Bippity Do)/Twist Me
   'Round Your Finger (Corlyn 117)

Castaways Five
   It's Over It's Over/Revenge (Raol 001-002)

Chain Reaction
   You'll Never Know/G.Y.S. (Get You Some Lovin')
   (Blank 67-764)

Chosen Few
   Forget About The Past/Another Goodbye

(Power International 872)
[Charted In Tampa in April, 1966.]

Daybreakers
I'm In Love/Like Me Like You (SLR 983)
[Top three hit in Jacksonville in July, 1967.]

Diamond Four
Anny Fanny/Chicken Honk (RCA Victor 9588)

Donna And The Dees
Happy Holiday/Hunkey Was Doing The Monkey
(B.C.S. 102)

Eighth Day
Hey Boy! (This Girl's In Love With You)/A Million
Lights (Kapp 862) (PS)
Raining Sunshine/That Good Old Fashioned Way
(Kapp 894)
Glory/Building With A Steeple (Kapp 916)
(LP) *On The 8th Day* (Kapp 3554)

Finders Keepers
(We Wear) Lavender Blue/Raggedy Ann
(Challenge 59338)
Don't Give In To Him/I've Done All I Can
(Challenge 59364)

Bill Friel & Fabulous Furies
Fort Lauderdale, U.S.A./Johnny Come Home
(Joker 1009)

Group
Land Of Lakes/Just In Case (Troupe 5467)

Kords
Boris The Spider/It's All In My Mind (Laurie 3403)

Luv'd Ones
Yeah I'm Feelin' Fine/Up Down Sue
(White Oak 759101)
[Although the above carries a Dania, Florida,
address, it was pressed in Chicago... and yes,
these ARE the same girls who recorded for the
Chicago-based Dunwich label.]

Mark V
    Over You/Fish Tracks-Purple And Green
    (Mark V no #)

Dean Morgan
    Good Rockin' Tonight/Rockin' My Blues Away
    (Rare 101)
    Little Maggie/Climb The Wall (Rare 102)
    [Totally bizarre mid-'60s grunge with strong
    rockabilly influence; but where's it from? The label
    graphics sure resemble those of a Miami record!]

Mumy
    Don't Let The Sun Catch You Crying/I Wake Up
    Crying (Mumy 1218)

Outer Mongolian Heard
    Hey Joe/I Want To Love You (Daisy 4846/7)

Queiros
    Something Tells Me/Cry, Cry, Cry
    (Panther 1001/2)
    [Let's get this straight: The record company is
    named Panther. The publishing company is
    Tampa Music. The group's title is in broken
    Spanish. How could this NOT be suspected of
    being from Florida?]

Randy & Road Runners
    Starvin'/I Broke A Rule (Ranco 1500)

Randy & The Rest
    Confusion/Dreaming (Jade 767)
    The Vacuum/Dreaming (SSS Intl. 720)

Randy's World
    Over Again/I Love A Girl (SSS Intl. 734)

Roosters
    Love Machine/I'm Suspectin'
    (Philips 40504)
    Home Down Right/Good Good Lovin' (Philips
    40559)
    [Long-suspected of originating from the

Jacksonville area, but there's never been any proof.]

Shades Of Jade
Why Does It Feel So Right/Rainy Sunday
(Dore 806)
[B-side of the above is not by The Shades Of Jade.]

Daniel E. Skidmore, III
Little Old Groovemaker/Listen To The Wind
(Parkway 131)
[You could just about put money on this being the Broward kid who sang with The Coachmen, Las Olas Brass, and so many other show bands. Skidmore later turned up fronting records by Free Fare and The Bloody Truth.]

Smack
Susie Q/Hit The Road Jack (Garland 2015)
[Garland is an Oregon label, but George Walden of Smack once told me he remembers his band cutting a heavy version of "Susie Q."]

Sounds Of Tyme
To Understand Mankind/Sold Out Show
(Bowmar 1001)
[Bowmar was a North Carolina label, but of course, that doesn't really mean anything. I have photos of a Sounds Of Tyme playing at the Ft. Lauderdale Armory.]

Spectres
Depression/8 2/3   (Melbourne 3230)

Squires
Wondren/Pieces (Crestline 15668)
Wonderin'/ (Anaconda 15268)
[I've never seen the above pressing, so I can't vouch for it.]

Teddy Bears
Miss To Mrs./ (Keystone Pavilion)
[Top 20 hit in Jacksonville in July, 1967.]

Thrashers
  Fort Lauderdale, U.S.A./Sledge Hammer
  (Clearview 1001)
Tikis
  At least seven singles and one album on labels
  such as Dial, Ascot, and Minaret. Possibly from
  Georgia or Alabama, although the Tikis did make
  it as far south as Miami and WERE connected
  with the late Florida producer Finley Duncan.
Us Four
  The Alligator/By My Side (Rising Sons 701)
Vanguards IV
  Blue Skies/Corkscrew (Chariot, Inc. 92360)
  [Chuck Kaniss of the Impacs wrote the B-side of
  these early instrumentals.]
What's Left?
  He Was A Friend Of Mine/You're A Better Man
  Than I (What's Left? 101)

17

THE SOUTH FLORIDA
SOUL SCENE

SOUL MUSIC is no stranger to South Florida. Unlike their rock 'n roll counterparts who struggled in obscurity for so many years, South Florida's major soul acts generally fared well, thanks in no small part to the ubiquitous hand of Henry Stone. Stone, who was partly responsible for the success of such influential acts as Ray Charles and James Brown, has had the magic touch for cultivating soulful talent for over 40 years. One can't help but be amazed at what Stone has accomplished — from being the first to record Sam and Dave in the early '60s to launching the most successful independent disco label of the '70s.

Stone has always managed to be a step ahead of the crowd. And Miami's prolific soul community has certainly benefited from this.

To understand the evolution of Miami's soul scene, one must first understand the structure of Miami's entertainment community in the early '60s. Back then there was no such thing as integration. The most luxurious clubs belonged to whites; the better hotels belonged to whites; it wasn't even all that easy for a black act to get booked into one of Miami Beach's many hotels. (If they did, they'd still have to prepare for that late-night drive across the bridge, back into Liberty City or Overtown.) That's one reason why so much musical activity was concentrated in the inner-city area. With racism running as high as it did back then, it was a lot safer — and a lot more practical — to stick to one's own backyard.

When you hear the names Liberty City and Overtown, you probably think of riots... racial violence... poverty... it's unfortunate that all the negative things that happened have been so widely publicized while the positive has gone almost completely unnoticed. I can think of little that's more positive than the inner-city club scene of the '60s — Clyde Killens' Knight Beat, Harlem Square, Fiesta, and Island Clubs — are all just memories today, but decades ago every major rhythm and blues act that passed through the South passed through those doors. In a way, Killens' clubs could be compared to New York's Apollo Theatre, with Count Basie, Dinah Washington, Ray Charles, and just about everyone else in between having shared the stage with Sam and Dave, Dizzy Jones, Frank Williams' Rocketeers, and the rest of Miami's finest. Other small clubs, such as the Continental and the Club Royal, also kept the big beat sound going strong.

Record company executives were starting to become aware of the potential bonanza that existed in these clubs, and a lot of acts were finding themselves inside recording studios, on the road, and sometimes even on the charts. As the '60s "soul boom" continued, spurred on by the incredible popularity (and across-the-board acceptance) of Motown, more and more artists were being signed to major labels. Some, such as Sam and Dave, did extremely well. Others, like Ella Washington, Della Humphrey, and Helene Smith, did fairly well. Others weren't quite as lucky, trying for many years without ever achieving a hit record.

One such group was the Marvells (Annette Snell, Loretta Letlo, Mattie Lovett, Addie Williams), who provided backup vocals for the Delmiras, Steve Alaimo, and many others. The Marvells later changed their name to the Fabulettes and recorded for national labels in Muscle Shoals, Nashville, and of course, Miami. Annette Snell left the group in 1969 and continued to record up until her death in a plane crash in

1977. The Fabulettes tried three other vocalists after Snell's departure (including Patricia Miles Bendroff from the Twans) before eventually breaking up in 1971.

Another group with an interesting history is the Prolifics, who had a local number one record under their original name, the Moovers. The Prolifics continued to record throughout the late '70s, including a release on United Artists under the name Living Proof. In addition to the nucleus of the Moovers, the Prolifics included a former member of the Delmiras, the early '60s vocal group that gave South Florida its first look at Clarence Reid.

The Delmiras were sort of a maverick in the world of vocal groups, thanks to Reid's sometimes unorthodox approach to harmony. (Who else would ask his group's first tenor to sing baritone?) The Delmiras' biggest hit, "Sooner Or Later," actually featured Paul Kelly despite the fact the label credited "Clarence Reed And The Delmiros" (sic) as the artist. Reid came down with laryngitis just prior to the recording session, and at the last moment Kelly was called upon to fill in. Two years later, Kelly would have his first solo hit, "Chills And Fever," while Reid would also embark on a solo career — one that would take a lot of strange twists and turns through the years.

Reid recorded for many national labels (Dial, Wand, Phil-L.A. Of Soul, Tay-Ster) but wasn't able to score a major smash until 1969 when "Nobody But You Babe," an infectious dance number based on the Isley Brothers' "It's Your Thing," set off a string of similar-sounding, yet nonetheless enjoyable records. Ironically, Reid's greatest claim to fame may be "Blowfly," a character he created one day while messing around in the recording studio. Blowfly's sharp, irreverent wit turned more than a few heads — especially in Pineville, Louisiana, where a record retailer was arrested just for selling a Blowfly album to a minor! (This happened more than a decade before the 2 Live Crew obscenity squabble.) Reid's alter ego was banned and bandied about, but despite all of his nastiness, Blowfly never forgot that soul music was supposed to be fun... and his albums are still the life of the party to this day.

Reid's talent was not just confined to the front of a microphone; he was also an excellent songwriter and found the perfect partner in fellow writer-producer Willie Clarke. The Clarke-Reid team formed one of the most creative, exciting collaborations in the history of soul music, lasting well into the '70s and culminating in a trio of gold records. The pair first got together while Clarke (a school teacher) and another faculty member, Johnny Pearsall, were operating Miami's first independent black production company. Clarke and Pearsall were the brains behind a number of local labels, including Deep City (named for an off-campus club in Tallahassee), Lloyd (which took its moniker from Pearsall's middle name), and Green Gold (what the pair had hoped to make). Helene Smith, a student at Northwestern Senior High (and future Mrs. Pearsall), was the first artist signed by the duo. Paul Kelly was the second. Eventually, Clarke and Pearsall would go their separate ways, but not before making what was to be a most-important discovery.

It all started the day an 11-year-old girl walked into Johnny Pearsall's record store to claim a prize she had won from a local radio station. As the girl started singing the prize-winning song out loud (Billy Stewart's "Summertime"), Clarke and Pearsall looked on in disbelief. The little girl sang with such power and conviction... she was just too good to be true. And because of her young age, her story almost ended before it began. But eventually, her reluctant parents agreed to sign a contract... and the career of Betty Wright was ready to begin.

Wright was put to the test singing background vocals for some local sessions before eventually recording her first solo disc, the excellent "Paralyzed" (of which the flip side, "Good Lovin'," was a sizable hit in Tampa).

Wright's second release, "Mr. Lucky," barely sold a dozen copies. But her third recording, "Girls Can't Do What The Guys Do," carried a message that teenage girls everywhere could identify with... and it paid off in both requests and

record sales. "Girls Can't Do What The Guys Do" was a
smash on both the soul and top 40 charts... and started
Wright on a career that's still going strong. It also meant the
start of something big for Reid and Clarke, the song's writers,
who then joined Henry Stone's Tone/TK family, where they
remained until TK's bankruptcy in 1981.

The heart and soul of the TK family. We're talking some serious talent here!
BACK ROW: Betty Wright, Clarence "Blowfly" Reid, Henry Stone. FRONT ROW:
Willie Clarke, Steve Alaimo. *Photo courtesy Henry Stone*

Many of Wright's early sides featured a backup section
that's a virtual supergroup, with three-fifths of the
Birdwatchers and two-thirds of the 31st of February joining
other TK stalwarts, including Reid himself on piano. Without
a doubt, Henry Stone was really starting to cook. Reid and
Clarke were writing hit after hit, and WRBD disc jockey Joe
Fisher, obviously a great judge of talent, was bringing future
stars such as J. P. Robinson and George and Gwen McCrae
to Stone's attention. All were releasing excellent records, and
it certainly seemed that the local soul scene would thrive
forever. It almost did.

The discography that follows bears an arbitrary cut-off date of Summer, 1970. Unlike the rock scene that kept changing (and regressing) as time passed, the soul scene continued to feature basically the same artists, writers, and producers as during its late '60s heyday. But as the rhythms started turning toward the mid-tempo and the sound grew funkier and funkier, it was becoming clear that the gritty, sweaty soul music that we all knew and loved was becoming less important than the need to dance.

Disco in its earliest forms was fast, funky, and often mindless, but it accomplished what it set out to do. It induced movement, and at times even approached the excitement level. But as dances changed and disco took on a lazy, mid-tempo beat (to accommodate such monstrosities as the hustle), the basic elements of soul continued to disappear. Disco is fine when it retains its soulful impetus and energy base; when this essence is depleted, all that remains is a dissonant jumble. It was only natural that a disco backlash would occur, as many older blacks could in no way relate to the sounds on the radio. "Boogie Oogie Oogie," "Ring My Bell," "Dance Dance Dance Yowsah Yowsah," and the like had very little, if anything, in common with Otis Redding or James Brown, and that, my friends, is hardly soul.

In defense of Miami's black sound of the '70s, it must be noted that local disco did not bow to some of the more putrid excesses of the genre, such as strings and over-orchestrated mush. If there is one thing that characterizes the Miami '70s sound, it is an emphasis on succinct rhythms, with backup vocals, and sometimes brass, seeming to dominate the song itself. Percussion, too, is dominant, with excesses such as violins being virtually nonexistent. In other words, one can usually distinguish a Miami TK record from one produced by a New York company. In almost all cases, the Miami disc is far more palatable... yet there was always something missing. The lacking element may have seemed intangible at times, but it always was there. But even as you read this, the cast of characters is still basically intact. Clarence Reid...

Willie Clarke... Benny Latimore... they're all still around. If there will indeed be a soul renaissance, it is a safe bet that Miami will be there. And where Miami soul goes, so does Henry Stone. Wanna bet we haven't heard the last of him?

18

THE SOUTH FLORIDA SOUL SCENE

Singles Discography
(through Summer, 1970)

Sammy Ambrose
    Soul Shout Limbo/Limbo Like Me (Mala 460)   (63)
    This Diamond Ring/Bad Night (Musicor 1061)   (12-64)
    Monkey See, Monkey Do/Welcome To Dreamsville
    (Musicor 1072)   (3-65)

Sammy Ambrose & Afro-Beats
    The Canadian Twist/Nitty Gritty (West-Side 1001)

Sammy Ambrose & Friend
    Ram-Ram/They'll Be Coming (Crazy Horse 1315)   (69)

Annetta
    Since There's No More Of You/Get Away Boy
    (Love Hill 001)   (6-69)
    Since There Is No More You/Get Away Boy
    (Juggy 404)   (6-70)
    [Annette Snell's first solo recordings after leaving
    the Fabulettes. Her final tracks were on board the
    Southern Express plane that crashed in 1977,
    taking her life.]

Bell Brothers
    Don't You Know She's Alright/Not Your Kind Of

Love (Sure Shot 5012)   (66)
Pity Me/Look At Me (Sure Shot 5023)   (9-66)
Tell Him No/ (Sure Shot 5038)
Chanteers
Jungle Twist/The Life Of Pepe Lococo
She's Coming Home/Mr. Zebra (Mercury 71979) (6-62)
I Waited/Just A Little Boy (Mercury 72037)   (9-62)
[Early West Palm Beach vocal group which
featured singer J. P. Robinson and influential disc
jockey Joe Fisher.]
Cliffs Of Rhythms Band
The Boogaloo Popeye/Jumping (Dit Dot 0002)   (67)
Wayne Cochran - See separate discography.
Cornelius Bros.
Things Are Gonna Change (one-sided demo)
(Gulfstream no #)
Cornelius Bros. & Sister Rose
Treat Her Like A Lady/Over At My Place
(Platinum 105-106)   (7-70)
Treat Her Like A Lady/Over At My Place
(United Artists 50721)   (12-70)
[Many later releases on United Artists, including
the national smash "Too Late To Turn Back Now."]
Bobby Darnell & Dorells
Tell Me How To Find True Love/Baby Check
Yourself (Bronze 101)
[Also see The Dorells.]
Delmiras
The Big Sound/Dry Your Eyes (Dade 1821)
[For future releases, see Clarence Reid & Delmiras.]
Dorells with the Rocketeers
I Need Someone To Love Me/You're Gonna Want
Me (Bronze 102)   (9-65)
Eddie And The Tropics
We've Got Something/Don't Monkey With Another
Monkey's Monkey (Josie 930)   (65)
One Hundred Pounds Of Clay/Will You Love Me

Tomorrow (Bird Bowl Lounge 3539)   (10-65)
I Don't Know/For Sentimental Reasons
(Universal demo)
[Also see Eddie Lovette.]

Fabulettes
Mister Policeman/The Bigger They Are
(The Harder They Fall) (Monument 901)   (7-65)
Try The Worryin' Way/Money (Sound Stage 7
2558)   (66)
Screamin' And Shoutin'/I'm In The Mood For Love
(Sound Stage 7 2576)   (12-66)
Because Of Love/If The Morning Ever Comes
(Kangi 102)   (69)
Because Of Love/If The Morning Ever Comes
(Phil-L.A. Of Soul 336)   (70)
Muddy Waters/Stickin Kind Of Man (Access 1002) (71)
[Formerly The Marvells.]

Five Steps
These Boots Are Made For Walkin'/Tightin Up
(issued on Scott 26, Dade 26, and Dade 2001)   (3-66)

Freddy & The Kinfolk
The Goat/Blabbermouth (Dade 45-217) - local   (1-68)
The Goat/Blabbermouth (Dade 2016) - national   (1-68)
Mashed Potato, Pop Corn/Last Take (Dade 2024)(11-69)
[Also see Freddy Scott.]

Arthur Freeman
No Hard Feelings/Shirley (Dade 1852)   (64)
Played Out Playgirl/I Can't Understand
(Regal 7257)   (64)
[Art's long career also saw releases on Jumbo,
Fame, and Excello.]

George & Gwen
Three Hearts In A Tangle/One Of These Days
(Alston 4576) - national   (7-69)
Three Hearts In A Tangle/One Of These Days
(Alston 4577) - local   (7-69)
Like Yesterday Our Love Is Gone/Stranded In This
. . . (Alston 4579)   (10-69)

No One Left To Come Home To/Stranded In This
Broken Heart Of Mine (Alston 4586)   (4-70)
[George and Gwen McCrae issued solo singles in
the early '70s on United Artists and Columbia,
respectively, before scoring mid-'70s disco hits for
TK-related labels.]

Freda Gray & Rocketeers
Stay Away From My Johnny/Rocketeers -
Stay Away From My Johnny (Deep City 2366)   (5-66)

Little Jimmy Griffin
If Things Don't Change/I'm Searchin' (R 508)   (62)
[Very early release by a future member of The
Kinfolk. Griffin, a top soul/R&B disc jockey for
more than two decades, recorded these sides for a
Kansas City label.]

Edw. Hamilton & Arabians
I Love You So/Now You Have To Cry Alone
(Lanrod 1605)
[Hamilton also had at least half-a-dozen releases
for Detroit labels. The above, for some reason,
bears a Miami Beach address.]

Odessa Harris
The Color Of His Love Is Blue/Driving Wheels
(JEB 101)   (5-65)
The Color Of His Love Is Blue/Driving Wheels
(Uptown 711)   (5-65)
Since I Fell For You/You're What I Need
(Uptown 720)
[Odessa also had an earlier release on Capitol
4881: "Rockin' Good Way" b/w "Nothing In The
World," although it's not likely this 1962 recording
is of local origin.]

Don Hollinger
I Had A Nightmare/Where The Young Folks Go
(Jato 7000)   (4-66)
Until I Find You/Cruel World (Atco 6492)   (6-67)
Wild Side Of Life/Wild Side Of Life (Kelane 691)
[Don had many later releases throughout the '70s.]

Eddie Holloway
   I Had A Good Time/I'm Standing By (Gem 102)   (7-70)
   [Also see The Third Guitar.]

Willie Hopkins
   If I Were A Carpenter/Goin Out Of My Head-Can't
   Take My Eyes Off You (W-H 7219)   (10-69)

Jimmy "Bo" Horne
   I Can't Speak/Street Corners (Dade 2025)   (12-69)
   Hey There Jim/Don't Throw Your Love Away
   (Dig 901)   (7-70)
   [Jimmy kept the beat going throughout the '70s
   and '80s.]

Louis Howard & Rocketeers
   I'm A Happy Man/Please Forgive Me
   (Bronze 108)   (10-67)

Della Humphrey
   Don't Make The Good Girls Go Bad/Your Love Is
   All I Need (Arctic 144)   (10-68)
   (Girls Have Feelings) Just Like The Boys Do/
   Over The Tracks (Arctic 155)   (8-69)
   Will You Love Me Tomorrow/Let's Wait Until Dark
   (Arctic 159)   (4-70)
   [Della had at least one more release in the early
   '70s.]

Mary Hylor
   Runnin'/We Walked Down The Aisle
   (El-Lor 1057/58)

Paul Kelly
   It's My Baby/The Upset (Lloyd no #)   (4-65)
   Chills And Fever/Only Your Love (Lloyd 007)   (9-65)
   Chills And Fever/Only Your Love (Dial 4021)   (11-65)
   Since I Found You/Can't Help It
   (Dial 4025) (with The Rocketeers)   (2-66)
   Nine Out Of Ten Times/I Need Your Love So Bad
   (Philips 40409) (PS)   (11-66)
   Sweet Sweet Lovin'/Cryin' For My Baby
   (Philips 40457)   (5- 67)

If This Old House Could Talk/You Don't Know,
You Just Don't Know (Philips 40480)   (9-67)
My Love Is Growing Stronger/Glad To Be Sad
(Philips 40513)   (12-67)
Call Another Doctor/We're Gonna Make It
(Dial 4088)   (11- 68)
[Many more nonlocal releases in the '70s and '80s,
including the 1970 national hit "Stealing In The
Name Of The Lord." Also see Clarence Reid & The
Delmiras and The Valladeers.]

James Knight & Butlers
There Goes My Baby-VOCAL/INSTRUMENTAL
(Concho 2250)   (8- 69)
Save Me/El Chicken (Cat 245/246)   (3-70)
Baby Please Pretty Please/Space Guitar
(Cat 1972)   (8-70)
Funky Cat/Nothin' (Cat 1976)

Johnny Larand
Don't Get Mad/Heaven To Me (Octavia 0005)
[Johnny also recorded a song called "The Eel" on
Reginald 1401, backed by The Internes.]

Benny Latimore
Snap Your Fingers/Peggy Thompson - I Sold My
Heart To The Junkman (Hit 15)
I Can't Go On Anymore/Rain From The Sky
(Blade 701)   (12-66)
Girl I Got News For You/Ain't Gonna Cry No More
(Dade 2013)   (5-67)
There She Is/It Was So Nice While It Lasted
(Dade 2014)   (67)
It's Just A Matter Of Time/Let's Move & Groove
Together (Dade 215) - local   (11-67)
It's Just A Matter Of Time/Let's Move & Groove
Together (Dade 2015) - national   (12-67)
The Power And The Glory/Love Don't Love Me
(Dade 45-217) - local   (6-68)
The Power And The Glory/Love Don't Love Me
(Dade 2017) - national   (7-68)

Have A Little Faith/I'm A Believer (Dade 2020)
I Pity The Fool/I'm Just An Ordinary Man
(Dade 2022)   (5-69)
I Pity The Fool/I'm Just An Ordinary Man
(Atlantic 2639)   (6-69)
I'll Be Good To You/Life's Little Ups & Downs
(Dade 2026) - local   (2-70)
I'll Be Good To You/Life's Little Ups & Downs
(Dade 2025) - national   (3-70)
[Many more releases throughout the '70s and '80s
as Latimore.]

Nickie Lee
Ten Commandments Of Man/Late Shadows
(Dade 2011)   (1-67)
I Want To Get Next To You/Nickie Lee Orch. -
Nick's Kick (Dade 2014)   (6-67)
And Black Is Beautiful/Faith Within
(Dade 2018)   (10-68)
And Black Is Beautiful/Faith Within
(Mala 12025)   (11-68)
Dream Of The People Part 1/Part 2 (Dade 2021)   (4-69)
Do Something About My Dream Part 1/Part 2
(Mala 12039)   (5-69)
["The Nick With A Positive Kick" was a popular
disc jockey on WAME and WRIZ.]

Little Beaver
I Feel My Love/Frank Williams - Git It
(Octavia 0006)   (5- 67)
Soul Stuff Part 1/Part 2 (Phil-L.A. Of Soul 306) (9-67)
Do It To Me One More Time/Blind Man
(Saadia 2331)
Do It To Me One More Time/Blind Man
(Saadia 5784)
Do Right Man/These Blues Are Getting Me Down
(Saadia 5283)   (7-70)
[Many more releases on Saadia and Cat.]

Eddie Lovette
By-Ooh-Pa-Ooh-Pa-Pa-Ya/You're My Girl

(Steady 122)   (12-68)
Too Experienced/You're My Girl (Steady 124)   (4-69)
Little Bluebird/By-Ooh-Pa-Ooh-Pa-Pa-Ya
(Steady 002)   (69)
Together/Boomerang (Steady 004)   (69)
Look At Me/Unemployed Heart (Steady 005)   (12-69)
[Eddie kept the island beat going strong clear
through the 1970s and 1980s.]

Johnnie Marie & Delvations
I've Got A Feeling/Love Is Like A Flower
(Sweet Soul 005/006)

Marvells
How Do I Keep The Girls Away/Go On And Have
Yourself A Ball (Angie 1005)   (63)
Go On And Have Yourself A Ball/How Do I Keep
The Girls Away (Butane 778)   (63)
This Can't Go On/Dizzy Jones Birdland (Yorey
1002)
["Dizzy Jones Birdland" was originally issued by
The Laddins on Butane 779. Also see The
Fabulettes.]

Mighty Dogcatchers
It's Gonna Be A Mess Pt. 1/Pt. 2
(Green Gold 6969)

Mona Lisa
They Don't Know Part 1/Part 2 (Dade 2002)   (3-66)
I Can't Stand Myself/I Love Me (Dade 2010)   (1-67)

Moovers
One Little Dance/Someone To Fulfill My Needs
(Deep City 2367)   (7-66)
I Love You Baby/One Little Dance
(Deep City 2374)   (4-67)
I Love You Baby/One Little Dance (Brent 7065) (5-67)
[The Moovers later became known as The Prolifics.]

Judson Moore, Jr., & Gayroy Students
I Got To Do What I Can/Un Un Yi Yi
(Mor-Top 204/205)

Mousetrap
    Spinning Wheel/Rhymetyme (Scott 402)   (5-69)
    [A very feeble attempt at soul by The Birdwatchers.]

Nasty Dog Catchers
    Nasty Dog Part 1/Part 2 (Reedsville 1970)   (66)
    Nasty Dog Part 1/Part 2 (Jato 7001)
    (as The Dog Catchers)   (4-66)

Original Cousins
    Eggman/Sock-It (Reid 2746)   (64)

Prolifics
    If Only I Could Fly/Keep On Raining Rain
    (Drive 6001)   (12- 68)
    [Later releases in the '70s on Konduko, Avco
    Embassy, and United Artists. The Prolifics also
    recorded under the name Living Proof.]

Red Rooster
    Like A Baby Part 1/Part 2 (Deep City 300)

Reflections
    You Don't Love Me/I Need Your Love (Went 001)   (68)

Clarence Reid
    There'll Come A Day/I Got My Share (Dial 3018) (1-64)
    Carry On/ (Reid)   (5-65)
    I Refuse To Give Up/Somebody Will (Dial 4019)   (11-65)
    I Refuse To Give Up/Somebody Will (Wand 1106) (12-65)
    Your Love Is All The Help I Need/I'm Your Yes Man
    (Wand 1121)   (66)
    Part Of Your Love/Gimme A Try (Dial 4040)   (9-66)
    Cadillac Annie/Tired Blood (Deep City 2372)   (2-67)
    Cadillac Annie/Tired Blood
    (Phil-L.A. Of Soul 301)   (3-67)
    No Way Out/ (Deep City)
    Soul Party/ (Reedsville)
    Let Those Soul Sounds Play/I'm Sorry Baby
    (Tay-Ster 6013)   (7-67)
    Heaven's Gonna Welcome You/The Price I Have To
    Pay (Tay-Ster 6014)   (1-68)
    Along Came A Woman/Something Special About

My Woman (Tay-Ster 6022)   (68)
Part Time Lover/Fools Are Not Born
(They Are Made) (Alston 4572)   (12-68)
Nobody But You Babe/Send Me Back My Money
(Alston 4574)   (6-69)
Nobody But You Babe/Send Me Back My Money
(Alston 4576)   (6-69)
I'm Gonna Tear You A New Heart/I'm A Man
Of My Word (Alston 4578)   (10-69)
I've Been Tryin'/Don't Look Too Hard
(Alston 4582)   (12-69)
Chicken Hawk/That's How It Is (Alston 4584)   (2-70)
Masterpiece/Down The Road Of Love
(Alston 4588)   (8-70)
[Clarence went on to record many other releases
throughout the '70s and '80s.]

Clarence Reid & Delmiras
I Don't Want The Leftovers/Anything That's Good
To You (Nuria 45-119)
Sooner Or Later/Down With It Can't Quit It
(Selma 4002)   (5-63)
Push A Little Harder/Like White On Rice
(Dade 1855)   (64)
I Refuse To Give Up/Somebody Will (Reid 2744)   (3-65)

Rick & The Delvations
I Want A Feeling/Hippie (Pal 007)   (68)

Road Show
Well I Know Too Well/If You Ain't Got It, Forget It
(Warner Bros.-7 Arts 7281)   (4-69)

J. P. Robinson
Only Be True To Me/I've Got A Long Way To Go
(Alston 4570)   (10-68)
You Can Be A Lady/Love Is Not A Stranger
(Alston 4574)   (12-68)
You Got Your Thing On A String/Love Is Not A
Stranger (Alston 4577)   (8-69)
What Can I Tell Her/Doggone It (Alston 4583)   (2-70)
Please Accept My Call/Say It (Alston 4587)-local   (4-70)

Please Accept My Call/Say It (Alston
4585)-national   (5-70)
[Many more subsequent releases, including a great
version of Bob Dylan's "George Jackson" on Atco
6879.]

Audrey Royal & Reid Singers
Come On Playboy/Playboy Instrumental
(Alston 4575)   (69)

Sam And Dave - See separate discography.

Freddy Scott
Same Ol' Beat/Take A Rest (Dade 1900)   (8-65)
Same Ole Beat/Take A Rest (Marlin 16002)   (9-65)
Hangin' Out/First Things First (Marlin 1906) -
local   (2- 66)
Hangin' Out/First Things First (Marlin 16003) -
national   (3-66)
Pow City/Quiet Time (Marlin 16004)   (7-66)
It's Not Unusual/The Thing (Marlin 16005)   (10-66)
[Also see Freddy & The Kinfolk.]

Frankie Seay
I Came A Long Way To Get To You/Hold On
(Tropical 108)   (8-69)
Baby Please/All I Want Is Loving You
(Tropical 112)   (70)
[The A-side of the above is an excellent garage-soul
remake of Wayne Cochran's "Somebody Please."
Frankie and his group, The Contact High, played
often at the Inner Circle Lounge in Miami Beach in
the early '70s.]

Frankie Seay & Soul Riders
Soul Food/Black Jack (Tropical 107)   (69)

Helene Smith
The Pot Can't Talk About The Kettle/ (Blue Star)
Demonstrate Your Love/Somebody Tell Me
(Dade 1853) (with the Backbeats)
Thrills & Chills/I Am Controlled By Your Love
(Lloyd 009)   (3-66)

A Woman Will Do Wrong/Like A Baby
(Deep City 2368)   (8-66)
A Woman Will Do Wrong/Like A Baby
(Phil-L.A. Of Soul 300)   (67)
True Love Don't Grow On Trees/Sure Thing
(Deep City 2375)   (5-67)
Wrong Or Right He's My Baby/Sure Thing
(Deep City 2380)   (10-67)
What's In The Lovin'/China Melody
(Deep City 2381)   (68)
You Got To Do Your Share/Willing And Able
(Deep City 2743)   (68)
Pain In My Heart/You Got To Be A Man
(Deep City 2390)   (68)
(Without) Some Kind Of A Man/You Got To Be A
Man (Phil-L.A. Of Soul 325)   (1-69)
You Got To Be A Man/And Away We Go
(Phil-L.A. Of Soul 330)   (69)
Let's Wait Until Dark/Too Good To Be True
(Phil-L.A. Of Soul 335)   (11-69)
[Helene also had a couple of releases on the local
Dash label in the mid-'70s.]

Soul Pleasers
I Found A Love/Baby Don't Cry
(Living Legend 102)   (11-65)

Tommy Strand & Upper Hand
Real Appeal/Little Tear (Living Legend 107)   (9-66)
Real Appeal/Little Tear (Epic 10100)   (11-66)
 (Above two releases shown as simply by The
Upper Hand.)
The Trik - Vocal/Instrumental (R 1515)
Funky Way To Treat Somebody/Instant Reaction
(Fame 1462)   (1-70)
I Wanna Testify/Am I Grooving You (Fame 1480) (1-71)

Jeb Stuart
I've Got To Cut You Loose/Sitba
(King 6033) (with The Reflextions)   (4-66)
Dreamer's Hall Of Fame/You're Playing With Fire

(Eureka 1001)   (7-66)
Soul Jerk It, Baby/I Don't Want To Leave You,
Darling (King 6117)   (9-67)
Please Give Me Another Chance/Your Good Lovin'
(Great American 1001)   (68)
Cause I Got Soul/You're Mine (By This Act
Of Fate) (Great American 601)
(Above shown as Soul Ful Jeb Stuart)   (9-69)
[Miami-based recordings only. Jeb was originally
from Memphis where he started his career with
the legendary Philips International label. Jeb is
still recording to this day.]

Eddie Taylor
Just The Way You Are/The State Song
(Tropical 101)   (12-65)

Them Two
Am I A Good Man/Love Has Taken Wings
(Deep City 2379)   (7-67)

Third Guitar
Lovin' Lies/Sad Girl (Rojac 120)
Baby Don't Cry/Don't Take Your Love From Me
(Rojac 123)   (68)
Down To The River/Been So Long (Rojac 127)
[Featuring Eddie Holloway. "Lovin' Lies" is
incredible, mixing trippy psychedelia with the
Motown sound!]

Treetop & Soul Branches
Inside Out/Don't Go Away (Tropical 116)   (5-70)

Twans
I Can't See Him Again/Darling Tell Me Why
(Dade 1903)   (1-66)

Valladeers
I'll String Along With You/Mexican Hop
[Early '60s recording featuring Paul Kelly on lead
vocals.]

Ella Washington
Nightmare/Tanzotic All Stars - The Grass Always

Seems Greener (Octavia 0002)   (4-66)
Bye, Bye, Baby/The Grass Always Seems Greener
(Octavia 0003)   (11-66)
The Grass Is Always Greener/Bye, Bye, Baby
(Atlantic 2382)   (1-67)
I Can't Afford To Lose Him - Vocal/Instrumental
(SS7 2597)   (11-67)
Starving For Love/I Done Made It Up In My Mind
(SS7 2611)   (5-68)
He Called Me Baby/You're Gonna Cry, Cry, Cry
(SS7 2621)   (11-68)
Stop Giving Your Man Away/The Affair
(SS7 2632)   (6-69)
I Want To Walk Through This Life With
You/Fragile (Handle With Care) (SS7 2642)   (9-69)
Sweeter And Sweeter/Doing The Best I Can
(SS7 2650)   (12- 69)
He'll Be Back/Sweet Talkin' Candy Man
(SS7 2659)   (4-70)
Trying To Make You Love Me/I Can't Afford To
Lose Him (SS7 2665)   (6-70)
[Ella had many more releases in the '70s and '80s.]

Billy Wells & Invaders
  This Heart These Hands/True Love
  (Sweet Soul 003/004)

Frank Williams Rocketeers
  Good Thing Part 1/Part 2 (Lloyd 008)   (1-66)
  It's All Over/Show Me What You Got
  (Lloyd 0010)   (5-66)
  You Got To Be A Man/The Spanish Fly
  (Deep City 2369)   (11-66)
  The Spanish Flyer/You Got To Be A Man
  (Phil-L.A. Of Soul 304)   (67)
  Git It/Little Beaver - I Feel My Love
  (Octavia 0006)   (5- 67)
  [The Rocketeers backed a countless number of
  Florida soul acts.]

Betty Wright
  Paralyzed/Good Lovin' (Deep City 2378)   (7-67)
  Mr. Lucky/Thank You Baby (Solid Soul 3030)
  Girls Can't Do What The Guys Do/Sweet Lovin'
  Daddy (Alston 4001) - local   (6-68)
  Girls Can't Do What The Guys Do/Sweet Lovin'
  Daddy (Alston 4569) - national   (7-68)
  He's Bad Bad Bad/Watch Out Love
  (Alston 4571)   (10-68)
  The Best Girls Don't Always Win/Circle Of Heart
  Break (Alston 4573)   (12-68)
  After The Smoke Is Gone/I'm Thankful (Atco 6659)
  (The above is a duet with Steve Alaimo.)   (3-69)
  The Joy Of Becoming A Woman/The Wrong Girl
  (Alston 4575)   (7-69)
  I'm Not Free Hearted/A Woman Was Made For
  One Man (Alston 4580)   (11-69)
  Soldier Boy/A Woman Was Made For One Man
  (Alston 4581)   (12-69)
  Pure Love/If You Ain't Got It
  (Alston 4585) - local   (3/70)
  Pure Love/If You Ain't Got It
  (Alston 4587) - national   (70)
  [Betty had many more releases throughout the
  '70s and '80s.]

Wrong Bros.
  Baby Baby Please/All I Want Is You (Glades 7001) (1-66)

Special mention should also be made of three veteran
performers whose music predated the "soul era," yet whose
contributions should not go unnoticed:

Rufus Beacham
  My Baby And Me/Hey Pretty Baby (S.I.W. 624)
  Since I Fell For You/Do You Know How To Boogie
  (Jax 300)   (51)
  Sad Feelings/I Want You So (Jax 303)
  Love Have Mercy/My Baby And Me (King 4807)   (5-55)
  Let Me Be/What Has Happened To Me (King 4820)
  Good Woman/Don't Say You Love Me (Chart 617)

I Can't Believe/All Right (Chart 627)
I Need Your Love/When You Call My Name
(Scepter 1209)   (9- 60)
Take It Easy Baby/No Man Is King (Scepter 1214)   (60)
Just One More Chance/Summertime (Scepter
1215)   (61)
Lead Me On/Do You Have A Good Woman
(Tropical 119)   (69)

Davey Jones
A Night To Remember/Don't Leave Me Baby
(Chart 641)
The Love I Missed/Don't Let Her Know (Chart 647)
The Love I Missed/If I Ever Loved A Woman
(Argo 5271)   (57)
Love Your Way/Come On And Love Me (APT
25013)   (58)
Our Love/Change Your Mind (Marlin 6062)
No More Tears/Tootsie Wootsie (Glades 601)
I Was Blind/The Chase (Glades 605)
Love Me Some More/The Real Thing (Dade 1801)   (60)
I've Got A New Love/Come On And Get It (Old
Town 1095)   (60)
I'm In Pain/Let's Do It (APT 25064)
Baby Please Love Me/Where There's Life There's
Hope (Dade 1835)   (63)

Davey Jones & His Continentals
Bobbin'/Mack The Knife (Dade 1850)

Dizzy Jones
You Left Me Here To Cry/I'm Comin' Home To You
(Chart 701)
Come On And Love Me/Unexplainable
(Blue Rock 4009)   (1-65)
Let Me Talk To You/I Don't Care (Blue Rock 4024) (65)
Why Me/Just As Sure (As You Play, You
Must Pay) (New Breed 1101)   (66)

[The late "Dizzy" Jones is a South Florida legend and no
doubt had other releases through the years. Jones not only
sang great but also served as personal manager for singing

groups (like the Marvells) and managed nightclubs (such as Dizzy Jones' Birdland, which was co-owned by singer Little Willie John). Dizzy was also one of James Brown's closest friends and remained so until his death in December, 1977.]

John McArthur - This mysterious
   writer/singer/photographer is the stuff legends
   are made of. Henry Stone once said of McArthur,
   "He has the talent, but not the discipline," and
   who could argue? McArthur rarely used the same
   name on more than one recording, making the
   task of compiling his discography as difficult as it
   is fascinating. Suffice it to say, his '50s group
   effort is one of the best and rarest, and his
   mid-'60s recordings managed to combine the teen
   garage band sound and soul music with
   surprisingly successful results. I guess there must
   be more to life than discipline!
   (with the Majestics) - Cave Man Rock/Nitey Nite
   (Marlin 802)   (56)
   (as John "Mr. Soul" McArthur) - Bad Business
   Baby/Play The Thing (Columbia 42218)
   (Flip side is by The Marlowe Morris Quintet)   (1-62)
   (as King John) - I Won't Take You
   Back/Something On My Mind (NA-R-CO 2871-48)   (65)
   (with Dr. T. & The Undertakers) - It's Easy
   Child/Times Have Changed (Target 4610)   (4-67)
   (as Johnny Mack) - Let Them Talk/I Want To Live
   Every Day For Your Love (JMA 0001/02)   (69)
   (as Sir John Henry) - Let Them Talk/Live Everyday
   For Your Love (Lonnie 801)   (69)
   (as John Henry) - Who Am I/ (Brownstone)   (12-70)
   [John later recorded in the '70s under the names
   "John Rootman Henry," "John Rootman
   McArthur," and "John Henry McArthur."]

SAM AND DAVE
Singles Discography

Keep A Walkin'/I Need Love (Marlin 6100)   (61)
No More Pain/My Love Belongs To You
(Marlin 6104)   (61)
Keep A Walkin'/I Need Love (Roulette 4419)   (3-62)
No More Pain/My Love Belongs To You
(Roulette 4445)   (8-62)
It Feels So Nice/She's Alright (Roulette 4461)(12-62)
It Was So Nice While It Lasted/You Ain't No
Big Thing Baby (Roulette 4480)   (2-63)
If She'll Still Have Me/Listening For My Name
(Roulette 4508)   (8-63)
I Got A Thing Goin' On/I Found Out
(Roulette 4533)   (1-64)
Never, Never/Lotta Lovin' (Alston 777)   (64)
Goodnight Baby/A Place Nobody Can Find
(Stax 168)   (3-65)
I Take What I Want/Sweet Home (Stax 175)   (7-65)
You Don't Know Like I Know/Blame Me
(Stax 180)   (1-66)
Hold On I'm Comin'/I Got Everything I Need
(Stax 189) (A- side of the above also issued as
"Hold On I'm A-Comin'")   (4-66)
It Feels So Nice/It Was So Nice While It Lasted
(Roulette 4671)   (5-66)
Said I Wasn't Gonna Tell Nobody/If You've Got
The Lovin' (I've Got The Time) (Stax 198)   (9-66)
You Got Me Hummin'/Sleep Good Tonight
(Stax 204)   (12-66)
When Something Is Wrong With My
Baby/Small Portion Of Your Love (Stax 210)   (2-67)
Soothe Me/I Can't Stand For Fallin' Down
(Stax 218) (Above 45 recorded live in London.) (6-67)
Soul Man/May I Baby (Stax 231)   (9-67)
I Thank You/Wrap It Up (Stax 242)   (1-68)
You Don't Know What You Mean To Me/This Is
Your World (Atlantic 2517)   (5-68)

Can't You Find Another Way (Of Doing It)/Still
Is The Night (Atlantic 2540)   (8-68)
Everybody Got To Believe In Somebody/If I
Didn't Have A Girl Like You (Atlantic 2568)   (11-68)
Soul Sister, Brown Sugar/Come On In
(Atlantic 2590)   (12-68)
Born Again/Get It (Atlantic 2608)   (3-69)
Ooh Ooh Ooh/Holding On (Atlantic 2668)   (10-69)
Baby Baby Don't Stop Now/I'm Not an Indian
Giver (Atlantic 2714)   (2-70)
One Part Love-Two Parts Pain/When You Steal
From Me (You're Only Cheating Yourself)
(Atlantic 2728)   (3-70)
Knock It Out The Park/You Easily Excite Me
(Atlantic 2733) (with Dixie Flyers)   (4-70)
Don't Pull Your Love/Jody Ryder Got Killed
(Atlantic 2839)   (9-71)
A Little Bit Of Good (Cures A Whole Lot Of
Bad)/Blinded By Love (United Artists 438)   (12-74)
Under The Boardwalk/Give It What You Can
(United Artists 531)   (6-75)
We Can Work It Out/Why Did You Do It
(Contempo 7004)   (1-78)
Hold On I'm Coming/I Thank You
(Atlantic 13091) - reissue
Soul Man/When Something Is Wrong With My
Baby (Atlantic 13092) - reissue
Hold On I'm Coming/Soul Man (Gusto 2028)
(re-recording)

Sam Moore
  Tennessee Waltz/Give You Plenty Lovin'
  (Atlantic 2762)   (8-70)
  Stop/Keep On Sockin' It To Me (Atlantic 2791) (2-71)
  Shop Around/If I Should Lose Your Love
  (Atlantic 2814)   (6-71)

Sammie Moore
  No Particular Place To Go (A-side only) (Hit 125)   (6-64)

Dave Prater
  Keep My Fingers Crossed/Love Business
  (Alston 4596)   (2-71)
  [Prater died in April, 1988, when his car slammed
  into a tree. He was on his way to Ocilla, Georgia,
  to pay a surprise visit to his mother.]

19

'60s SOUL LPs

Eddie Lovette - *Sings Reggae/Little Bluebird Too Experienced* (Steady 101)   (69)
Little Bluebird/Unemployed Heart/A Little Love/Together/Boomerang/Too Experienced/You're My Girl/Red Red Wine/I Heard It Through The Grapevine/By-Ooh-Pa-Ooh-Pa-Pa-Ya

Clarence Reid - *Dancin' With Nobody But You Babe* (Alston/Atco 33-307)   (69)
Nobody But You Babe/Twenty-five Miles/Doggone It/Get Back/Don't Look Too Hard/I've Been Trying/Tear You A New Heart/Part Time Lover/Shop Around/Fools Are Not Born/Polk Salad Annie/Send Me Back My Money
Nobody But You Babe (Tay-Ster 3333)   (8-69)
Nobody But You Babe/Something Special About My Baby/Let The Soul Sounds Play/Mark My Word/I'm Sorry Baby/Skunks Hogs And Dogs/Along Came a Woman/Heaven Will Welcome You/Good Lovin' My Middle Name/The Price I Have To Pay/I Wish It Were Me

Sam And Dave - *Sam And Dave* (Roulette 25323)   (8-63)
It Feels So Nice/I Got A Thing Goin' On/My Love Belongs To You/Listening For My Name/No More

Pain/I Found Out/It Was So Nice/You Ain't No Big
Thing/I Need Love/She's Alright/Keep A Walkin'/If
She'll Still Have Me
Hold On, I'm Comin' (Stax 708)   (8-66)
Hold On, I'm Comin'/If You Got The Lovin'/I Take
What I Want/Ease Me/I Got Everything I
Need/Don't Make It So Hard On Me/It's A
Wonder/Don't Help Me Out/Just Me/You Got It
Made/You Don't Know Like I Know/Blame Me
Double Dynamite (Stax 712)   (12-66)
You Got me Hummin'/Said I Wasn't Gonna Tell
Nobody/That's The Way It's Gotta Be/When
Something Is Wrong With My Baby/Soothe
Me/Can't Get Enough/Sweet Pain/I'm Your
Puppet/Sleep Good Tonight/I Don't Need
Nobody/Home At Last/Use Me
Soul Men (Stax 725)   (11-67)
Soul Man/May I Baby/Let It Be Me/Broke Down
Piece Of Man/Hold It Baby/I'm With You/Don't
Knock It/Just Keep Holdin' On/The Good Runs
The Bad Away/Rich Kind Of Poverty/I've Seen
What Loneliness Can Do
I Thank You (Atlantic 8205)   (6-68)
I Thank You/Everybody's Got To Believe In
Somebody/These Arms Of Mine/Wrap It Up/If I
Didn't Have A Girl Like You/You Don't Know What
You Mean To Me/Don't Turn Your Heater On/Talk
To The Man/Love Is After Me/Ain't That A Lot Of
Love/Don't Waste Your Love On Him/That Lucky
Old Sun
The Best Of Sam And Dave (Atlantic 8218)   (2-69)
Hold On, I'm Comin'/When Something Is Wrong
With My Baby/You Don't Know Like I Know/May I
Baby/Soul Man/Soothe Me/I Thank You/I Take
What I Want/Wrap It Up/You Don't Know What
You Mean To Me/Small Portion Of Your Love/You
Got Me Hummin'/Can't You Find Another Way Of
Doing It/Said I Wasn't Gonna Tell Nobody

Excerpts From 'The Best Of Sam And Dave'
(Atlantic 136)   (2-69)
The above is an in-store promotional album with
one side devoted to Sam And Dave and the other
containing excerpts from Wilson Pickett's *Hey
Jude* album. Titles: Hold On, I'm Comin'/Soul
Man/Soothe Me/I Thank You/I Take What I
Want/You Got Me Hummin'.)
Sam And Dave also appear on a number of various
artists albums, including *Stax-Volt Revue, Volume
1* (Stax 721), *Stax-Volt Revue, Volume 2* (Stax 722),
Stay In School (Stax A-11), *Memphis Gold Volume 1*
(Stax 710), and *The Super Hits* (Atlantic 501).

Helene Smith - *Sings Sweet Soul* (Deep City 1001) (12-67)
A Woman Will Do Wrong/Thrills and Chills/Wrong
Or Right, He's My Baby/You Got To Be A
Man/Sure Thing/Willing and Able/It's What's In
The Loving/Like A Baby/China Melody/True Love
Don't Grow On Trees/You Got To Do Your
Share/I'm Controlled By Your Love

Ella Washington - *Ella Washington*
(Sound Stage 7 15007)   (69)
Stop Giving Your Man Away/Sit Down And
Cry/Sweeter And Sweeter/Starving For
Love/Fragile (Handle With Care)/He Called Me
Baby/I Want To Walk Through This Life With
You/Doing The Best I Can/The Affair/All The
Time/This Bitter Earth

Betty Wright - *My First Time Around*
(Alston/Atco 33-260)   (69)
Girls Can't Do What The Guys Do/Funny How
Love Grows Cold/I'm Gonna Hate Myself In The
Morning/Circle Of Heartbreak/Sweet Lovin'
Daddy/Cry Like A Baby/Watch Out Love/He's
Bad, Bad, Bad/I Can't Stop My Heart/I'm
Thankful/The Best Girls Don't Always Win/Just
You

SAVAGE LOST

NOTE: Reid, Wright, and Sam And Dave continued to issue albums well past the '60s, although these were not quite as exciting as their earlier releases.

"A Woman Will Do Wrong" by Helene Smith and "Don't Make The Good Girls Go Bad" by Della Humphrey both appear on *Old 'N Golden* (Jamie 3031), a fine late '60s compilation that includes everyone from Duane Eddy to the Kit Kats!

"Chills And Fever" by Paul Kelly and "They Don't Know" by Mona Lisa appear on a rare 1966 compilation called *SURhythm And BluesOUM* (Atlantic 820040), apparently issued only in France!

SOUL IN OTHER
PARTS OF FLORIDA

Recently, I was watching an old episode of *Leave It To Beaver* when a certain scene caught my eye. Wally and the Beaver were searching through their father's old war chest when they came upon what Wally called "a picture of two bearded women." Upon further inspection, it was determined that it was actually a photo of "Dad with another man," at which point Ward Cleaver chimed in (as he was so often prone to do), "Why, that man is Charlie Vickers. He was one of the best architects around."

The point of all this is that the mythical Charlie Vickers may have been an excellent architect during World War II, but years later, many miles away in the town of Daytona Beach, a very real Charlie Vickers was pursuing a much different path.

Vickers, who was born in 1948, had been singing since the age of six, when he joined other children in a musical program at Daytona's Bethune-Cookman College. Vickers' first break came through Bob Quimby, owner of Tropical Records, for whom Vickers recorded extensively throughout the '60s and '70s. Despite a national release on King and a number of fine recordings throughout the years, Vickers was never able to establish himself on a national level. Today

Vickers is singing primarily gospel and enjoyed a scattered success with his album, *Heaven Is Just Over The Hill*.

Also "just over the hill" was Pensacola's Papa Don Studios where the likes of Mighty Sam and Oscar Toney, Jr., recorded their finest works. Pensacola's hottest act by far was James and Bobby Purify (actually James Purify and friend Robert Lee Dickey) who enjoyed a long string of hits with cover version after cover version — Dan Penn's "I'm Your Puppet," Spooner & The Spoons' "Wish You Didn't Have To Go," the Rubber Band's "Let Love Come Between Us," Sam And Dave's "I Take What I Want," the Tams' "Untie Me," and the oft-recorded "Shake A Tail Feather"... there really was no need for the Purifys to even try to write a tune with so many great songs just waiting to be interpreted. James Purify attempted a comeback in the middle '70s with a new "Bobby" (actually Ben Moore), releasing seven singles and one over-looked album. Unfortunately, the market had changed radically by then, and the Purify's vocal blendings were left sounding like echoes from a distant era.

One artist still going strong in our present era is Jackie Moore, a gospel-tinged vocalist from Jacksonville. Moore recorded three singles in Philadelphia before teaming up with her cousin, Atlantic Records' producer Dave Crawford, at North Miami's Criteria Studios. From those sessions came "Precious Precious," originally a B-side until a Florida disc jockey wisely flipped the record over. Moore now lives in Tampa, where she's still recording, and is still capable of hitting the top at any time.

Another project of Crawford's was a trio from Tampa that briefly made the big time... but had to take the long way around. Zulema Cousseaux and Brenda Hilliard were members of the 5 Crystals, a typical teenage singing group that could be seen at a sockhop on Saturday night and back in class on Monday morning. But there comes a time when a performer has to make a decision as to whether she's playing the game... or playing for keeps. Choosing the latter, Zulema and Brenda formed a new group with a local singer, Albert Bailey.

As the Lovelles, the trio recorded for two national labels, but didn't make much noise until Crawford introduced them to Van McCoy, an influential writer/producer, who took the trio to see Bob Crewe, an even MORE influential writer/producer. Crewe liked what he heard, but didn't like the group's outdated name... but that was no problem. The first time he saw them, he reportedly said they looked like "Faith, Hope & Charity," so that naturally became their brand new name.

The first single for Crewe's Maxwell label, "So Much Love," became a national hit. But Maxwell's financial difficulties forced the trio to switch to Sussex Records, and then RCA, where their recording of "To Each His Own" went on to become a major disco hit. Zulema by then had embarked on a solo career while producer Dave Crawford went on to work with a host of nationally known artists, including Esther Phillips, B. B. King, and Wilson Pickett.

If it seems Florida's other soul scenes were eclipsed by what was happening in Miami, you aren't imagining things. This was a definite fact. Miami was where the studios, backing, and labels were, and artists from all over the state (including Pensacola's Gwen McCrae and Jacksonville's Freddy Scott) made the trek to become part of South Florida's greener pastures. Perhaps Benny Latimore described it best when the Tennessee native settled here with "visions of orange trees and palm trees," not to mention freedom from cold, cold winters. Let us also not forget that soul legends ranging from Ray Charles to Wilbert Harrison (originally from North Carolina) found Florida to be more than a small boost to their careers.

There's no denying that Florida's soulsters didn't have quite as strong an impact as some of their Georgia neighbors (most notably James Brown and Otis Redding)... that's an indisputable fact. Yet Florida soul had its own magic, taking the groundwork laid by the boys from Georgia and adding a unique regional spice to the gritty rhythm. Florida soul "cooked"... it moved and grooved... it shook, it rattled, and it rolled. It made us dance and it made us smile, and years later, it still has the ability to do just that.

Perhaps Martha and The Vandellas put it best when they sang, "Summer's here and the time is right for dancing in the streets." In Florida it's almost always summer... and, somehow, the time always seems to be right.

SOUL IN OTHER PARTS OF FLORIDA SINGLES DISCOGRAPHY, 1964 - SUMMER, 1970

Lewis Clark
   Dog (Ain't A Man's Best Friend)/I Need You Baby
   (Brent 7071)   (6-67)
   Green Power/Here's My Heart (Fuller 0031)   (67)
   Red Man's Revenge/Love Can Save (Ultimate
   7280/81)   (70)
   I Got My Eyes On You/Everything's Gonna Be
   Alright (Red Ram no #)
   [Long-enduring Tampa soul man. Instrumental
   backing on "I Need Your Love So Bad" is courtesy
   of The Jesters IV.]

Lewis Clark & Explorers
   Let's Do It Now/I Need Your Lovin' So Bad
   (Tigertown 002)   (66)
   Here's My Heart/If You Ever Ever Leave Me
   (Tigertown 004)   (66)

Faith Hope & Charity
   So Much Love/Let's Try It Over (Maxwell 805)   (3-70)
   [Many later releases on Maxwell, Sussex, RCA, and
   20th Century Fox. This Tampa group was formerly
   known as The Lovelles.]

5-Souls
   Baby-3 Times/The Wedding Must Go On
   (Shelly 0005)
   [Straight from the garage! The A-side is a direct
   steal of Chuck Jackson's "I Don't Wanna Cry,"
   while the B-side is reminiscent of Percy Sledge.

Despite its extremely raw sound, this Orlando
release is probably from the early '70s.]

Johnny "K"
Come Out/A Few Precious Moments (AJP 1514)
[Johnny and his band came from Tampa. Later
Johnny K releases could be found on labels such
as Drive and Buddah.]

Johnny K. & Dynamites
Don't You Believe/Make The Nights A Little Longer
(Phono 101)   (66)

Johnny K. Killens & Dynamites
I Don't Need Help/Frenchy The Tickler
(Deep City 2370)   (2-67)

Tommy Knight
It's Real/Say You Do (Atco 6209)   (8-61)
That's All I Ask/There's No Pain (Gold Eagle 1801)
Ha Ha Ha And Oh Oh Oh/Yes Yes Go On
(Emerson 2104)
[Tommy obviously tried to be the next Jackie
Wilson. The influence is unmistakable! From the
town of DeLand, which later gave the world
Terence Trent D'Arby.]

Lemon Twisters
Hey Little Baby/Pretty Rosa Lee (Arlingwood 8607) (64)
Lemon Juice/Please
(R & D Productions 6559/5326)
[From the Jacksonville area.]

Lovelles
Here Come The Heartaches/My Time To Cry
(Brent 7073)   (67)
I'm Comin' Today/Pretending Dear (Atco 6670)   (4-69)
[An early version of Faith Hope & Charity.
Formerly known as The 5 Crystals.]

Buddy McKnight & Soul Brothers
I've Got To Move/Baby Baby (PH 120)
[Otis Redding-influenced soul from the Orlando
area.]

Gene Middleton
  Stop Where You Are/ (D And B)   (12-66)
  When A Boy Becomes A Man/You Need Love
  (D And B 103)   (67)
  A Man Will Do Anything/ (Soul Town 1)
  [This Tampa soul singer continued to record well
  into the '70s.]

Mighty Sam
  Sweet Dreams Of You/Good Humor Man
  (Amy 957)   (6-66)
  Fannie Mae/Badmouthin' (Amy 963)   (8-66)
  I'm A Man/Georgia Pines (Amy 973)   (12-66)
  Talk To Me, Talk To Me/I Need A Lot Of Lovin'
  (Amy 984)   (2-67)
  In The Same Old Way/Silent Tears (Amy 990)   (67)
  When She Touches Me (Nothing Else
  Matters)/Just Like Old Times (Amy 11001)   (10-67)
  (EP) In The Same Old Way/Talk To Me, Talk To
  Me/Just Like Old Times/I'm A Man (Amy EP-001)   (67)
  I Just Came To Get My Baby Out Of Jail/Baby
  Come On Home (Amy 11022)   (4-68)
  I Who Have Nothing/Papa True Love (Amy 11044)   (69)
  I've Got Enough Heartaches/Love Bones
  (Atlantic 2707)   (1- 70)
  Evil Woman/Your Love Is Amazing (Atlantic 2711) (2-70)
  ["Mighty Sam" McClain was born in Monroe,
  Louisiana, but came to Florida in 1963, where he
  sang with groups such as The Dothan Sextet and
  The Rounders. Sam also had at least two later
  releases in the '70s. Much of his material is now
  available on the 1988 compilation album *Nothing
  But The Truth* on Charly 1189.]

Jackie Moore
  Dear John/Here I Am (Shout 232)   (6-68)
  Why Don't You Call On Me - Vocal/Instrumental
  (Shout 239)   (11-68)
  Who Told You/Loser Again (Wand 11204)   (69)
  Willpower/Precious Precious (Atlantic 2681)   (11-69)

SOUL IN OTHER PARTS OF FLORIDA   249

["Precious Precious" was reissued as the A-side a
few months later and went on to become a big
national hit. Jackie still actively records today.]

James & Bobby Purify

I'm Your Puppet/So Many Reasons (Bell 648)	(8-66)
Wish You Didn't Have To Go/You Can't Keep A Good Man Down (Bell 660)	(1-67)
Shake A Tail Feather/Goodness Gracious (Bell 669)	(3-67)
I Take What I Want/Sixteen Tons (Bell 680)	(6-67)
Let Love Come Between Us/I Don't Want To Have To Wait (Bell 685)	(8-67)
I'm Your Puppet/Goodness Gracious (Hip Pocket 28) (PS) (The above is a miniature flexi-disc issued by the Philco-Ford Corporation.)	(11-67)
Do Unto Me/Everybody Needs Somebody (Bell 700)	(12-67)
I Can Remember/I Was Born To Lose Out (Bell 721)	(3-68)
Help Yourself (To All My Lovin')/Last Piece Of Love (Bell 735)	(8-68)
Untie Me/We're Finally Gonna Make It (Bell 751)	(11-68)
Section C/I Don't Know What It Is You Got (Bell 774)	(4- 69)
I'm Your Puppet/Everybody Needs Somebody (Sphere Sound 77,004)	
(LP) James & Bobby Purify (Bell 6003)	(66)
(LP) Pure Sound Of (Bell 6010)	(9-67)

[James and Bobby also had seven 45s on
Casablanca and Mercury between 1975 and 1977,
and one album, You And Me Together Forever
(Casablanca 7011), issued in March, 1975.]

Rounders

Small Town Girl/Foolish Lover (Jora 1001)	(65)

John Standberry, Jr.

Lonely Man/Marie (Barry 112)	(2-65)

[Other releases on numerous labels, including
Hart, Cypress, and Jayville. John was a big part of

the Jacksonville black music scene since the
1950s, singing with The Fabulous Imperials and
Five Knights, and writing for acts such as The
King Crooners. John died in 1989.]

Jimmy & Louise Tig & Co.
    Who Can I Turn To/A Love That Never Grows Old
    (Bell 708)   (2-68)
    [Jimmy, whose real last name is Tigner, wrote and
    recorded with The Rounders. His boy Eric turned
    up in 1973 with a single on Hi Records.]

Charles Vickers
    Play Love/ (Glenn 1001)   (8-59)
    Little Sally Walker/Friendly Advice (Carellen 111)
    Are You For Me Or Agin' Me/He's My Everything
    (Carellen 6)
    Double Knott/Who's Putting Stardust In Your
    Eyes (Carellen 10)
    These Two Eyes/Mary Tippins - You Were Not
    With Me (Staff 102/101)   (63)
    Paths Of Glory (National Songwriters Guild)
    (one-sided demo)   (63)
    (EP) Sad Sad Memories/Everyone Has A
    Heartache/+2 by The Earthmen (National Guild
    EP 102)   (68)
    Do Me Good/Lost My Faith In You (King 6128)   (2-68)
    Another Dawn/Man Can Not Live By Bread Alone
    (Roach 103/104)   (5-68)
    [See Tropical Records discography in the Daytona
    Beach section for numerous other Vickers'
    releases.]

Noble Watts
    F.L.A./Thingamajic (Brunswick 55382)   (6-68)
    [From DeLand, Florida, Noble Watts was a member
    of the '40s and '50s group Charles Brantly & The
    Honeydippers, which also included Frank
    Shellman of The Skyliners, and a then-unknown
    piano player named Ray Charles. Noble also
    recorded many, many earlier singles on labels

such as Arrawak, Baton, Clamike, Cub, Deluxe, Enjoy, Jell, Peanut, Sir, and Vee Jay.]

NOBLE "THIN MAN" WATTS

Personal Manager
CLARENCE JACKSON

DeLand's top saxaphone player, **Noble "Thin Man" Watts**, a recording star since the early '50s. His recording of "Hard Times (The Slop)" reached #44 on the national charts in December 1957.

21

SOUL MUSIC . . . ON THE RADIO

South Florida soul of the 1960s revolved around two extremely important and powerful sources: Henry Stone's family of labels and WAME Radio. Stone's role in the evolution of local soul is examined in detail throughout this book; suffice it to say that if Stone's ventures were the lifeblood of Miami's soul scene, Whammy Radio was the circulatory system that enabled it to prosper and thrive.

WAME's air personalities included the legendary Fred Hanna, the infamous Wildman Steve, Dade-Mala recording artist Nickie Lee ("The Nick With A Positive Kick"), Rockin' Rogers, Butterball, and Les Brown. Whammy was personality radio at its finest, with a combination of announcers, music, and lively production work that has yet to be topped in this market.

WAME's reign came to an end in 1969 when Mission Broadcasting Company of San Antonio acquired the station. Mission owner Jack Roth, who also owned WWOK in Charlotte, North Carolina, decided to switch the two stations around with the Charlotte station taking on the call letters WAME, and the 1260 frequency in Miami becoming WWOK, a fledgling country music station. This paved the way for WMBM, long Miami's number two soul music station, to become the new kingpin of local black radio.

WMBM wore the crown well, carrying the tradition of

liberal music programming and strong personality radio into the early '80s. Ratings pressure from stronger, trendier FM competitor WEDR (which switched to a black music format in July, 1971, after years as Miami's top FM progressive outlet) contributed to WMBM's change to a news and talk-oriented format in 1980 and signaled the end of another legendary Florida music station. (WMBM has since switched to an all-gospel music format.)

The following is a list of Florida-based soul records that reached the top ten on either WAME or WMBM, along with the month and year when the record reached its peak position. Entries denoted with a * went all the way to number one during the designated month.

Freddy Scott - Same Ole Beat	9-65*
Paul Kelly - Chills And Fever	10-65
Sam And Dave - You Don't Know Like I Know	12-65
Frank Williams Rocketeers - Good Thing	2-66
Mona Lisa - They Don't Know Pt. II	3-66
Sam And Dave - Hold On! I'm Comin'	4-66
Steve Alaimo - So Much Love	5-66
Ella Washington - Nightmare	5-66
Freddy Scott - Pow City	8-66
Arthur Freeman - Can't Get You Out Of My Mind	10-66
Mighty Sam - Fannie Mae	10-66
Sam And Dave - Said I Wasn't Gonna Tell Nobody	10-66
Ella Washington - The Grass Always Seems Greener	12-66
Sam And Dave - You Got Me Hummin'	1-67
James & Bobby Purify - Wish You Didn't Have To Go	2-67
Sam And Dave - When Something Is Wrong With My Baby	2-67*
James & Bobby Purify - Shake A Tail Feather	5-67
Little Beaver - I Feel My Love	5-67
Moovers - I Love You Baby	6-67*
Benny Latimore - Girl I Got News For You	6-67

Sam And Dave - Soothe Me	7-67
Paul Kelly - Sweet Sweet Lovin'	7-67
James & Bobby Purify - Let Love Come Between Us	10-67
Sam And Dave - Soul Man	10-67*
Benny Latimore - It's Just A Matter Of Time	12-67
Ella Washington - I Can't Afford To Lose Him	1-68
Sam And Dave - I Thank You	2-68*
Betty Wright - Girls Can't Do What The Guys Do	7-68*
Benny Latimore - The Power And The Glory	7-68
Jackie Moore - Dear John	8-68
Nickie Lee - And Black Is Beautiful	10-68
J. P. Robinson - Only Be True To Me	10-68
Della Humphrey - Don't Make The Good Girls Go Bad	11-68
Betty Wright - He's Bad Bad Bad	11-68
James & Bobby Purify - Untie Me	12-68
Ella Washington - He Called Me Baby	12-68
Clarence Reid - Part Time Lover	1-69
Betty Wright - The Best Girls Don't Always Win	1-69
J. P. Robinson - You Can Be A Lady	2-69
Steve Alaimo & Betty Wright - After The Smoke Is Gone	4-69
Clarence Reid - Nobody But You Babe	7-69
Betty Wright - Soldier Boy	1-70
J. P. Robinson - What Can I Tell Her	4-70
James Knight & Butlers - Save Me	5-70
Betty Wright - Pure Love	5-70
J. P. Robinson - Please Accept My Call	8-70*

22

MIAMI TOP 40
RESPONSE
TO
FLORIDA SOUL 45s

Record & Artist	Month of Peak Popularity	Billboard	WQAM	WFUN
Same Ole Beat - Freddy Scott	10-65		37	32
Chills And Fever - Paul Kelly	11-65	123	28	41
These Boots Are Made For Walkin' - Five Steps	3-66		—	56
Hold On I'm Comin' - Sam And Dave	6-66	21	17	12
Pow City - Freddy Scott	8-66		39	15
Said I Wasn't Gonna Tell Nobody - Sam And Dave	8-66	64	—	56
I'm Your Puppet - James & Bobby Purify (Pensacola)	11-66	6	17	10
Wish You Didn't Have To Go - James & Bobby Purify (Pen.)	2-67	38	—	54
When Something Is Wrong With My Baby - Sam And Dave	2-67	42	—	66
Shake A Tail Feather - James & Bobby Purify (Pensacola)	5-67	25	24	33
Girl I Got News For You - Benny Latimore	6-67		20	32
Soothe Me - Sam And Dave	7-67	56	—	57
I Take What I Want - James & Bobby Purify (Pensacola)	8-67	41	—	39
Soul Man - Sam And Dave	11-67	2	5	4
Let Love Come Between Us - James & Bobby Purify (Pen.)	11-67	23	24	18

Record & Artist	Month of Peak Popularity	Billboard	WQAM	WFUN
The Goat - Freddy and the Kinfolk	3-68		33	—
I Thank You - Sam And Dave	3-68	9	12	9
I Can Remember - James & Bobby Purify (Pensacola)	5-68	51	40	33
You Don't Know What You Mean To Me - Sam And Dave	6-68	48	33	37
Girls Can't Do What The Guys Do - Betty Wright	7-68	33	2	4
Don't Make The Good Girls Go Bad - Della Humphrey	11-68	79	—	35
He's Bad Bad Bad-Betty Wright	11-68	103	—	23
After The Smoke Is Gone - Steve Alaimo & Betty Wright	4-69		28	—
Nobody But You Babe - Clarence Reid	8-69	40	14	18
Soldier Boy - Betty Wright	1-70		12	29
So Much Love - Faith, Hope & Charity (Tampa)	6-70	51	—	33
Please Accept My Call - J. P. Robinson	8-70		9	29

23

SOULFUL BITS AND PIECES

Clarence Reid wrote and produced a number of sides for Big Maybelle on New York's Rojac label, although he never received any label credit...

Two of Helene Smith's best releases were "answer" records: "Thrills & Chills," an answer to Paul Kelly's "Chills And Fever," and the nationally successful "A Woman Will Do Wrong," which answered Percy Sledge's "When A Man Loves A Woman"... Paul Kelly is responsible for writing Karla Bonoff's 1981 top 20 hit "Personally." Kelly has also written for Jackie Moore, Ella Washington, Margie Joseph, Carl Carlton, Leslie West, the Staples Singers, and many others...

A very young Timmy Thomas was reportedly one of the session musicians on the Mar-Keys' 1961 smash "Last Night"... Benny Latimore started out as a member of Joe "Snap Your Fingers" Henderson's band... Eddie Hope and Rocky Mizell are among the esteemed musicians to have played on Jeb Stuart's King recordings ...

One very important early soul/dance hit was "The Cow" by Bill Robinson & The Quails. "The Cow" was a giant hit on local rock 'n roll stations, placing at number 38 for the year on WQAM's Top Hits of 1963 list...

Betty Wright gained a reputation throughout the mid-'70s as queen of "advice records" with "Girls Can't Do What The Guys Do," "He's Bad Bad Bad," "The Best Girls Don't Always

Win," "Clean Up Woman," "Is It You Girl," "Baby Sitter," and "Secretary" all following in that suit...

Jimmy "Bo" Horne's nickname was given to him by his schoolmates who used to tease him because of his bowlegs...

A great soul group of the '70s that is definitely worth mentioning is the Mystic Five, whose "Sweet Brown Frame" (GWS/Twin 10732) may have been stolen from the Four Tops' "It's The Same Old Song," but is still one of the best sweet soul records of its era. The Mystic Five later recorded for the Leo and Unity labels...

With the exception of Sam and Dave (who consistently scored on a national level), no two local soul records seemed to dominate the charts more than Betty Wright's "Girls Can't Do What The Guys Do" and J. P. Robinson's "Please Accept My Call," both on the Alston label...

Benny Latimore (right) shares a golden moment with Henry Stone. He'd come a long way from his early days, and songs such as "Snap Your Fingers." *Photo courtesy Henry Stone.*

An old television toothpaste ad featuring a beaver brushing its teeth and singing "brusha brusha brusha" prompted friends of young Willie Hale to nickname him "Little Beaver." Considering the fact that Hale had two big front teeth and was always the youngest musician around, it was only natural that the name would stick... Some of Little Beaver's early groups were the Savoys (which included tenor saxophonist Clifton Walker) and Birdlegs & Pauline, who had a national hit with "Spring" in 1963. Beaver's guitar licks have graced countless sessions at Tone/TK Studios, including Betty Wright's influential "Clean Up Woman"...

Ella Washington attempted a comeback of sorts in 1980 with "The Ballad Of Arthur McDuffie" (K 1003), which concerned itself with the black insurance salesman whose beating death by half a dozen white police officers was a precursor to the May, 1980, Miami riots. One of the co-writers of the tune was Luther Dixon, a one-time member of RCA recording group the Four Buddies, and writer of many hit tunes, including "Mama Said" and "Soldier Boy" for the Shirelles... Dixon also co-wrote most of Eddie Lovette's recordings, including "Too Experienced," which reached the Billboard Hot 100 in 1969, yet was never able to crack the local top 40 charts...

Freddy Scott, known for his solo work as well as his stints with the Kinfolk and Miami, was once the drummer in Lloyd Price's band. Freddy's association with the late Dizzy Jones signaled the start of his South Florida career... Another former member of the Kinfolk is Jimmy Griffin, a popular disc jockey on WEDR. Griffin also backed-up Otis Redding and Hank Ballard...

Part of Sam and Dave's early backing band later went on to the popular '70s & '80s group LTD... Sam and Dave used to play at the King of Hearts nightclub, operated by future Sunrise Mayor John Lomelo, who was later convicted of racketeering and mail fraud...

How low can you go? Local limbo dancer Sammy Ambrose might have been able to shake up a crowd at the Place

Pigalle, but he couldn't shake a lust for heroin that landed him in jail on murder charges...

Both Joey Gilmore and Little Beaver were featured vocalists with Frank Williams' Rocketeers, who at one time backed-up just about every major name in town... Loretta Letlo of the Marvells/Fabulettes was the cousin of singing star Little Esther Phillips...

Birdwatchers leader Bobby Puccetti wrote songs for the Prolifics and Betty Wright, and recently played in former Marvell Addie Williams' backing band...

It's too late to turn back now for Carter Cornelius, who gave up touring with his brother (and Sister Rose) in favor of the Yahweh religious cult. Cornelius' new name: Prince Gideon Israel.

24

SOUTH FLORIDA COUNTRY

(Or "Don't Knock The Twang, Gang")

Back in the days when country music meant REAL country music (and not just Urban Cowchips), Miami had WOAH. Now, WOAH was not just another modified country jukebox that churned out the hits — it was an exciting, personality-oriented station and the home of Miami's granddaddy of country music, Happy Harold — the man who discovered Charlie McCoy and so many others — and the man who ably anchored the 1220 Radio Ranch, which also featured Jim Drummond, Charlie Davis, Bill Smithson, Dave Edwards, and George Daye. (Daye was later associated with WGOS, a noble experiment in FM country radio that debuted in the mid-to-late '60s, but never really got off the ground.)

WOAH virtually owned local country radio until WWOK began its decade-long reign of the country airwaves in Summer, 1969. WWOK began with a real bang, providing South Florida with some of the best country radio it had ever been treated to. (Not to mention some of the best personalities ever, in George Means, Bob Cole, and others who truly loved their work.) But then came WWOK's downfall in the late '70s, starting with Mission Broadcasting's lack of money and ending with the departures of Program Director Ted Cramer and General Manager Cy Russell. I worked at WWOK while a college student in the late '70s, witnessing first-hand the fall of a giant, sadly doing my midnight-to-six shift on the FM side, unable to save a good thing from buckling to the Urban Cowboy Blues.

So WWOK turned Latin in 1980; its FM became "Super Q," and the door swung wide open for former rock giant WQAM to step in and take over the crown. WQAM blew it early, and FM's trendy Kiss Radio soon became Miami's top country station, at least according to the ratings. Trendy FM'ers seemed to have forgotten where country music originated: the hills — and what a vital role hillbilly (mixed with gospel and rhythm and blues) played in forming rock 'n roll. When some stations instituted "no twang" policies (which even banned Hank Williams in some areas, the Chuck Berry of country-western music! Is there no shame?), it was clear that C&W music had suffered the same essence-depleting devastation as its rock 'n roll and rhythm and blues counterparts. Country without western is like rock without roll. Country means steel guitars, not syrupy strings. More power to Ricky Skaggs, Dwight Yoakam, and the "new traditionalists" who are finally making radio say yes to bluegrass and no to Las Vegas production numbers!

The selective discography that follows makes no pretense as to being complete; rather, it presents a look at just a few of the outstanding country releases from this area. Needless to say, these are all REAL country records with no trace of Kenny Rogers or Anne Murray in any of them.

Bill Alexander & Le Sabras
   F.L.A./Hiway #1 (no label name #101)   (64)

Russ "Big Daddy" Anders, Fabulous Four
   Dear God Bring Our Boys Back Home/Three To
   One (Anbee 3500)   (11-67)

Pat Canavan with Bob McGehe & Florida Trail Blazers
   It Seems So Wrong/Don't Know Where I Stand
   With You (Florida 929)   (68)

Anne Christine
   Kitty Up Go/I'd Fight The World (HBR 464)   (66)

Anne Christine & Kentuckians
   Kitty Up Go/I'd Fight The World (Phonographics 102)   (66)
   [Anne continued to record well into the '70s.]

Ann Clark
   A Girl That Works In A Bar/He'll Never Cheat No
   More (Pantage 16)   (8-67)
   Secretly You're Mine/The Damage Has Been Done
   (Pantage 16)   (11-67)

George Clark
   It's My Life, Let Me Live It/Women Can't Be
   Satisfied (Pantage 102)   (8-67)

Rusty Diamond
   I Guess I'd Better Get Up And Go Home/The
   Lonely Sentry (Zodiac 3508/3509)   (11-65)
   [B-side also features Maryanne Mail. I personally
   feel that this Jack Blanchard production/
   composition is the best country record ever to
   come out of Florida.]

Trooper Jim Foster
   Four On The Floor (And A "Fifth" Under The
   Seat)/Don't Call Me (I'll Call You)
   (United Artists 844)   (3-65)
   My Friend Jack/I Guess I Had It Coming
   (United Artists 905)   (8-65)
   Bring 'Em Back Alive/Four Chrome Wheels
   (Turret 109)   (7- 67)
   [Trooper Jim — a member of the Florida Highway
   Patrol — had at least three later singles and an
   album on Country Artists Records.]

King Houston
   Steppin' On My Heart/Silver Flowers (Marianna
   4506)   (2- 67)
   Steppin' On My Heart/Silver Flowers (King 6096)   (4-67)

Freddie King
   (LP) *A Girl Like You* (Freddie King Records 4)   (71)

Hank Lindsey
   Bad Cat/She Thinks I'm Wondering (I.R.P. 101)

Brock McCoy
  Way Down In Southern Florida/This Feeling In My
  Heart (Venus 521)   (65)

Misty Morgan & Jack Blanchard
  Bethlehem Steel/No Sign Of Love (Those Darn
  Records 2041/42)   (6-68)
  Bethlehem Steel/No Sign Of Love (Wayside 1024)   (68)
  [Many later releases, including the national hits
  "Tennessee Birdwalk" and "Humphrey The Camel."
  Blanchard is one of Miami's most important
  country writer/producer/singers and is not only
  responsible for some of the best discs on this page,
  but also one of the early releases on the legendary
  Mida label.]

Bob Racino with The Country Four
  Cry, Cry, Cry Baby, Cry/House Without Love
  (Hilltop 1)

Jim Reid
  Instantly/Ballad Of The Hungry (Air 1555)

Jimmy Roberts
  Lonesome Fool/A Passing Love Affair (Venus 520)   (65)

Joe Sanns
  Wondering Remembering/Riding High Blues
  (Kelane 1)

Marion Skinner
  Gunman's Repentance/You Fooled Me Once
  (Roxie 306)

Tommy Spurlin
  No Time For Heartaches/ (Art 131)

Tommy Spurlin & Southern Boys
  There Might Have Been A Love Song/Tomorrow I'll
  Be Gone (Perfect 108)

25

SOUTH FLORIDA ROCKABILLY DISCOGRAPHY

Hasil Adkins & His Happy Guitar
    She's Mine/Chicken Walk (Air 5045-1) (PS)
    The Hunch/She's Gone (Roxie 5134)
    [Hasil hailed from West Virginia, but these
    primitive rockabilly classics were somehow issued
    on Miami labels. Hasil also recorded for Jody,
    Avenue, Hub, and ARC, and his wild, wild works
    are again available to melt your turntable, thanks
    to the crazy folks at Norton Records.]

Steve Alaimo & Redcoats - See separate discography.

Bill Bell & 4 Unknowns
    Little Bitty Girl/Fearless (Mida 112)

Lou Chester, Jr., with the Stardusters
    Let's Fall In Love To Stay/Teasin' (Young 1001)

Curley Jim & Billy Rocks
    Rock & Roll Itch/Air Force Blues (Metro 100)
    Rock & Roll Itch/Air Force Blues (Mida 100)
    Sloppy, Sloppy Susie/Didn't I Tell You (Mida 108)
    [The Metro and Mida takes of "Rock & Roll Itch"
    are different. Lead singer "Curley" Jim Morrison
    later recorded four non-rockabilly singles in
    1963-64 for the Tennessee-based Curley Q label.]

Steve Alaimo as a '60s pop idol on the TV show Where The Action Is — far away from his rockabilly days as leader of the Redcoats. *Photo courtesy Henry Stone*

Chuck Darty
    Can't You See/My Steady Girl (Chart 649)
    Can't You See/My Steady Girl (Rama 229)
    [Henry Stone tells me that Darty — whose real
    name was Dougherty — was a pioneer disc jockey
    on WQAM in the 1950s. Chuck also recorded
    "Lumberjack"/"Reluctantly" on Roulette 4159 in
    1959.]

Wally Dean & His Flips
    Cool Cool Daddy/ (Globe 238)
    Drag On/Rockin' With Rosie (Arctic 102)
    Saddle Up A Satellite/Should've Been Me
    (Artic 103)

In The Jailhouse Now/Drinkin' Wine,
Spo-Dee-O-Dee (Artic 65221/2)
[Wally's last name is shown as both "Dean" and
"Deane," while his label is shown as both "Artic" and
"Arctic." No wonder Wally's band is doing FLIPS!]

Carlos Diaz
Sugaree/Only One Love (Triangle 1000)
[Carlos turned up a few years later with a group
called Los Dinamitas del Twist, doing a great
rocking "What'd I Say" (actually "Oye Lo Que Te
Digo"), backed by "Perfidia Twist" (Miami 5060).]

Doug Dickens & Fireballs
Lucy's Graveside/Raw Deal (Vulco 1506)

Billy Eldridge & Fireballs
Let's Go Baby/My Blue Tears (Vulco 1501)
Let's Go Baby/My Blue Tears (Unart 2011)
Half A Heart/Take My Love (Vulco 1507)

Frantics Four (Vocals By Bobby Shane)
T.V. Mama/Down By The Old Mill Stream
(Gulfstream 1000)

Bobby Gay & Sparkletones
Let's Dance/You're Mine (Mida 104)

Jack Gillen & His Orchestra
Early One Morning/How Is The World Treating
You (S And S 1)
  [Jack later played a major role in labels such as
ABCO and Zodiac. He's the guy behind that
mysterious Shaggs single with Perry Gordon and
Cynthia Williams.]

Jack Gillen & Internationals
Don't Treat Me This Way/Treat Me Nice
(Provencher 1001) (PS)

Wes Hardin & Roxters
Anyway/A Thing Called Love (AFS 302)

Wesley Hardin
Honky Tonk Man/Cry Cry Cry (Perfect 110)
[This early rockabilly band included future

members of The Birdwatchers and Razor's Edge.
Also see The Roxters.]

Jim Holt
Paralyzed/Brown Eyed Handsome Man
(Gulfstream 1061)

[See the Gulfstream label discography for later releases by
Holt.]

Buddy Howard
Be Sure You Know/Take Your Hands Off Me, Baby
(Mida 15)

Art Law
Run Baby Run/Big Train (Gulfstream 1050) (PS)
Kitty Kat Rock/Yodeling Blues (Gulfstream 1051) (PS)

Randy Luck (Tommy Miles Guitar)
I Was A Teen-Age Caveman/Twelve O'Clock (Art
170)

Ross Minini
Baby Rock/Oh! Janet (Gulfstream 7269)

Texas "Red" Rhodes
Go Cats Go/Won't You Say (Echo 1001)

Rhythm Rockets (Vocal Ray Pate)
My Shadow/Lucky Day (Gulfstream 6654/55)
[Classic tracks featuring Ray Pate and his little
brother Donny.]

Pat Richmond & Fireballs
Don't Stop The Rockin'/Honey Bee Baby (Vulco
1500)

Don "Red" Roberts
Only One/Don't Say Maybe (Chart 643)
Only One/Don't Say Maybe (Rama 230)
Only One/Don't Say Maybe (Apex 76155 - Canada)

Roxsters
So Long/Goodbye Baby (Art 175)
[See Related South Florida Releases section for
more on this early band.]

Mike Shaw & Sons Of Drifting Sands
Long Gone Baby/Frankie & Johnny (Perfect 111)
[Mike's later releases include "O Bee O By O Baby
O"/"My Friend" on Regal 7507.]

Tommy Spurlin & Southern Boys
Hang Loose/One-Eyed Sam (Perfect 109)
[See South Florida Country discography for
Tommy's hillbilly releases.]

Jimmie Tennant with Buddy Lucas & His Dynatones
The Witness/Giggle Wiggle (Thunder 1000)
[It's hard to believe that the maker of this hot
rocker later went on to become balladeer Jimmy
Velvet!]

Eddie Thorpe
Just Call My Name/I'll Be Different (Scott 1401)

Buck Trail
Honky Tonk On Second Street/Beneath Miami
Skies (Trail 100)
The Knocked Out Joint On Mars/The Blues Keep
Knockin' (Trail 103)
[Current South Florida rockabilly star Larry Joe
Miller does a sizzling live version of "Honky Tonk
On Second Street" and in 1983 included a cover of
"Knocked Out Joint On Mars" on his "Rub A
Bucket" cassette!]

Jimmy Voytek
Kitten/Searching For You (Scott 1404)

Jimmy Voytek & Knights
Close Your Eyes/Why (Caper 1551)
[Backing on the Scott release is by The Beltones.
Jimmy started out as part of Miami's Old South
Jamboree, sharing the stage with Charlie McCoy
and Donny ("Johnny Paycheck") Young. In later
years Jimmy cut straight country recordings and
even wound up as a City of Miami police officer. A
heart attack took Jimmy Voytek's life in June,
1980. He was barely in his 40s.]

Kent Westberry
   No Place To Park/My Baby Don't Rock Me Now
   (Trail 103)
   No Place To Park/My Baby Don't Rock Me Now
   (Art 172)
   Turkish Doghouse Rock/Popcorn And Candy Bars
   (Art 174)
   [Kent went on to become a country
   singer/songwriter, perhaps best known for writing
   Gene Watson's mid-'70s country smash "Love in
   The Hot Afternoon."]

POSSIBLE
SOUTH FLORIDA ROCKABILLY

Chuck Harrod & Anteaters
   They Wanna Fight/Sandy (Champion 1013)
Reggie Perkins
   Date Bait Baby/High School Caesar (Ray-Note S-9)
Reggie Perkins & His Rockin' Maniacs
   Pretty Kitty/Saturday Night Party (Gem 1201)
   [Coincidentally, both Chuck and Reggie make an
   appearance on the 1988 bootleg album *Teen-Age
   Riot!* released on Atomic Passion 1957. Does
   anybody know where these two called home?]

26

ROCKABILLY AROUND FLORIDA

Big Four
 All Keyed Up/Outa Tune (Moon 306)   (59)
 [Instrumentals by Allen Page's band. See Allen
 Page for more.]

Bob And Vic with Kool Kats
 Cross Eyed Susie Wakeup/Let Me Hear You Say
 (Sky 115)
 [Also see Bob Hooks & the Kool Kats.]

Rocky Davis & Sky Rockers
 Hot Rod Baby/ (Blue Sky 102)

Jack Harrell
 Rock Around The Christmas Tree/Rock Rock
 Who's There (Vim 1089)   (57)
 [Vim was a Jacksonville label.]

Bob Hooks & Kool Kats
 Baby Baby Baby/Exotic Baby (Sky)
 [Bob also recorded "Daddy Let Me Go"/"Sputnik"
 with Anita Veal On Sky 112 and "Cinch Bug
 Blues"/"Why Should I Lie" with Chuck Benoit on
 Sky 111. Unfortunately, "Cinch Bug Blues" (from
 1957) is as lame as it sounds.]

Benny Joy
 Hey... High School Baby/Spin The Bottle
 (Tri-Dec 8667)

Steady With Betty/Spin The Bottle (Dixie 2001)
Little Red Book/Crash The Party (Antler No #)
Ittie Bittie Everything/Money Money (Ram 1000)
(Above recorded as Benny Joy-Big John Taylor.)
Sincerely Your Friend/New York, Hey Hey
(Decca 31199)   (1- 61)
(EP) *Celanese Presents Datesetters U.S.A. 1961*
(Decca ED9- 38292) (PS)
[Four-song EP includes "Sincerely Your Friend" by
Benny Joy.]
Birds Of A Feather Fly Together/You Go Your Way
(And I'll Go Mine) (Decca 31280)   (6-61)
[Benny later recorded country tunes for labels
ranging from Dot to Mercury. His early rockabilly
recordings were reissued often, and why not? They
were great. We lost Benny on October 28, 1988, at
the age of 52. He may well have been the king of
Florida rockabilly.]

Bobby Lord - More than a dozen early 45s on
   Columbia, including "Everybody's Rockin' But Me"
   (Columbia 21539). From the Tampa area.

Billy Match & Starfires
   I Want My Baby/Girl Of Mine (Starfire 664)
   [Also a 45 on Impala. Billy J. Killen is the man
   responsible for this Orlando killer.]

Larry McKenzie with Buddy Roberts & His Space Men
   There's Always Room/Chubie Dubie (Vim 1091)   (58)

Gene Norman & Rockin' Rockets
   Snaggletooth Ann/Long Gone Night Train
   (Snag 101)   (58)

Allen Page
   High School Sweater/Honeysuckle (Moon 301)   (58)
   Dateless Night/I Wish You Were Wishing
   (Moon 302)   (58)
   She's The One That's Got It/Sugar Tree
   (Moon 303)   (58)
   Oh Baby/I Wish You Were Wishing (Moon 307)   (59)

[Real name: Allen Wingate. Allen and the Big Four
hailed from Daytona Beach.]

Tracy Pendarvis
It Don't Pay/One Of These Days (Scott 1202)
(& The Blue Notes)   (4-58)
All You Gotta Do/Give Me Lovin' (Scott 1203)   (7-58)
A Thousand Guitars/Is It Too Late (Sun 335)
(& The Swampers)   (2-60)
Is It Me/South Bound Line (Sun 345)
(& The Swampers)   (11- 60)
Belle Of The Suwannee/Eternally (Sun 359)   (5-61)
I Feel A Teardrop/First Love (DesCant 1234)   (3-62)
Philadelphia Filly/Don't Wait On Love
(DesCant 1235)   (5- 62)
[Tracy is a veteran Florida rockabilly artist who
started his career in Gainesville in the late '50s.
Pendarvis is also responsible for writing Wynn
Stewart's 1970 country hit "It's A Beautiful Day"
and is reputed to have recorded a version of "You
Don't Know What You've Got" in 1961.]

Ralph Pruitt
Someone Like You/Louise (B.B. 226)

Ralph Pruitt with His Rhythm Boys
Hey, Mr. Porter/This Heart Within Me
(Lark 1506/7)
Hey, Mr. Porter/This Heart Within Me
(Meridian 1506/7)
[I hear Ralph's "Ballad Of Joseph Robinette" on
K-Ark is also supposed to be good.]

Johnny Redd
Fixed For Life/Rockin' Peg (Carellen 106)   (2-61)
I Flipped My Top/ (Carellen 11)
[Johnny, whose real name was John Stetham, cut
demos by the score for Bob Quimby's National
Songwriters Guild. Two of the best — "Jungle
Rock" and "Kiss Me" — were cut in DeLand on
September 1, 1958.]

Rhythm Rousers
   Just Because/ (Rouser 7423)
   [From Cocoa Beach.]

Ricky Ryal & Rebelairs
   Sycamore Lane/Is It Wrong (Sound Labs 259/260)

Charles Walton & Kool Kats
   Teen Age Blues/Four Four Time (Sky 114)
   [More from the cryptic St. Pete label.]

Gene Watson
   My Rockin' Baby/ (Tri-Dec 8357)
   I'll Always Love You/Life's Valley (Dixie 2003)

Lewis Weber & Hi-Fis
   The Time Is Right/Tell Me Baby (Tatoo 7452/53)   (58)
   [Weber's 1959 release on Scottie and 1960 single
   for Magnum both fail to shake it up the way this
   Jacksonville giant does.]

Rod Willis
   Somebody's Been Rocking My Baby/Old Man
   Moses (Chic 1010)
   The Cat/The Title (NRC 020)
   [Rod reportedly lived on Florida's west coast.
   "The Cat" really cooks!]

SOUTH FLORIDA ROCKABILLY ALBUMS

Bill Adler - *C'Mon Everybody With Bill Adler*
   (Universal 104)
   C'Mon Everybody/The Joker/Marilyn/Fire
   Water/Pickin' Time/That Old Gang Of Mine/The
   12th Of Never/Pink Pedal Pushers/Slow
   Down/The Fox/Joe Cool/Toot Toot Tootsie

Steve Alaimo - *Sensational Steve Alaimo* (Crown 382)
   [February, 1963, reissue of Steve's early Dade and
   Marlin recordings, most of which were rockabilly
   flavored. Eight of the ten tracks on this album also
   appear on the budget album *Johnny Rivers &
   Steve Alaimo*, issued on Custom 1100.]

Tracy Pendarvis - *Bison Bop* (Bison Bop 2004)
[This late '70s West German pressing includes
both of Pendarvis' Scott releases, plus ten other
tracks recorded in 1961 at Atlanta's NRC Studios.]

Various Artists - *Miami Rockabilly Volumes 1
Through 3* (AFS)
[These albums consist primarily of rare tracks
from the vaults of Gulfstream and Art/AFS
Records. Highly recommended!]

Various Artists - *The Publisher's Favorite Songs*
(Air 5063)
[Very rare early '60s LP issued by Active Music of
Miami. Includes three rockabilly tracks: "Bubble
Gum Betty" by Sonny Marshall, and two good cuts
from Roger Smith ("Be-Bop Boogie" and "Roll On").
The other 15 tracks on the album range from
straight pop to country western.]

27

HOW TO IDENTIFY A SOUTH FLORIDA RECORD

Let's say you're out hunting for records, and you think you've found one from Florida. How do you know for sure? There are many guidelines you can follow — they're not all conclusive, but they do make it possible to identify most Florida releases with little more than a glance.

1. PUBLISHING COMPANIES: Any song published by Sherlyn, Tracer or Bodean Music is more than likely of local origin.

2. PRODUCERS: Anything produced by Jim Sessody, Bob Archibald, Willie Clarke, or Steve and Vince Palmer is bound to be local, while many singles produced by Steve Alaimo, Brad Shapiro, or Gary Stites quality as well.

3. DEAD WAX MARKINGS: Look for the name "DUKOFF"' in the dead wax portion of the record between the grooves and the label. In addition to being an accomplished saxophone player, Bobby Dukoff was a local recording engineer whose name appears on many releases. Also, the initials "JD," coupled with a four-digit number in parentheses, appears in the dead wax of many Florida pressings.

4. LABELS: The following record companies all had a lot of local South Florida material:

THAMES: All releases are by groups that were connected with the Florida Bandstand in 1966. Jim Sessody and/or the Palmers were involved with every local release.

THAMES DISCOGRAPHY

100/101   Clefs Of Lavender Hill - Stop! Get A
          Ticket/First Tell Me Why

102   Montells - Daddy Rolling Stone/You Can't Make
          Me

103   Tropics - For A Long Time/Black Jacket Woman

104   Legends - Raining In My Heart/How Can I Find
          Her

105   Echoes Of Carnaby Street - No Place or
          Time/Baby Doesn't Know

MARLIN: Most pre-1975 releases are local. At one time distributed by London, but generally a part of the TK/Tone family.

SCOTT: Also part of Henry Stone's family of labels. Like Marlin, Scott was an excellent outlet for local rock and soul artists, with the Birdwatchers, Nightcrawlers, and Proctor Amusement Company among the artists to have recorded for Scott.

DADE: Basically a soul label, featuring artists ranging from Nat Kendrick & The Swans to Benny Latimore. Releases were usually local.

ALSTON: Also an outlet for soul artists. All early releases (pre-3700 series) are local, with the exception of the Bahamian group Beginning Of The End.

LLOYD & DEEP CITY: Fine mid-60s soul labels run by Willie Clarke, Johnny Pearsall, and later Clarence Reid. All releases are local and epitomize the gritty mid-'60s Miami soul sound.

LIVING LEGEND: Had many local releases, most of which involved Gary Stites. If the song was published by "ILUVLORI MUSIC" or produced by Stites, the record is Florida-based.

TRIP UNIVERSAL: Formed in early 1969, Trip Universal Records was based both in Miami and Nashville. Most Miami releases on the label were produced by local hotshot Bill Stith.

PLATINUM: This Miami label featured everything from metal to mellow with a little bit of everything in between. Platinum, an offshoot of the Music Factory Inc., is best known as the label that first recorded Gene Cotton and The Cornelius Brothers & Sister Rose, both of whom went on to become successful artists in the 1970s.

BLUE SAINT: Manager Steve Palmer's 1965 label, prior to the formation of Thames. Blue Saint had but two releases:

1001 H.M. Subjects (Montells) - Don't Put Me Down
       Censored/Uncensored

1002 Squires V - Bucket Of Tears/I'm Thru

GULFSTREAM: Formed in the 1950s by musician Vincent Fiorino. Gulfstream's early releases included some wild rockabilly tracks.

Many other less-interesting labels existed, including ART (sometimes brilliant, but basically schlock), AIR (mainly country or pop with an occasional rockabilly release), PAL, BRA (ska/rock steady and soul), BART, ABCO, MALISSA, KANGI, TWIN, GWS, and countless others.

As is the case with every area, many local South Florida singles show no marks to indicate their origin. Fortunately, this is the exception rather than the rule, as the bulk of local material tends to fall into one of the above categories.

28

MARLIN RECORDS:
A History

From Henry Stone's first single on the Rockin' label to the latest releases on Esync Ocular, a wide variety of record companies have originated from South Florida. While a few are fortunate enough to have survived for a decade or more (Art, Alston), most labels lasted for merely a release or two (Winterhurst, Blue Saint) before dissolving. Of all the labels to emerge from South Florida in the past forty years, perhaps the most interesting is Hialeah-based Marlin, formed four decades ago as an outlet for local black talent.

Marlin's first four releases, beginning with Skinny Dynamo (an obvious Fats Domino takeoff), are all excellent and highly collectible, particularly Eddie Hope's bluesy "A Fool No More/Lost Child" and the Majestics' "Nitey Nite," which epitomizes the southern street sound of the 1950s. Marlin's early release schedule was extremely erratic, as local artists were generally consigned to one of Stone's four main labels (Marlin, Dade, Chart, and Glades) with some artists (i.e., Davey Jones, Sonny Thompson) recording for two or more labels concurrently. By 1960, Dade became Stone's prominent label, with the others turning out only sporadic releases.

In the late '50s, a University of Miami medical student named Steve Alaimo formed a singing group called the

Redcoats and gave Marlin its first local hit with "I Want You To Love Me." Alaimo's interest in music spanned beyond performing, and soon he joined Stone's staff as a producer, working closely with former Redcoat Brad Shapiro.

One of Alaimo's first projects for Marlin was a duo he and Stone saw causing a commotion in the inner city clubs. Sam Moore and Dave Prater, better known simply as Sam And Dave, first met in Miami when nightclub owner John Lomelo suggested that they combine their singing talents. The duo's first tracks were recorded for Marlin and leased to Roulette Records in New York where poor promotion kept them from getting off the ground. Three fine singles were issued locally (two on Marlin, one on Alston), but the duo met with little commercial success until their middle '60s recordings for Stax broke nationally. Still, it was Alaimo's keen ear that was responsible for Sam And Dave's first exposure to the recording public.

With the coming of the middle '60s, Alaimo (then a member of Dick Clark's *Where The Action Is* cast) and Brad Shapiro continued to produce local rock and soul artists. Alston and Glades were temporarily discontinued, with Dade, Marlin, and Scott releasing the brunt of Stone's material. While Dade was concerned primarily with soul music, Scott and Marlin provided an excellent outlet for local rock 'n roll bands.

Among the artists to record for both Marlin and Scott were the Birdwatchers, Miami's most commercially successful band, and Daytona Beach's versatile Nightcrawlers, further chronicled in Blitz Magazine #30. Marlin also released numerous singles by Freddy Scott, later a member of the disco/funk band Miami (which also included former members of the Kinfolk), and the Unknowns, a fine studio offshoot of the *Where The Action Is* program.

With the reborn Alston label breathing new life into Henry Stone's pocketbook in 1969, Marlin and Scott were quietly discontinued. Marlin was resurrected in 1975 as a disco/jazz label, scoring chart successes with such abysmal artists as the Ritchie Family and Voyage. These lackluster releases made it clear that the local rockers who once filled the airwaves were gone, leaving a rich, illustrious past just begging to be discovered.

LOCAL LABEL DISCOGRAPHIES

MARLIN

[Does not include the 3300 disco/jazz series resurrected in 1975.]

801 Skinny Dynamo - You Know This Story/Baby Baby Mine

802 Majestics - Cave Man Rock/Nitey Nite

803 Little Iris Culmer - Frankie My Eyes Are On You/

804 Eddie Hope & Manish Boys - A Fool No More/Lost Child

6062 Davey Jones - Our Love/Change Your Mind

6064 Steve Alaimo & Redcoats - I Want You To Love Me/Blue Skies

6065 Steve Alaimo & Redcoats - The Weekend's Over/Girls Girls Girls

6066 Sammy Early - If You Really Love Me/I'm Gonna Find Me A Girl

6067 Steve Alaimo & Redcoats - She's My Baby/Should I Care

6068

6069

6070 Joy Mann - Up To The Mountain/Tell Me

6100 Sam And Dave - Keep A'Walkin'/I Need Love

6101 Berj Vaughn Quartet - Truck Stop/Pass The
      Goodies

6102

6103 Count Stephen - Spooky/The Redcoats Are
      Coming

6104 Sam And Dave - No More Pain/My Love Belongs
      To You

1900 Freddy Scott & Four Steps - Same Ol'
      Beat/Take A Rest (Dade Records)

1901 King Coleman - It's Dance Time
      Vocal/Instrumental (Dade Records)

1902 Birdwatchers - It's A Long Way Home/It Doesn't
      Matter

1903 The Twans - I Can't See Him Again/Darling Tell
      Me Why (Dade Records)

1904 Nightcrawlers - A Basket Of Flowers/Washboard

1905 Don Goldie - Pop Corn/

1906 Freddy Scott & Five Steps - Hangin' Out/First
      Things First

1907 Buddy Canova - Why Torture Me/Never In Love

1908

1909

1910 Senders - Chintz And Rubies/What's Your
      Sister's Name

      Security Blankets - Schroeder/ (number
      unknown)

16001 The Charmettes - Surrendering My Love/One
       More Time

16002 Freddy Scott & Four Steps - Same Ole
       Beat/Take A Rest

16003 Freddy Scott's Orchestra - Hangin' Out/First
       Things First

16004 Freddy Scott & Orchestra -
       Pow City/Quiet Time

16005   Freddy Scott & Seven Steps - It's Not
        Unusual/The Thing

16006   Conlon & The Crawlers - I Won't Tell/You're
        Comin' On

16007   Chuck Conlon - Won't You Say Yes To Me,
        Girl/Midnight Reader

16008   The Unknowns - Tighter/
        Young Enough To Cry

2301   Mercy - Feelin' Easy/To Whom It May Involve

[NOTE: All Marlin releases were locally distributed except the 16000 series, which was distributed nationally by London Records. Of this series, #16001 was released in 1962; the remaining seven were issued between 1965 and 1967.]

ALSTON RECORDS
Through 4500 Series

[NOTE: Alston and Dade both had a tendency to issue a record locally prior to releasing it on a national level. As a result, it was not uncommon for a record to have two different serial numbers or for a number to have two different releases connected with it. Needless to say, this makes matters considerably difficult for discographers!]

235   Ginny Dale - Wishful Thinking/Just Thinking Of
       You (local)

777   Sam And Dave - Never, Never/Lotta Lovin' (local)

4001   Betty Wright - Girls Can't Do What The Guys
       Do/Sweet Lovin' Daddy (local)

4569   Betty Wright - Girls Can't Do What The Guys
       Do/Sweet Lovin' Daddy (national)

4570   J. P. Robinson - Only Be True To Me/I've Got A
       Long Way To Go(local and national)

4571   Betty Wright - He's Bad Bad Bad/Watch Out
       Love (national)

4572   Clarence Reid - Part Time Lover/Fools Are Not
       Born (local and national)

4573 Betty Wright - The Best Girls Don't Always
Win/Circle Of Heart Break (local and national)

4574 J. P. Robinson - You Can Be A Lady/Love Is Not
A Stranger (local)
Clarence Reid - Nobody But You Babe/Send
Me Back My Money (national and local*)

4575 Audrey Royal & Reid Singers - Come On
Playboy/Playboy Instrumental (local)
Betty Wright - The Joy Of Becoming A
Woman/The Wrong Girl (local and national)

4576 Clarence Reid - Nobody But You Babe/Send Me
Back My Money (local*)
George & Gwen - Three Hearts In A
Tangle/One Of These Days (national)

4577 George & Gwen - Three Hearts In A Tangle/One
Of These Days (local)
J. P. Robinson - You Got Your Thing On A
String/Love Is Not A Stranger (national)

4578 Clarence Reid - I'm Gonna Tear You A New
Heart/I'm A Man Of My Word (national)

4579 George & Gwen - Like Yesterday Our Love Is
Gone/Stranded In This Broken Heart

4580 Betty Wright - I'm Not Free Hearted/A Woman
Was Made For One Man (local)

4581 Betty Wright - Soldier Boy/A Woman Was Made
For One Man (national and local)

4582 Clarence Reid - I've Been Tryin'/Don't Look Too
Hard

4583 J. P. Robinson - What Can I Tell Her/Doggone It
(local and national)

4584 Clarence Reid - Chicken Hawk/That's How It Is
(national and local)

4585 Betty Wright - Pure Love/If You Ain't Got It (local)
J. P. Robinson - Please Accept My Call/Say It
(national)

* Local versions of Clarence Reid's soul smash "Nobody But You
Babe" were issued with both the numbers 4574 and 4576.

4586 George & Gwen - No One Left To Come Home
To/Stranded In This Broken Heart Of Mine
(local)

4587 J. P. Robinson - Please Accept My Call/Say It
(local)
Betty Wright - Pure Love/If You Ain't Got It
(national)

4588 Clarence Reid - Masterpiece/Down The Road Of
Love (local and national)

4589 Betty Wright - I Found That Guy/If You Love Me
(Like I Love You)(national and local)

4590 J. P. Robinson - Keep On Holding On/Hot Love
(local)
Diamonettes - Rules Are Made To Be
Broken/Don't Be Surprised (national)

4591 Famous Chromes - Baby, Let Me Love You/I
Gotta Groove On (local)

4592 Clarence Reid - Direct Me/You Knock Me Out
(local and national)

4593 J. P. Robinson - If It Wasn't For
Tomorrow/Can't Find Happiness

4594 Betty Wright - I Love The Way You Love/When
We Get Together Again (local and national)

4595 Beginning Of The End - Funky Nassau Pt. 1/Pt.
2 (national)

4596 Dave Prater - Keep My Fingers Crossed/Love
Business (local and national)

4597 Clarence Reid - Three Is A Crowd/You Got To
Fight (local and national)

4598 Clarence Reid - I Get My Kicks/Gonna Take It
Home To Mother

4599 Beginning Of The End - Monkey Tamarind/Hey
Pretty Girl

CHART

201   Crystal Ball - It's Love It's Love/Be My Baby, Be

601   Sonny Jones - Can't You See/My Baby's Crying

602   Champions - Annie Met Henry/Keep A-Rockin'

603   Paul Tate - You Know I Tried/How Can I Love You

604   Rudy Ferguson - Darling, Come Back To
      Me/Together

605   Evergreens - Very Truly Yours/Guitar Player

606   Roy Gaines - I'm Setting You Free/Loud Mouth
      Lucy

607   Calvin Vaughn - I Love A Liar/Weak Minded Baby

608   Charms - Love's Our Inspiration/Love, Love,
      Stick Stov

609   John Lee Hooker - Going South/Wobbling Baby

610   Jimmy Wilson - Louise/Alley Blues

611   Champions featuring Sonny Thompson - It's Love
      It's Love/Mexico Bound

612   Sonny Thompson - Slow Rock Part 1/Part 2

613   Charms - Heart Of A Rose/I Offer You

614   John Lee Hooker - I Ain't Got
      Nobody/Misbelieving Baby

615   Piccadilly Pipers - Where's My Baby/I Loved Only
      You

616   Johnny & Marsha - Be Mine/You Want Me

617   Rufus Beacham - Good Woman/Don't Say You
      Love Me

618   David Brooks - Bus Ride/Foot Stompin'

619   Piccadilly Pipers & Pic-A-Dillies - A Lonely Lovers
      Prayer/Mr. Butterball

620   Champions - Pay Me Some Attention/The Same
      Old Story

621   Johnny & Marsha - Friends Until The End/After
      School Date

622

623 Charms - Boom Diddy Boom Boom/I'll Be True

624 Elder Beck - Rock And Roll Sermon/

625

626 Wilbert Harrison - Cool Water/Calypso Man
     [Artist's first name erroneously shown as
     Wilburt on label.]

627 Rufus Beacham - I Can't Believe/All Right

628 Johnny & Mark - Do Be You/I Want To Tell You
     Why

629 Jimmy Wilson - Send Me Your Key/Poor Poor
     Lover

630

631 Champions and Sonny Thompson - Come
     On/Big Bad Beulah

632 Wally Futch - She Loves Me So/My Baby's
     Comin' Home

633 Sonny Thompson - Juke Joint Part 1/Part 2

634 Tru-Tones - Magic/Tears In My Eyes

635

636 Lightnin' Hopkins - Walkin' The Streets/Mussy
     Haired Woman

637 Sonny Thompson - Drive In/Drive Out

638 T.N.T. Tribble - T.N.T./Riff Alley

639

640 Wally Futch (shown on label as Fitch) - Little
     Girl/You Don't Have To Worry

641 Davey Jones - A Night To Remember/Don't Leave
     Me Baby

642 Sonny Thompson - Candy Part 1/Part 2

643 Don "Red" Roberts - Only One/Don't Say Maybe

644 Wally Futch (shown on label as Fitch) - I Cried All
     The Way Home/Our Love Will Never Die

645 Sonny Thompson - Hi-Ho/Day Break Blues

646 Alec Davis - Stand By Baby

647 Davey Jones - The Love I Missed/Don't Let Her
     Know

648 Sonny Thompson - Caribbean Cruise/Night
     Watch

649 Chuck Darty - Can't You See/My Steady Girl

701 Dizzy Jones - You Left Me Here To Cry/I'm
     Comin' Home To You

DADE

1800 Steve Alaimo with The Redcoats - Home By
     Eleven/

1801 Davey Jones - Love Me Somemore/The Real
     Thing

1802

1803 The Trends - Rockin'/Runaway

1804 Nat Kendrick & The Swans - Do The Mashed
     Potatoes Part 1/Part 2 (later reissued in 1964
     as Oldies 45 #145)

1805 Steve Alaimo with The Redcoats - You Can Fall
     In Love/Love Letters

1806 R-Dells - You Say/You Know Baby

1807 King Coleman - Loo-Key Doo-Key Part 1/Part 2

1808 Nat Kendrick & The Swans - Dish Rag Part
     1/Part 2

1809 The Baby - Wait And See/ I Need Love (also
     issued on Atco 6175 as Baby Lloyd)

1810 King Coleman - My Mother Told Me/

1811 Percy Welch - Back Door Man/Throw This Poor
     Dog A Bone

1812 Nat Kendrick & The Swans - Slowdown/Hot
     Chile

1813 Johnny Shaw - May's Shuffle/Any May

1814

1815 Sonny Thompson - Hangout Part 1/Part 2

1816

1817

1818

1819

1820 King Coleman - Do The Hully Gully Part 1/Part 2 (also issued on Atlantic 2125)

1821 Delmiras - The Big Sound/Dry Your Eyes

1822 Sam Early - Question Mark/Trust Me Baby

1835 Davey Jones - Baby Please Love Me/Where There's Life There's Hope

5000 Ted Taylor - I Lost The Best Thing I Ever Had/Darling If You Must Leave

5001 Jimmy Paris - Esmerelda/Lost Love (also issued on KC 113)

5002 Sonny Til - Someone Up And Told Me/Sonny And Virgil - Open Up Your Heart

1850 Davey Jones & His Continentals - Bobbin'/Mack The Knife

1851 Yvonne Fair - Straighten Up/Say Yeah Yeah! (local)

1852 Arthur Freeman - No Hard Feelings/Shirley

1853 Helen Smith & The Backbeats - Demonstrate Your Love/Somebody Tell Me

1854

1855 Clarence Reid and The Delmiras - Push A Little Harder/Like White On Rice

5003 Nat Kendrick & The Swans - Wobble Wobble Part 1/Part 2 (national)

5004 Nat Kendrick & The Swans - Do The Mashed Potatoes Part 1/Part 2 (national)

5005 Kitty Love - The Power Of Love/You Gotta Change (national)

5006 Yvonne Fair - Straighten Up/Say Yeah Yeah! (national)

1900 Freddy Scott & Four Steps - Same Ol' Beat/Take A Rest (also issued on Marlin 16002)

1901 King Coleman - It's Dance Time
      Vocal/Instrumental

1902 See Marlin Discography.

1903 The Twans - I Can't See Him Again/Darling Tell
      Me Why

1904 See Marlin Discography.

26   Five Steps - These Boots Are Made For
      Walkin'/Tightin Up (also issued on Scott 26)

2001 Five Steps - These Boots Are Made For
      Walkin'/Tightin Up

2002 Mona Lisa - They Don't Know Part 1/Part 2

2010 Mona Lisa - I Can't Stand Myself/I Love Me

2011 Nickie Lee - The Ten Commandments Of
      Man/Late Shadows

2012 Stranger & Patsy - Tonight/Give Me The Right

2013 Benny Latimore - Girl I Got News For You/Ain't
      Gonna Cry No More

2014 Nickie Lee - I Want To Get Next To You/Nickie
      Lee Orch. - Nick's Kick (local)
      Benny Latimore - There She Is/It Was So Nice
      While It Lasted (national)

215   Benny Latimore - It's Just A Matter Of
      Time/Move And Groove Together(local)

2015 Benny Latimore - It's Just A Matter Of
      Time/Let's Move & Groove Together (national)

2016 Mark McIver - Soul Thing/The Tic Of The Clock
      (local)
      Freddy And The Kinfolk - The
      Goat/Blabbermouth (national)

217   Freddy And The Kinfolk - The
      Goat/Blabbermouth (local)
      Benny Latimore - The Power And The
      Glory/Love Don't Love Me (local)

2017 Benny Latimore - The Power And The
      Glory/Love Don't Love Me (national)

2018 Nickie Lee - And Black Is Beautiful/Faith
     Within (local) (also issued on Mala 12025)
     Red Tam - Red Tam Is A Lover/Red & White
     Blues (national)

2019 Red Tam - Red Tam Is A Lover/Red & White
     Blues (local)

2020 Benny Latimore - Have A Little Faith/I'm A
     Believer (local)

2021 Nickie Lee - The Dream Of The People Part
     1/Part 2 (local) (also issued on Mala 12039)

2022 Benny Latimore - I Pity The Fool/I'm Just An
     Ordinary Man (local) (also issued on Atlantic
     2639)

2023 H. Dee & The Stones - Potato Chips/Last Take
     (local)

2024 Freddy And The Kinfolk - Mashed Potato, Pop
     Corn/Last Take (national)

2025 Jimmie "Bo" Horne - I Can't Speak/Street
     Corners (local)
     Benny Latimore - I'll Be Good To You/Life's
     Little Ups And Downs (national)

2026 Benny Latimore - I'll Be Good To You/Life's
     Little Ups And Downs (local)

2027 Arnold Albury And The Casuals - Funky
     Yolk/Thanks For Waiting (local)

2028 Arnold Albury And The Casuals - My Baby
     Don't Understand/Feel It (local)

2029 Arnold Albury And The Casuals - That's A
     Bet/My Baby Don't Understand

2030 Lynn Williams - I'll Except/Tears In My Eyes
     (local)

2031 Jimmy "Bo" Horne - Clean Up Man/Down The
     Road Of Love (also issued on Alston 4606)

2032

2033

no # Lynn Williams - You Are The Greatest/It Takes
      Two

2040 Lynn Williams - Is It Possible/Theme For
      Vanilla (national)

2041 Jackey Beavers - Trying To Get Back To You
      Girl Part 1/Part 2 (national)

[NOTE: All nationally issued Dade singles were distributed
by Atlantic, except for 2040 and 2041, which were distributed by TK.]

DEAUVILLE

[Miami-based label of the early '60s specializing in twist
and dance-oriented records.]

1000 Lawrence Cook - The Old Piano Roll Blues/

1001 Bud Messner & His Skyline Boys - Slippin'
      Around With Jole Blon/Bud Messner & Molly
      Darr - Tell Her You Love Her Today

1002 Bobby Marshall - Call Me Darling/It's A Great,
      Great Pleasure

1003

1004 The Peridots - Hully Gully All Nite Long/It's The
      Bomp

1005 The Crazy Kats - Makin' Whoopee/The Candy
      Stik Twist

1006 Skip Poulsen & Beach Continentals - A Pretzel
      Ain't Nothin' But A Twist Pt. 1/2

1007 Gene The Hat - (Pass) The Bug Part 1/Part 2

OTHER EARLY '60s DANCE RECORDS

Frank Du Boise
    Chicken Scratch/Cause We Can't Get Along
    (United Artists 444)
    Knight Beat/I Need Someone (United Artists 445)
    (also Ascot 2110)

[Frank was part of the house band at the Knight Beat Club in downtown Miami's Sir John's Hotel.]

Doug Fowlkes & His Airdales
Wild Irish Rock/Dicla (Viva 63)
(LP) *The Airdale Walk* (Atco 33-145)

Gene The Hat
Ram-Bunk-Sush/Jelly Beans (Walden 101)
Ram-Bunk-Sush/Jelly Beans (Checker 960)
Big Cigar/Hush Puppy (Purl 903)
(Pass) The Bug Part 1/Part 2 (Gee 1078)

Impacs - See Tampa/St. Petersburg discography.

King Coleman - Tampa-born singer/drummer who started out with the R&B group the Skyliners. Coleman recorded numerous sides for labels such as Dade, Symbol, Kenco, Sylvia, Togo, Fairmount, Port, Karen, King, Columbia, and Big Apple, and provided the vocal shouts on Nat Kendrick & The Swans' 1960 smash, "(Do The) Mashed Potatoes" (Dade 1804).

Lincolns
Night Drag/Vagabonds - Baby Face McCall (Abco 1001)
["Night Drag" is actually "The Candy Stik Twist" with drag racing sound effects dubbed in. "Baby Face McCall" was originally issued on Viva 62 and is basically a worthless folk- pop ballad.]

Los Dinamitas Del Twist
Oye Lo Que Te Digo/Perfidia Twist (Miami 5060)
[The A-side is the wildest version of "What'd I Say" ever put to wax!]

John McCormick & Beach Continentals
Yoo Hoo Spin/Beach Continentals - Something Else (Versatile 114)
["Yoo Hoo Spin," like "The Chicken Scratch" and "The Bug," was a dance that rose to prominence on Bill Wyler's *Saturday Hop* television show in the early '60s. Max C. Freedman, who co-wrote the

song, also co-wrote Bill Haley's classic "Rock
Around The Clock."]

Peridots
Twistin' The Bop/Winky Blinky (Twist 15201)

Bill Robinson & Quails
The Cow/Take Me Back, Baby (American 1023)
The Cow/Take Me Back, Baby (American 6000)
Congo Dance Party/You're Mine (American 1024)
[Other later releases, including one for the
nationally distributed Date label. Bill & The Quails
also had six or so 1950s releases on Deluxe
Records.]

Bobby Sands & His Soul Twisters
(EP) *Live At The 007 1/2 Go Go* (Art 2005)
[includes "Wildest Go Go Show Ever Recorded,"
"Caravan," "Wake Up," and "Where Did You Go."]

Sophisticates
When Elvis Marches Home Again/Woody's Place
(Viva 61)
["Woody's Place" is actually the earliest-known
version of the song that later became "The Candy
Stik Twist."]

Twisters
Street Dance/Elvis Leaves Sorrento (Campus 125)

Berj Vaughn Quartet
Pass The Goodies/Truck Stop (Marlin 6101)

GULFSTREAM

6654/55 Rhythm Rockets (Vocal Ray Pate) -
My Shadow/Lucky Day

7226 Bob Sparks/Vince Fiorino Orch. - You Have Not
Gone/Crying My Heart Out For You

7269 Ross Minimi - Baby Rock/Oh! Janet

1000 Frantics Four (Vocals by Bobby Shane) -
TV Mama/Down By The Old Mill Stream

1001 Fort Pierce Master Singers - (EP) Seal Of Heaven
     On My Soul/Gloryland/Jesus Set Me
     Free/Heaven On My Mind

1050 Art Law - Run Baby Run/Big Train (PS)

1051 Art Law - Yodeling Blues/Kitty Kat Rock (PS)

1052 Joey Dade Trio - Jeepers Creepers/Bobby Oliver
     - My Babe

1053 Joey Dade - Jet My Love/Bobby Oliver -
     La Bomba

1054

1055

1056 Pete Dollard - Malaguena/Star Dreams

1057 Tic Tac 'N Toe Plus Ray Wood - Good Time
     Jazz/Beau James

1058 Tom & The Craftsmen - Roses Are Red/The
     Work Song (PS)

1059 Riccardo Bertoni - Tira Lla Lla/Wondering Why

1060

1061 Jim Holt - Paralyzed/Brown Eyed Handsome
     Man

1062 Jim Holt - Money/Melody D'Amour

1063

1064 Jim Holt - Oh! My Linda/You Just Can't Win

1065 John Amory - Pink Champagne/Bad

1066 Cathy Kent - All I Care/Just A Minute Away

1067

1068 Jim Holt - Walk Away From Me Darlin'/Life
     Span

1069

1070

1071 Fern Hall - Who Put The Turtle In Myrtle's
     Girdle/I'm Gonna Bump My Baby Tonight

1072

1073

1074

1075

1076 Tom Collins - Cuttin' Out/Just Like Me

1077

1078 Big Daddy Fabulous Four (Vocal by Russ
     Anders) - Dear God Bring Our Boys Back
     Home/Three To One

1079

1080 Becky Dee (Jack Wyatt Trio) - A Day In The Life
     Of A Fool/Satin Doll

1097 Bill Wallace - Sam Dog/Big Old Black Dog
     [The above 33 1/3 disc has no number on the
     actual label, but the number 1097 etched in
     vinyl.]

no # Joey Murcia & Kingsmen - Can't Sit Down/
     Since You're Gone (acetate)

(blank label acetate) George W. Handlon & Boss
     Beats - Sugaree/Unchained Melody
     [The above pressing is also 33 1/3.]

no # Barbara King - Pool Of Love/Big Sweet Man

no # Cornelius Bros. - Things Are Gonna Change
     (one- sided demo)

no # Lucia Pamela -*Into Outer Space With* (LP)

[Basically an outlet for tracks recorded at Gulfstream
Studios, located at 5614 Taylor Street in Hollywood.
Gulfstream's earliest releases feature some of the hottest
rockabilly tracks ever recorded in Florida.]

LIVING LEGEND

100 Mor-Loks - There Goes Life/Elaine

101 Gary Stites & Birdwatchers - Real Appeal/While
     I'm Gone

102 Soul Pleasers - I Found A Love/Baby Don't Cry

103

104

105

106

107   Upper Hand - Real Appeal/Little Tear

108   Evil - Whatcha Gonna Do About It/Always
       Runnin' Around

109

110   Gents Five - I'll Remember You/Legendary Street
       Singers - While I'm Gone

111   Custer's Last Band - Another Year/Mind Rhymes
       [#110 and #111 are on Legend Records.]

ABCO

1001   Lincolns - Night Drag/Vagabonds - Baby Face
       McCall

1002   Cynthia Williams & Shaggs - It's Too Late/Perry
       Gordon & Shaggs - Anytime

1003   Jack Gillen & His Combo - These Boots Are
       Made For Walkin'/Good Luck Charm

MIDA

100   Curley Jim & Billey Rocks - Rock And Roll
       Itch/Air Force Blues (slightly different version
       originally issued as Metro 100.)

101   Ric Castle & Jim Patterson Orch. - Don't Do This
       And Don't Do That/Our Love

102   Ric Castle & Jim Patterson Orch. - Swing Time
       Waltz/I Just Fell In Love With You

103

104   Bobby Gay & Sparkletones - Let's Dance/You're
       Nice

105   Jim Preddy & Orchestra with The Dreamers - I'll
       Be The One In Your Dreams/Our Memories

106   Donel Austin & Sensational Dellos - So
       Shy/Donel Austin & Rockin' Impallas - That's
       Why I'm Dreamin'

107   James & Richard The Two Tones - I'll Cry/My
       Love And I

108   Curley Jim & Billey Rocks - Sloppy Sloppy
       Susie/Didn't I Tell You

109   Sensational Dellos - Lost Love/So Don't Go

110   Jessie Lee with Ed Row's Band - Lonely Broken
       Heart/Jessie Lee with The Rhythmaires -
       Won't Have To... Any More

111   Jackie Blanchard & Rockin' Impallas - The King
       O'Hearts/Only A Fool

112   Bill Bell & 4 Unknowns - Little Bitty Girl/Fearless

113   Donel Austin & Rockin' Impallas - Baby You Are
       Mine Tonight/Get With It

114   Glenn Powell - I Die A Thousand Ways/I'm Going
       Back To South Carolina

15   Buddy Howard - Be Sure You Know/Take Your
       Hands Off Me, Baby

  [One of the greatest labels of the 1950s.
  MIDA was short for Miami-Dade.]

SCOTT

1201   Champions with Sonny Thompson - It's Love It's
       Love/Mexico Bound

1202   Tracy Pendarvis & Blue Notes - It Don't
       Pay/One Of These Days

1203   Tracy Pendarvis - Give Me Lovin'/All You Gotta
       Do

1204   Ray & The Quarter Notes - Rose/

1205   Pyramiders - Don't Ever Leave Me/How It Feels

1206   Freddie & The Heartaches - Blue
       Tomorrow/Womp-Womp

1401 Eddie Thorpe - Just Call My Name/I'll Be
      Different

1404 Jimmy Voytek - Kitten/Searching For You

26   Five Steps - These Boots Are Made For
      Walkin'/Tightin' Up

27   Birdwatchers - Girl I Got News For You/Eddie's
      Tune

28   Nightcrawlers - I Don't Remember/What Time Is It

168   Proctor Amusement Co. - Heard You Went
      Away/Call Out My Name

29   Birdwatchers - Turn Around Girl/You Got It

30   Birdwatchers - Put A Little Sunshine In My
      Day/Than You Say Boh Bah

31   Proctor Amusement Co. - You Don't Need A
      Reason/Two Wonderful Girls

401   New Rock Band - Rock Steady/Little David

402   Mousetrap - Spinning Wheel/Rhymetyme

GLADES

601   Davey Jones - No More Tears/Tootsie Wootsie

602

603   Wilbert Harrison - Gonna Tell You A Story/Letter
      Edged In Black

604

605   Davey Jones - I Was Blind/The Chase

7001 Wrong Bros. - Baby Baby Please/All I Want Is
      You

[Glades was resurrected by Henry Stone in the 1970s and
is best known as the label Timmy Thomas' top ten hit "Why
Can't We Live Together" appeared on.]

TRIP UNIVERSAL RECORDS, INC.
(Through March, 1970)

101

102 Neighborhood Of Love - Count Yourself Out Of
Bounds/Miss Blue Three Quarter

103 Changing Image - Awakening Dream/The Happy
Girl

104 Steve Greenberg - Big Bruce/Man Is Dead
[Reissued with "Run To You" on the B-side as
Trip 3000.]

105

106

107

108

109

110 The Squiremen - Who In The World/Secrets

11

12 Generation Gap - Trumpets/Movin' On Strong

13

14

15 Six Pak - There Was A Time/Midnight Brew

16 Heroes Of Cranberry Farm - Fellow John (Has A
Vision)/Who In The World

17 Guy Drake - Welfare Cadillac/Keep Off My Grass

18 Heroes Of Cranberry Farm - Man/Secrets

19 Generation Gap - Letter From Seattle/Ball

20

21 Still Life - Dear Robert/Midnight Brew

22 Heroes Of Cranberry Farm - Will You Love Me
Tomorrow/Fellow John (Has A Vision)

23 Common Market - Wouldn't It Be Nice/If You're
Ever In Miami

24

25

26   Melvin Carter - Welfare Cadillac/Midnight Brew

27

28   New Society Band - Margie May/Minek A Szoke
      Ennekem

29   Glass Tears Band - Midnight Brew/

[Outside of a great neo-rockabilly tune by Bredice Mays, appropriately entitled "Miami Boogie" (Twin 38), and a few stray Heroes Of Cranberry Farm singles, you can pretty much kiss off future Trip/Twin/GWS releases — unless you have this strange need to sample '70s mediocrity.]

TROPICAL

[Miami-based soul label, totally unrelated to the better-known Tropical in DeLand, Florida.]

101   Eddie Taylor - Just The Way You Are/The State
      Song

102

103

104

105

106

107   Frankie Seay & Soul Riders - Soul Food/Black
      Jack

108   Frankie Seay & Soul Riders - I Came A Long Way
      To Get To You/Hold On

109   Florida Stars - Call On Doctor Jesus/If He Calls,
      Would You Answer

110   Missionaires - Clouds Hanging Low/

111   Caravans - Break Bread Together/One Baptism
      (Gospel Gold Records)

112   Frankie Seay - Baby Please/All I Want is Loving
      You

113

114

115

116   Treetop And The Soul Branches - Inside
        Out/Don't Go Away

117

118

119   Rufus "Mr. Soul" Beacham - Lead Me On/Do You
        Have A Good Woman?

120

121

122

1038   Willie Wilson & Renegades - Little Girl/Return
        To Love

unknown - Creative Voices - Sincere People/

unknown - Southern Echoes - Each Day And
        Every Hour/

VULCO

[1950s-'60s label based in Palm Beach County]

1   Flaming Hearts - Baby/I Don't Mind

2   Tornados - Ramblin' Man/

3   Clyde Williams - Anymore/

1500   Pat Richmond & Fireballs - Don't Stop The
        Rockin'/Honey Bee Baby

1501   Billy Eldridge & Fireballs - Let's Go Baby/My
        Blue Tears
        [The above was later released on Unart 2011.]

1502

1503

1504

1505

1506   Doug Dickens & Fireballs - Lucy's
        Graveside/Raw Deal

1507   Billy Eldridge & Fireballs - Half A Heart/Take
        My Heart

1508

1509

1510 No Artist Listed-Arranged by Vern Strickland - Sneaky/Maria Elena

1600 Tiny York's Band featuring Donald Scott - Too Young/You Change My Love

30

DEAD WAX MARKINGS

I always look a strange sight while hunting for records; not because of WHAT I'm examining, but HOW. While most people take records out of their sleeves to check for surface wear or warpage, I take records out of their sleeves to read the "dead wax;" that is, the markings between the grooves and outer portion of the label. Few people realize it, but in many cases, the very history of a musical scene can be found simply by reading between the lines. Or behind them. The real trick is tracking the tiny marks left behind by engineers, masterers, platers, and pressers so many moons ago.

You won't become a deacon of dead wax overnight. It took me years to crack some of these numbering systems; others still remain a confusing succession of digits. This book probably would have been finished long ago had I not become obsessed with finding the differences between "SO" and "SON" or learning what's right about the Rite pressing plant. Knowing the difference between RCA and QCA and distinguishing ZTSB from ZTSC means the difference between listing an artist's recordings in order, by month and year... or just listing them randomly. My obsession, although time-consuming, paid off when I was able to date nearly every record listed in this book, almost to the very day of release.

Some will find the following dead wax guide confusing. Others will find it essential. But remember, just as a record has to be IN the groove to be worth its salt, so it goes BEYOND those grooves... for there lies the hidden secrets of where and when America's garages rang out and sang out with a twist and a shout.

♩D

I mentioned this symbol briefly in the record labels section. As funny-looking as it is, it's a Florida collector's best friend. If you find this symbol (a bunched-together "JD," the initials of master masterer Jack Davis), you've found a Miami pressing! No questions asked! There was a lot of garbage mixed in with the great stuff (when isn't there?), but the treasures far outweigh the trash... and think of how many numbers still have yet to be found!

♩D

JD DISCOGRAPHY

2454 Chessmen - The Lycra Stretch/One And Only
(Suncrest 2454)   (64)

2716 King John - I Won't Take You Back/Something
On My Mind (Na-R-Co 2871-48)

2746 Original Cousins - Eggman/Sock It (Reid 2746)

2774 Clarence Reid & Delmiras - Push A Little
Harder/Like White On Rice (Dade 1855)

2824 Carlos Montiel - Flagler Street/Oye
(Blue Bell 100)

3137/20 Byron Lee & Dragonaires - River Bank
Jump Up/And I Love Her (Bra 501)

3191 Odessa Harris - The Color Of His Love Is
Blue/Driving Wheel (JEB 101)   (6-65)

3220 Spyders - New Boy Came To Our School/Just
For You (Spyder 3220)

3241 Gary Stites & Birdwatchers - Real Appeal/While
     I'm Gone (Living Legend 101)   (7-65)

3341 Jack Blanchard Group - Gemini/New World
     (Zodiac 3341)

3344 Invaders - She's A Tiger/"Honda" Come Back
     (Suncrest 3344)   (9-65)

3402 Eye Zooms - She's Gone/On The Line (Atila 213)

3410 Dorells - I Need Someone To Love Me/You're
     Gonna Want Me (Bronze 102)

3412 King Coleman - It's Dance Time
     Vocal/Instrumental (Dade 1901)

3456 (LP) Various - *Jam Session Goes Latino* (593)

3491 Birdwatchers - It's A Long Way Home/It Doesn't
     Matter (Marlin 1902)

3508/09 Rusty Diamond - I Guess I'd Better Get Up
     And Go Home/The Lonely Sentry
     (Zodiac 3508/09)

3539 Eddie & Tropics - One Hundred Pounds Of
     Clay/Will You Love Me Tomorrow (Bird Bowl
     Lounge 3539)

3554 Mysteries - My True Love/Pink Panther
     (JDL 3554)   (11-65)

3560 Soul Pleasers - I Found A Love/Baby Don't Cry
     (Living Legend 102)

3574 Eddie Taylor - Just The Way You Are/The State
     Song (Tropical 101)

3606 Fabulous Thunder - So Hold Me Tight/Jealous
     Of You (Tight 3606)

3622 Bees - Shy Boy/Jadoo (Bees 3622)

3630 Frank Williams Rocketeers - Good Thing Part
     1/Part 2 (Lloyd 008)   (1-66)

3638 Lee Hazen - Plantation Isle/An Orchid In The
     Moonlight (Harry's Songs 3638)

3680 We The People - My Brother, The Man/Proceed
     With Caution (Hotline 3680)

3697 Satans - Gone From Me/Big Boss Man
(Seller 007)

3720 Dark Horsemen - You Lied/Girl, Stand By Me
(The Dark Horsemen 3720)

3781 Jacques Kayal - (EP) *Pour Vous* (Preview 3781)
(PS)

3820 Nick Bartell - Jezebel/I Can't Get You Out Of
My Heart (Bart 3820)

3822 Billy Sandlin & Interns - Poor Rich Girl/Here
Comes That Feeling (Royale 326)

3881 Ella Washington - Nightmare/Tanzotic All Stars
- The Grass Always Seems Greener
(Octavia 0002)   (4-66)

3889 Gang Of Saints - Yes, It's Too Bad/This Feeling
(PKB's 000)

3893 Clefs Of Lavender Hill - Stop! Get A Ticket/First
Tell Me Why (Thames 100/101)

3903 Don Hollinger - I Had A Nightmare/Where The
Young Folks Go (Jato 7000)

3904 Nasty Dog Catchers - Nasty Dog
Part 1/Part 2 (Jato 7001)

3956 Limeys With London Sounds - Come
Back/Green And Blue (Sherwood 1715) (PS)   (5-66)

3959 Frank Williams Rocketeers - It's All Over/Show
Me What You Got (Lloyd 0010)

3960 Baskerville Hounds - Here I Am Miami
(A-side only) (Tema no #)

4021 Freda Gray & Rocketeers - Stay Away From My
Johnny Vocal/Instrumental (Deep City 2366)

4035 Tropics - For A Long Time/Black Jacket Woman
(Thames 103)

4044 Legends - Raining In My Heart/How Can I Find
Her (Thames 104)

4096 Bobby Naylor & Bees - Shy Boy/Where Is My
Baby (Sunville 495)

4101 Banana Monkies/Los Monstruos/Los
      Temerarios/Los Yenka - (LP) *Exitos A Go Go*
      (Son-Art 103)

4122 Joe Ruggiero - Italian Theme
      Part 1/Part 2 (Malissa 147)

4180 Frankie Scott - (LP) *You're In My Act!* (Arco 501)

4224 Bob Roberts - The Lonesome End/Wind From
      The Wilderness (White Oak no #)

4225 Mark Markham & Jesters - Goin' Back To
      Marlboro Country/I Don't Need You
      (Power 4225)   (9-66)

4228 Frank Williams Rocketeers - You Got To Be A
      Man/The Spanish Fly (Deep City 2369)

4255 Ella Washington - Bye Bye Baby/The Grass
      Always Seems Greener (Octavia 0003)   (11-66)

4274 Bobby Cash & Niteflyers - Nobody Knows/Only
      With You (Kap-Tal 1001/02)

4295 Novas - Whenever You're Ready/Please Ask Her
      (Chelle 162)   (1-67)

4442 Non-Pareils - Willow Tree/Painter Man
      (Five Star 101)

4462 U.S. Male - It's Gonna Be So Hard/Is This Guy
      (U.A.P. 1002)

4506 King Houston - Steppin' On My Heart/Silver
      Flowers (Marianna 4506)

4523 Johnny K. Killens - I Don't Need Help/Frenchy
      The Tickler (Deep City 2370)

4581 The New Clarence Reid - Cadillac Annie/Tired
      Blood (Deep City 2372)   (2-67)

4589 Americana Brass - Venetian Blue/Americana
      Weekend (A & B 4589)

4604 Shades Inc. - Who Loved Her/Sights
      (Abstract 4604)   (3-67)

4610 Dr. T. & Undertakers - It's Easy Child/Times
      Have Changed (Target 4610)   (4-67)

4663 Soul Tenders - Somebody Help Me/Silver &
Gold (JD 4663)

4667 Gents Five - A Wave Awaits/Straight Shooter
(March 7734)

4720 Byron Lee & Dragonaires - (LP) *Rock Steady*
(BRA 3101)

4737 Evil - Whatcha Gonna Do About It/Always
Running Around (Living Legend 108)

4758 Newports - Life Must Go On/Feelin' Low
(Zebb 155)   (5-67)

4817 Squiremen IV - What's On Your Mind/Bitter
End (Squire 14-15)   (6-67)

4874 Young Strangers - She's Gone/You Are (TYS 1)

4878 Betty Wright - Paralyzed/Good Lovin' (Deep City
2378)

4878 Them Two - Am I A Good Man/Love Has Taken
Wings (Deep City 2379)

[The above pair of Deep City releases shared the
same matrix number.]

4919 Ann Clark - A Girl That Works In A Bar/He'll
Never Cheat No More (Pantage 16)

4932 Razor's Edge - Get Yourself Together/Cloudy
Day (Power 4932)   (8-67)

4936/63 Kollektion - Savage Lost/My World Is
Empty Without You (Heads Up 101)

4970 (EP) *University Of Miami Fight Songs* (PS)

4992 Tasmanians - I Can't Explain This Feeling/If I
Don't (Power 4933)

5027 Shaggs - Hummin/I Who Have Nothing
(Power 103)   (9-67)

5053 Helene Smith - Wrong Or Right He's My
Baby/Sure Thing (Deep City 2380)   (10-67)

5056 Louis Howard & Rocketeers - I'm A Happy
Man/Please Forgive Me (Bronze 108)

5134 Russ "Big Daddy" Anders, Fabulous Four - Dear
God, Bring Our Boys Back Home/Three To
One (Anbee 3500)

5146 Birdwatchers - Put A Little Sunshine In My
Day/Than You Say Boh Bah (Scott 30)

5228 Other Side - Wild Rebels/Come See About Me
(Sundi 103/104) (PS)   (11-67)

5242/3 New Chains III - The End/Like A Friend
(Enterprise 5242/3)

5257 Scott Thomson - Merry Christmas/Time For
Love (Pantage 5257)

5283 Little Beaver - Do Right Man/These Blues Are
Getting Me Down (Saadia 5283)

5320/03 Edie Walker - Baby Angel/Your Unusual
Love (Mew 103)

5362 Jacqueline Hyde & Moonfolk - Strange New
World/Runaway (Zodiac 1040/41)

5391 Graduates - Right Or Wrong/Theme For A Little
Girl (Penni 5391)

5488 Pat Canavan - It Seems So Wrong/Don't Know
Where I Stand With You (Florida 929)

5566 Reflections - You Don't Love Me/I Need Your
Lovin' (Went 001)

5582 Misty Morgan & Jack Blanchard - Bethlehem
Steel/No Sign Of Love (Those Darn Records
2041/2)

5607 Benny Latimore - The Power And The
Glory/Love Don't Love Me (Dade 45-217)   (6-68)

5680 Rhodes Brothers - (LP) *Rhodes Brothers*
(Pan-O-Ram 5680)

5698 Monopoly - There's Gotta Be Some
Goodtimes/Shame (Power no #)

5769 Jeb Stuart - Please Give Me Another
Chance/Your Good Lovin'
(Great American 1001)

5784 Little Beaver - Blind Man/Do It To Me One More
Time (Saadia 5784)

5833 Blues Image - Can't You Believe In
Forever/Parchmant Farm (Image 5833)   (9-68)

5969 Tiny Kennedy - Fireball Jungle/Please Don't
Give Him My Love (Americana 5969)

6403 Minority - Where Was My Mind/High Flyer
(Hyperbolic 105)

6421 Tom Carlile - (LP) *The Original Sounds Of Tom
Carlile* (Cherry 101)

6479 Rick Shaw - A Message To All Teenagers From
Universal Record Shop
(one-sided) (Universal Record Shop 1)

6519 The Yak - Every Little Thing/Eric Cleveland
(Tooth 533)

6549 James Knight & Butlers - There Goes My Baby
Vocal/Instrumental (Concho 2250)

6593 Speed Limit - You're Too Young To Know/Speed
(Hyperbolic 108)

6609 Soul Ful Jeb Stuart - (Gonna Keep On Dancin')
Cause I Got Soul/You're Mine (By This Act Of
Fate) (Great American 601)   (9-69)

6681 Nick Bartell - The Chair/Wild Flowers
(Banana 25)

[By this point, the JD symbol was interchangeable with
the initials CTW, but don't let that throw you. The numbering
system, thankfully, remains the same.]

RCA PRESSINGS

You can't discuss the history of records without mentioning RCA, generally credited with issuing the first commercially available 45 RPM records. RCA also handled custom pressings for labels big and small: everything from Motown and Laurie to Black Cat and Sundi. Many labels carry a three-digit number followed by a letter, which in turn is followed by another series of digits/letters. That first three-

digit number, generally a 600, 700, 800, or 900 series, tells
you the region of the country the record is being pressed for.
All 600 and 700 numbers belong to southern clients. 800
numbers correspond to the North and Midwest. The only
inconsistency is the 900 series, which includes Tiara
Records from Hollywood, Florida. Most other 900s are a
continuation of the 800 series, serving Ohio, Michigan,
Indiana, Minnesota, and the like. (Interestingly enough, New
York clients didn't get a three-digit prefix... and as of this
writing, I've never seen an RCA pressing for a West Coast
act. Strange but true.)

Now, before this gets too confusing, let's take a real RCA
pressing and closely examine its mastering number. A typical example would be "Grasshopper Pizza" b/w "It Won't Be
Long" by Don & The Holidays: 634K - T4KM 9780. It all looks
like gibberish, but it makes perfectly good sense. Really. 634
is the RCA client number; in this case, Kam Records from
Orlando. Other releases on the label also bear this number.
The "K" that follows the number (and this is where the fun
begins!) tells you the first letter of the client's name; in this
case, Kam! As for those other funny notations on RCA
pressings — the N8OWs, SK4Ms, etc. — boy, are you about
to have fun. The first letter corresponds to the year in which
the disc was mastered while the four-digit number also
follows a consecutive pattern. With this chart, RCA mastering codes will make sense. Trust me!

F - 1955	R - 1964
G - 1956	S - 1965
H - 1957	T - 1966
J - 1958	U - 1967
K - 1959	W - 1968
L - 1960	X - 1969
M - 1961	Z - 1970
N - 1962	A - 1971
P - 1963	

So in the case of Don & The Holidays, T4KM, by virtue of
its first initial, means the record was mastered in 1966. By

comparing the number that follows (9780) with other T4KM pressings, we find a mid-66 mastering date (and in almost all cases, release date). Believe it or not, this system works. More examples: Paris Tower 125, 126, 127, 128, 129, and 130 were all released in November, 1967, (UK4M 2337 through 2416) as was the Male Bachs on Truce (UK4M 3351/2). So was "Snoopy's Christmas" by the Royal Guardsmen (UK4M 0782). RCA pressings are wonderful. The West Coast didn't know what it was missing!

Here's where California girls (and boys) get us back for leaving them out of the RCA picture. One of the nation's most successful plating/pressing plants was Monarch, located in funky ol' L.A. The folks at Monarch deserve their weight in gold for giving us the "delta number:" a triangle, followed by a matrix number, that has graced about 100,000 sides since 1954. And here's the beautiful part: All 100,000 or so numbers are in chronological order according to the time the record was mastered and/or plated!

You won't find many small Florida labels with delta numbers since few were pressed on the West Coast. But as far as major labels go... watch out! Delta numbers tell us Billy J. Killen on the Roulette-distributed Meridian 1510 (delta symbol 29620/2) goes all the way back to May, 1959. The Roemans on ABC-Paramount 10583 (delta symbol 53707/08) came to us from late July, 1964. And in case you were wondering about the Legends on Parrot 45010, one glance at the delta number (delta symbol 56564) tells us April, 1965, was a rockin' good date for a rockin' good record. One word of caution: Many big-label releases were pressed on both coasts, and your East Coast pressings will NOT have a delta number. Generally, your Atco, Dot, or Dunhill labels with LARGE PRINT will have delta numbers. Small print labels will not.

APPROXIMATE DELTA DATES

(With thanks to Warren "Blob" Cook for first breaking this
code two decades ago.)

January, 1956	8253	January, 1963	46238
January, 1957	13634	January, 1964	51227
January, 1958	19980	January, 1965	55884
January, 1959	26912	January, 1966	60101
January, 1960	34320	January, 1967	64616
January, 1961	37697	January, 1968	69696
January, 1962	41698	January, 1969	74380

NASHVILLE MATRIX

If very few Florida records were pressed on the West Coast,
you can blame both economic and geographic reasons.
Nashville offered studios, labels, and pressing plants galore
and was the place of choice for the majority of southern
one-shot big shots. The largest masterer, by far, was Nashville Matrix, which did us all a great favor by assigning all
its clients their own mastering code (sort of like the 600 -
900 numbers assigned by RCA's custom plants). This code
is found strictly on the dead wax — never on the label — and
in many cases gives a dead giveaway of the record's origin
(lucky for us!).

All the Bee Jay/Tener stuff was mastered by Nashville
Matrix with a code number of 84. The Pine Hills label (PH)
bears the number 103. You'll find the number 67 on the
Argee label (well, not exactly ON the label... you get the
picture!). But that's just the beginning. Other Nashville
Matrix clients included Motown (number 10), Hit (number
15), SSS (113), Monument (125), Paula (127)... plus two
numbers assigned to tiny Detroit labels: 77 and 95! But for
now, we'll concentrate on clients that concentrated on the
South: DOVER (client number 86), SO (client 5), PRP (client
161), and my personal favorite, SON ("Sound of Nashville,"
client 18).

Not to take anything away from the acknowledged music capitals, but Nashville isn't called "Music City U.S.A." for nothing. If you think the home of the Grand Ole Opry is strictly a one-horse country town, check out the following very incomplete discographies. Then pack your bags for Music City, where Nashville cats turned garages into gold... and the gold rush has just begun!

SO
(Nashville Matrix Client 5)

381/2   Starlighters - Whomp Whomp!/Until You Return (Suncoast 1001)

489/90 Flash Terry - She's My Baby/It's All Over Now (Suncoast 1003)

966/7   Dorinda Duncan & Capris - You're Something Special/Caddy Daddy (Glendale 1011)

1099/2000 Jimmy Velvit - Sometimes At Night/Look At Me (Division 102)

1473/4 Jimmy Velvit - You're Mine & We Belong Together/I'm Gonna Try (Witch 115)

1565/6 Wayne Cochran - Monkey Monkey/Little Orphan Annie (Deck 151)

1872/3 Jimmy Velvit - Wisdom Of A Fool/I Want To Be Loved (Startime 103)

2327/8 Jimmy Velvit - Donna/Her Love (Abnak 108)

[To further complicate matters, it appears both singers who used the name Jimmy Velvit/Velvet had records that were SO pressings!]

3535/6 Ray Yeager - Mama's Radio/Secret Agent Garbage Man (Tiara 102)

4238/4166 Wilson Messer - I'll Love Again someday/ The Laugh's On Me Tonight (Eagle no #)

4360/1 Jim Foster - Bring 'Em Back Alive/Four Chrome Wheels (Turret 109)   (6-67)

4803   Jimmy Velvet 5 - Good Good Lovin'/Broken Hearted Misery (Velvet Tone 114)

5690/1 Lauri Beth - Happiness/Pathways (Twin 101)

5732/3 Neighborhood Of Love - Count Yourself Out
Of Bounds/Miss Blue Three Quarter

[Issued in two different versions on Trip 102 and
Twin 102.]

5772/3 Changing Image - Awakening Dream/The
Happy Girl (Trip 103)

5774/5 Steve Greenberg - Big Bruce/Man Is Dead
(Trip 104)

5830/1 Coal Flask - Stop/Concept In Your Mind
(Trip 105)

6200/1 Enalpria - Rose Water/Shredded Heat
(Enko 6200/01)

6274/5 Crystalline Silence - Space Kid's Science Fair
Project/Papa's Hung Up On The TV
Newsman (Twin Oaks)

6346/7 Blues People - (EP) *Blame It On Florida*
(GP 6346/47)

6420/1 Squiremen - Who In The World/Secrets
(Trip 110)

6504/5 Generation Gap - Trumpets/Movin' On
Strong (Trip 12)

6520/30 Heroes Of Cranberry Farm - Fellow John
(Has A Vision)/Who In The World (Trip 16)

6590/1 Guy Drake - Welfare Cadillac/Keep Off My
Grass (Trip 17)

6646/7 Harry - Emily, My Darlin'/If You're Ever In
Miami (Case 001)

6648/6421 Heroes Of Cranberry Farm -
Man/Secrets (Trip 18)

6650/1 Generation Gap - Letter From Seattle/Ball
(Trip 19)

6746/6521 Still Life - Dear Robert/
Midnight Brew (Trip 21)

6810/6530 Heroes of Cranberry Farm -
Will You Love Me Tomorrow/Fellow
John (Has A Vision) (Trip 22)

6862/6658 Common Market - Wouldn't It Be Nice/
If You're Ever In Miami (Trip 23)

6988/9 Common Market - Going Nowhere
Vocal/Instrumental (Twin Oaks 009)

6996/6300 Mike Moore - Letter From Seattle/
Fellow John (Twin Oaks 010)

7008/9 New Society Band - Margie May/Minek A
Szoke Ennekem (Trip 28)

7280/1 Lewis Clark - Red Man's Revenge/Love Can
Save (Ultimate 7280/1)

7354/5 Babel - Think Me Strange/Summertime
(Trip 38)

7356/7 Babel - Under My Thumb/4 Until Late
(Trip 39)

7402/3 World of Matter - No Such Thing/What's Your
Name (Trip 41)

7508/9 Nancy Grahm - The Bones (Trip 44)

7580/1 Aragon Exchange - Raise Up Your
Voices/Boat Master (Trip 48)

7750/1 Jim McCartney & Koincidence -
Rock-A-Tum-Tum/Leave Us Alone
(Twin Oaks 12)

7856/7 Third Condition - Monday In May/Nickel
(Sundi 6815)

7918/9 Heroes Of Cranberry Farm -
Christians/Children (Trip 61)

8422/8214 Jimmy Velvet - A Woman/Wasted Years
(Sundi 7101)

8646/7 Bob Newkirk - Man Is Dead/Time (Trip 82)

8976/7 Dave Brockman - My Angel's Gone To
Hell/Six 10's And An 8 (Pea-Nut 1001)

10274/5 Fabulettes - Muddy Waters/
Stickin Kind Of Man (Access 1002)

[Notable SO pressings from states other than Florida
include releases by Ernie K-Doe, The Showmen, Floyd Dakil
Combo, Citations, Del-Rays, K-Otics, Torquays, Distortions,
Villagers, Preachers, Vikings, Bugs, Five Americans,
Shambrels, 4th Amendment, Rockin' Rebellions, The News,
Electric Love, The Bridge, Wild Vybrashun, Jaguars, Che-
ques, Tories, Rogues, and so many others. Many releases
shown here have the number "5" in the dead wax with a
Nashville Matrix designation instead of the actual letters
"SO." It should be mentioned that the two are interchange-
able, with the numbering system consistent throughout.]

SON
(Nashville Matrix Client 18)

436   (LP) *Night At The Hootenanny Coffee House*
       (various local folk artists) (Yale 1001)

536   Jim Morrison & Band - The Used Car Blues/My
       Old Stand By (Curley Q 5707)

560   Sand Fleas - The Maid Of Destin/Miracle Strip
       USA (Exclusive 2284)

705   Jim Morrison & Band - The Campfire Song/You
       Made Me Happy Again (Curley Q 5709)   (64)

955   Bill Alexander & La Sabres -
       F.L.A./Hiway #1   (no label name 101)

1083/671 Chalker McKay & Backroom Boys -
          Lost Stop Sign/T. Zero (Amphion 101)

2254   Sugar Beats - Have You Ever Had The
       Blues/What Am I Doing Here (Knight 101)

2297   Travis Rogers & Continentals - Why/Rheumatiz
       (T 'N T 2001)

2512   Eye Zooms - She's Gone/On The Line
       (Atila 213)   (10-65)

2718   Ray Yeager - Country Boy/Empty Bottle
       (Tiara 100)

3654 Johnny "K" & Dynamites - Don't You
      Believe/Make The Nights A Little Longer
      (Phono 101)

3656 Don Barrie - Our Song/Tomorrow This Will Be
      Yesterday (Tiara 660)

3766 Kleen-Kuts - (You're My) Summer Love/I've
      Found A New Love (Vitality 701)

4253 Teddy Lee - Rainbow Mender/A Place
      (Or-Sum 1001)

9918 5-Souls - Baby-3 Times/The Wedding Must Go
      On (Shelly 0005)

[Florida-related releases only are listed above. Notable
SON pressings from other states include releases by The
Continentals, Bassmen, Revlons, Dave & The Stalkers, In-
vaders, Jerry Waugh & Skeptics, Realistics, Distortions,
Fabulous Four, Saharas, The "In", Malibus, Dynatones,
Reasons Why, Group Therapy, Versatiles, Melinda & The
Misfits, Classmen, Bo & Weevils, Fourth Amendment, Dept.
Of Sound, and '60s samplers from Ohio and Kentucky!]

PRP
(Nashville Matrix Client 161)

78   Allen Hensley - If I'd Left The Bottle Alone/
      I'm Sorry For It All (Florida 67-849)

141   Lewis Clark - Green Power/Here's My Heart
      (Fuller 0021)

162   The Crypt - You Keep Me Hanging On/Love,
      I'll Never Know (The Crypt 68-940)

482   Mouse & The Boys - Xcedrin Headache #69/
      Love Is Free (Rubiat 68-1043)

594   Shy Guys - Goodbye To You/Black Lightening
      Light (M-U 5941/2)

834   Joey Ray & Shays - For A Little Of Her
      Sunshine/Would I Still Be Loving You
      (Sundi 6812)

1527 Good Bad & Ugly - I'll Never Let Her Go/
The Meaning Of Love (Seyah 001)

1811 Third Condition - Charisma (Sundi 6814)

2180 Linda McFaye & Doc Castellana - Cream Cheese
& Jelly (Gulf Coast 45-101)

2840 Charles Vickers - Thunder Bay/Yes-es Of
Yesterday (Tropical 171)

2844 Bill Rogers & Arrangers - Wrong As Can
Be/Believe It Or Not (Mark 0337)

2851 Euphoria - Everloving People/The Nicest Words
(Hit 1005)

3038 Charles Vickers - Let There Be Another
Tomorrow/Let's Go Back (Tropical 172)

3163 Front Woods - It's Gonna Be Alright/Higher (Lee
1000)

3565 Dan Feather - Touch And Go/Memories
(Tropical 177)

3592 Arthur Freeman - Here I Am/Played Out Play
Girl (Excello 2322)

[Notable PRP pressings from states other than Florida
include releases by the Debuts, Ballantraes, Chateaus,
Reverbs, Movement, Mishaps, Celtics, Palace Guard, Sweet
Acids, Offbeats, Black River Circus, Beau Allen, Wet Paint,
Bitter Creek, Ace Song Service, and many others. All numbers listed were followed by the digit 1 or 2, denoting the A
and B sides.]

DOVER
(Nashville Matrix Client 86)

2265/6 Painted Faces - Anxious Color/Things We See
(Manhattan 808) (251)

2285   Jesters - Unchain My Heart/Blue Feeling
(Qualicon 5003) (133)

2380/1 Painted Faces - I Lost You In My Mind/I
Think I'm Going Mad (Manhattan 811) (258)

2448/9 Painted Faces - In The Heat Of The
Night/Don't Say She's Gone (Manhattan
814) (258)

2472/3 Mysteries - Please Agree/I Find It's True Love
(Manhattan 815) (258)

2540/1 Mysteries - I Can't Wait For Love/Satisfaction
Guaranteed (Manhattan 817) (258)

[There'll be bluebirds over the white labels of Dover! Yeah,
this Louisiana legend was kind enough to use a consistent
four-digit number for each of its releases, as well as a "client
number" preceding it, to help us determine where the record
is from. Obviously, "258" belonged to a pair of Florida acts
on the Manhattan label. Other client numbers are harder to
figure out, such as "133," which not only included The
Jesters from Naples/Ft. Myers (see above) but also bands
from Alabama, Louisiana, and possibly Tennessee. Not as
hard to figure out are Dover clients 219 (the Busy B label)
and 239 (RAP Records from Mississippi)... and '60s collectors
will want to check out Dovers from all over the South by
bands such as The Satans, Nomads, Swinging Medallions,
Rapids, Distortions, Rusty Gaytz, Better Half Dozen, Souls
Of The Slain, Palace Guards, and Substantial Evidence.]

ZTSB

Can't say I know what the "ZTS" stands for: you've seen
variations of it on all your Columbia records and lots of major
minors. The real story is the "B," which for some untold
reason denotes a Nashville pressing. ("ZTSC" records are
generally from Chicago or Detroit, while "ZTSP" is found
mainly on New York labels.) It appears ZTSB sometimes
assigned numbers out of order, depending on the client, as
witnessed by the 96000 series for Florida acts; ditto the
111000 series found on at least three great Tampa discs.
Nevertheless, the selective discography that follows is a good
starting point, and I know you'll have fun filling in the
missing numbers!

ZTSB
Florida Discography

83441/2   Wayne Cochran - Monkey Monkey/
          Little Orphan Annie (Deck 151)

93975   Sammie Moore - No Particular Place To Go
          (Hit 125)

95952/3   Bill Meadows - I've Been Seasick/
          I Won't Be Here (Meadow 9003)

96064/5   Savages - Everynight/So Much In Love
          (National 2001)

96068/9   Tropics - I Want More/Goodbye My Love
          (Knight 102)

96080/1   Savages - Little Miss Sad/If You Left Me
          (National 2002)

96096/7   Members - Wish I Never Met You/Jenny
          Jenny (Label 101)

96098/9   Ty B & Johnny - Doubtful Baby/Bony
          Moronie (Red Wing 706)

99137/8   Ty B & Johnny - Meaner Than An
          Alligator/You Don't Have To Cry (Red
          Wing 705)

101382/3 Canadian Rogues - Have You Found
          Somebody New/You Better Stop (Fuller
          2597)

111011/2 Wrong Numbers - The Way I Feel/I Wonder
          Why (Hit Cat 201)

111026/7 Senders - Party Line/Love Me Too
          (Leopard 201)

111033/4 Outsiders - Just Let Me Be/She's Comin'
          On Stronger (Knight 103)

111380/1 Missing Links - Run And Hide/I Really
          Ought To Go (Bamboo 111380/1)

120421/2 Don Barrie - Our Song/Tomorrow This Will
          Be Yesterday (Tiara 660)

125113/4 Don Barrie - Indian Wedding Day/Looking
For A Rainbow (Tiara 665)

127520/1 Monarchs - Girl, You Know/Do You Love
Me (Bruno 539)

129235/6 Canadian Rogues - Do You Love
Me/Mickey's Monkey (Rogue 1967)

[Notable ZTSB pressings from states other than Florida include releases by The Spades, Gentrys, Torques, Commanches, Newbeats, XL's, Donovan, Bassmen, Dalton Boys, Skeptics, Realistics, Chateaus, Bandits, Gants, K-Otics, Link Cromwell, James Gang, Rugbys, Soul Inc., Sparkles, Temptashuns, Lawson & 4 More, The In, Shadows, Sam The Sham, Neal Ford & Fanatics, Billy Lee Riley, WC Dorns, Robin & Three Hoods, Wee Juns, Booker T. & MG's, Goodees, 5 Emprees, Rebellion, Bryllig & Nymbol Swabes, Delrays, Johnnie Taylor, Eddie Floyd, and countless others.]

RITE

Here is one of the music industry's truly amazing stories. Rite was one of the nation's most prolific pressing plants... that's the good news. It was also the nation's least-successful, chart-wise! Hands down. No competition.

For more than twenty years, Rite cranked out releases for just about every state in the union. Cheaply. (1,000 singles with a picture sleeve, for as low as $229, way back in 1959!)

Amazingly enough, Rite had NO HITS, and we're not just talking national here. I've never even seen a REGIONAL hit come from a Rite pressing! Anywhere! A ZERO SUCCESS RATE! Compare that with all the regional SO, SON, ZTSB smashes. The only thing green Rite ever saw was the musicians they recorded. It's no wonder some of the crudest garage discs were pressed there. From a collector's standpoint, Rite lives up to its name. But for anyone who truly wanted a hit, Rite couldn't have been more WRONG!

[For more on RITE, get REBEL TEEN MAGAZINE, issues one and two, from George Gell, 624 Boston Post Road #13, Marlborough, MA 01752.]

RITE PRESSINGS, Florida releases only:

2869/70   Tiny York's Band featuring Donald Scott -
          Too Young/You Change My Love
          (Vulco 1600)

4190   Jewell Timmons & Ralph Sullivan with The
          Que-Tones - All The Time/Feel So Good
          (At The Martinique 502)

4227/28   Diplomats - On The Beach Down In
          Pompano Pt. 1/Pt. 2 (Pompano 105)

4953/54   Cara Stewart & Gold Coast Boys - You're My
          Honey/I Want You To Know (Roxie 247)

5079/80   Johnny Redd - Fixed For Life/Rockin' Peg
          (Carellen 106)

6243/44   Bill Friel & Fab. Furies - Fort Lauderdale
          USA/Johnny Come Home (Joker 1009)

6309/10   Wayne Cochran - Last Kiss/Funny Feeling
          (Gala 117)

7011/12   Betty Jayne - Dreamy/Dudley (Carellen 112)

7013/14   Charles Vickers - Little Sally
          Walker/Friendly Advice (Carellen 111)

8279/80   Billy Jones - The More I See You/Teenager's
          Dream (Carellen 7)

8527/28   Jimmy Simms Thunderbirds - Twistin On
          The Beach/Shuffle Twist (Peppermint
          34542/3) (62)

8911/12   Charles Vickers - Are Ya For Me Or Agin'
          Me/He's My Everything (Carellen 6)

9193/94   Betty Jayne - In The Darkness/Charles
          Vickers - Come On, Baby (Tropical 106)

10825/26 Mary Tippins - You Were Not With
          Me/Charles Vickers - These Two Eyes
          (Staff 101/102)

11883/84 Little Junior & Butler-Aires - Jackie, Don't
          You Weep/That's The Matter With The
          Church Today (Fuller 6438)

12061/62 Lee Hazen - Don't Know A Thing About
Love/Rayna - One More Lesson
(Tropical 108)

12279/80 OFfBeEts - Double Trouble/She Lied
(Tropical 109)

13059/60 Nick Bartell - Temptation/You Are
Beautiful (Bart 500)

13383/84 Houston & Dorsey - Wreck Of The John
B./Hootenanny Annie (Carellen 125)

14057/58 Jimmy Roberts - Lonesome Fool/A Passing
Love Affair (Venus 520)

14539/40 Nightcrawlers - Cry/Marie (Lee 101)

14731/32 Charles Conlon - When God Come To
Call/Charles Vickers - He'll Understand
(Tropical 112)

15033/34 Brock McCoy - Way Down In Southern
Florida/This Feeling In My Heart
(Venus 521)

15626/27 Rayna - The Bank Of Love/Lee Hazen - My
Love For You Has Come Back Again
(Tropical 116)

17419/20 Laney Jones & Chordvettes - Almost
Persuaded Him/Little Heartthrob
(Tropical no #)

18591/92 Mixed Emotions - I Lied/Marie
(Tropical 18591/92)

18803/04 Ron Fraiser & Consolidations - Summer
With You/Another Girl (Catalina 335)

18993/94 (EP) *Earthmen & Charles Vickers*
(National Guild 101)

19063/64 2/3rds - All Cried Out/2/3 Baby (April 101)

19067/68 Newports - Life Must Go On/Feelin' Low
(Zebb 155)

19453/54 Reason Why - Sweetest One Around/One
More Time (Strike 001)

19493/94 Hoss & His Hammond - What Now My
         Love/There Will Never Be Another You
         (Coe West 001)

20297/98 Earthmen - Back Again-I Want Me A Purty
         Woman/Charles Vickers - Sad Sad
         Memories-Everyone Has A Heartache
         (National Guild EP 102)

20323/24 Surftones - Secret Admirer/Charles
         Vickers - Mammy Lou (Tropical 124)

20493/94 Deadbeats - Trust Me/Can't Go On This
         Way (Coe West 002)

20837/38 Guy Williams - I Cried Over You/Foolin'
         Around (Romano no #)

20901/02 Charles Vickers - Where Do The Teardrops
         Go?/I'm Trying To Believe I'm Through
         (Tropical 125)

20999/21000 Enalpria - You Keep Me Hanging On/
             Purple Haze (Moonport 100)

21329/30 Brewed - Lifeless Love/State Of Mind
         (Tropical 126)

21783/84 Wally Cosgren - I'll Hold You In My
         Heart/Blue, Stay Away From My Door
         (WABR no #)

21785/86 Mary Tippins - You're My
         Necessity/Surftones - So Long Blues,
         Hello Love (National Guild)

22915/16 Mark & Clark Seymour - (LP) *From The
         Inside Out* (Twin Co. 521/2)

23039/40 Bobby Williams & Mar Kings - Darling,
         Here Is My Heart/All The Time
         (Tropical 130)

23713/14 Houston & Dorsey - Little Conch
         Train/Key West (Key West no #)

24963/64 Pancho & Cherie - Danny Boy/El Rancho
         Grande (Tropical 146)

25089/90 Roger Hamilton & Odds & Ends - I'm A
          Mojo Man/Something's Wrong
          (Tropical 147)

25185/86 Pat Henry - (LP) *Lookin' For A Free-Way*
          (Sundi 6801)

25529/30 Buddy DeLaney With Candy Soupe - Girl/I
          Love That Girl (De-Shane no #)

25887/88 Whipperdoos - Playback/Daytona Beach
          (Tropical 154)

26303/04 Charles Vickers - I've Got A Mind (To Keep
          On Running)/I'm Gonna Take That Long,
          Long Journey (Lord Of Lords 0101)

27187/88 Enalpria - Speed Limit/Sliding
          (Ron Sound 128)

A few later-'70s releases:

29961/62 Blackfoot - That Ain't The Way It Is/And
          You (Blackfoot 29961/62)   (8-3-72)

32157/58 Strange - A Thousand Miles From
          Nowhere/Annihilation (Outer Galaxie 102)
          (1973!)

35487/88 Whipperdoos - Let Freedom Ring!/Charles
          Vickers - How Many Times? (Tropical 208)

36101/02 Avolanche - You Know My Love/Good Seed
          (Big A 006)

36217/18 Charles Vickers - An April Fool/I'm Lonely
          (Pyramid 1003)   (1976)

36219/20 Charles Vickers - Swamp Angel/For Your
          Love (Pyramid 1002)   (1976)

40255/56 Ronnie-D - Office Lounge/Hey Lawdy
          Mama (Tropical 217)   (4-2-79)

QCA

Three small initials resulting in scores of dynamite
records, most of which captured the edge of psychedelia as

it gyrated across garages from Youngstown to your town. QCA, like Rite, was/is based in Cincinnati and attracted some wildly whacked-out clients. Bands such as the Live Wires, Nomads, Temple Of The Barons, and loads of Ohio acts, ranging from Blues Inc., to The Daze Ends.

Florida wasn't left out, but it came awfully close. Outside of Yak and Terry Brooks & Strange (both from the Orlando area), you won't find many Florida QCA releases. But here's the news that will cure your blues: the first number in the mastering code tells you the year when the particular platter climbed off its ladder. So in the case of the Yak, #90868 means a 1969 release. Terry Brooks & Strange's "Jimi" saw the light of day in 1973, judging from its 305322 number. QCA's best-known release was a dreadful Elvis eulogy called "Elvis Has Left The Building" by Felton Jarvis. Years later, magic records by the Magic Sounds, Crystal Rain, and Cole & The Embers have also left the building, so don't expect QCA to ever sound as good as those days when the Yak yakety-yaked their way into vinyl vaults.

Still, if you love mid-'60s gems (and you wouldn't be reading this if you didn't), look out for QCA pressings with numbers beginning with 5, 6, 7, 8, or 9. Otherwise, you might find yourself caught out in the Crystal Rain!

31

COVER ME!

["Cover" versions — remakes, updates, and the like — of songs first recorded by Florida acts; all by artists from OUTSIDE the state... artists who knew a good thing when they heard it!]

A WOMAN WILL DO WRONG - Esther Phillips
  (Atlantic 2783)
  Dee Dee Sharpe (Atco 6576)
  Irma Thomas (Chess 2017)
  [Originally recorded by Helene Smith.]

BIG CITY MISS RUTH ANN - Gallery (Sussex 248.
  Also on the LP *Gallery*, Sussex 7017.)
  Freddie Leigh King (Lancelot 04)
  [Originally recorded by the Heroes Of Cranberry
  Farm.]

BLACK JACKET WOMAN - Yorkshire Puddin
  (Dellwood 1)
  Zone V (Caravan 21449)
  [Written for the Tropics by St. Petersburg college
  student Rick Swain.]

BUON NATALE - Nat King Cole (Capitol 4301)
  [Co-written by the late Miami studio owner Frank
  Linale, and first performed by Sonny Bloch's
  Coralairs — the vocal group that included future
  disc jockey/TV host Arnie Warren.]

CAN'T STOP LOVING YOU - Wild Prophets
(Kustom 1001)
[Originally recorded by the Last Word.]

CHILLS AND FEVER - Teacho (Okeh 7234)
[Originally recorded by Paul Kelly.]

EL ULTIMO BESO (LAST KISS) - Los Americans
(from the LP *Exitos Del Rock And Roll*, Disma 8460,
Mexico.)
Polo (from the LP *Inolvidables En Ritmo*, Eco
25725, Mexico.)
[Originally recorded by Wayne Cochran. Also see
"LAST KISS."]

FOLLOW ME BACK TO LOUISVILLE - Heather
(Chatham 0002)
[Originally recorded by We The People.]

GET DOWN WITH IT - King Midas & Mufflers
(Chrome 104)
Tradewinds Five, Inc. (Franklin 6179. Also
released in Germany on Ariola 14098.)
[Made famous by Wayne Cochran.]

GIRL I GOT NEWS FOR YOU - Aesop's Fables
(Atco 6508)
Cherokee (ABC 11304)
Iron Brigade Quickstep (Decca 32854)
Mardi Gras (Map City 303)
[All of the above covers are closer in style to Benny
Latimore's bluesy rendition than the Birdwatchers'
1966 original. The Mardi Gras release was the
most successful version, rising all the way to
number two in France in October, 1970.]

GIRLS CAN'T DO WHAT THE GUYS DO - Judy White
(Buddah 62)
[Originally recorded by Betty Wright.]

GOIN' BACK TO MIAMI - Blues Brothers (Atlantic
3802. Also on the LPs *Made In America*, Atlantic
16025, and *Best Of*, Atlantic 19331.)
Chris Owens (from the LP *An Evening With Chris*

Owens, Watch 80901.)
Spectacle (Fish 2353)
Spirit Of St. Louis (Philips 40545)
Dave Taylor & Clique (Zodiac Intl. 339. Also on
the LP *Miami To Las Vegas*,
Zodiac Intl. Aquarius 1.)
Unchained Mynds (released on three different
labels: Trans- Action 705, Teen Town 109, and
Buddah 111.)
[Originally recorded by Wayne Cochran.]

HERE COMES THE PAIN/SUMMERTIME BLUES -
Shandells (Studio City 1037)
["Here Comes The Pain" was written and first
recorded by the Legends — who also recorded a
version of "Summertime Blues."]

HEY HIGH SCHOOL BABY - Tav Falco's Panther
Burns (from the LP *Behind The Magnolia Curtain*,
Frenzi 4000/Rough Trade US 16.)
[Originally recorded by Benny Joy.]

HOLD ON I"M COMIN' - Fontella Bass (Gusto 9022)
Cliff Bennett (Parlophone 5466, UK)
Sharon Benson (Malaco 12" 2100)
Bette Bright & Illuminations (Radar 18, UK)
Casinos (from the LP *Then You Can Tell Me
Goodbye*, Fraternity 719.)
Checkmates (from the LP *Live At Caesar's Palace*,
Capitol 2840.)
Child (from the LP *Child*, Jubilee 8029.)
Bob Dobyne & Barefacts (Crown Ltd. 120)
Aretha Franklin (from the LP *Love All The Hurt
Away*, Arista 8146.)
Johnny Gee & Gee Men (Nu-Child 102)
Greenmen (JR 91166)
Haunted (as part of the song "Horror Show")
Heartbreakers (Tomi 119)
Instincts (from the LP *Loving Sandwich Live*, TCS
3952)
Chuck Jackson & Maxine Brown (Wand 1148)

Python Lee Jackson (CBS 221385, Australia)
Waylon Jennings & Jerry Reed (RCA 13580. Also
on the LP *Waylon And Company*, RCA 4826.)
Jon & Robin (from the LP *The Soul Of A Boy And
Girl*, Abnak 2068.)
Tom Jones (from the LP *Fever Zone*, Parrot
61019/71019.)
King Curtis (from the LP *Plays The Great Memphis
Hits*, Atco 211.)
Billy Larkin & Delegates (World Pacific 77844.
Also on the LP *Hold On*, World Pacific 1850.)
Dave Lewis (from the LP *MMM MMM MMM*, First
American 7733.)
Lively Ones (from the LP *Bugalo Party*,
MGM 4449.)
Mammals (from the LP *Nobody But Me*,
Gateway 3012.)
Herbie Mann (Atlantic 2661. Also on the LPs
Memphis Underground, Atco 1522, and *Glory Of
Love*, A&M 9-3003.)
Mauds (Dunwich 160 & Mercury 72694)
Tracy Nelson (from the LP *Come See About Me*,
Flying Fish 209.)
Paul Nero (from the LP *Soul Party*, Liberty 7586.)
Pied Pipers (WAM 5948)
Fred Ramirez (Warner Bros. 7081)
Doc Rand & Purple Blues (Lance 119)
Righteous Bros. (Verve 10521. Also on the LP
Sayin' Something, Verve 5010.)
Rocky Roberts & Airedales (from the LP *Rocky
Roberts & Airedales*, Brunswick 754133. Also
issued on Durium 9223 in Italy.)
Sarah Simpson (Soul-Po-Tion 105)
Sole Inspiration (Soulsville USA 1003)
Solid Gold (Matawan 5051)
Sonset (from the LP *Discoteca Sonset*,
Hit Parade 007- Mexico.)
Soul Children (Stax 0062. Also on the LP

Chronicle, Stax 4120.)
Steel Wool (White Whale 358)
T-Bones (from the LP *Everyone's Gone To The
Moon*, Liberty 3471/7471.)
Tempters (from the LP *Live*, Am-Cue SLP 2.)
Total Eclipse (from the LP *Symphony For Soul*,
Imperial 9353/12353.)
Spyder Turner (from the LP *Stand By Me*, MGM.)
Victors (Sage 101)
Geno Washington & Ramjam Band (from the UK
LP *Hand Clappin' - Foot Stompin' - Funky Butt -
Live!*.)
Pamela Webb (Liberty 56102)
Wild Thing (from the LP *Partyin'*, Elektra 74059.)
[Originally recorded by Sam And Dave.]

HOW MANY TIMES - Plan 9 (Voxx 1005. Also on the
LP *Frustration*, Voxx 200.007.)
[Originally recorded by the Rovin' Flames.]

HUMMIN' - Magic Plant (Majic-L 519
& Crazy Horse 1311)
[Originally recorded by Sam And Dave. Also see
"You Got Me Hummin'."]

I CAN'T AFFORD TO LOSE HIM - Baby Washington
(Cotillion 44047)
[Originally recorded by Ella Washington.]

I CAN'T STAND UP FOR FALLIN' DOWN - Elvis
Costello (Columbia 11194. Also on Columbia EP
11251 and the LP *Get Happy*, Columbia 36347.)
[Originally recorded by Sam And Dave.]

I TAKE WHAT I WANT - Artwoods (Decca 12384-UK)
Aretha Franklin (from the LP *Aretha Now*,
Atlantic 8186.)
Groov-U (from the LP *The Groov-U On Campus*,
Gateway 3010.)
Night-Dreamers (Frog Death 67-1)
[Originally recorded by Sam And Dave.]

I THANK YOU - Bar-Kays (Volt 4033)
Carnage (from the LP *History Of Syracuse Music,
Volume 5*, Ecelp 21012. Part of a live medley that
also includes "Hold On I'm Coming" and "Soul
Man.")
Four-Um (from the LP *Just Us*, Libra 7 7008.)
Donny Hathaway & June Conquest (Curtom 1971)
Bonnie Raitt (from the LP *The Glow*,
Warner Bros. 3369.)
Valentine Brothers (A&M 2642)
Young Brass (from the LP *Rhythm & Brass*,
Dot 25913.)
ZZ Top (from the LP *DeGuello*, Warner Bros. 3361.)
[Originally recorded by Sam And Dave.]

I WANT TO WALK THROUGH THIS LIFE WITH YOU -
Tiffany (SSS Intl. 836)
[Originally recorded by Ella Washington.]

IN THE PAST - Chocolate Watchband (from the LP
The Inner Mystique, Tower 5106.)
[Originally recorded by We The People.]

IT'S A WONDER - Human Beans
(Columbia 8230, UK)
Python Lee Jackson (CBS 221425, Australia)
O'Hara's Playboys (from the LP *Get Ready!*,
Fontana 67581.)
Geno Washington & Ramjam Band (from the UK
album *Hipsters, Flipsters, Fingerpoppin' Daddies*.)
[Originally recorded by Sam And Dave.]

LAST KISS - Mike Hogan & Microwave (Le Cam 330)
Wednesday (Sussex 507)
J. Frank Wilson & Cavaliers (originally issued on
Josie 923. Reissued in various forms on Vertigo
506, Eric 130, and Charay 13, the latter as "Last
Kiss '69." This top-two hit also inspired an album
entitled *Last Kiss* on Josie 4006.)
[Originally recorded by Wayne Cochran.]

LET'S CALL IT A DAY GIRL - Bobby Vee (Liberty
    56124)
    [Originally recorded by the Razor's Edge.]

THE LITTLE BLACK EGG - Buckeye Boys
    (Allied no # - demo)
    Bebe Buell (from the EP *Covers Girl*,
    Rhino RNEP 600.)
    Conchords (AGA 102266)
    Creations (Hull 1067)
    Forgotten Tymes (Night Owl 678)
    Fourth Amendment (4 Sons 16801)
    Kommotions (on the compilation album
    Ear-Piercing Punk, Trash 0001.)
    Wayne Lacadisi (Bell 630)
    Jamie Lyons (Laurie 3409)
    Marquis (from Hillside LP 1, an untitled 1966
    sampler of Ohio bands.)
    Music Explosion (Attack 1404 & Laurie 3500)
    Next Five (Destination 637)
    Tone Benders (from the LP *Northland Battle Of
    The Bands*, Magnetic.)
    [Originally recorded by the Nightcrawlers. You'll
    even find this classic on the Chant's 1985 release,
    Three Sheets To The Wind on the local Safety Net
    label.]

L.O.D. (LOVE ON DELIVERY) - Lenne & The Lee
    Kings (Gazell C-173, Sweden)
    The Lee Kings (Gazell EP-68, Sweden. Also on the
    Swedish LP *Stop The Music*, Grand Prix 9911.)
    [Originally recorded as a demo by Rayna Leggett,
    at Bob Quimby's DeLand studio.]

LOVE CAN MAKE YOU HAPPY - Ray Bloch Singers
    (from the LP *Love Can Make You Happy*,
    Ambassador 98085.)
    California Poppy Pickers (from the LP *Today's
    Chart Busters*, Alshire 5163.)
    [Originally recorded by Mercy.]

MARLBORO COUNTRY - Charlie Pickett & The Eggs
(from the 12" EP *COWBOY JUNKIE AU GO GO*,
Open Big 2.)
[Originally recorded by Charlie's cousin, Mark
Markham, with the Jesters. I know Charlie's a
Florida artist, but since this record isn't listed
elsewhere, and since it's so good, I figured I'd
make this one exception!]

NO MORE PAIN - Champells (Pacific 1001)
[Originally recorded by Sam And Dave.]

PART OF YOUR LOVE - Daydreams (Dial 4029)
[Originally recorded by Clarence Reid.]

PURPLE HEART - Free Fare (Showcase 1001)
[Originally recorded by Noah's Ark.]

RIDE CAPTAIN RIDE - Spitfire (Sonic 221)
[Originally recorded by Blues Image.]

SAID I WASN'T GONNA TELL NOBODY - The Gruve
(Liberty 56034)
[Originally recorded by Sam And Dave.]

SAME OL' BEAT - Teacho & The Students
(Okeh 7234)
[Originally recorded by Freddy Scott.]

SANDCASTLES - Merrilee Rush (from the LP *Angel
Of The Morning*, Bell 6020.)
[Originally recorded by the 31st Of February.]

SHE'S MY BABY - Mojo Men (Autumn 27 & Reprise
0486. Also on the LP *San Francisco Roots*, Vault
119.)
[Originally recorded by Steve Alaimo — whose
cousin Jim was a member of San Francisco's Mojo
Men. Jim Alaimo also recorded under the names
Jimmy Summers and Jimmy Paris.]

SINCERELY YOUR FRIEND - Sheila Ellis (San 1510)
Buddy Miller (Bandbox 223)
Eddy Raven (La Louisianne 8100)
[Originally recorded by Benny Joy.]

SNOOPY VS. THE RED BARON - Chords (Hit 272)
  Hotshots (Mercury 73409)
  Peter Pan Pop Band & Chorus (from the LP
  Snoopy Vs. The Red Baron, Peter Pan 8054.)
  Rolling Dogs (BASF 11858)
  Ventures (from the LP *Guitar Freakout*, Dolton
  2050/8050.)
  [Originally recorded by the Royal Guardsmen.]
SOUL MAN - Bagatelle (from the LP 11 *AM Saturday*,
  ABC 646.)
  Blues Brothers (Atlantic 3545. Also on the LPs
  Briefcase Full Of Blues Atlantic 19217, and *Best
  Of*, Atlantic 19331.)
  Jimmy Brown (Abet 9426)
  Denis Bryant (Discreet 1323)
  Calhoon (Warner-Spector 0407 & Warner-Spector
  12" 45 #PRO 627)
  Drifters (from the LP *Too Hot*, 51 West Q-16242.)
  Five By Five (from the LP *Next Exit*, Paula 2202.)
  John R (USD 1041)
  Kazoos Brothers (from the LP *Circus Royale*,
  Rhino 007.)
  Bob Kuban (Reprise 0937)
  Ramsey Lewis (Cadet 5583. Also on the LPs *Up
  Pops*, Cadet 799, and *Solid Ivory*, Chess 9001.)
  Paul Nero (from the LP *Soul Party*, Liberty 7586.)
  Paul Revere & Raiders (from the LP *Goin' To
  Memphis*, Columbia 2805/9605.)
  Rotary Connection (Cadet Concept 7002. Also on
  the LP *Rotary Connection*, Cadet Concept 312.)
  Shirley, Squirrely, & Melvin (from the LP *Live*,
  Excelsior 88009.)
  Soulovations (Beach Town 1072)
  Young Brass (from the LP *Rhythm & Brass*, Dot
  25913.)
  [Originally recorded by Sam And Dave.]
STOMP - Humming Bird (Agape 9007)
  [Actually the band Chessman Square from St.

Joseph, Missouri. This is the only NRBQ cover listed here since all other known covers are of '70s and '80s tracks.]

STOP! GET A TICKET - Statesmen (Tema 137) [Cleveland, Ohio's legendary Baskerville Hounds also recorded a demo of this Clefs Of Lavender Hill tune.]

WATCHING THE TRAINS GO BY - Tommy Overstreet (Dot 17189) [Originally recorded by Steve Alaimo.]

WHEN SOMETHING IS WRONG WITH MY BABY - Jewel Akens
Jackie Beavers Show (Mainstream 713)
Blue Eyed Soul (Sand City 2101)
Joe Cocker (from the LP Mad Dogs And Englishmen, A&M 6002.)
King Curtis (Atco 6476)
Billy Eckstine (Enterprise 9046)
Johnny Gill (from the LP Johnny Gill, Cotillion 90103.)
Groov-U (from the LP The Groov-U On Campus, Gateway 3010.)
Sonny James (Columbia 10335)
Mauds (Mercury 72750)
Bill Medley (from the LP Soft And Soulful, MGM 4603.)
Otis & Carla (Atco 6665. Also on the LP King And Queen, Stax 716)
Lea Roberts (Minit 32069)
Linda Ronstadt & Aaron Neville (from the LP Cry Like A Rainstorm, Howl Like The Wind, Elektra 60872.)
Joe Stampley
Sweet Inspirations (Atlantic 2418)
Tuane & Rose Mary (RCA 0441)
[Originally recorded by Sam And Dave.]

WRAP IT UP - Eurythmics (from the LP Sweet Dreams, RCA 4681.)

Fabulous Thunderbirds (Columbia 06270. Also on the LP *Tuff Enough*, Columbia 40304.)
[Originally recorded by Sam And Dave.]

THE YELLOW BRICK ROAD - Lemonade Charade (Epic 10216)
[Written, but never released, by We The People's Wayne Proctor. Other Proctor compositions were recorded by Patti Drew and Tom And Jerry.)

YOU DON'T KNOW LIKE I KNOW - Ambertones (White Whale 242)
Changing Tydes Revue (Night Owl 6837)
Chic And The Diplomats (Ivanhoe 500)
Cordells (Casket 50111)
Exceptions (Capitol 2120)
Fabulous Apostles (Shana 097)
Fagan-Williams (Torch 29571)
Peter Frampton (from the LP *Peter Frampton*, A&M 3710.)
Gentry (Venture 133)
H. P. & Grass Route Movement (BBTC 3021)
Catfish Hodge (from the LP *Bout With The Blues*, Adelphi 4126.)
Jimmy James & Vagabonds (from the UK LP *London Swings Live*.)
Koffie (Philips 40554. This is a medley with the song "Get Ready.")
O'Hara's Playboys (from the LP *Get Ready!*, Fontana 67581.)
Pied Pipers (Hamlin Town 2510)
Shady Daze (It's A Gass 6831)
Shirt Tail Relation (Mobie 3432)
Sound System (Worldwide 6767)
Sweet Smoke (Amy 11053)
Tempests (from the LP *Would You Believe*, Smash 27098/67098.)
Traces Of Blue (Artist 2184)
Geno Washington & Ramjam Band (from the UK LP *Hand Clappin' - Foot Stompin' - Funky Butt -*

Live!)

[Originally recorded by Sam And Dave.]

YOU GOT ME HUMMIN' - Cold Blood (San Francisco
60. Also on the LP *Cold Blood*, San Francisco SF
200, and the 4-song EP San Francisco 33091.)
Hassles (United Artists 50215. Also on the LP *The
Hassles*, United Artists 6631. This recording
features pop superstar Billy Joel.)
The Id (Spin EK 1730, Australia)
Kombination (Prestige 338)
Delbert McClinton (from the LP *Wake Up Baby*,
Accord SN- 7145.)
Sandy Nelson (Imperial 66253. Also on the LP
Cheetah Beat, Imperial LP-9340.)
[Originally recorded by Sam And Dave.]

YOUR SUN NEEDS TO SHINE - Lemonade Charade
(Bell 742)
[Another We The People composition that was
never released by that group.]

[NOTE: Cover versions of James & Bobby Purify tunes are
not included, as these were all remakes to begin with. Also
excluded is Fred Neil, the prolific folk artist whose compositions, particularly "Candy Man," "Everybody's Talkin'," "The
Dolphins," and "The Other Side Of This Life," have been
covered by literally over a hundred artists.]

32

DON'T TOUCH THAT DIAL!

Manual typewriters; black and white TVs; AM radios; their obsolescence is assured by our thirst for progress and convenience. Sure, AM radio is kicking and screaming and refusing to die, but then again, so did drive-in movies and roller hamburger joints. Obsolescence is the American way since it keeps us buying new and better products. Well, in radio's case, we'll leave that at newer. In the next few chapters, I'll show you what BETTER really meant.

* * * * * * *

Our perception of the mid-'50s more likely conjures up a teenage heaven than a teenage wilderness: splishing and splashing and rocking 'round the clock. Unfortunately, things weren't always that simple. There would have been trouble in paradise had radio pioneer Todd Storz not breathed top 40 life into WQAM with his incredible epiphany of a 5,000 watt jukebox, live and blasting into your living room. Storz and company rocked first and rocked best in the half-decade or so before WFUN entered the "more music" sweepstakes; a half-decade in which many imitators tried their hand at grabbing the attention of Sweet Little Sixteen.

WAME was one of the the BETTER stations. Prior to its switch to a soul music format, Whammy 1260 Radio rocked to a 60-song playlist (MORE music, remember?); tunes played by the likes of Fred Hohl, Sid Knight, Ted Clark (later of WQAM), and Bruce Bradley. Across town WINZ had *The Late Date Show* and some soon- to-become-legendary voices: Bob Green (Mr. Anita Bryant) and Bruce Morrow (after WINS in New York City, and prior to WABC. "Cousin Brucie" does not remember his Miami days with much affection). In 1961, you could also hear Johnny Bell, Bob Booker, Kirby Brooks, and Lee Taylor of 940 WINZ sailing those time-checks across Biscayne Bay and mixing hot singles with hot jingles until you and the summer sun just had to set in a blaze of red heat. And then there was the early '60s crew at WCKR 610 Radio ("Never a dull minute, and you're really in it"): Rick Shaw (pre-WQAM), the late Biggie Nevins, Buddy Holiday, Pete Connors (pre-WFUN), and Bobby Lyons. Who could forget the "Wacker Buitoni Spaghetti Twist" (or better yet, who can remember it)?

All these small stations were fast forgotten during the great frequency swap of 1961 when WMBM gave up its position on the dial (800 AM), shifting over to WFEC's old 1220 spot. That cleared the way for the brand new WFUN to debut at 790 on the dial — Danny Dark, Pete Connors, Frank Ward, Jim Tucker, Gary Stevens, Bill Deane, and Johnny Gilbert were about to make history on South Miami's amazing new voice. (If those seven names aren't familiar, don't feel bad. All had "returned to sender" by the end of 1962 — a far cry from more stable WQAM where Charlie Murdock ruled the roost for a full eight years — from 1957 to 1965.) WQAM, it should be noted, was among the last stops for legendary deejay Alan Freed, who would prove to be a mere shell of himself during his less-than-spectacular Miami stop.

I've said a lot about WFUN's music and deejays, but what about the earliest "FUNdamental" *news* team? News director Mark Adams, Jay McKay, Terry Parker (actually local talk show host Larry Kent), and Paul Henderson always told us what was going on with tons of reverb, pops, zings, bells, and whistles. News was never so much fun to listen to. It's almost ironic that WFUN would sign off the air for good on January 8, 1976 — only to be replaced by WNWS — an all news and talk station. It was strange for me to work there in 1978, actually operating the old, custom- made WFUN air panel. You'd almost expect the ghost of Dick Starr to appear and order everyone to play Canadian Legends records. WINZ also made the news/talk switch, and somewhere in their halls it would seem appropriate for a ghost or two to lurk around the production room, just waiting to sneak a classic jingle into the control room; or perhaps to pop an old rocker or two in your ear, just for your old Cousin Brucie, you dig?

Our next stop: the mid-'60s.

33

FOR WHOM THE TIGER ROARED

"Snicklefritz." It sounds like something you'd find near the pumpernickel in your local deli, but it's actually a word/sound/name that once had the power to stop a swirling robot. "Maximillian The Mechanical Money Monster" he was called, and every night in September 1965, he came alive on the *Rick Shaw Show* on WQAM. Listeners had no way of knowing Maximillian had no tubes or tin-plated armor and didn't really roam wild within the walls of WQAM. He was simply a distorted voice on a tape cartridge, spitting out prizes one-by-one: a Corning Ware set, a 6-transistor radio. To win, you'd have to say "snicklefritz" while Mechanical Max was listing the available prizes, and the very next words from his tape recorder-tongue would be yours. Five out of six times, it was the infamous 6-transistor radio, which cost the station peanuts, yet, to the average fifth-grade listener was a gift as good as gold.

I was actually a third-grade listener at the time, riding my ferry across the Mersey, getting married to the widow next door (who'd been married seven times before), and looking for that place where the music was fine and the lights were always low. It was for me that "Snicklefritz" sang out, even if it would be ten more years, when Rick Shaw spoke to my freshman broadcasting class, before I'd learn what it really means: "It's just a name my father used when I was a little

346

teeny kid," Shaw recalls. "Just a crazy name he invented that stuck with me all those years."

Maximillian, along with the Beatle Trip to Jacksonville and WQAM Money Matchbooks, were among Rick Shaw's favorite contests from the many the crazy Tiger DJ's took part in. And I do mean crazy.

Like the time disc jockey Ronnie Grant sailed up the Intracoastal Waterway from Miami to Ft. Lauderdale in response to an Irishman's claim that a 13th century monk could have been the first man to sail to America. Ex-WQAM program director Dan Chandler remembers thousands of people lining the bridges with big WQAM banners while 55 powerboats joined in the "Boatercade," all to jokingly show that "a Jewish rabbi could have just as easily brought civilization to America." It was all just good fun in Chandler's words. Life was simpler then, and the games we played made us forget how frightening fractions could be, or how taxing syntax felt, day after day.

We all had our favorite contests and promotions, and Dan Chandler had his: "The Fifth Monkee Contest where Rick Shaw got some friends to stuff the ballot box and narrowly beat me! The Surfari Weekend, where we gave away a woodie, and attracted 25,000 people to the beach on a flat day, when Roby Yonge magically made waves! I don't know how it happened! And Chickenman — Dorsey Harrell — lived in a Volkswagen Coupe painted like a big chicken, sitting on a nest for one week!" No wonder the Tiger roared as loud as it did!

Which is not to say rival station WFUN didn't have ITS share of kooky contests, always enunciated emphatically in a hurried breath, mixed with rapid-fire call letters (as in "WFUN Boss Birthday Brain Time"). Many's the time we'd try to guess which Boss Jock would win the night's Dee Jay Derby, racing down the stretch with the flair and finesse Secretariat would show a decade later. One night Tom Campbell would win. On another, Dick Starr, or maybe Dutch Holland. My sister always picked Mike E. Harvey because she thought he was cute. Who could have known the results were controlled by the man on the air who could pick the winner with the single push of a button? To us, the derby took skill. In reality, it was just more snicklefritz, as was WQAM's "Fortune Phone," in which a lucky listener was phoned at random and offered a chance to win big bucks. If that listener's phone wasn't temporarily disconnected, as more often than not, it seems an operator's voice would drive home the point that yes, once again, no one was home.

Winning was everything, for as Dan Chandler ably noted, "Contests and promotions are the lifeblood of a good rock 'n roll station." So when the WQAM jocks raced their GTO's down the street (Lee Sherwood won) or gave away Tiger Camaros and Mustangs, WFUN had to dig even deeper, giving us "WFUN Win-A- Boss-Dune-Buggy Time." Everything moved faster. Everything felt fresher. When WQAM gave us Chickenman, WFUN had to look for Amazon Ace. When a WFUN jock got married on the air, WQAM had to counter with a fake feud between Rick Shaw and Charlie Murdock, with Shaw pretending to lock himself in the studio all night, defiantly playing nothing but oldies. Of course, it was all planned simply as a way to take the wind out of the competition's wedding ploy. Who could do the most record hops or pep rallies? It really seemed to matter. Whether it was WQAM's Money Matchbooks or WFUN's Icee Bear collecting contest, we took it in and took part in it, and it will always be a part of us.

Gone are the days of "Starr In The Car," "Stop The Music," or spotting the "Eye In The Sky." Gone is the night WFUN's Greggo Warren rode nonstop on a ferris wheel at the Dade County Youth Fair. Or the time WQAM's Jim Dunlap nearly got trampled at the Miami premiere of *A Hard Day's Night* while trying to give away free movie cameras. Or the night WFUN smuggled six containers of helium and balloons into the Miami Beach Convention Center where WQAM was the true, legitimate sponsor of the Monkees/Jimi Hendrix Experience concert. The plan was to release balloons with banners reading "The Monkees Are Coming To Town For FUN," just as Rick Shaw was introducing the band for rival

WQAM. Finally the helium canisters were confiscated — curses, foiled again — and Shaw seized the moment by thanking the Boss Jocks for helping make HIS show a great success. Kind Of A Drag for some — a Little Bit 'O Soul for others. The Kind Of Hush that always kept us Groovin'.

WFUN's Amazon Ace: Chickenman meets the Red Baron!

Years later, on the night WFUN bowed off the air for good, Roby Yonge would praise the Boss Jocks for keeping the Tigers on their toes... and almost kicking their behinds. "WQAM had to spend a quarter of a million dollars on promotion, just to keep up with you guys," he confessed, stating publicly for the first time how WFUN scared his station out of a brief stint with automation and burying the hatchet to the point of calling WFUN "one of America's great radio stations." It was a poignant moment, hearing a Tiger legend praise the competition, after years of pummeling them through ploys and promotions. Yonge's observations couldn't have been more on the money.

So what was it all really about? "At the heart of it all was fun, and at the heart of that fun was the music we all danced to and lived to," says Dan Chandler, in a reflection as "true and accurate" as an old Fab 56 survey. "It was the kind of thing that made you wanna kick off your shoes and dance." Those dances have changed, and so has the music, but outlandish promotions haven't disappeared completely. So maybe we're not "Q'ing In Our Cars" anymore; all it takes is a little jingle jangle, and a lot of imagination to keep our mojos working, whether we're fourteen years old or forty-four.

Rise up and tell your favorite radio station you're tired of coasting. Let them know you want to cook!

34

1960s DISC JOCKEY SCHEDULES

These are the men that helped make it happen — the voices that brought the sound of rock 'n roll to a generation of South Floridians...

WQAM

Early 1962
Don Armstrong
Johnny Prince
Bob Kaye
Bill Holley
Charlie Murdock
(since 8/57)

March 1963
Jerry Goodwin (6-9AM)
Ted Clark (9AM-12 Noon)
Bob Green (12 Noon-3PM)
Charlie Murdock (3-6PM)
Tom Campbell (6-10PM)
Jim Dunlap (1-6AM)

June 1963
Jerry Goodwin (6-9AM)
Ted Clark (9-12N)
Bob Green (12N-3PM)
Charlie Murdock (3-6PM)
Jim Dunlap (6-10PM)
Alan Courtney (Talk)
(10PM-1AM)
Jack Sorbi (1-6AM)

July 1963
Jerry Goodwin (6-9AM)
Ted Clark (9AM-12N)
Bob Green (12N-4PM)
Charlie Murdock (4-7PM)
Jim Dunlap (7-11PM)
Alan Courtney (Talk)
(11PM-2AM)
Jack Sorbi (2-6AM)
(replaced by Lee Sher-
wood, August, 1963.)

352

SAVAGE LOST

October 1963
Lee Sherwood (6-9AM)
Ted Clark (9AM-12N)
Bob Green (12N-4PM)
Charlie Murdock (4-7PM)
Rick Shaw (7-11PM)
Jim Dunlap (2-6AM)
Alan Courtney (Talk)
(11PM-2AM)

Nov. '63/Jan. '64
Lee Sherwood (6-9AM)
Ted Clark (9-12N)
Jerry Goodwin (12N-4PM)
Charlie Murdock (4-7PM)
Rick Shaw (7-11PM)
Alan Courtney
(11PM-2AM) (Talk)
Jim Dunlap (2-6AM)

March 1964
Lee Sherwood (6-9AM)
Ted Clark (9-12N)
Jim Dunlap (12N-4PM
since Feb.)
Charlie Murdock (4-7PM)
Rick Shaw (7-11PM)
Jack Sorbi (2-6AM)
(Also Ron King in May, 1964)

October 1964
Lee Sherwood (6-9AM)
Ted Clark (9-12N)
Jim Dunlap (12N-4PM)
Charlie Murdock (4-7PM)
Rick Shaw (7-11PM)
Jack Sorbi (2-6AM)
Bill Winters (Weekends)
Jack Sorbi exits after October. Roby Yonge enters
January, 1965. Charlie
Murdock exits July, 1965.

July 1965
Roby Yonge (6-9AM)
Ted Clark (9AM-12N)
Jim Dunlap (12N-4PM)
Lee Sherwood (4-7PM)
Rick Shaw (7-11Pm)
Mac Allen (2-6AM)
Bill Winters (Weekends)
Stu Bowers (Sundays)
Lee Vogel (talk) (11PM-2AM)
Steve Clark replaces
Ted Clark in September, 1965.

November 1965
Roby Yonge (6-9AM)
Steve Clark (9AM-12N)
Jim Dunlap (12N-3PM)
Lee Sherwood (3-6PM)
Rick Shaw (6-9PM)
Stu Bowers (9-11PM)
Mac Allen (2-6AM)
Lee Vogel (talk) (11PM-2AM)

February 1966
Lee Sherwood (6-9AM)
Steve Clark (9AM-12N)
Jim Dunlap (12N-3PM)
Roby Yonge (3-6PM, 9-11PM)
Rick Shaw (6-9PM)
Mac Allen (2-6AM)
Stu Bowers
(Sunday, 12N-6PM)
Lee Vogel (talk) (11PM-2AM)

March 1966
Same as above with
John Powers doing
6-9PM Sunday.
Dan Chandler replaces
Steve Clark.

October 1966
Roby Yonge (6-9AM)
Dan Chandler (9AM-12N)
Jim Dunlap (12N-3PM)
Lee Sherwood (3-6PM)
Rick Shaw (6-9PM)
John Powers (9-11PM)
Mac Allen (2-6AM)
Lee Vogel (talk) (11PM-2AM)

February 1967
Roby Yonge (6-9AM)
Dan Chandler (9AM-12N)
Jim Dunlap (12N-3PM)
Lee Sherwood (3-6PM)
Rick Shaw (6-9PM)
Johnny Knox (9-11PM)
Tom Adams (2-6AM)

August 1967
Jim Dunlap (6-9AM)
(since June)
Dan Chandler (9AM-12N)
Roby Yonge (12N-3PM)
Lee Sherwood (3-6PM)
Rick Shaw (6-9PM)
Johnny Knox
Clarke Moore
Tom Adams (2-6AM)
Roby Yonge leaves October, 1967.

April 1968
Jim Dunlap (6-9AM)
Dan Chandler (9AM-12N)
Tom Tyler (12N-3PM)
Lee Sherwood (PD)
Rick Shaw
Clarke Moore
Johnny Knox

October 1968
Jim Dunlap (6-10AM)
Ronnie Grant (10AM-2PM)
Johnny Knox Gold Reserve
(2-3PM)
Rick Shaw &
Johnny Knox (3-9PM)
John Paul Roberts
(9PM-1AM)
Clarke Moore (1-6AM)
Dan Chandler (PD)

May 1969
Jim Dunlap (6-10AM
through July, 1978)
Ronnie Grant(10AM-2PM)
Rick Shaw (2-6PM)
Johnny Knox (6-9PM)
John Paul Roberts
(9PM-1AM)
Clarke Moore (1-6AM)
Dan Chandler (PD)

October 1969
Exactly the same as May
with Dan Chandler also doing 10AM- 2PM Saturday.

WFUN DISC JOCKEY SCHEDULES

1961
Danny Dark (6-9AM)
Pete Connors (9AM-12 Noon)
Frank Ward (12 Noon-3PM)
Jim Tucker (3-6PM)
Gary Stevens (6-9PM)
Bill Deane (9-12 Mid)
Johnny Gilbert (12 Mid-6AM)

May 1962
Jack Purrington (6-9AM)
Ted Clark (9AM-12 Noon)
Bruce Bartley
(12 Noon-3PM)
Jim Howell (3PM-6PM)
Johnny Gilbert
(6PM-9PM)
Greg Warren (9-12 Mid)
Mitch Price (12 Mid-6AM)

1963
Jack Purrington (6-9AM)
Bob Gordon (9AM-12 Noon)
Dick Starr (12 Noon-3PM)
(since Jan.)
Jim Howell (3-6PM)
Bill Holley (6-9PM)
Greggo Warren
(9PM-12 Mid)
Rock Robbins (12 Mid-6AM)

August 1964
Jim Howell
Al Dunaway
Dick Starr
Bill Holley
Greg Warren
Jimmy Bey (all night)

Oct.-Dec. 1964
Jim Howell (6-9AM)
Al Dunaway (9AM-1PM)
Dick Starr (1-4PM)
Bill Holley (4-7PM)
Greg Warren (7-11PM)
Mac Allen (all night)
Jack Wilder (weekends)
Dave Archard (weekends)

April 1965
Jim Howell (6-9AM)
Davey O'Donnell
(9AM-12 Noon)
Dick Starr (12 Noon-3PM)
Doc Downey (3-7PM)
(since January)
Dutch Holland
(7PM-12 Mid)
Jesse James (12 Mid-6AM)
Jack Wilder (weekends)

May 1965
SAME, except:
Jim Howell (5-9AM)
Jesse James (12Mid-5AM)
(Doc Downey quits in
controversy, 7/65.)
(Dutch Holland's hours
in 8/65; 6-11PM)

October 1965
Davey O'Donnell (6-9AM)
Jim Howell (9AM-12 Noon)
Dutch Holland
(12 Noon-4PM)
Dick Starr (4-7PM)
Tom Campbell (7PM-12
Mid) Jack Armstrong (12
Mid-6AM)

April 1966
Same as above with
Mike E. Harvey
(12 Mid-6AM) replacing
Jack Armstrong.

August 1966
Bob Gordon (6-9AM)
Jim Howell (9AM-12 Noon)
Dutch Holland
(12 Noon-4PM)
Dick Starr (4-7PM)
Mike E. Harvey
(7PM-12 Mid)

Oct.-Nov. 1966
Bob Gordon (6-9AM)
Jim Howell (9AM-12Noon)
Jerry Smithwick
(12 Noon-4PM)
Dick Starr (4-7PM)
Mike E. Harvey (7PM-12 Mid)
Johnny Summer (12 Mid-6AM)

March thru Oct. 1967
Chris Edwards (6-9AM)
Jim Howell (9AM-12 Noon)
Bob Gordon (12 N-4PM)
Dick Starr (4-7PM)
Mike Harvey (7PM-12 M)
Stephen W. Morgan (12
Mid-6AM)

November 1967
Chris Edwards (5-9AM)
Bob Gordon (9AM-12 Noon)
Jim Howell (12 Noon-3PM)
Dick Starr (3-6PM)
(through 1/26/68)
Mike E. Harvey (6-11PM)
Stephen W. Morgan
(11PM-5AM)
Andy Winston (weekends)

March 1968
Bob Gordon (6-9AM)
Jack Merker
(9AM-12 Noon) (PD)
Jim Howell (12 Noon-3PM)
Mike E. Harvey (3-6PM)
Jay Mack (6-9PM)
Stephen W. Morgan
(9PM-12 Mid)
Bob Rado (12 Mid-6AM)
Pete Berlin (weekends)
(since Dec.,1967) (Berlin
also worked the 9PM-12
Mid shift for a while.)

May 1968
Bob Gordon (6-9AM)
Michael W. Morgan
(9AM-12 Noon)
Bob Rado (12 Noon-3PM)
Mike E. Harvey (3-6PM)
Jay Mack (6-9PM)
Big Bob Baker (9PM-1AM)
(Newsman Ken Scott did the
1-6AM shift in June; Gary
Nelson took over in July.)

August 1968
Bob Gordon (6-9AM)
Michael W. Morgan
(9AM-12 Noon)
Jay Mack (12 Noon-3PM)
Mike E. Harvey (3-6PM)
Jack Armstrong (6-9PM)
Jon Fox (9PM-1AM) (since
July)
Gary Nelson (1-6AM)

October 1968
Same as above except:
Bob Gordon (5-9AM)
Jon Fox (9PM-12 Mid)
Jerry Peterson (12 Mid-5AM)
replacing Gary Nelson

January 1969
Bob Gordon (5-9AM)
Michael W. Morgan
(9AM-12 Noon)
Jack Armstrong
(12 Noon-3 PM)
Mike E. Harvey (3-6PM)
Jon Fox (6-9PM)
Jerry Peterson (9PM-1AM)
Bobby Holiday (1-5AM)

January 1969 *(Continued)*
(Denney Murray also worked 1-5AM for a very short time.)

May 1969
Bob Gordon (6-9AM)
Larry Dean (9-12 Noon)
Jack Armstrong
(12 Noon-3PM)
Mike E. Harvey (3-6PM)
Bill Barry (6-9PM)
(AKA Don Wright)
Jerry Peterson (9PM-1AM)
Bobby Holiday (1-6AM)

July 1969
Bob Gordon (6-9AM)
Larry Dean (9AM-12 Noon)
Jack Armstrong (12 Noon-3PM)
Mike E. Harvey (3-6PM)
Jerry Peterson (6-9PM)
Don Wright (9PM-12 Mid)
Gary Allen (weekends)

December 1969
Bob Gordon (6-9AM)
Larry Dean (9AM-12 Noon)
Tom Kennington
(12 Noon-4PM)
Mike E. Harvey (4-7PM)
Don Wright (7PM-12 Mid)
Gary Allen (12 Mid-6AM)

July 1970
Bob Gordon (6-9AM)
(replaced 1/71 by Richard Ward Fatherley)
Larry Dean (9AM-12 Noon)
Tom Kennington (12 Noon-3PM) (PD)
Mike E. Harvey (3-7PM)
Don Wright (7PM-12 Mid)
(Wright eventually replaced Kennington as program director and remained with WFUN until the bitter end, 1/8/76.)
Alan Sands (12 Mid-6AM)
Greg Dunne (weekends)

The WFUN Boss Jocks in December, 1966: Front Row: Dick Starr, Jerry Smith-wick, Bob Gordon, Jim Howell. Back Row: Johnny Summer (Actually WQAM's Johnny Knox!), Mike E. Harvey.

35

THE LIVERPOOL LOUDMOUTH

THE FALL AND RISE OF
MORTON DOWNEY, JR.

Smoke fills the stage, but not the dry ice variety you find at oh-so-many rock concerts. Some of this smoke is coming from the cigarette it seems the acid-tongued host never ever puts down, while the rest seems to be osmotically flowing from the heads of feminists and their foes, Guardian Angels and their adversaries, or right-to-lifers and those convinced they're wrong. Tonight the topic could be pornography, politics, or even the Pope. The rhetoric will include four-letter words, some choice five-letter words, and spicy syllogism the audience will never hear over the censor beeps. But then again, beeps and bleeps are nothing new to the show's host, who two-and-a-half decades ago was virtually run out of Miami over a censored single and a territorial battle of the airwaves that remains perhaps the nastiest ever seen in South Florida.

Back then, no one could have possible known there would ever be a syndicated *Morton Downey, Jr. Show*, soaring via satellite from coast to coast. Heck, few of us knew of satellites beyond what Huntley & Brinkley told us on their nightly reports. Back then we cared more about our six-transistor radios, tucked under our pillows at low, low volume, so Mom and Dad wouldn't know we'd rather hear the Searchers than go to sleep. In between commercials for Aktex ("Hi, we're Bocky & The Visions"), or Coca Cola ("Hi, we're Wayne Fontana & The Mindbenders"), or everybody's favorite, Great Shakes (featuring a ferocious blast of beautiful noise from the likes of the Who and the Yardbirds), there was no way we could put our radios down. Damn, the commercials were every bit as good as the latest records from Liverpool, London, or the group living down the street. And those jingles, "Tiger Radio Swings!" "More fun, more music!" Yeah, teenage heaven was a place on earth, and it was yours 24 hours a day for the mere price of a battery. Our radios took us Downtown, gave us Satisfaction, made it Just A Little Bit Better, All Day and All Of The Night. She's in love with me, and yeah, it sure felt fine.

April of 1965, the top hits around the nation included "Ticket To Ride," "Mrs. Brown You've Got A Lovely Daughter," "I'm Telling You Now," and "Game Of Love," all by English artists. But it didn't take an oracle to know the odyssey of American acts was starting to crystallize in a big way. April, 1965, also saw the coming of "She's About A Mover" by the Sir Douglas Quintet, "Land Of 1,000 Dances" by Cannibal & The Headhunters, and that tortilla-twisting classic by Sam The Sham & The Pharaohs, "Wooly Bully." In South Florida it also brought the chart debut of "Just In Case" by the Canadian Legends, those transplanted Milwaukeeans who just a year earlier packed everything up and headed south for Miami, never passing "Go" until they reached what was then the apex of vacation spots, Miami Beach. The Canadian Legends were still very young, but not to the many high school students who watched them play. To them, the Legends were "pros," too musically proficient to even think about competing in the Battle Of The Bands (which, of course, belonged to teenagers, right?). The Legends even had a regional midwest number one hit way back in the (gasp?) **early** '60s. So if the average 15-year-old guitarist couldn't identify with the Canadian Legends, he could at least emulate them and try to duplicate their unprecedented success.

And that's where a 32-year-old man with a 320-RPM brain enters the picture.

Sean Morton Downey, Jr., was born into a show business family. His mother, Barbara Bennett, was an actress; his father, a well-known tenor whose voice warbled in tune with Paul Whiteman's Orchestra. But blood isn't always thicker than venom. Downey Senior would not tolerate his son's attempts to share the family thunder, and ruthlessly fought it tooth and nail, often with a heart of stone. Downey Junior wasn't looking for trouble when he wrote a poem about his parents' marital problems ("Money Marbles & Chalk"); still, he was dragged to a psychiatrist. When he sang "Boulevard Of Broken Dreams" (his first recording) on Dick Clark's TV Show, he was told by his father that he "sounded off key." But despite all the parental discouragement, the younger Downey's **dreams** wouldn't break. For years he recorded teenage melodramas; lightweight, often moribund pap such as "The Ballad Of Billy Brown," which told the story of the shocking death of a high school hotshot. Few radio programmers noticed "Billy Brown" when it first appeared in 1961 (even though it was produced by singer Johnny Burnette), so Downey decided to take matters into his own hands. Four years later, he played the record **himself**, while rocking Miami from the studios of Boss Radio WFUN. "A screaming, ranting, raving disc jockey" (his words) was born.

Downey fine-tuned his fast-talking announcing style at WONE in Dayton, Ohio, where he worked double duty as Morton Downey, Jr., in the daytime, and "Doctor D." at night — the latter persona evolving into "Doc" Downey by the time he'd found his way to South Florida. WFUN and Doc Downey would come together for a mere seven months; 29 turbulent weeks of intense acrimony and clashing egos that would end with innocent lives dangerously disrupted in the darkest hour of an otherwise resplendent radio rivalry.

It all started when a group of shaggy Southwest High boys refused to cut their hair. Two days earlier, Gregory Shaw, drummer for the Shaggs, was forced to trim his long locks by order of Southwest Principal E. Hugh Allsworth, and now the edict had been issued for the members of another of the school's growing rock 'n roll bands. The Montells they called themselves, and their mission, it seemed, was to shake up the squares, taking every moment to its maximum maximum.

If the Montells walked into a restaurant, it was a safe bet that a food fight wouldn't be too far behind. Lead singer Carter Ragsdale, in particular, struck terror into the hearts of waitresses everywhere, especially at the old Pizza Palace on Bird Road, where a collective groan could be heard when these five moptops entered the building! Later the Montells would cause a stir with their clothes (Drummer Jeffrey Allen tried in vain to wear a Nazi uniform on stage) and just about anything unconventional they could try as long as it put them on the cutting edge, in the music they played, in how they played it, and with an attitude that never failed to turn the kids on and the adults off.

But not the deejays at WFUN. The Montells' Jeffrey Allen and George Walden used to spend hour after wondrous hour at the old South Miami studios, often staying all night to watch announcer Jesse James in action (when Allen and Walden weren't sneaking in to see the movie *Blood Feast*, which they must have watched together two dozen times). But most of the time, it was their fellow teens watching **them** at the old Police Athletic Bandstand building, where a Friday night dance became a trip upon a magic swirling ship — and you didn't even need drugs for your senses to be enlightened. Oh, that music: gnashing, smashing, not-fade- away ferocity, melting with the night humidity in a glorious state of rhythm and raunch, coming at you with a Marshall amp attack that could even shake the horses at nearby Tropical Park.

If the Montells had it above the other local bands at the time (and they did), it was their uncanny perception of what was about to be big — before it happened. As previously mentioned, drummer Jeffrey Allen visited England several times to check out the club scene (watching in person bands such as the Pretty Things, the Poets, the Who, and the

Fairies), and of course, no trip would be complete without exciting new English releases to bring back home. Imagine the amazement of their fellow high schoolers when the Montells introduced "Gloria," "Little Red Rooster," and countless other tunes that their classmates (mere mortals) hadn't heard before. Sweet dreams are made of this.

It was May of 1965, and a revolution was shaking; an evolution of sound and fury. Gone was the notion of bands being required to wear suits on stage. Forget those tied-to-the-office- looking ties. The time had come to let freedom ring, and baby let your hair hang down. In this spirit, the Montells entered Dukoff Studios to record four songs; one, "Watch Out For That Guy," sounded more like Herman's Hermits than the Montells' usual British mod/R & B influences. Two others, "I Can't Explain," and "For Your Love," were virtually unknown at the time, but would soon ring out on radios by their original artists (as they had in England just prior). Then there was "Don't Bring Me Down," an obscure Pretty Things song that owed more to Bo Diddley than it did to the Beatles (but then again, would there have been a British invasion without Bo and his Bros?). Carter Ragsdale didn't bother to copy down the lyrics, instead ad libbing in the studio (including the clearly-articulated, much-repeated line "and when I laid her on the ground"). Something clicked like a Kodak in Doc Downey's brain the first time he heard the finished product. He wasted no time in rushing "Don't Bring Me Down" onto his radio show and told the boys "I'm going to make you as big as the Canadian Legends." It was an offer no teenage musician could possibly turn down. But as Morton Downey, Jr., and the Montells entered into their fateful alliance, their rolling stone would soon gather more than just moss — and what started as careless whispers, would soon become nothing less than headline news.

If you lived in Miami in the summer of 1965, you know about the infamous censor beeps that became as much a part of the record's sound as George Walden's guitar solo. Some claim Downey added the beeps in appropriate places to calm protests about the "lay" lyrics; other say it was merely a ploy to boost sales by making buyers have to flip the record over to hear the true lyrics. Nevertheless, "Don't Bring Me Down" first hit WFUN's "Official Top 40 Survey" on June 13, 1965, debuting at the very bottom — but not for long.

Beep beep! **The Montells'** fortunes were forever changed by a fast-talking Miami deejay. Even a name change (to **Her Majesty's Subjects**) couldn't set them free. *Concert flyer courtesy Jeffrey Allen*

The Montells (then sporting the more British-sounding moniker "Her Majesty's Subjects") found themselves with a platter pulling in no fewer requests than "Help Me Rhonda," "I Can't Help Myself," "Seventh Son," or even "I'm Henry VIII, I Am," which Downey played as an album cut while Herman's Hermits were still riding high with "Wonderful World." (Jeffrey Allen recalls the time Downey played "Henry VIII" for one full hour, back-to-back, with nothing in between.) By June 20, "Don't Bring Me Down" zoomed fourteen points in one week to number 26. By June 27, it was already in the top ten, and by the following week — only its fourth on the chart — it was at number five, trailing only "I'm Henry VIII, I Am" (naturally), "Yes, I'm Ready," "Satisfaction," and "What's New Pussycat," and AHEAD of acts such as Gary Lewis & The Playboys, the Kinks, and the Dave Clark Five. The single sold so fast, a number of white-colored, hand-written labels had to be pressed up according to Allen, who recalls seeing a sign proclaiming "We Have The Montells Record" in the window of one Coral Gables record store!

Anytime a record zooms from 40 to 26 to 10 to 5 in consecutive weeks, you know you're looking at a future number one hit — NOT a song likely to drop to number 34 the following week. But on July 6, 1965, the sky began to fall for Morton "Doc" Downey and his teenage proteges. The storm clouds rolled in quickly, and like a soaked shepherd in the Sudan, no one could do anything to stop the torrential downpour that followed. And it all started with two simple words.

When parents complained about their kids listening to this "dirty record," Downey reportedly went on the air and called them "fuddy duddies; the type who ride around in a horse and buggy!" Well, talk like that didn't end the protests, but fueled them all the way to the desk of South Miami's then-City Manager Richard Barton, who was asked to do something about the Liverpool Loudmouth. It wasn't long before the squabble came to the attention of *The Guide*, a small newspaper which started the snowball rolling. That was on July 7th. The very next day *The Miami Herald* got its two cents in, charging forth with a headline which read "Parents Denounce Suggestive Record." Then somebody (WQAM perhaps?) did a little digging and discovered Downey had a financial interest in the very record he was playing on his radio show... reaping a cool penny-and-a-half for every copy sold. Downey, who had previously condemned announcers who accepted payola, suddenly had a lot of explaining to do. But if it looked like cool cat Downey was finding himself in hot water, this was only the beginning. The real mess was about to hit the fan in a downright dangerous way.

* * * * * *

In the '70s we all learned "you don't mess around with Jim," an offense, according to the hit tune, as bad as "tugging on Superman's cape." Well, Downey spit into the wind in the summer of '65 when he messed around with WQAM's operations manager, and an institution-of-sorts, Charlie Murdock. Downey was intent on dethroning Murdock as top dog in the afternoon ratings race; Murdock, apparently, was just as intent on keeping that from happening. Who fired the first salvo is still unclear all these years later, but WQAM's head honchos were convinced Downey fired first by telling his listeners they could "talk to famous rock stars" if they dialed a certain telephone number. That number belonged to Charlie Murdock.

Listeners, as you'd expect, thinking perhaps Peter Noone, George Harrison, or Mick Jagger might be on the other end of the line, dialed the number night and day. While Murdock and his wife slept. While Mrs. Murdock was ill and badly in need of rest. Finally Murdock took his case before the F.C.C., which reportedly kept the complaint on file, for possible use when WFUN's license came up for renewal.

Downey vehemently denied ever giving out the number, ever making derogatory remarks about Murdock's wife, or knowingly sharing in the profits of the Montells' record. Still, WFUN General Manager Arnold Kaufman thought it in the best interests of everyone involved to suspend Downey from the air while it conducted an "investigation." (No, there were no independent counsels at that time!) Downey also asked that the thousand-or-so copies of "Don't Bring Me Down," just pressed to meet its expected number one ranking on the chart, be embargoed. So the records stayed at a warehouse while WFUN quietly had to let the record die. Instead of 40-26-10-5-1, the Montells had to settle for the crushing chronology 40-26-10-5-34, their record stopped dead in its tracks, and for all intents and purposes, banned from the airwaves for good.

WFUN's investigation took a mere four days; the station's attorneys concluding Downey had no financial interest whatsoever in the doomed disc. Downey returned to his afternoon slot on Monday, July 19, but by Thursday, July 22, he was off the airwaves again. This time it was his choice. The reason: harassment.

"I remember going to Doc Downey's house one day, and it was broken into," recalls Jeffrey Allen. "Ransacked. Things all over the place." Carter Ragsdale, the Montells' vocalist, remembers him looking "in pretty bad shape." Indeed, Downey's apartment had been broken into, and in his words, "turned upside down." He told police how cushions and his baby's crib mattress were slashed with a knife, and outside, someone scratched four-letter words (including "WQAM") into the paint of his car. Downey blamed "inflamed kids" for the vandalism and told a *Miami Herald* reporter he was "through with top 40 radio for as long as I live. God help radio if it continues on its present course. It won't need any Federal Communications Commission to kill it. It will fight itself to death."

Ironically/coincidentally/unexpectedly (take your pick since people used all three terms at the time), Downey's cross-town nemesis also packed his bags around the same time. Charlie Murdock left WQAM after eight years, accepting a job in Cincinnati. Was the timing mere coincidence? Years later, there's little doubt it was, but at the time there were those who firmly believed Downey ran Murdock out of Miami, the last straw being a private tape between Murdock and a fan, allegedly played by Downey on his radio show. Downey says the incident never happened. Still, in a matter of days the two most powerful afternoon deejays in the state of Florida were gone, replaced by Lee Sherwood (on WQAM) and Tom Campbell (on WFUN), although Dick Starr, fast becoming as popular as a warm pizza and a cold Pepsi, was given Downey's afternoon spot, substituting the popular *Liverpool Hour* with the just-as-popular *Jet Set*, which brought hits from around the world to the Miami airwaves; hits we never would have heard anyway, anyhow, anywhere without his innovative program.

Downey soon decided WQAM alone didn't inflame the kids who trashed his apartment, and by late July filed suit against two newspapers, which he claimed libeled him by reporting Murdock's unproven allegations. Even the record industry magazine *Billboard* carried the story in its July 24, 1965, edition in an article entitled "Disk Tie Charges Denied By Downey." The publicity may have seemed detrimental at first, but any good publicist will tell you how time will leave the masses merely remembering your name, or at least coming away with a slight sense of recollection. Allegations fade into the atmosphere. Facts fade with the falling of a leaf. And innuendo swims across the sky, fleeing more swiftly with each successive Auld Lang Syne. But seeds can be planted, and sometimes they even grow. Morton Downey, Jr., wouldn't shy away from controversy. He would run to meet it with the open arms of an octopus who has finally found, and will ardently savor, the perfect prey.

* * * * * *

If there were any real losers in this battle royale, no doubt it was our boys from Southwest High. First, the Montells were deprived of a number one hit when copies of "Don't Bring Me Down" were left to waste away in a warehouse. Their planned second release through Downey, Van Morrison's "Gloria," was also placed on permanent hold. Nine months later, the Shadows Of Knight took "Gloria" all the way to the national top ten in a version nearly everyone in Miami insists sounds like Mantovani next to the Montells' sizzling signature tune. Later, when local promoter Rick Tyson (a future writer for the Shaggs and Heroes Of Cranberry Farm) tried to hawk "Don't Bring Me Down" to Capitol Records, he was told by producer Marvin Holtzman in a letter dated January 4, 1966, "I feel this particular sound is a little old." Of course, the record had everything and more of what would become THE sound of 1966, the year of "Dirty Water," "Psychotic Reaction," "7 and 7 Is," "We Ain't Got Nothin' Yet," and of course, "Gloria." You might call it a Capitol offense — or maybe just the shortsightedness of an industry obsessed with Carnaby Street, and still nearly a year away from discovering Haight Street, and the soon-to-come, soon- to-swelter Summer Of Love.

Also lost in the shuffle was another Southwest High band with sweet dreams of conquering the Boss 40. Many believed the Modds were halfway there when "Don't Be Late" appeared one day on Downey's Liverpool Hour — but it was never to appear in record stores. The demo, with properly-punked-out vocals by Dean Liapis, and the type of four- and five-word verses so popular at the time, remains unissued to this day, Downey's downer probably doing little to help it along. (And yes, rumors persist of a tape out there of Doc Downey playing this unknown gem on the air. Downey himself claims to have no WFUN tapes among his archives.)

Downey might have quit Top 40 radio, but the urge to conquer its highest reaches didn't quit him overnight. As a producer, he gave us a horrible dirge-like ballad by Tommy Dawn & The Sunsets that reached #70 on WFUN in October, 1966. "Poor Little Ugly" told the morbid tale of a damsel with a damaged face who saves the life of a beautiful baby, and while dying, somehow in the process becomes beautiful herself. Divinely disgusting. Far more listenable was a June, 1967, recording by the Flower Children, "Marching Lovers," which Downey co-authored. Fans of '60s garage bands still believe in this B-side, but radio programmers didn't, and Downey's dream of becoming the next Andrew Loog Oldham jumped, and flashed Down The Road Apiece.

So what's a frustrated singer-announcer-promoter to do next? Well, there were more recordings, but no more sappy ballads about dying football players. The Downey of the '70s brought politics to his platters, celebrating the Bicentennial with "I Believe America," and playing up a well-publicized stunt by Richard Nixon in "He Played A Yo-Yo in Nashville." Downey-the-singer's last stand (until just recently) came in 1979 with a tune called "Family Tree" for Private Stock Records, backed with a cover of the '60s standard "Spanish Harlem." That record, like the others, went about as far as an environmentalist at an oil driller's convention, flaming out like a great Yellowstone spring in a Greenhouse summer.

The tunes might have stopped coming for Downey, but not the talk. A stint at radio station WDBO in Orlando ended

— what else — in controversy but led to his growing reputation as a renegade rabble-rouser. Morton Downey, Jr., was perfect for the TV talk spot created by WWOR-TV, in an age of Bernhard Goetz, and Baby M. Downey took comfort in knowing he'd no longer have to waste his time in sales, public relations, or money-making schemes turned sour. You can knock his journalism all you want (as you should), but keep in mind he never claimed to be anything more than an entertainer and an activist. If he relishes the role of the courtroom prosecutor, he makes no bones about it. And if the press wants to label his show as "Tabloid TV" and accuse him of instigating the ignorant, more power to them. It merely means more power for him.

Nothing lasts forever as Downey the deejay discovered. But it's not likely ol' Doc will have to return to his lounge lizard roots. "I think he's going to be president some day," insists Jeffrey Allen. While most may disagree, it's clear Downey has at least accomplished one goal: something his proteges never really could claim. Love him or hate him, he's certainly become a heck of a lot bigger than the Canadian Legends!

* * * * * *

AUTHOR'S UPDATE: I met with Mort Downey on December 27, 1990, at which time he shared his memories of his days as "the fastest mouth in the South:"

"Charlie Murdock, or 'Mudrock' as I called him, was the number one honcho in town when I came here — he had a 38.1 rating, which was unheard of. He was unbeatable... but I'm very competitive, and I wanted to beat him. I was determined to beat him."

So Downey reached into his bag of tricks:

"I announced that I had hidden a TV — one of those transistor sister things — and I gave out directions that led to Murdock's street. Instead of telling listeners to go left, which would have put them in an empty lot, I told them to go right: right into Charlie Murdock's front lawn! And they dug up all of his bushes, his plants. At the time, I said, 'Jeez, I made a mistake!'"

Did Downey give Murdock's home number on the air? Did he ever! "I told listeners that was the number a big group — maybe the Animals — would be staying at while in town," he finally admits more than 25 years later. During our interview, Downey looked straight into the lens of the camera, and said, "Gee, Charl, I honest to God — I sincerely — I say — I'm sorry!" all the while laughing and grinning as if to say he'd do it all again if given the chance!

One thing Downey wants to make clear all these years later is that he donated all his profits from the Montells' record to a musician's rehearsal hall and never walked away with a penny. "I just wanted to entertain and have fun," he told me, "but it turned into the biggest rock 'n roll war in the history of radio." Fans of Miami radio look back at that war with fondness and smiles, despite its sometimes ugly nature. Doc Downey wouldn't have it any other way.

36

SOUTH FLORIDA RADIO RESPONSE TO LOCAL 45s

1964 — Summer, 1970

NOTES: The month and year listed beside each song title in this section indicates the month in which the song enjoyed its greatest popularity, not the date of release.

*   This is the highest position known. As more surveys turn up, an adjusted position can be determined.

** "Sandcastles" was erroneously dropped from WFUN's survey listing and replaced by the Box Tops' "Choo Choo Train," when it fact it was "Sandcastles" that was supposed to be listed. Number five was the deserved position with this mistake taken into consideration; ten was the actual highest listed position.

	Month of Peak Popularity	Billboard	WQAM	WFUN
Wishful Thinking — Ginny Dale	1-64		38*	
He Was A Friend Of Mine — Briarwood Singers	1-64	126	48*	
Dream Baby — The Laddins	1-64		56	
Mary Lou — Harrison Freese	2-64		46*	
You've Known So Many — Gary Stites	3-64		15	
Love's Gonna Live Here/Let Her Go — Steve Alaimo	4-64		25*	28
Love Tastes Like Strawberries — Briarwood Singers	4-64		52	
Don't Be Unkind — American Beetles	4-64		43	35*
Love is A Many Splendored Thing — Steve Alaimo	6-64		18*	35*
To The Aisle — Jimmy Velvet	6-64	118	55*	
My Babe — Charlie McCoy	7-64		42	
Here Comes The Pain — (Canadian) Legends	8-64			17
I Don't Know — Steve Alaimo	9-64	103	2	4*

*   This is the highest position known. As more surveys turn up, an adjusted position can be determined.

** "Sandcastles" was erroneously dropped from WFUN's survey listing and replaced by the Box Tops' "Choo Choo Train," when in fact it was "Sandcastles" that was supposed to be listed. Number five was the deserved position with this mistake taken into consideration; ten was the actual highest listed position.

	Month of Peak Popularity	Billboard	WQAM	WFUN
Love, Emotion, Desire — The Birdwatchers	9-64		31	35
His Lips Get In The Way — Bernadette Castro	9-64	123	22	
Blue Suede Shoes — The Birdwatchers	11-64		31*	
Happy/Everybody Knows But Her — Steve Alaimo	12-64		17*	25*
A Girl In Love Forgives — Bernadette Castro	1-65		18	
Real Live Girl — Steve Alaimo	2-65	77	16*	11
Ballad Of Billy Brown — Mort (Doc) Downey, Jr.	2-65			23
Diane From Manchester Square — Tommy Roe & Roemans (Clearwater)	3-65		20*	33
Tomorrow Is Another Day — Steve Alaimo	4-65		37	29
Just In Case — (Canadian) Legends	5-65		29	10
It's Almost Tomorrow — Jimmy Velvet	5-65	93	9*	31*
Cast Your Fate To The Wind — Steve Alaimo	5-65	89	2	11
Don't Bring Me Down — H.M. Subjects (Montells)	7-65			5
Alright — (Canadian) Legends	7-65			20
Blowin' In The Wind — Steve Alaimo	8-65		36	

Title	Date			
Real Appeal — Gary Stites & The Birdwatchers	8-65		22	
Take What I Got — The Twilights	8-65			16
There Goes Life — The Mor-Loks	9-65		23	
The Little Black Egg — The Nightcrawlers (Daytona)	10-65	85	3	4
I'm A Nut — Jon Jon Lewis	1-66		5	11
Bucket Of Tears — Squires V	1-66			37
Wish I'd Never Met You — The Members (Tampa)	1-66			78
Once A Day — Steve Alaimo	2-66		34	59
Times Have Changed — Dr. T. & The Undertakers	3-66			49
A Basket Of Flowers — The Nightcrawlers (Daytona)	3-66		22	20
Love Me Too — The Senders (Tampa)	3-66			72
Girl I Got News For You/Eddie's Tune — The Birdwatchers	4-66		4	1
Stop! Get A Ticket — Clefs Of Lavender Hill	5-66	80	7	4
So Much Love — Steve Alaimo	5-66	92	19	27
Get Down With It — Wayne Cochran	5-66		25	19

* This is the highest position known. As more surveys turn up, an adjusted position can be determined.

** "Sandcastles" was erroneously dropped from WFUN's survey listing and replaced by the Box Tops' "Choo Choo Train," when it fact it was "Sandcastles" that was supposed to be listed. Number five was the deserved position with this mistake taken into consideration; ten was the actual highest listed position.

	Month of Peak Popularity	Billboard	WQAM	WFUN
Raining In My Heart — The Legends	6-66		18	7
Daddy Rolling Stone/You Can't Make Me — The Montells	6-66			14
Happy — Steve Alaimo	7-66		4	10
I Know — The Illusions (Palatka)	7-66			40
I Don't Remember — The Nightcrawlers (Daytona)	7-66			56
I'm Gonna Love You Anyway — The Birdwatchers	8-66	125	3	2
Let's Call It A Day Girl — The Razor's Edge	9-66	77	11	14
Melody For An Unknown Girl — Unknowns (FL related)	9-66	74	13	25
Blue Blue Feeling — Dr. T. & The Undertakers	9-66			50
No Place Or Time — Echoes of Carnaby Street	9-66			52
One More Time — Clefs Of Lavender Hill	9-66	114		17
Pollyanna — The Classics (Jacksonville)	9-66	106		28
Hurting — Gary Stites	9-66	123	14	26
For A Long Time — The Tropics (Tampa)	9-66			60
Wings Like A Dove — The Rhodes Brothers	9-66			55

Midnight Reader — Ron & The Starfires (Auburndale)	9-66			62
Goin' Back To Marlboro Country — Mark Markham & Jesters	10-66			22
Real Appeal — Upper Hand	10-66		37	74
Pardon Me (It's My First Day Alone) — Steve Alaimo	11-66		16	24
Goin' Back To Miami — Wayne Cochran	11-66		18	23
I'm Gonna Do It To You — The Birdwatchers	12-66		11	16
Snoopy Vs. The Red Baron — Royal Guardsmen (Ocala)	12-66	2	1	1
Schroeder — Security Blankets	2-67			72
Leave Me Alone — Jesters (Ft. Myers)	3-67			42
Return Of The Red Baron — Royal Guardsmen (Ocala)	3-67	15	16	20
I Won't Lead You On — The Minute Men	3-67			26
Mary Mary (It's To You That I Belong) — The Birdwatchers	4-67		12	72
You Don't Know Like I Know — Steve Alaimo	4-67		11	9
I Won't Tell — Conlon & The Crawlers (Daytona)	4-67			58
It's Easy Child — Dr. T. & The Undertakers	5-67			53

* This is the highest position known. As more surveys turn up, an adjusted position can be determined.

** "Sandcastles" was erroneously dropped from WFUN's survey listing and replaced by the Box Tops' "Choo Choo Train," when it fact it was "Sandcastles" that was supposed to be listed. Number five was the deserved position with this mistake taken into consideration; ten was the actual highest listed position.

	Month of Peak Popularity	Billboard	WQAM	WFUN
Whatcha Gonna Do About It — Evil	6-67		7	7
Airplane Song — Royal Guardsmen (Ocala)	6-67	46	15	22
What's On Your Mind — Squiremen Four	7-67			38
Heard You Went Away — Proctor Amusement Company	8-67		15	7
Can't Stop Loving You — The Last Word	8-67	78	3	4
Turn Around Girl — The Birdwatchers	8-67		28	19
So Right/Wednesday — Royal Guardsmen (Ocala)	9-67	97		78
New Orleans/Ooh Poo Pah Doo — Steve Alaimo	9-67	126		39
Get Yourself Together — Razor's Edge	9-67			56
Hummin' — The Shaggs	10-67			28
Savage Lost — The Kollektion	10-67		7	
Heartbeat — Hour Glass (Florida-related)	10-67			73
Get Ready — Wayne Cochran	11-67		3	39
Snoopy's Christmas — Royal Guardsmen (Ocala)	12-67		10	6
I Wish I Had Time — The Last Word	1-68	105	23	

Title	Date			
Spooky — Classics IV (Jacksonville)	2-68	3	4	3
Denver — Steve Alaimo	3-68	118	27	27
I Say Love — Royal Guardsmen (Ocala)	3-68	72	20	18
Soul Train — Classics IV (Jacksonville)	4-68	90		
Backwards And Forwards — December's Children (Orlando)	5-68	123	18	24
Sandcastles — 31st Of February (Jacksonville)	7-68		5	5/10**
Snoopy For President — Royal Guardsmen (Ocala)	7-68	85		
Baby Let's Wait — Royal Guardsmen (Ocala)	11-68	35	4	15
Watching The Trains Go By — Steve Alaimo	11-68		28	
Stormy — Classics IV (Jacksonville)	12-68	5	4	4
Rock Steady — New Rock Band	12-68		27	
Traces — Classics IV (Jacksonville)	2-69	2	2	5
Love (Can Make You Happy) — Mercy (Tampa)	4-69	2	2	1
Take Your Love (And Shove It) — Kanes Cousins	6-69	116	1	24
Everyday With You Girl — Classics IV (Jacksonville)	7-69	19	2	18

* This is the highest position known. As more surveys turn up, an adjusted position can be determined.

** "Sandcastles" was erroneously dropped from WFUN's survey listing and replaced by the Box Tops' "Choo Choo Train," when it fact it was "Sandcastles" that was supposed to be listed. Number five was the deserved position with this mistake taken into consideration; ten was the actual highest listed position.

	Month of Peak Popularity	Billboard	WQAM	WFUN
Forever — Mercy (Tampa)	7-69	79	46	
One Woman — Steve Alaimo	9-69	101	38	30
Change Of Heart — Classics IV (Jacksonville)	9-69	49	48	
Midnight — Classics IV (Jacksonville)	11-69	58		39
Will You Love Me Tomorrow — Heroes Of Cranberry Farm	2-70			28
Tennessee Birdwalk — Jack Blanchard & Misty Morgan	4-70	23	23	19
Ride Captain Ride — Blues Image (Tampa)	6-70	4	2	1
Stoned Cowboy — Fantasy	8-70	77	1	1
Gas Lamps And Clay — Blues Image (Tampa)	9-70	81		18

* This is the highest position known. As more surveys turn up, an adjusted position can be determined.

** "Sandcastles" was erroneously dropped from WFUN's survey listing and replaced by the Box Tops' "Choo Choo Train," when it fact it was "Sandcastles" that was supposed to be listed. Number five was the deserved position with this mistake taken into consideration; ten was the actual highest listed position.

OTHER RADIO NOTES

— "Lavender Blue" by Finders Keepers reached #40 on WQAM and #41 on WFUN during the second week of October, 1966. I have not yet been able to determine whether or not this is the same Finders Keepers that played at Miami's Palmetto Bandstand.

— WSRF in Ft. Lauderdale was a small, liberal-minded station that played a number of Florida releases that were ignored by both WQAM and WFUN. The following local records were hits in Dade and Broward Counties strictly on WSRF:

	Month of Peak Popularity
Shadows — The Echoes	8-68
Can't You Believe In Forever — Blues Image(Tampa)	10-68
Mother Where's Your Daughter — Royal Guardsmen (Ocala)	4-69
Stomp — NRBQ	6-69
C'Mon Everybody — NRBQ	9-69
You Got Your Thing On A String — J. P. Robinson	9-69
Keep On Movin' On — Magic	12-69

37

RADIO IN OTHER
PARTS OF FLORIDA

South Florida was certainly not the only area of the state to feature an exciting radio scene. Other stations around the peninsula, such as WLOF and WHOO in Orlando, WALT, WLCY, and WFSO in Tampa-St. Petersburg, and WYND in Sarasota featured exciting, original music programming.

WYND, in particular, was so incredible that chapter upon chapter could be devoted to the multitude of obscure records they played. A look at WYND's mid-to-late '60s music surveys provides some staggering realizations. Examples? Not only did WYND play nearly everything by Mouse & The Traps and the 13th Floor Elevators, but these artists made the top five with amazing regularity. A look at the January 20, 1968, chart reveals the following top five:

(4)	1.	Sunshine Of Your Love/SWLABR	Cream
(12)	2.	I'll Do Anything	Uniques
(23)	3.	L.O.V.E. Love	Mouse & The Traps
(14)	4.	She Lives	13th Floor Elevators
(1)	5.	Midnight Confessions	Evergreen Blues

Further down this chart, we see "Flower People" by the Cobblestones, "Freedom Now" by the Knack, "Come Ride Come Ride" by the Merry Go Round (on its way to number four), "Aries The Fire-Fighter" by the Zodiac Cosmic Sounds, and other similar obscurities. And this was not an isolated chart — WYND was this great for years!

As far as local records are concerned, they couldn't be beat. WYND even played records by South Florida artists that never got as much as a spin in Miami or Ft. Lauderdale! "You Don't Need A Reason" by the Proctor Amusement Company got all the way to number nine; "Dreaming In The Rain" by the Glass Bubble (alias the Birdwatchers) was a top 20 hit; I could go on and on and on. Suffice it to say that WYND really couldn't care less how a record did on the national charts; if Sarasota liked it, they played it! Perhaps the best example is the week of February 14th, 1969, when "Close The Barn Door" by the 49th Parallel was not only one of the biggest hits on WYND — it was the number one song of the week! Kurt Curtis of Daytona Beach recalls that they were Florida's hottest station back in the 1960s, but I think I can take it a step farther. WYND was not only Florida's best station — they were AMERICA'S hottest station!

Radio-wise, the rest of Florida was well represented as well. WALT in Tampa played nearly every Tropics and Outsiders release, with the Tropics never being too far away from that top spot. Let us also not forget WLCY, where the Roemans were even bigger than the Beatles for a while. (From August, 1965, to January, 1966, the Roemans had no less than three top four hits, with "Listen To Me" clocking in at number one on January 22, 1966). WLCY also played a number of South Florida bands, including the Birdwatchers, Clefs of Lavender Hill, and Evil, and also granted airplay to Tampa area bands such as Sir Michael and the Sounds and the U.S. Male (which featured a young Kent Lavoie on vocals in his pre-Lobo days).

WHOO and WLOF in Orlando were the stations to turn to for the legendary band We The People, whose "St. John's Shop" on Challenge hit number four on WLOF during the

last week of 1966. (This chart also featured Gayle Haness'
classic "Johnny Ander" and obscurities by the Montanas,
"E" Types, Hogs, Count Five, and Orlando's own Little Willie
and the Adolescents.) We The People also scored major hits
on WHOO, with "Follow Me Back To Louisville" reaching the
top ten in September, 1967, and "The Day She Dies" going
all the way to number two in January, 1968. WHOO also
made major hits out of "Flower Girl" by Orlando's Plant Life
(alias the Go-Mads) and "Please Agree" by the Mysteries,
another area band.

And let's not forget Jacksonville, where WPDQ battled "the
Big Ape" for teenage supremacy. WPDQ's Dino Summerlin
(himself a recording artist for the Dial label) made sure
EVERYTHING recorded by the Dalton Gang (released or
unreleased) made it onto the station's playlist. But the big
story is WAPE — who could forget those ape calls! — or the
way local records could be heard night and day. WAPE deejay
Ken Fuller used to play bass in the band Deep Six (pre-
Mouse & The Boys), and as you'd expect, Mouse's crew
consistently hit the top ten. ("Love Is Free" on Rubiat even
reached NUMBER ONE on October 21, 1968, sending "Hey
Jude" by the Beatles to the runner-up spot!) "PDQ" and "the
Big Ape" also sent obscurities by the Coronados, Illusions,
Daybreakers, and Teddy Bears streaking toward the top ten
— just imagine that happening today!

There were, of course, more great stations and more great
local hits, but these were some of the best. Combined with
Palm Beach's WIRK (which made "Shadows" by the Miami-
based Echoes a top ten hit) and South Florida's two rock
powerhouses, it's clear that Florida radio of the 1960s could
not be beat.

38

FROM CHORDS... TO DISCORD

Picking which songs to play — that may sound rather simple, and for most mid-'60s bands, I guess it was. Songs which featured no more than three chords — generally C-F-G or A-D-E ("Louie Louie," "Wild Thing," et al) were just that — simple, and for that reason the obvious choice of many band members. But there was more to the mid-'60s music selection than may at first meet the ear. Sure, there was a certain amount of repetition in what groups of the day played, but each band's repertoire was uniquely its own, based upon any number of factors.

The Montells, my all-time favorite local band, leaned heavily toward the British R&B sound of the Pretty Things, Fairies, and Yardbirds, and favored material of that nature. Their high school rivals, the Shaggs, preferred the harmonic sounds of Beatlesque groups, and tunes that allowed them to show off their exceptional singing abilities. The Aerovons were an obvious Beach Boys-influenced group, although in their early days they played everything from the Zombies to Ray Charles. (To quote Chuck Kirkpatrick in the Aerovons' diary: "We frankly prefer the Beatles — their stuff is easy to play!")

The point of all this is that there's no way to pigeonhole just what made bands select the material they performed. Groups would hear songs on the radio — practice them —

learn them — and from time-to-time write "originals" based on these songs. But there **were** certain things that did help influence song selection, such as disc jockey Rick Shaw's early-morning television show, conveniently scheduled at 7:00 a.m., right before all the young hipsters had to leave for school. In addition to performances by local bands, Shaw featured a cast of lip-synchers pretending to sing the top hit tunes of the day. (Who could ever forget Steve Marcus' embarrassing mimic of "Winchester Cathedral," or Nilda Rice's countless impersonations of Petula Clark?) One of the most memorable film clips on the show starred Shaw's young son, prior to receiving a haircut, bouncing around to the Barbarians' "Are You A Boy Or A Girl." This film clip aired for many years, and not coincidentally, so did the song, in garages all around South Florida.

What were the most-covered tunes or artists? If you guessed the Beatles and Rolling Stones, you wouldn't be too far off. Their entire catalogues plus the usual standards — "Gloria," "I'm A Man," and the like — were heard on every street every day. But there were other songs that were especially popular in this region — particularly those introduced by the more influential of the area's bands. "Alright," a local hit by the Canadian Legends, was almost mandatory at many dances. Ditto "The Little Black Egg," probably THE most widely heard song of late 1965-early 1966 (with the possible exception of "Day Tripper"). "LSD," an otherwise obscure Pretty Things track, was turned into a household tune by the Montells, whose excellent rendition inspired not only many covers, but even imitations such as "ESP" by Ft. Lauderdale's Beaver Patrol.

By mid-1966, "Hold On I'm Coming" became the most overheard, overplayed, but not surprisingly, also the most danceable tune in town. The Young Rascals were also making their mark as a group whose tracks had the knack to make people dance. "Come On Up," "Mustang Sally," and later "Groovin'," were all accessible to white teen bands that aspired to play soul — and there were countless numbers of them, just waiting to break into the local dance scene.

As the first love-in was flowering in San Francisco in January, 1967, the bulk of Florida bands were still clinging to the most commercial exponents of blue-eyed soul. Bands were about to find themselves caught between two worlds — trying to be hip while still feeling compelled to play top 40. Never was this more evident than in August, 1967, when WFUN staged (and the key word is "staged") a "Barefoot In The Park" Love-In. There were lots of flowers... lots of love beads, sitars, and even a "foot painting contest"... but beneath all the hair and hoopla, it was just an ersatz imitation of what was happening in Haight- Ashbury.

Just a week or two earlier, the Thingies (as legend has it) brought Miami's first light show to the World (one of Miami's top teen clubs), but even then most bands were not yet sure which musical world they were in. That is why there were so many great records (from a '60s garage standpoint) still coming from this area as late as 1967. Amidst the changing world around them, kids still just wanted to play music — whether it be outdated from a California standpoint or not. But there was just so long that this sort of limbo could go on. Eventually, the hippie world won out... eventually, people got caught up in what they **thought** was "their own thing"... eventually, the whole essence of the scene got lost — and I do mean lost. Savage Lost.

Long hair and a wild light show:
The **Thingies** made hippies happy during their short South Florida stay.

39

LIFE IN THE BLOODSTREAM

"It's not enough just to talk of what happens;
A stream of conscious thoughts, a never-ending flow.
Some patterns rise,
    Some hypnotize,
      But where do they go?"

(Angel Rissoff & Richie Chimelis, from the Kollektion's classic "Savage Lost.")

One very vital element in '60s rock 'n roll culture has been rather conspicuous in its absence from this book so far. While the use and abuse of drugs was a major factor in what transpired musically in this area, it is certainly not my intention to run down drug use schedules of each band or performer. That would be quite irrelevant as what really matters is the music that was created by these artists, not a checklist of the substances that may have inhabited their bloodstreams at one time or another. Yet, drugs are a factor that has to be explored if one is to understand the radical changes in music that were taking place in the mid-to-late '60s, particularly the mind-altering chemicals that outwardly changed the perception of what was being created or heard.

First off, let's stifle any impression that every '60s band relied on drugs to provide creative inspiration — there were numerous bands that deplored the prevalent drug use of their peers and openly denounced such use. (The leader of one long- enduring band recently expressed pleasure at how his group never so much as tried marijuana through the years.) Some bands encountered internal dissension between drug users and non-users, with one major group coming to mind as losing many original members through smoker vs. nonsmoker confrontations. A lot of this may seem silly today, but keep in mind that in 1966, drugs in Miami were basically an unknown quantity, feared by adults and intriguing to many teenagers. The horror stories of heroin addiction and bad LSD trips that we've heard ad nauseam throughout the years were certainly not in general circulation. Drugs appeared glamorous to young people as a means not only to rebel, but also to experience sights and sounds in a way that the naked senses never could.

Marijuana use was still in its infancy stages. In fact, at a July, 1965, Columbia Records convention in Miami Beach, Rolling Stones manager Andrew Loog Oldham decided he wanted some marijuana and sent some members of a popular local band out to "find" some. Logically, the place to go for drugs in those days was Coconut Grove, but even a trip to the Grove couldn't always guarantee a successful score. The boys in the band came up empty, failing in their attempt to impress their newly-found, famous acquaintance.

Glue sniffing was quite popular in the early days. One band recalled that its members used to frequent the Royal Castle at the corner of Bird Road and Galloway because "their paper bags were the best for sniffing glue." A diverse array of drugs came into prominence as the decade wore on, but none would to prove as devastating as heroin and acid, two that continue to rear their heads into the '90s.

Heroin addiction cost the lives and/or minds of way too many musicians, with one young guitarist coming to mind as having died before being able to see his group score a runaway smash hit. A handful of people are still fighting heroin addiction to this day; a sad, sad testimonial to the awesome power of this chemical monster.

I've come across a few people who still praise the glories of acid, but these few are definitely the exception. A big turning point for a lot of people was the mammoth three-day Miami Pop Festival that occurred late in 1968. To say that drugs were rampant at this festival would be like saying that Hank Aaron hit a home run or two. The acid tripping that went on during the festival proved to be just too heavy for a few people, including the lead guitarist of a BIG local band who decided to quit the group following the festival. The three-day event may have been just a musical experience to some, but to others it was the turning point of a lifetime... either a high point or a low point, depending on whom you speak to.

The Miami Pop Festival: Trippin' in the Florida sun.
The height of hippiedom for South Florida.

Actually, what may well be the most important drug-related event to affect the local rock 'n roll community happened several months prior to the festival. One of Miami's top progressive bands was busted for possession of marijuana at a Biscayne Boulevard motel, something that was considered absolutely shocking by adults at the time. As parents throughout the city began to get wind of this bust, it was then that the "drug problem" began to hit a little closer to home. All of a sudden, parents would not allow their kids to frequent the places where this band was playing. I guess it was a little hard for them to understand why drug use was as widespread as it was, and a lot of them revived the pathetic anti-rock 'n roll stance that was once so popular. Whether this helped reduce attendance at local show-dances

is a matter of speculation; one thing that **is** for certain is that
in no way did it make any kind of a dent in teenage drug use.
(One can also point to the March, 1969, Jim Morrison Dinner
Key "indecent exposure" episode as an important factor in
shaping parents' attitudes toward youthful music, although
by then the seed had long been firmly planted.)

A major consequence of increasing drug awareness was
the provocative new perspective in song lyrics that came
about. "Mary Mary" by the Birdwatchers, "Love So Dear" by
the Undertakers, and the Kollektion's amazing "Savage Lost"
are the obvious examples. Parents and lecturers argued that
rock 'n roll lyrics in general were making kids turn on, but
this was really not the case. Drug- related lyrics (especially
the more subtle examples) spoke to the initiated; those
turned-on kids who knew exactly what was going on. For
those that didn't understand, it just didn't make any difference. "Mary Mary" could have been just another love song
just as "White Rabbit" might as well have been another
simple children's story for those to whom "feed your head"
was not a way of life.

Drug-lyric paranoia turned everything from the innocuous ("Puff The Magic Dragon" and "Yellow Submarine")
to the esoteric ("Lucy In The Sky With Diamonds," based on
a painting by Julian Lennon and NOT about LSD, although
some people even today just won't listen) into open invita-
tions to turn on and tune in. Someone once suggested that
even "Row Row Row Your Boat" could be construed as a drug
song, and indeed it could! Sure, drug lyrics were a reality of
the era, but no drug lyric ever made a person take drugs.
Music was the perfect scapegoat for the problem of which it
was merely a symptom: the problem itself being a misguided
youth movement that placed a disproportionate importance
on the consumption of drugs. Naturally, as musicians were
prone to write lyrics that reflected upon their reality, refer-
ence to drugs couldn't be avoided. But I see it more as a
reflection upon this reality and of the individual's lifestyle
rather than the tool of a crusade to turn the whole world into
drug users. Unfortunately, a good number of people couldn't

understand this and took it upon themselves to label drug lyrics as "harmful" and "immoral." They couldn't see the culture as it was; all they saw was a so-called threat to whatever value they deemed fragile at the time.

But enough about lyrics. The music itself was changing too, and not necessarily for the better. One of the most negative aspects of the drug era was the twisting inside-out of rock 'n roll rhythms. The fast rhythms (generally in 4/4 time) that typified the most exciting rock 'n roll since its very inception were, well, a little difficult to handle for a 17-year-old kid on an acid trip. So the rhythms got slower; no, not slow, but slower ... twisted... tortured... it was a new, developing form of rock, but certainly not rock 'n roll, at least not in any pure form. Much of this new music was dubbed "psychedelic" or, in some cases, even "acid rock," and much of it, particularly in its earliest stages, was very good. But the folk-rock boom that came into prominence in the mid-'60s opened the door for ex-beatniks and folkies to invade the domain of rock 'n roll, and much of the music that came from these drugged-out ex-beatniks was far from good. Folk-rock at its most exciting was a hybrid of rock 'n roll and folk with rock 'n roll remaining the dominant element. But let's face it — when jangling guitars give way to jug band instrumentation and drum rolls are replaced by bongos and the like, there is just no way the result is going to sound anything like real rock 'n roll. Coffeehouse musicians who never played rock 'n roll in their lives were turning up in neo-psychedelic bands, playing music that may have had merit on its own terms, but certainly had no validity as rock 'n roll, despite the fact that it was generally labeled as such. In many cases, being "heavy" was considered more important than the beat or hook that normally would have accentuated or dominated the song, and without a strong beat or hook, you cannot have rock 'n roll. It just isn't possible.

All kinds of incredible (or was it incorrigible) things continued to happen to rock 'n roll as the decade wore on. Rock (the new all-encompassing term) became psychedelicized, mellowed, jazzed up, slowed down, classicalized, orchestrated, and generally wounded almost beyond recognition. Drugs, peer pressure, and a number of pretensions (often masquerading under the guise of "awareness") all helped delete the honesty and energy level that has always exemplified real rock 'n roll. As stated previously, some of the music resulting from these hybrids was decent (and in some cases extremely good), but for the most part, the very essence (aka guts/soul) of the music was stripped or deleted. Rock just wasn't allowed to be fun anymore.

The passing of time has a way of putting things into perspective and making the once obscure and once fast-changing world of the late '60s seem so clear and, in so many ways, so trivial. It's a common joke today to refer to a person stuck in this era as a "60's burnout;" these people are easy to recognize with their trademark look, demeanor, and speech patterns. Yet there's nothing funny about a 1990s flower child who hasn't yet realized that the revolution is over. All those peace rallies, be-ins, and overindulgent musical jam sessions didn't change a damn thing. If you don't believe me, ask the next 14-year-old you see to describe his or her youth culture to you. Somehow I don't think that video games, designer jeans, and mass-manufactured rock T-shirts were what the hippies had in mind. Somewhere along the line we lost our way, and the first nail in the coffin came when we let rock 'n roll slip away.

There is no way to bring back the performers who were lost to drugs, just as we can't go back in time and reverse the musical trends of the late '60s and '70s. We also can't bring back the wasted careers of drugged-out musicians who are now nearing 50 years of age. Those years are gone forever, and all we can do now is learn. Doubtlessly, there are exceptions to the rule, but one thing remains eminently clear through the toil and rubble of the passing years: hard drugs and rock 'n roll do not mix. They never did... they never will.

40

SO MUCH FOR THE '70S

America slept for a decade. We stuck a feather in our sleeping caps and called it the '70s. We lit a fire in our pipes, but did not stir a spark within our souls. If the '60s were psychedelic, the '70s were prosaic, caught up in a rebellion against responsibility that was more cop-out than cool.

Oh, it was fun... at the time. But not much was accomplished. 1970 ran into 1971 which ran into 1972 (which ran into 1973), and we kinda crawled back from it all. It was fun to watch dozens of bands jam for peace at the YMHA (Young Men's Hebrew Association) — but who really remembers the difference between Moon and Rain?, Rubber Band, and Rubber Soul? This book is about groundbreakers and chance-takers — not lollygaggers. The early '70s were a lollygagger's delight, perfect for jammin' and rollin' and tokin', but little else. Still, a few decent tunes managed to sneak out of the '70s, so let me briefly mention some of them. Briefly.

First there's Tiger Tiger's "Dog Legs/Red Man" (Miccosukee Hopanke 1003), wonderfully out of place in 1975 and easily one of my favorite local records of the '70s. "Everlovin' People" by Euphoria (Hit 1005) sounds more like 1969 than 1971 (its actual release date) as does the garagey, dark "It's Gonna Be Alright" from the Front Woods (Lee 1000). Masalla conjures up images of Led Zeppelin-meets-

MC 5 on their 1970 recording "Burnin' Feelin'" (Climax 1001). Frenzy succeeds with "I Need Your Love/A Little Love" on Art 218 as does Ice with "Wally" on Cindri 9257. Bolder Damn's album on Hit 5061 is highly sought after, although I can't figure out why... and the less said about the Blood Sweat & Tears styling of the 9th Floor Symfony (Cypress House 9657) the better.

For a good laugh, you must check out Maxima's "Four Dead In Ohio" (GWS 42). Despite some excellent musicians and a caring co-producer in Dave Hieronymus, this stands out as the most blatant example of what was WRONG with the early '70s: "No longer can I sit idly by while the arrows of outrageous indifference pierce the lungs of my brothers!" So perfectly pretentious — it's a must-own, if for no other reason than to remind us what happens when we allow an entire decade — ten precious years of our lives — to whirl by so uninspired. Fortunately, a new generation — still untainted and not yet bored — was there to pick up the pieces. **Their** story is the '80s.

41

THE '80S:
A RETURN TO CLUBLAND?

1979: Max Demian and Keith Herman make it onto major labels and get national airplay.

1989: Nuclear Valdez makes it onto a major label and gets national airplay.

It's not deja vu. From the Coralairs in the '50s, to the Clefs Of Lavender Hill in the '60s, to Critical Mass in the '80s, South Florida's musical history is filled with the ranks of the nearly-was and almost-rans. Did ANYTHING change in the '80s: a decade in which great clubs opened and great clubs closed; great acts recorded and then broke up? A decade in which the good and the bad alike enthusiastically tried to create a scene from the ashes of the self-indulgent '70s. Did anyone succeed?

Let's start at the beginning: 1980. To the south, we find Z-Cars doing the Time Warp at Rollo's, gloriously evoking the long-lost energy of the Kinks and Easybeats. To the north, the Cichlids are serenading pink tourists with their songs about life and lifeguards. At the Agora Ballroom, the Reactions play like their lives depend on it, competing against Freewheel and the Kids at the September 28th Rising Star competition. And the Eat, punks all the way, with songs about Nixon's Binoculars and Communist Radio — they never did take the stage at the John Lennon tribute concert

at Bicentennial Park, but at least we got to hear the Rubber
Thongs rocking up "Day Tripper" (in between the filibuster-
ing of local politicos). And let's not forget Critical Mass' big
break with MCA Records ending acrimoniously, with radio
programmers snubbing the band, just to get back at its
manager (radio Svengali Lee Abrams). At least we had *Mouth
Of The Rat*, a fanzine willing to take a chance.

We toast 1981 at the Tight Squeeze Club.

1981

Monday nights belong to Eric Moss' *Radio Free Living
Room* — amateur hour for sure, but what really matters:
being slick or being cool? Thanks to the insight of this
in-tune show (on public radio WLRN), there's finally an
alternative to FM radio's obsession with the mellow and the
mundane. "In Society" by the Reactions becomes the best-
sounding Miami radio song since "Whatcha Gonna Do About
It" by Evil (May, 1967). Used People and Sheer Smegma (the
awesomely wicked "Club Night") also sound great on the
radio. The word of the year is "oi!"

Around town, we dance to the Eat, Essentials, and the
Eggs at the Polish American Club. On the fanzine front, *The
Boringtonal Journal* and *Suburban Relapse* do what they can
to shape out a scene. Channel 4's *PM Magazine* wins an
Emmy for its segment on former Game/Proctor Amusement
Company star Chuck Kirkpatrick (and his one-man Beach
Boys medley). We toast 1982 at the New Wave Lounge.

1982

"27 Birds"; what a place. One night it's the Front and the
X-Conz. The next night it's the U.S. Furys (with Isaac from
the Reactions)... or maybe the Throbs... or maybe even
Einstein's Riceboys (from Milwaukee), immersing the
audience with "Milk Of Amnesia." Cats on Holiday, with Ray
from Z-Cars, tries but fails to break free from its inherent
mediocrity — while the ever-faithful Fat Chance Blues Band
gets competition from the up-and-coming Fleet Starbuck

(former member of '60s band The Stoned!). Tobacco Road lives!

Fanzines? My vote goes to *Alternative Rhythms*. LPs? Two cheers for Open Records. Prior to moving from Ft. Lauderdale to North Miami Beach, they treat us to Charlie Pickett's *Live At The Button* and the highly-eclectic *Land That Time Forgot* (the first South Florida rock sampler EVER). But the real record gem of 1982 comes from the Screamin' Sneakers: my choice for the best local 12-incher of the entire decade. Oh, Lisa Nash — tattooed yet tender — to hear her sing "To Sir With Love" is to melt. Could she possibly show us more flesh?

Let's toast 1983 at Finder's.

1983

Flynn's is happening! Wow — the best local club since The Place in the '60s! All kinds of bands dazzle the senses — from the Spanish Dogs to the Psycho Daisies to the Sleep Of Reason (sharing the bill with Love Tractor!). Larry Joe Miller & The Rockabilly Rockets give a sizzling set at Open Records — go cat go!

South Florida gets its first look at Nuclear Valdez — signs of good things to come. Over on the Ft. Lauderdale strip, the best cover band of the '80s is smoking its way through the Byrds' "My Back Pages." Of course, I'm talking about the Rockerfellas (see *Rag*, March, 1984 issue). Too bad their originals (including "She's That Kind Of Girl") never came out. In Tampa, Avatar becomes Savatage and attracts national attention while the Triple X Girls, A New Personality, and Deloris Telescope travel the state searching for shakes. South Florida's hard rockers from Roxx to Slyder keep hanging in. Me... I'll be toasting 1984 at Flynn's.

1984

The big sound is coming from the Chant — my choice for best local live band of the '80s. They'd soon go on to cut an album, but "Jonesboro" and "Small House" were meant to

be heard LIVE! Good cover versions, too, and a great R.E.M.
cop in "Heaven Assumes." THE BEST! Too good to stay —
the Chant would take off for Atlanta, a year or so after R.B.T.
— originally from Binghamton, New York — would do just
the opposite — relocating to South Florida.

As for Charlie Pickett, superstardom eludes, but just
imagine the feeling of being called on stage by R.E.M. (to join
in a cover of the Velvet Underground's "There She Goes
Again"). Would you be able to sleep for a week?

Over at Flynn's: The Bobs... Roach Motel... True West
(from L.A.). Almost paradise. Channel 6 goes live with Z-Toyz
the night their "Miami Breakdown" video made the finals of
MTV's *Basement Tapes! Florida's New Video Beat* debuts on
West Palm Beach TV screens. The Screamin' Sneakers become Poison Pack. The Heroes exploit the nostalgia market
as the Backbeats. The Wind calls it quits. Gypsy Queen
continues to mix hard rock with sensuality.

Where to toast 1985? The choice is obvious!

The **Chant**: Rickenbacker guitars, feedback, and inspired songwriting. If only
they'd stuck around. L-R: Walter Czachowski, vocals and guitar; Todd Barry,
drums; Rich DeFinis, lead guitar; James B. Johnson, bass. *Photo courtesy Safety
Net Records.*

1985-86

Nuclear Valdez wins WSHE's Local Shot competition on March 2, 1985 — one bright spot — otherwise, it's all starting to fall apart. Flynn's closes down over an insurance squabble. Fire & Ice gets too trendy. The clubs on the Ft. Lauderdale strip fail to inspire. Power 96 Radio is on the rise, promoting "track music": Are we going to stand around and let Sequal and Secret Society become "The Miami Sound?" What would YOU rather listen to — Exposé, or the Eat?

I toast 1987 at home listening to my stereo.

1987

Slowly, clubs are springing up on South Beach. The Cameo Theatre takes a stand with its "Rock To Walk" benefit, led by Nuclear Valdez and Agony In The Garden. Amazing Grace ALMOST gets on TV's *Miami Vice*. Jaco Pastorius is killed outside a Broward bottle club. Kru and Apex release new 12-inchers. New 'zines *Screen!* and *Metal Scene* keep South Florida's hard rockers happy. Naiomi's Hair makes dazzling stops at Penrod's in Ft. Lauderdale and the Banal Club in North Miami. NRBQ makes the cover of *Rag* (July, 1987 issue). And then there's the amazing story of a woman who was trampled at the Broward County Fair and how her tragedy inspired Power 96's #1 song of 1987 ("Dreaming" by Will To Power). Let's toast the new year at a club those in the know are buzzing about — hail Churchill's Hideaway!

1988

Tough times for Charlie Pickett: He opens for the Silos (ex-Eggs/Psycho Daisies/Vulgar Boatmen) at Churchills but can't quite get along with guitarist John Salton. Imagine what it's like getting blown off the stage by what's essentially your former backing band!

The "alternative band" scene grows, but track music still dominates the airwaves. Four FM stations (the most ever in South Florida) play bits and pieces of local music — mainly bits — while the commercial stations still won't give in. Still, "Birdie" by KRU and just about anything by Saigon Kick sound great, even if it's only on college radio. We're not giving up.

We welcome 1989 at Club Beirut.

1989

The Goods officially come together on January 13th and quickly catch the media's eye with their infamous condom giveaway. Their Christmas show at Churchill's (with another excellent band, the Mavericks) had to be seen to be believed — rock theatre WITHOUT pretension! Not to forget their spellbinding "Psycho Ponies" performance in which they imitated/immortalized their fellow local bands — from Vesper Sparrow to Fruit Fly to Scraping Teeth! The Goods are what legends are made of. No late-'80s band did more to promote the local scene than the Goods; no band did more to involve their audiences; no band deserves success more.

Bands saying adios to South Florida in 1989 included Paint (don't worry — their music is MUCH BETTER than their name, as New Yorkers would soon find out) and the socially-conscious Hoosegow (joining the Chant in Georgia).

Other cool bands in 1989 included Another Nation (who, along with Vociferous Mutes, helped promote industrial sounds), Broken Spectacles, Forget The Name, thrashers FWA, Powerhouse, and the Believers, and surf instrumental twangers the Randies! On TV, local videos make the airwaves on Metro-Dade Cable's *South Florida Rock 'N Roll Showcase*, even if it seems they show the same eight or ten videos over and over again. (Do they really believe the Biscaynes and Split Image are the only bands in town?) Gainesville's Genitorturers and Tampa's Pink Lincolns thrash their way through the state. Gainesville/Orlando's Naiomi's Hair makes the finals of the Snickers New Music Search. Even if you don't believe Snickers satisfies, there's little doubt this energetic trio DOES... and they're not alone as the '80s end in a FLOURISH of power chords.

* *

So it sounds like it's been a good decade, right? South Florida made a HUGE musical comeback in the 1980s, but the step forward — while fun to behold and often exciting — realistically remains a miniscule one. The best bands of the 1980s remained virtually underground, hidden away in the half-a-dozen-or-so clubs willing to take a chance and radio stations to the left of your dial with a collective rating of 1.3. 99% of the people living here never heard of the Reactions in 1980, just as they had no clue who the Goods were in 1990. So while this community's musicians made great strides, let's not lose our perspective. Until Miami's consciousness is turned away from Sound Machines and dressed-to-be-seen divas, we're all going to have to work even harder in the years ahead — just to KEEP what gains we've been able to make.

But there's a bigger story here — one that's mind-boggling in a way. Think about this for a minute: Question Reality, Coral Gables, and Quit (in the 1990s) would inhabit the very same turf that so recently (the 1980s) belonged to the Cichlids and Critical Mass. There's been a COMPLETE turnaround. Just as there was no sign of the 1967 Miami in 1977, so was the case in 1987... and TODAY's bands are so young they barely remember the original Flynn's, 27 Birds, OR the bands that rumbled across their stages! But although generations replace generations, the beat goes on. It's up to the NEXT generation to rehearse. To rebel. To realize we're all counting on them. It's THEIR turn now.

30 FROM THE '80s

(The coolest local garage records/cassettes of the '80s)

1. The Eat - (CASS.) *Scattered Wahoo Action* (Jeterboy 2) (82)

2. Screamin' Sneakers - (12") *Marching Orders* (S.S. no #) (82)

3. Naiomi's Hair - (LP/CASS) *Tara* (Figurehead) (89)

4. The Chant - (CD) *Two Car Mirage* (incl. *Three Sheets To The Wind*) (Safety Net 12) (89/85)

5. Reactions - (EP) *Official Release* (Reaction Recs no #) (80)

6. Charlie Pickett - (LP) *Route 33* (Twin Tone 8665) (86)

7. Lethal Yellow -(EP) *Declaration Of Retardation* (Stench 009) (84)

8. The Silos - (LP) *Cuba* (Record Collect 22) (87)

9. The Eat - (EP) *God Punishes The Eat* (Giggling Hitler no #) (80)

10. Reactions - (EP) *Love You* (Reaction Records no #) (81)

11. Principles - (45) "U.S.A. 423" (Dome no #) (80)

12. Nuclear Valdez - (LP/CD) *I Am I* (Epic 45354) (89)

13. Hoosegow - (CASS) *Big Wings* (Hoosegow no #) (89)

14. Charlie Pickett & Eggs - (LP)
    Live At The Button (Open 1)   (82)

15. Cichlids - (LP) *Be True To Your School*
    (Bold 306)   (80)

16. Mark Markham (with Tight Squeeze)- (LP)
    If This Is Love Then I Want My Money Back
    (Athens Free Ent. no #)   (81)

17. Various Artists - (CASS) *Jukebox 1*
    (Jeterboy 1)   (83)

18. Various Artists - (LP) *The Land That
    Time Forgot* (Open 2)   (82)

19. Trembles - (45) "Feel Alright/
    Stupid Fool" (Mental 108)   (86)

20. Larry Joe Miller - (CASS) *Rub A Bucket*
    (Jeterboy 003)   (83)

21. Essentials - (EP) *Fast Music In A
    Slow Town* (Safety Net 1)   (82)

22. Various Artists - (CASS) *Florida Explosion*
    (E-Sync ARE- 1)   (85)

23. The Goods - (CASS) *Play Rip Music*
    (The Goods no #)   (89)

24. Rugged Edge - (45) "Two Face/Gangs
    In Heat" (no label or #)   (87)

25. Various Artists - (EP) *We Can't Help It If
    We're From Florida* (Destroy 14710)   (83)

26. Black Box Approach - (45) "I'll Just Be
    There/Echo" (QQQQ 0001)   (82)

27. Used People - (EP) *Used People* (Edge no #)   (81)

28. Spanish Dogs - (EP) *Don't Sweat The
    Petty Things* (Rasta Dog 002)   (82)

29. FWA - (LP) *FWA* (FWA no #)   (88)

30. X-CONZ - (EP) *Do Dead People Tan* (Edge no #)   (81)

A band for the '90s: Nobody does it better than the **Goods**. Support them while you can! L-R: John Camacho, keyboards and vocals; Jim Camacho, bass and vocals; Tony Ohms, guitar; Kasmir Kujawa, drums. *Photo courtesy The Goods.*

43

OVERCOMING THE PREVAILING RIDICULOUSNESS
A Closing Editorial

So here we are, firmly entrenched in the '90s, and pondering the past, present, and future of Florida music. Surely a lot of mistakes have been made; it's easy to sit back with the usual hindsight and pick out incidents that could have resulted in much greater things. The "what ifs" could fill an entire book with row after row filled with mountains of debatable speculation. What if, for example, the Shaggs had a manager who could have directed their energies toward realizing their inert, exceptional talents? What if the Mor-Loks, Legends, and numerous others had not been victims of a senseless draft? What if Sammy Hall had remained with the Birdwatchers instead of giving in to his religious leanings? What if Capitol Records had realized just how stupendous the Evil master they purchased really was?

The possibilities are endless with the bottom line always remaining the same: The number of rock 'n roll acts originating from South Florida to score high on the national charts in the past thirty years can be counted on one finger! This failure is in no way related to the talent of the artists — the exterior forces in nearly all cases were just too great. Other parts of Florida fared much better, thanks to a 1970s fluke

in both timing and tastes called Southern Rock — although
with the exception of the Outlaws (ex-Four Letter Words) and
the Allman Bros. (ex- Allman Joys), these bands were far
removed from the golden age of (what was then) just a few
years back.

So what's to become of the '90s? Will a local artist be able
to make that national splash with a minimum of compromis-
ing, or will things sputter as they have for so long? Will more
of South Florida's most promising bands hitch a ride to New
York or Los Angeles, fed up with the gloomy prospects of
getting national attention from our southern shores? The
prevailing prejudices within the national media are without
question, with bands from New York and Los Angeles being
sucked up at will while South Florida bands continue to plug
away, night after night, in complete anonymity. It's no secret
why the Silos, Screamin' Sneakers, Wowii, and others
decided to try their fortunes in New York, or why the
Essentials opted to breathe the L.A. smog. That's the way it
was in the '60s, and it will probably continue to happen as
long as the media makes it that way.

I've always been an optimist, and I continue to believe that
South Florida will one day shed its disco image and receive
its rightful place in the annals of music capitals. That's what
keeps me here. That's what keeps young people continuing
to form bands and continuing to believe, despite the odds,
that good music will eventually prevail. It's an uphill battle
for sure, but the talent that this state has produced is
absolutely astounding. Anyone who chooses to pay attention
strictly to bands from media centers is only cheating himself.

So now it's our responsibility to remember the setbacks
of the '70s, the lost efforts of the '80s, and to make sure those
mistakes never happen again. Everytime a band as cool as
the Chant has to pack up and leave, or a place like the
original Flynn's, with its rock-of-ages excitement and sleeze,
has to permanently shut its doors, we're repeating the errors
that made the Montells today only fading memories. Those
who ignore history only repeat the same damn mistakes, and

don't think it won't still be happening on the eve of the year 2000 if we as rockers don't open our eyes and do something about what's forced into our ears.

Perhaps the main contributing factor to the magnitude of the '60s scenes was the interplay between radio and local bands. This cannot be overemphasized. While the Kollektion could appropriately be billed as "WQAM's Own Kollektion," the same could no doubt be said about WFUN and bands such as the Montells. This band-to-station relationship created a strong identity within the community, something that for the most part is not the case today. No game of "hi-lo," phone call-in contest or cash giveaway can do a tenth for a station what a local hit can. When a person could walk into a record store and pick up the latest weekly music survey, that person could decide AT THAT VERY MOMENT that he wants to listen to the station in question.

Seeing your favorite local band's name created a feeling of excitement and local pride; it helped not only the band, but the image of the station as well. These days most stations not only refrain from distributing weekly surveys, but also frown upon requests and new ideas. In other words, a local band that doesn't sound like the Miami Sound Machine or Exposé almost always has to go through the national level, procuring a *Billboard Magazine* review or an industry hype sheet recommendation, before the local program director will add the disc into rotation.

In 1990, two local FM'ers took the lead of college radio WVUM in setting aside time for local acts — a good gesture, guys, but why just Sunday nights? You seem to have no trouble programming bands from media centers on a daily basis, but when it comes to your own backyard, all we get is the graveyard shift. Bottom line: Radio is still unwilling to stretch out beyond that which is proven or safe. The growth of a youthful rock 'n roll scene revolves around radio living up to its role as both educator and entertainer; NOT merely an echo of what's conceived as popular or trendy.

Without the help of radio, the South Florida '60s scene would not have existed. No way. There would have been a

bunch of bands in Miami, Ft. Lauderdale, and West Palm
Beach with absolutely nothing in common. These bands
would have rarely crossed paths, content to play their
respective parties, teen dances, or shopping center open-
ings. Clearly, the Miami Bandstand and the Florida
Bandstand were more than just show-dances. They were the
glue — the cohesive force — that tied everything together.
They were the catalysts that turned a bunch of teen bands
into the spearheads of a vital, thriving scene. What is there
today to stimulate the growth of bands in this day and age
when radio station playlists are as tight as record company
budgets? A couple of exciting bands in bars and nightclubs
does not a scene make. It takes a little more than that.

Until the most unfortunate elements of recent eras give
way to spontaneity and logic (prerequisites to any kind of
positive musical change), let's not forget the incredible excitement that once existed: A time when a radio listener was
a person and not merely a demographic; a time that saw the
most exciting music ever created readily available to one and
all. A time forever hanging in the purgatories of "the past"...
unless we find it in our power to make it "the future."

We can all learn a lesson from the rise and fall of **Evil...** one of the many
incredible garage bands to record for a major label, only to be soon forgotten.
Photo courtesy Jeffrey Allen/Evil.

ACKNOWLEDGMENTS, ADDENDUM, AND A PAT ON THE BACK TO ROCK 'N ROLL

Savage Lost was made possible through the sharing of facts, opinions, and recollections by a number of people. A great debt of thanks is due the following, without whom this book would not have been possible.

Kenny Ahern
Ron Armstrong
Evan Chern
Willie Clarke
Carlton "King" Coleman
Burt Compton
Kurt Curtis
Dennis Dalcin
Bill DeMoya
John Doyle
Sally Duke
W. Patrick Ernst
The Goods
Randy Haynes
Dave Hieronymus
Mike Hughes
Cleve Johns & The Shaggs
Bill Kerti
Chuck Kirkpatrick
Tom Kounelis
Jeffrey Kramer

Mike Kusiak
John Mascaro
Dick Miller
Charles Molter
The Montells (Jeff, John, George, Carter, Danny)
Tom Murasso
Gary Myers
Robert Quimby
The Rockerfellas
Jim Sessody & The Legends
Stak-O-Wax (Ken Clee)
Tom Staley
Henry Stone
Jeff Teague
Richard Ulloa
Addie Williams
Bill Wyler (1931-1988)
Travis (Fairchild) Ximenes

A very special thank you is extended to Linda Neary, who initially steered me in the right direction and provided me with the impetus to pursue the inside story. Thanks is also due to each and every performer, disc jockey, and club owner who made the mid-'60s scene so downright magical. Your contributions will never be forgotten.

Those who wish to learn more about Florida music of the 1960s should keep an eye open for Kurt Curtis' forthcoming book, *The Illustrated History Of Florida Rock & Soul*. Kurt delves further into the histories of the Roemans, Tropics, Nightcrawlers, 31st Of February, We The People, and dozens upon dozens of other great bands from Central and Northern Florida (not to mention those dreaded '70s bands and disco acts that really didn't fit into this particular work!)

Other publications of interest to '60s fanatics include *Goldmine* (700 E. State Street, Iola, WI 54990), *Kicks* (Billy Miller, P.O. Box 646, Cooper Station, New York, NY 10003), *Rebel Teen* (George Gell, 624 Boston Post Road #13, Marlborough, MA 01752), *Outasite* (Greg Prevost, P.O. Box 17775, Rochester, NY 14617), and *Hoosier Hysteria* (Ron Simpson, P.O. Box 211, Roachdale, IN 46172). Those who enjoy wading through mountains of discographies should also check out *The Directory Of American 45 RPM Records* (Ken Clee, C/O Stak-O-Wax, P.O. Box 11412, Philadelphia, PA 19111), which includes discographies of thousands of labels, both large and minute.

I'd be remiss if I didn't mention the names of some of the Florida acts that for whatever reason (usually falling too early or too late) have not been previously mentioned. Really, guys, you didn't think I'd forget you, did you?

Cannonball Adderly
Herman Adelsohn
  (AKA Keith Herman)
Arthur, Hurley &
  Gottlieb
Axe
Richard Barone
  (The Bongos/Snails)
Perry Bernstein
  (Jane's Addiction)
Billion Dollar Band
Gary "US" Bonds
Henry Briggs
B. B. Brown
Jo Ann Campbell
Valerie Carter
Judy Cheeks

Desmond Child & Rouge
Bill Conti
Crossfire Choir
Teri DeSario
Stephen Dees
Dixie Dregs
Fortress
Four In Legion
Goldust Twins
Gil Hamilton (AKA
  Johnny Thunder)
Hearts Of Stone
Hopney
Hot City
David Hudson
Roy Hytower

Impact Of Brass	Rising Sun
(AKA Power Of Brass)	Cal Roberts
Don Jarrells	Roxx Gang
Glenn Jones	Silver Platinum
George Kerr	Charlie "Hoss" Singleton
Gloria Loring	Barry Smith
Los Vivos	Benny Spellman
Mantra	Gary Stewart
Pat Metheny	Terry & Pirates
Johnny Milanese	.38 Special
& Interludes	Three Thirds
Molly Hatchet	Thunder Lightning & Rain
Robert Moore	Johnny Tillotson
David Oliver	Nestor Torres
Milt Oshins	Universals
Patti Jo (Demps)	Terry Weiss
Red Cheek	Eugene Wilde

If there's anyone I may have left out, or a little-known Florida release you'd like to share, drop me a line. There's little I love discussing more than obscure '60s rock 'n roll (especially of the Florida variety), so if you have any newspaper clippings, music surveys, records, or just plain recollections to share, feel free to reach me c/o Distinctive Publishing Corporation, P.O. Box 17868, Plantation, FL 33318-7868. I'm only the messenger — it's the music that really matters. It's the reason I chose to devote my "20s" to researching this book... and the reason behind my closing thoughts, which I hope come through as clear as an old top 40 countdown.

Rock 'n roll is not meant to sell cars, cosmetics, or corn chips. It's not meant to baby-sit latch-key kids while their parents are out "doing lobster." Rock 'n roll was born of a rebellion that had to happen. I wasn't there at the beginning, and maybe you weren't, either. But it's up to us now. Combat musical mediocrity. Support local bands. Support fanzines. Support anyone who strives to educate the public about the most exciting force ever created.

Rock 'n roll isn't nostalgia. It's an experience every one of your senses is waiting for RIGHT NOW. It's time to stop reading... and start listening. It's time to start experiencing!

About Jeffrey Lemlich

Jeffrey Lemlich, a WCIX-TV news producer, has won awards in broadcast journalism: *Broadcaster of the Year* in 1975-76 at Miami-Dade Community College, *The Florida EMMY* for Best News Series in 1989 and Best Public Affairs Program Series in 1990 (presented by the NATIONAL ACADEMY OF TELEVISION ARTS AND SCIENCES); and also in 1990, the *Blakeslee Award for Journalistic Excellence*, presented by the AMERICAN HEART ASSOCIATION National Branch, and the *Steve Yates Award* for media Public Service, presented by the Florida Chapter of the AMERICAN HEART ASSOCIATION.

In spite of such accomplishments, being a television news producer is not Jeff's ultimate aim in life. His heart's ambition began as a gleam in the soul of a young boy in 1966.

On that fateful day, Jeff picked up his first WQAM Top 56 Survey. It changed his life. He realized that he could own a copy of each of his favorite songs for a mere 66 cents each, and now he awaited his tenth birthday with greater anticipation than usual. When May 11 arrived at last, an excited ten-year-old spent every penny of his birthday money on 45's — everything from "Paint It Black" by the Rolling Stones to "Girl I Got News For You" by the Birdwatchers.

Over and over, he played the rock 'n roll discs, fantasizing that he was on the radio like his idol, disc jockey Roby Yonge. Jeff and his sister fabricated imaginary radio stations, and printed counterfeit surveys with their favorite songs listed. He also invented bands — with names like The Nations, 14th Tornadoes, and Orangepeel Minority — writing songs that these bands would perform nightly in a radio station in his mind. There was nothing he wanted more than to make his dream a reality.

Unfortunately, when he was old enough to get his first paying disc jockey gig, it was January 1977, a time when the rock 'n roll sounds Jeff lived so much had completely disappeared from the airwaves. At WIGL-FM, using the air name Jeff McGraw, he played records by Helen Reddy, John Denver, and the Captain and Tennille — all the while, longing to play the Razor's Edge and the Ramones. He empathized completely with Brian Wilson, whose "I Just Wasn't Made For These Times" (from the wonderful *Pet Sounds* album) became his motto.

After one year, WIGL went off the air, and there wasn't much market for an out-of-work, 21-year-old would-be rock jock. he settled for a job at WNWS, the station which, ironically, had once been rock giant WFUN. At WNWS, Jeff learned the basics of news broadcasting, moving on to WCIX-TV two years later.

At WCIX, Channel 6 in Miami, Jeff has perfected his news skills, rising from his position in electronic graphics to news producer. He has put together nearly every kind of news show, special, and series conceivable. His series on dangerous jet ski areas was awarded a Florida EMMY in 1989. Although he's proud of his news broadcasting accomplishments, rock 'n roll is still his first love. He's never lost his enthusiasm for record and survey collecting, and still dreams of being a "boss jock." In fact, Jeff has what is believed to be the most extensive Florida record collection and one of the best '60s record collections in the country.

Savage Lost was born out of the love of rock 'n roll. After reading his book, you'll swear you can hear him: "...And now, here's our pick hit! Can you dig it? New from the Birdwatchers..."

To order additional copies of
SAVAGE LOST
by Jeffrey M. Lemlich,
send $19.95 plus $3.00 shipping/handling
for each copy ordered to:
Distinctive Publishing Corp.
P.O. Box 17868
Plantation FL 33318-7868

Quantity discounts are also available from the publisher.